DATE DUE FOR

Anticipations of the General Theory?

And Other Essays on Keynes

Don Patinkin

Anticipations of the General Theory?

And Other Essays on Keynes

Basil Blackwell • Oxford

© 1982 by The University of Chicago

First published in the United Kingdom 1982 by
Basil Blackwell Publisher
108 Cowley Road
Oxford OX4 1JF
England

British Library Cataloguing in Publication Data

Patinkin, Don
  Anticipations of the General Theory?
  1. Keynes, John Maynard
  2. Keynesian economics
  I. Title
  330.15′6   HB99.7

  ISBN 0-631-13156-6

Printed in the United States of America

לזכר אחי נחמן

In memory of my brother Nachman

Contents

Preface

Parts I and II of this book represent an extensive reworking, elaboration, and refinement of four public lectures given at the University of Chicago in the fall of 1978 under the auspices of the Graduate School of Business. Parts III and IV reproduce—with some revisions and additions—four already published articles. Major additions to these articles appear as postscripts; lesser ones are in most (though not all) cases set off by boldface square brackets.

The chapters of Parts II–IV are each self-contained. However, as indicated by the numerous cross-references between them and the chapters of Part I, they are more closely related to the latter than might at first sight appear. Thus Part II on Keynes' theory of effective demand provides a detailed examination of what is identified in Part I as the central message of the *General Theory*. In the course of identifying this message, it turns out to be essential to distinguish between it and two other aspects of Keynes' teachings: the multiplier, the history of which is the subject of chapter 7 of Part II; and Keynes' policy views, which are the subject of chapter 8. Chapter 6 provides an earlier and as yet not fully developed application of the notion of "central message" (without use of the term) that is so much emphasized in Part I. In these ways the three chapters of Part III provide background material for and elaboration of various points discussed in Part I.

Concurrent with the revolution in macroeconomic theory analyzed in Part I was one in macroeconomic measurement (read, national income statistics), and it is the complex interactions between these two revolutions that are studied in Part IV. The original stimulus for this study was one of Simon Kuznets' characteristically penetrating observations that remained tucked away in the back of my mind after I first heard it more than a quarter of a century ago: namely, that a history of economic ideas is not complete unless it also examines the nature of the economic facts that were known by the economists whose writings are being analyzed. In a related manner, this study also illustrates the general circumstance that the interaction between developments in theory and developments in the tools of measurement is a crucial feature of scientific progress.

The concern of this book with the development and simultaneity of ideas makes chronology of the essence. I have therefore cited all works by the original date of publication. For the convenience of the reader, however, the page references of a reprinted or translated work are to the pages of the reprint or translation in question. The simple rule is that the page references always relate to that version of a work that appears last in its listing in the relevant bibliography. Thus, for example, the reference on page 53 below to "Ohlin 1933a, p. 368" refers to page 368 of the 1978 translation of Ohlin's 1933 article as listed in the bibliography on page 113.

All page references to the writings of Keynes are to the relevant volumes of the Royal Economic Society's edition of his *Collected Writings*. For simplicity, the following short titles are sometimes used; *Tract* for the *Tract on Monetary Reform; Treatise* I (II) or *TM* I (II) for the respective volumes of the *Treatise on Money;* and *General Theory* or *GT* for the *General Theory of Employment Interest and Money*. As a help to the reader, corresponding page references to the original editions of the *Tract* and *Treatise* are provided in the Appendix on pages 271–72. The other volumes of the *Collected Writings* are referred to as *JMK* XIII, *JMK* XXIX, and so forth. For convenience, I have also used the acronym *KMT* to refer to my *Keynes' Monetary Thought*.

The work on Part I has led me into problems of the sociology of science—and I am deeply grateful to my Jerusalem colleague Joseph Ben-David, who first guided my reading in this field and who has continued to be a constant source of good advice. I am also grateful to him and to Yehuda Elkana for valuable comments on an early draft of this part. And I have a special debt to Robert K. Merton for his detailed and provocative criticisms of a subsequent draft, his fruitful suggestions, and, not least, his encouragement to make the "central message" my central message. Other individuals to whom I am indebted for comments on earlier drafts of Part I as well as other help in connection with it are Sidney Davidson, Stanley Fischer, Zvi Griliches, Frank Hahn, Samuel Hollander, Peter Howitt, David Laidler, Abba Lerner, and Stanislaw Wellisz. I have also benefited from the comments of participants in seminars at various universities in Israel and abroad where, as the work progressed, I presented different portions of the material in Part I.

The work on Part I has led me into new territory in yet another dimension: that of literature in Swedish and Polish. In the course of the work, parts of this literature turned out to be relevant and were translated for me by various individuals; in this connection I wish to thank Moshe Apelblat, Yossi Ben-Akiva, Finn Borg, Henryk Francuz, Pearl and Arcadius Kahan, Barbara Kaminski, Avraham Sheshinski-Shani, and Lewis Taylor. But one who is restricted to translations and cannot directly examine a body of literature is in more danger than usual of overlooking some essential parts of it. For valuable comments and criticisms that inter alia reduced this danger with respect to my treatment of the Stockholm School, I am indebted to Bent Hansen, Assar Lindbeck, Erik Lundberg, Otto Steiger, and the late Bertil Ohlin; and I have a similar debt to Kazimierz Laski and especially Jerzy Osiatyński with respect to my treatment of Kalecki. As will, however, be seen, significant differences of opinion remain between some of these individuals and myself as to the proper interpretation of relevant texts. My discussions with Hansen also provided much valuable background information about the Stockholm School. Similarly, I am indebted to Alexander Erlich, on whose encyclopedic knowledge I have repeatedly drawn so as to feel more at home in the world of Kalecki in Poland of the 1930s.

The work on this book, and on Part I in particular has been greatly facilitated by the availability of the Royal Economic Society's edition of Keynes' *Collected Writings* and the Polish Academy of Sciences' edition of Kalecki's *Dzieła* [Works]. To Sir Austin Robinson and Donald Moggridge, editors of the former, and Jerzy Osiatyński, editor of the latter, I have an additional debt of gratitude for the kind and cooperative way they have always responded to my requests for clarification or for additional materials, as well as for permission to reproduce materials. For such permission I am also indebted to Lord Kahn, Keynes' literary executor.

The aforementioned public lectures at the University of Chicago were given during a year (1978–79) that I served there as Ford Foundation Visiting Research Professor. During that year I had the extreme good fortune of having Mark Levin as my research assistant. In this capacity he carried out a heavy burden of library work with great accuracy, initiative, and responsibility. He also undertook the initial responsibility for putting the bibliographies of this book on the computer. In this connection I am also grateful for the advice and assistance of Faye Citron, Robert Graves, William Hupp, and Gary Skoog of the Graduate School of Business. I would also like to thank Marie Marchese for her most efficient typing assistance during my visit to Chicago. Similar thanks to Laurie Bland and Theresa Caverhill for their assistance during a brief visit to the University of Western Ontario.

After my return to Jerusalem in the fall of 1979, I benefited greatly from the assistance of Dale Knisely. He was succeeded the following year by Bette Gorden, who in a most pleasant and efficient way provided essential help in all aspects of the work: in the library, in the computer room, and at the typewriter. I am particularly grateful to her for many helpful suggestions and for the care, patience, and accuracy with which she collated and proofread the successive drafts of the manuscripts. My thanks too to Daniel Braniss of the Department of Computer Science at the Hebrew University, who brought the computerizing of the bibliographies to a successful completion. For help in this regard I am also indebted to Yaakov Kop.

The final touches on the book as well as the checking of its page proofs were carried out at Columbia University during the fall term of 1981, when I served as Wesley C. Mitchell Visiting Research Professor. In the work there I was much aided by Robert Graboyes, who was also responsible for the preparation of the Appendix on pages 271–72. My thanks also to Yuval Cohen, Lisa Levine, and Silvine Oesman for technical assistance. Finally, let me express my sincerest appreciation to Barbara Lowe of Cambridge, England, for preparing the indexes to the book.

For permission to reproduce (in part or whole) already published articles of mine, I am indebted to the following journals and organizations: *Econometrica, Economic Inquiry, History of Political Economy,* the Israel Economic Association, the Macmillan Press Ltd., *The Manchester School,* the MIT Press, the Oxford University Press, and the *Scandinavian Journal of Economics.*

Most of the work on Parts I–II of this book was carried out under a grant from the Ford Foundation, administered by the Maurice Falk Institute for Economic Research in Israel. During my visit to the University of Chicago, the work was supported by National Science Foundation grants nos. Soc 77-12212 and Soc 79-08281, as well as grants from the Department of Economics and the Graduate School of Business; similar grants were provided by the Departments of Economics of Columbia University and the University of Western Ontario during my visits there. The work on Parts III–IV during 1972–76 also received support from the Central Research Fund of the Hebrew University of Jerusalem, the Israel Commission for Basic Research, and the Israel Foundation Trustees (on behalf of the Ford Foundation). I wish to express my thanks to all these institutions for this support over the years. My deepest thanks also to the Israel Academy of Sciences and Humanities, in whose quiet atmosphere, so conducive to scholarly endeavors, I have over the past decade carried out most of the work that has culminated in this book.

This book is dedicated to the memory of my brother Norman—or Nachman as he was known to his family and friends: a graduate of the school under whose auspices these lectures were given and a lecturer on its staff for many years afterward. We were to live and work together in Jerusalem, but fate decreed otherwise: "For you shall see the land before you, but you shall not go there." In his professional life in operations research, his emphasis was naturally on the practical; but he was also interested in *Torah lishmah*—in learning for the sake of learning. So I feel that he would have found interest in this book too.

Dramatis Personae as of 1933

(in alphabetical order)

Colin Clark. Age 28. Educated at Dragon School, Oxford, Winchester College, and Brasenose College, Oxford. Specialized in chemistry, completing his undergraduate studies in 1924. Worked as an assistant on the Social Survey of London 1928–29, and of Merseyside 1929–30. Member of staff of Economic Advisory Council 1930–31. Lecturer in Statistics at Cambridge University from 1931. [(g), (h)]

Roy F. Harrod. Age 33. Educated at Westminster School and New College, Oxford. Specialized in classics, philosophy, and history, completing his undergraduate studies in 1922. Lecturer at Christ Church, Oxford 1922–24. Student of Christ Church from 1924 onward. Visited Cambridge during 1922–23 to study economics under Keynes. [(b), (o), (q)]

Hubert D. Henderson. Age 43. Educated at Rugby School and Emmanuel College, Cambridge. Specialized first in mathematics and then shifted to economics, in which context heard lectures by Pigou and Keynes. Took his B.A. in 1912. Secretary of the Cotton Control Board, 1917–19. Fellow of Clare College and Lecturer in Economics, Cambridge University 1919–23. Editor of the *Nation and Athenaeum*, 1923–30, during which period Keynes was Chairman of the Board. Joint Secretary of the Economic Advisory Council from 1930. Member of the Committee on Economic Information from 1931. [(e), (n), (q)]

J. R. Hicks. Age 29. Educated at Clifton College and Balliol College, Oxford. Studied P.P.E. and took his B.A. in 1925. Lecturer, London School of Economics from 1926. Did not have any significant contacts with Keynes until after publication of the *General Theory* [(d), (g), (o), (r)]

Richard F. Kahn. Age 28. Educated at St. Paul's School and King's College, Cambridge. Specialized first in mathematics and physics, taking his B.A. in 1927. Then studied economics as a pupil of Keynes. Fellow of King's College from 1930 onward. Co-Secretary of Committee of Economists of the Economic Advisory Council, 1930. [(e), (o), (r)]

Michał Kalecki, Age 34. Educated at Warsaw Polytechnic and Gdansk Polytechnic. Specialized in engineering but for family reasons had to discontinue studies before receiving a degree. Self-taught in economics. Member of Research Staff of Institute of Business Cycles and Prices, Warsaw, from 1929. [(g)]

John Maynard Keynes. Age 50. Educated at Eton and King's College, Cambridge. Specialized in mathematics and took his B.A. in 1905. Afterward, spent an additional year at Cambridge studying economics under Alfred Marshall (1842–1924) and A. C. Pigou. Fellow of King's College from 1909 onward. Appointed Lecturer in Economics at Cambridge in 1908, resigning in 1915 to take wartime position at Treasury. Resigned from Treasury in 1919 in protest against Versailles Treaty. Subsequently also active as publicist, in which context served as Chairman of the Board of the *Nation and Athenaeum* from 1923. Member of Committee on Finance and Industry (Macmillan Committee) 1929–31. Member of Economic Advisory Council from 1930, and Chairman of its Committee of Economists, 1930. [(b), (f)]

Simon S. Kuznets. Age 32. Educated at Columbia University, where he took his B.A. in 1923, M.A. in 1924, and Ph.D. in economics in 1926. Member of the research staff of the National Bureau of Economic Research from 1927. Assistant Professor of Economics and Statistics at University of Pennsylvania from 1930. [(g), (p)]

Abba P. Lerner. Age 30. Educated at London School of Economics, where he took his B.Sc. degree in 1932, continuing afterward with graduate studies. [(g)]

Erik Lindahl. Age 42. Educated at the University of Lund, where he studied under Wicksell and received his Ph.D. degree in 1919. Appointed Lecturer there in 1920. Moved in 1924 to the University of Uppsala and subsequently to the University of Stockholm, where he was also connected with its Institute for Social Sciences. Professor of Economics and Statistics at the Gothenburg School of Economics from 1932. [(j), (m)]

Erik Lundberg. Age 26. Educated at Stockholm High School (now University of Stockholm), where he received his fil. kand. degree in

1928 and fil. lic. in 1931. Rockefeller fellow in the United States 1931–33, after which he returned to Stockholm to complete work for Ph.D. [(k), (l)]

Gunnar Myrdal. Age 35. Educated at Stockholm University. Specialized in economics, receiving his doctorate in 1927. Lecturer in Political Economy at Stockholm University 1927–33. Rockefeller fellow in the United States, 1930. Professor of Political Economy at Stockholm University from 1933. [(g), (h)]

Bertil Ohlin. Age 34. Educated at University of Lund and the Stockholm School of Economics and Business Administration, taking his B.A. in 1919. Further studies at Harvard University (A.M. 1923) and Stockholm University (Ph.D. 1924). Professor, University of Copenhagen, 1925–29. Professor of Economics, Stockholm School of Economics and Business Administration from 1930. [(a), (g), (i)]

A. C. Pigou. Age 56. Educated at Harrow and King's College, Cambridge. Studied first history and then economics. Took his B.A. in 1899. Fellow of King's College from 1902 and onward. Succeeded Marshall as Professor of Political Economy in 1908, at the relatively young age of 31. Was one of Keynes' teachers. [(b), (f), (q)]

Dennis H. Robertson. Age 43. Educated at Eton and Trinity College, Cambridge. Specialized first in classics, taking his B.A. in 1910, then went on to study economics under Pigou and Keynes, the latter serving as his director of studies. Fellow of Trinity College from 1914 onward. Collaborated closely with Keynes during early and mid-1920s on questions of monetary theory. [(c), (f), (q)]

Joan Robinson. Age 30. Educated at St. Paul's Girls' School, London and Girton College, Cambridge. Specialized in economics and took her B.A. in 1925. Appointed Assistant Lecturer in Economics at Cambridge in 1931. [(b), (g), (o), (q)]

Jan Tinbergen. Age 30. Educated at University of Leiden. Specialized in physics, taking his Ph.D. in 1929. Worked on business cycle research for the Central Bureau of Statistics in the Hague from 1929. Part-time Lecturer in Statistics at the University of Amsterdam 1931–33. Part-time Professor Netherlands School of Economics from 1933. [(g)]

Bibliography for Dramatis Personae

(a) *Directory of Members of the American Economic Association. American Economic Review* 64 (Oct. 1974).

(b). Harrod, R. F. (1951). *The Life of John Maynard Keynes.* London: Macmillan. Reprinted, New York: Kelley, 1969.

(c) Hicks, J. R. (1966). "Dennis Holme Robertson, 1890–1963: A Memoir." In Robertson, *Essays in Money and Interest,* selected by Hicks (Manchester: Collins), pp. 9–22.

(d) Hicks, J. R. (1973). "Recollections and Documents." *Economica* 40 (Feb.): 2–11.

(e) Howson, Susan, and Donald Winch (1977). *The Economic Advisory Council 1930–1939.* Cambridge: Cambridge University Press.

(f) *International Encyclopedia of the Social Sciences* (1968). Edited by David L. Sills. New York: Macmillan and Free Press.

(g) *International Encyclopedia of the Social Sciences: Biographical Supplement* (1979). Edited by David L. Sills. New York: Free Press.

(h) *The International Who's Who 1967–68.* London: Europa Publications.

(i) Steiger, Otto (1981). "Bertil Ohlin, 1899–1979." *History of Political Economy* 13 (Summer): 179–88.

(j) *Svensk Upplagsbok* (1951). Malmö: Norden

(k) *Svenska man och kvinnor* (1949). Edited by Oscar Wieselgren and Bengt Hildebrand. Stockholm: Albert Bonniers boktryckeri.

(l) *Vem är Det 75* (1974). Stockholm: Kungliga Boktryckeriet, PA Narstedt & Soner.

(m) *Uppsala Universitets Matrikel: 1937–1950* (1953). Edited by A. Dintler and J. C. Sune Lindqvist. Uppsala: Almqvist & Wiksell.

(n) *Who Was Who, 1951–1960.* London: A. & C. Black.

(o) *Who's Who 1973.* London: A. & C. Black.

(p) *Who's Who in America 1976–77.* Chicago: Marquis Who's Who.

(q) College registrar records.

(r) Personal correspondence with individual in question.

Prologue

John Maynard Keynes:
A Biographical Sketch

John Maynard Keynes was one of the great intellectual innovators of the first half of our century, and certainly its greatest political economist. He was born in Cambridge, England, on June 5, 1883, and died in nearby Tilton on April 21, 1946. His father was John Neville Keynes, also an economist and later registrary of Cambridge University.

In accordance with the traditional British upper-middle-class pattern of the time, Keynes was educated at Eton and then at King's College, Cambridge, where he took a degree in mathematics in 1905. Afterward he spent an additional year at Cambridge studying economics under the then-doyen of British economics, Alfred Marshall, as well as under the latter's student and successor-to-be as Professor of Political Economy at Cambridge, Arthur C. Pigou. Keynes then entered the Civil Service, where he worked for over two years in the India Office, though he never actually visited India. Out of this work grew his first book in economics, *Indian Currency and Finance* (1913), which was largely descriptive in nature. This work also led to Keynes' first major participation in public life as a member of the Royal Commission on Indian Finance and Currency (1913–14).

In 1908 Keynes returned to Cambridge as a Lecturer in Economics. During that year he continued his work on *A Treatise on Probability,* which he successfully submitted to King's College as a fellowship dissertation in 1909. This dissertation was published in a revised form in 1921 and continues to be recognized as a pioneering work in the field.

Shortly after the outbreak of World War I, Keynes took a leave of absence from Cambridge to enter the Treasury. Here his exceptional ability and capacity for work led to his rapid advancement, and by 1919

Published originally in Hebrew in *Ha-encyclopedia Ha-ivrit* (Encyclopedia Hebraica) 29:643–46 (Jerusalem, 1977). Some minor additions and revisions have been made.

All of Keynes' writings referred to in this Prologue appear in his *Collected Writings.*

he was principal Treasury representative at the Peace Conference at Versailles. His passionate disagreement with what he considered to be the harsh clauses of the Versailles Peace Treaty led to his resignation from the British delegation and to the writing of his vehement denunciation of the treaty in his *Economic Consequences of the Peace* (1919), which overnight made him a world celebrity. From then on Keynes was a national figure whose voice was heard on all major economic problems that arose in Britain in the interwar period.

In 1925 Keynes married the Russian ballet dancer Lydia Lopokova. They had no children.

Keynes is primarily known for his fundamental contributions to monetary economics. His first important work in this field was his *Tract on Monetary Reform* (1923). For the most part, this is a slight revision and elaboration of a series of articles that he had published the year before in the *Manchester Guardian* dealing with the problems of inflation, deflation, and exchange-rate disequilibrium that beset Europe in the wake of World War I. Thus the primary emphasis of the book is on policy problems, and the limited theoretical discussion that it does contain is largely a recapitulation of the Cambridge form of the quantity theory of money as it had been developed by his teachers, Marshall and Pigou.

In the second half of the 1920s, Keynes began to work on what he planned to be his scientific *magnum opus*—his *Treatise on Money,* which was finally published in two volumes in 1930. In contrast with the *Tract*, this book was designed for an audience of professional economists. In style and organization it is accordingly the most systematic and scholarly of Keynes' economic writings.

The analysis of the *Treatise* (presented in its first volume, entitled *The Pure Theory of Money*) is based on the so-called fundamental equations. These analyze the relationship between the cost of production of a unit of output (including normal profits) and its market price. An economy is in full-employment equilibrium when these two are equal: that is, when cost-of-production = price. If, however, costs exceed price, then firms will be incurring losses and will accordingly contract output and thus generate unemployment. By means of his special definitions, Keynes then shows that such losses equal the excess of saving over investment. Correspondingly, Keynes' solution to the problem of unemployment is to have the central bank carry out policies that will reduce the rate of interest, hence stimulate investment, hence eliminate the aforementioned excess of savings and corresponding losses, and hence increase the level of employment. In the second volume of his *Treatise* (entitled *The Applied Theory of Money*), Keynes presented empirical estimates of the respective variables of his fundamental equations and also provided what he considered to be historical illustrations of their workings. In addition, he described the institutional aspects of both the domestic and the international financial systems, with emphasis in both contexts on the problems of "monetary management" by means of central-bank interest-rate policy.

Despite the high hopes with which Keynes presented his *Treatise* to the profession, it rapidly became clear that the theoretical part of the book was not a success. To a certain extent this was due to the fact (which Keynes had only in part recognized) that this theory had been largely adumbrated by the Swedish economist Knut Wicksell at the turn of the century. Even more so was it due to the criticism that, on the one hand, the "fundamental equations" were actually tautologies, and, on the other, that the *Treatise* had explained the forces that caused output to expand or contract, but had not explained what determines its actual level during any period.

As a result of this criticism, Keynes began within a relatively short time after the appearance of the *Treatise* to work on a new book. This book, which was of a purely theoretical nature and which ultimately bore the title *The General Theory of Employment Interest and Money*, was published in 1936 and had a revolutionary impact on macroeconomic theory. The major innovation of this book was its theory of aggregate demand. This consisted of a theory of the consumption function (determining the consumption component of aggregate demand as a function of the level of income), a theory of the marginal efficiency of capital (determining its investment component as a function of the rate of interest), and a theory of liquidity preference (determining the level of the rate of interest, and hence the level of investment). The equilibrium level of output in the economy is accordingly that level which brings the aggregate demand for output into equality with the output supplied. And Keynes' major contribution was to analyze the forces that brought this equilibrium about and to stress that the level of output so generated need not be one of full employment. Furthermore, monetary policy (i.e., central-bank operations to reduce the rate of interest) might not be able to stimulate investment expenditures sufficiently to generate full employment. In such cases, fiscal policy (i.e., increases in government expenditures) would be necessary to accomplish this purpose. Thus Keynes provided the theoretical underpinning for the policy of public-works expenditure which, though it had been advocated before (by himself as well), did not become widely accepted until after the appearance of the *General Theory*.

Despite the many criticisms and discussions of the *General Theory* that followed its publication, the basic analytical structure of the *General Theory* not only remained intact, but also defined the framework of both theoretical and empirical research in macroeconomics for decades to come. Truly a scientific achievement of the first order.

It would, however, be a mistake to think of Keynes as devoting his major efforts in the interwar period to writing these books in the quiet halls of academe. On the contrary, after he became a public figure in the wake of his *Economic Consequences of the Peace* (1919), he resigned his lectureship at Cambridge, though he continued as an active Fellow of King's College. Correspondingly, his normal routine became one in which he divided his time between London and Cambridge, living in the former during most of the week and coming down to Cambridge for long weekends, during which he dealt with both academic and (as bursar of King's) business matters. On Monday mornings of the fall term during most of the interwar years he also gave a course of lectures on monetary economics which were widely attended by students, faculty, and visitors, and in the process of which he expounded his new theories as he developed them. On Monday evenings he would then preside over the discussions of his famous Political Economy Club. And the following morning he would be back in London.

Keynes' intensive public activity with respect to the policy discussions of the interwar period was reflected in the more than three-hundred articles he wrote for the sophisticated news magazines of the time (particularly the *Nation and Athenaeum,* of whose board Keynes was chairman in the 1920s, and its successor, the *New Statesman and Nation*) as well as for the popular press. Many of the latter articles were syndicated in newspapers all over the world. A selection from these and similar writings was reissued by Keynes in 1931 under the title *Essays in Persuasion.* These are marked by a brilliant publicist style, truly the work of a literary craftsman. This brilliant style also characterizes his *Essays in Biography* (1933), in which Keynes reprinted his impressions of the leading political figures he had known as well as his biographical essays on various British economists. Most notable among the latter are his stimulating essay on Thomas Malthus and his perceptive and evocative memorial essay on his teacher Alfred Marshall.

At various critical junctures in the interwar period, Keynes also published influential pamphlets in which he analyzed the questions at issue and proclaimed his prescriptions. Such were his *Economic Consequences of Mr. Churchill,* in the times of trouble after the return to the gold standard in 1925; *Can Lloyd George Do It?* (written with Hubert Henderson), in support of the Liberal Party's pledge in the 1929 election campaign to combat unemployment by means of public works; the *Means to Prosperity,* in further support of public works (this time making use of the newly developed notion of the multiplier) as the depression deepened in the early 1930s; and *How to Pay for the War*, as in 1940 the problems of depression gave way to those of wartime finance (all of these pamphlets have been reproduced in *JMK* IX).

Keynes influenced policy not only through his journalistic activities, but also by his active membership in various official government bodies. Thus he was the leading figure of the Committee on Finance and Industry (the Macmillan Committee, 1929–31) and of the Economic Advisory Council (1930–39), and he also served as chairman of the Committee of Economists (1930)—all of which were charged with advising the British government on different aspects of the policies it should follow in order to overcome the serious depression in which Britain, together with the rest of the Western world, then found itself. Similarly, at the outbreak of World War II Keynes was appointed adviser to the Chancellor of the Exchequer, a position he held until his death. He also played a leading role in the negotiations with the United States government, first for lend-lease support in 1944, and then for a special postwar loan in 1945. Keynes was also one of the intellectual progenitors of the Bretton Woods Conference (1944), which established the International Monetary Fund and the International Bank for Reconstruction and Development (the World Bank). In the foregoing capacities, Keynes wrote countless letters, memoranda, reports, draft proposals, and the like, the major ones of which are being reproduced in the various volumes of his *Collected Writings*.

Keynes' concern with policy questions also exerted a strong influence on the direction of his scientific writings. This was clearly the case for his *Tract on Monetary Reform* (1923), which, as already noted, had its origins in newspaper articles that Keynes had written on current economic problems. Similarly, the predominant emphasis of the *Treatise on Money* (1930) on the problems of unemployment and of the workings of the international gold standard reflected the major economic concerns of the period, particularly in Britain. By the time the *General Theory* (1936) was being written, however, the gold standard had collapsed, while the problem of unemployment had become increasingly severe. Correspondingly, the *General Theory* is concerned almost exclusively with the problem of mass, long-run unemployment in a closed economy—that is, one not subject to the restrictions imposed by the gold standard.

Keynes' interests ranged far beyond the confines of economics. He was for many years a member of the famous Bloomsbury Circle. His cultural activities included the theater, the dance, paintings, and rare-book collecting. In all these ways he played a prominent role in the general British intellectual life of his time.

Bibliography for Prologue

Harrod, R. F. (1951). *The Life of John Maynard Keynes*. London: Macmillan. Reprinted, New York: Augustus M. Kelley, 1969.

Howson, Susan, and Donald Winch (1977). *The Economic Advisory Council 1930–1939*. Cambridge: Cambridge University Press.

Johnson, Elizabeth S., and Harry G. Johnson (1978). *The Shadow of Keynes: Understanding Keynes, Cambridge and Keynesian Economics*. Chicago: University of Chicago Press.

Keynes, John Maynard. *Collected Writings*. London: Macmillan, for the Royal Economic Society, 1971–.

Keynes, Milo, editor (1975). *Essays on John Maynard Keynes*. Cambridge: Cambridge University Press.

Klein, Lawrence (1966). *The Keynesian Revolution*. Revised edition. New York: Macmillan.

Lekachman, Robert, editor (1964). *Keynes' General Theory: Reports of Three Decades*. New York: St. Martin's Press.

Moggridge, D. E. (1980). *Keynes*. 2nd edition. London: Macmillan.

Patinkin, Don (1976). *Keynes' Monetary Thought: A Study of Its Development*. Durham, N.C.: Duke University Press.

Patinkin, Don, and J. Clark Leith, editors (1977). *Keynes, Cambridge and the General Theory: The Process of Criticism and Discussion Connected with the Development of the General Theory*. London: Macmillan.

Robinson, E. A. G. (1947). "John Maynard Keynes, 1883–1946." *Economic Journal* 57 (March): 1–68. As reprinted in Lekachman (1964), pp. 13–86.

Stein, Herbert (1969). *The Fiscal Revolution in America*. Chicago: University of Chicago Press.

Winch, Donald (1969). *Economics and Policy: A Historical Study*. London: Hodder and Stoughton.

I

Anticipations of the General Theory?

1

Anticipations of the General Theory? The Problem Defined

Those of us who live in Jerusalem need not be reminded of the words of a wise king who ruled in our city three thousand years ago that there is nothing new under the sun. Yet it is with a question of newness—more specifically, of scientific discovery—that I shall be dealing in these lectures. For though every scientific development is necessarily related to the stock of knowledge existing at the time it was made, there are some—and Keynes' *General Theory of Employment Interest and Money* is clearly an example—which by consensus are regarded as constituting a discovery, a new theory, if not a scientific revolution.[1] And it is, of course, with reference to such theories that the question of priority and the related question of multiple discovery arise.

In my discussion I take as given Merton's penetrating analysis (1957) of the role of priority in the reward system of science: that "the institution of science . . . defines originality as a supreme value and therefore makes recognition of one's originality a major concern" (ibid., p. 294). What I shall examine, by means of the *General Theory* as a case study, is Merton's further and well-known hypothesis that multiples—that is, "the multiple and independent appearance of the same scientific

For general acknowledgments with respect to Part I, see the Preface.

1. I am using this term metaphorically and not in the technical sense that Thomas Kuhn has attempted to define in his well-known monograph *The Structure of Scientific Revolutions* (1962). This monograph has been much criticized by other philosophers of science, thus leading Kuhn himself to retract many of its basic ideas in the second edition (1970). See Shapere (1964), Lakatos and Musgrave (1970), Toulmin (1972, pp. 96–130), Laudan (1977, pp. 73ff.), and the references there cited. See also Bronfenbrenner (1971) for a criticism of Kuhn's analysis, as applied to the history of economic thought, and to the *General Theory* in particular. See also Blaug's "Kuhn versus Lakatos *or* Paradigms versus Research Programmes in the History of Economics" (1976) for an illuminating survey of the literature and for an attempt to interpret the *General Theory* in terms of Lakatos' methodology of scientific research programs. For the reason just given, I have also not made use in these lectures of Kuhn's term "paradigm," which has become so fashionable in recent writings on the history of economic thought, especially in those dealing with the development of the *General Theory*.

discovery"—constitute the "dominant pattern" in science: that indeed "all scientific discoveries are in principle multiples" (Merton 1961, pp. 352, 356).

The question of multiple discovery is related to the broader question of the relative importance in scientific discovery of the individual scientist, on the one hand, and of historical processes, on the other. Clearly, both play a role. As Barber (1952, p. 265) has so aptly put it, "There emerge multiple discoveries by men whose activity is guided in part by the existing scientific heritage and in part by their creative imaginations." And Merton himself (1961, pp. 366–69) has emphasized that his hypothesis does not imply that all discoveries are the inevitable product of historical processes. At the same time, it would seem that the more scientific development is characterized by multiple discovery, the less important the role of the individual scientist.

Among the supporting examples for Merton's hypothesis that are customarily cited in our own discipline[2] are (1) the formulation of the law of diminishing returns by West and Malthus in 1815; (2) the discovery of marginal-utility theory by Jevons, Menger, and Walras in the early 1870s; (3) the development of the cash-balance approach to the quantity theory by Marshall, Walras, and Wicksell in the last decades of the nineteenth century; (4) the development of the theory of imperfect competition by Chamberlin and Joan Robinson in the early 1930s; (5) the demonstration of the balanced-budget-multiplier theorem by Haavelmo, Gelting, William Salant, and Samuelson in the early 1940s; and (6) the demonstration of the factor-price equalization theorem by Lerner and Samuelson in the 1930s and 1940s.[3] And the question to which I shall address myself in these lectures is whether to this list (which is not intended to be exhaustive) we can add the discovery of the General Theory—by which term, not italicized, I shall henceforth mean the theory presented in Keynes' book, the *General Theory*.

As a preliminary, let me note that whether we consider the progress of science to be determined by external, social needs or whether we consider it to proceed by a dynamics of its own (Laudan 1977, chap. 7),

2. But whether they are validly cited in this context is a question I defer to my concluding lecture (chap. 4 below).

3. For references, see the following: on (1), Cannan (1893, pp. 156–63), and Blaug (1978, pp. 79–80); on (2), Roll (1939, pp. 371–91), Schumpeter (1954, chap. 5) and Blaug (1978, chap. 5), which also discusses this case from the viewpoint of Merton's hypothesis; on (3), Marget (1931) and Patinkin (1956, 1965, suppl. notes C, E, and G); on (4), Chamberlin (1933) and Joan Robinson (1933a); on (5), Haavelmo (1945, 1946) and the symposium in the spring 1975 issue of *History of Political Economy*, with papers by Jørgen Gelting and William Salant, as well as Bent Hansen, Walter Salant, and Paul Samuelson; on (6), Samuelson (1948, 1949) and Lerner ([1933] 1952). The foregoing list overlaps partly with that presented by George Stigler (1980, pp. 143–44).

there are good reasons why we might a priori have expected the General Theory to have been simultaneously discovered by several economists, and even by economists in different countries. For, from the viewpoint of social needs, the pernicious problem of persistent depression and unemployment which formed the background of the General Theory was common to all of the Western world in the early 1930s; while, from the viewpoint of internal dynamics, the state of economics as a science in several of these countries (e.g., Britain, United States, Sweden) was not basically different at that time. So the general issue which concerns me in these lectures is whether this a priori expectation of a multiple discovery of the General Theory was fulfilled. And this will bring me to an examination of the frequently voiced claims that the General Theory was indeed independently discovered in the early 1930s by the economists of the so-called Stockholm School and/or by the Polish economist Michał Kalecki. To avoid any possible misunderstanding, let me at the outset emphasize that it is only from this specific viewpoint that I shall examine the writings of these economists; I make no pretense of presenting an exposition and evaluation of their respective theories as such.

To deal with this issue, it is necessary first to clarify three questions: first, the nature of the major contribution of the *General Theory;* second, the time Keynes first formulated this contribution; and, third, the time when he first published it. And it is to these questions that this introductory lecture is devoted.[4]

The first question is obviously the most important of all: for we cannot meaningfully discuss the possible multiple discovery of the General Theory unless we first specify what its major innovation was. Unfortunately—and largely (it is my impression) unlike the situation in discussions of discoveries in the natural sciences (but see pp. 91–92 below)—there is no unanimity on this question. Indeed, there seems to be more disagreement today than there was fifteen years ago, or at least I am now hearing interpretations of the *General Theory* that I never heard before (but see chap. 4, n. 8 below).

Clearly, the broader the specification of the innovative contribution of the *General Theory,* the greater the likelihood of finding this contribution anticipated. Thus, if we define this contribution as lying in its notion of aggregate demand coupled with the rejection of Say's law, and the corollary contention that aggregate demand can fall short of aggregate supply, thus generating unemployment, then—as Keynes himself noted in the *General Theory* (pp. 362–71)—this notion is to be

---

4. I have in the following drawn freely on the discussion in *KMT*, chaps. 7–11, which should be consulted for further details. See also Patinkin (1977).

found (albeit not fully developed) in the writings of Malthus in his famous debate with Ricardo on Say's law more than a century before, and in the writings of Mummery and Hobson (1889) toward the end of the nineteenth century. And to these I would add the name of Nicholas Johannsen and his *Neglected Point in Connection with Crises* (1908), to whom Keynes had referred in his *Treatise* (II, pp. 89–90), though puzzlingly enough not in the *General Theory*.

Similarly, if we instead identify Keynes' contribution as lying in his emphasis on the crucial role of fluctuations in investment in generating business cycles, then this theme is to be found at least as far back as the business-cycle theories of Tugan-Baranowsky (who in turn was influenced by Marx) and Spiethoff at the turn of the century (Hansen 1951, pp. 277–300; below, pp. 242–43). And if in a related manner we see Keynes' contribution as lying in his advocacy of government investment in the form of public works as a means of combating unemployment, then such policies had been advocated in Britain, Sweden, and other countries before World War I (Winch 1969, pp. 53–57; Ohlin 1981, p. 191). More to the point, by the end of the 1920s in Britain, as the unemployment generated by the return to the gold standard in 1925 at prewar parity dragged on, most British economists (including even Pigou) were advocating public works as a means of reducing unemployment (Hutchison 1953, pp. 409–23; idem 1968, pp. 277–79; Winch 1969, pp. 104–46, 145–97, 343).[5] Finally, if the contribution of the *General Theory* is its emphasis on the fact that economic decisions in the real world (and especially those related to investment) are made under conditions of uncertainty which are not subject to a probability calculus, then this notion of uncertainty had already been forcefully presented many years before that by Knight in his classic 1921 work *Risk, Uncertainty, and Profit*—or, if you wish (though I am not sure of its equivalence), by Keynes himself in his *Treatise on Probability*, published the same year, to which work he indeed refers in the *General Theory* (p. 141, n. 1) when discussing the uncertainty of expectations (cf. *KMT*, pp. 141–42).

Thus to my mind none of the foregoing constitutes the major contribution of the *General Theory*. And since so many claims of anticipation of the General Theory turn out on closer examination to be claims that public works were advocated by economists before Keynes (cf., e.g., Garvy 1975), let me in particular emphasize that Keynes could not possibly have perceived this advocacy as constituting the major contribution of his book. First of all, the *General Theory* is, as its name

5. A similar statement can be made for United States economists in the 1930s; see Stein (1969, chaps. 2, 7); Patinkin (1969, pp. 245–46); and Davis (1971). See also chap. 6 below, pp. 167–68.

indicates, a book concerned with theory; it contains only brief, passing discussions of policy, and of the policy of public-works expenditures in particular. Furthermore, already in 1929, in his influential election pamphlet with Hubert Henderson entitled *Can Lloyd George Do It?* Keynes had forcefully advocated this policy, and even here he was basically repeating views he had expressed five years earlier in the *Nation and Athenaeum* (*JMK* XIX, pp. 221–23; Hutchison 1953, pp. 418–19; cf. also chap. 8 below). Correspondingly, the advocacy per se of public-works expenditure was not the purpose of the *General Theory;* rather it was to provide a theory which would, among other things, rationalize such a policy.

What, then, was the major innovation of this theory? As a useful background against which to answer that question, let me first briefly characterize the major work which Keynes had published only five years before the *General Theory,* namely his *Treatise on Money* (1930).

In retrospect, the approach of the *Treatise* was a fairly simple one. It claimed that business cycles, or (to use the term of Keynes and his contemporaries) credit cycles, are caused by the alternation of profits and losses: profits cause firms to expand output, and losses to contract it. Now, profits are generated by the excess of the price of a product over its cost of production (including normal returns to capital), and losses by a shortfall. And so Keynes' analysis of the business cycle evolved into an analysis of what determines the price per unit of output relative to the cost per unit. This is the subject and the purpose of the so-called fundamental equations which Keynes regarded as the central message of his *Treatise:* his "novel means of approach to the fundamental problems of monetary theory" (*Treatise* I, preface, p. xvii). I will not bother you now with the obscure notation, so strange to us today, with which Keynes presented these equations. But when you finish examining them carefully, when you get down to their essence, what they say is the following:

index of price = index of cost of production + index of profits

—all per unit of output. And that is the fundamental equation!

Keynes recognized that this is an identity, and indeed said so. But he also claimed that it is an identity which is useful for classifying causal relationships. By means of his special definition of income (which excluded abnormal returns to capital), Keynes then showed—and this was the crucial point for him—that profits (as defined above) equal the excess of investment over saving. And he went on to proclaim that in analyzing the cycle in terms of the relation between these two quantities, he was "break[ing] away from the traditional method of setting out from the total quantity of money irrespective of the purposes on which it is employed" (*Treatise* I, p. 121). Note, however (and the significance of this will become clear in my next lecture), that Keynes of the *Treatise* used the relation between saving and investment to analyze in the first instance not changes in output, but changes in prices. Correspondingly, though as indicated he does discuss changes in output, he considers these to be derivative from the changes in prices.

I must also emphasize that though he recognized the tautological nature of his fundamental equations, Keynes inconsistently contended that they show that an excess of investment over savings *causes* prices to rise relative to costs, hence *causes* profits, and hence *causes* output to expand. But (as Keynes himself was later to point out in his preface to the *General Theory*) the *Treatise* did not explain the forces which determine by how much output would expand; and this was the major deficiency which the *General Theory* was designed to correct.

A more precise specification of the basic contribution of the *General Theory* can be obtained by letting Keynes speak for himself, as he did in a letter to Roy Harrod in August 1936, commenting on the latter's review article (1936) of the *General Theory*—a letter whose first and most important point largely repeats what Keynes had written Abba Lerner two months earlier on his (1936) review (see *JMK* XXIX, pp. 214–16):

> You don't mention *effective demand* or, more precisely, the demand schedule for output as a whole, except in so far as it is implicit in the multiplier. To me the most extraordinary thing, regarded historically, is the complete disappearance of the theory of demand and supply for output as a whole, i.e., the theory of employment, *after* it had been for a quarter of a century the most discussed thing in economics.[6] One of the most important transitions for me, after my *Treatise on Money* had been published, was suddenly realising this. It only came after I had enunciated to myself the psychological law that, when income increases, the gap between income and consumption will increase,—a conclusion of vast importance to my own thinking but not apparently, expressed just like that, to anyone else's. Then, appreciably later, came the notion of interest being the measure of liquidity preference, which became quite clear in my mind the moment I thought of it. And last of all, after an immense amount of muddling and many drafts, the proper definition of the marginal efficiency of capital linked up one thing with another. [*JMK* VII, p. xv, italics in original; see also *JMK* XIV, p. 85]

6. Presumably, the quarter-century between the beginning of the Ricardo-Malthus debate on the possibility of a "general glut in the market" in 1820 and the appearance of J. S. Mill's *Principles of Political Economy* in 1848. See also the reference to this period in the *General Theory* (pp. 32–34).

Now, in the *General Theory* (p. 141) Keynes himself had attributed priority for the notion of the marginal efficiency of capital to Fisher; and only recently have we (with the help of Paul Samuelson) learned the fascinating story of how this priority was brought to Keynes' attention by Redvers Opie at almost the last minute before publication (Patinkin and Leith 1977, pp. 87–89). Insofar as the theory of liquidity preference is concerned, this is clearly a contribution of Keynes, but it is one whose basic features had already been presented in the *Treatise* (*KMT*, pp. 37–41). This leaves the theory of effective demand as the distinctive analytical contribution of the *General Theory*.

That this is its central message is also clear from the *General Theory* itself. Thus Keynes tells us in its preface that, in contrast with his earlier *Treatise*, his new work is "primarily a study of the forces which determine changes in the scale of output and employment as a whole"; gives chapter 3 of "Book I: Introduction" the title "The Principle of Effective Demand" and presents in it a "summary of the theory of employment" that he will develop in the book (*GT*, p. 27); and devotes most of the remaining chapters of the *General Theory* to this development.

Figure 1 reproduces the familiar diagram which has served to transmit the central message of the *General Theory* to generations of economics students.[7] I wish, however, to refine the usual analysis which accompanies this diagram in one respect. In particular, what I mean by the theory of effective demand is not only that the intersection of the aggregate-demand curve $E = F(Y)$ with the 45° line determines equilibrium real output Y_0 at a level that may be below that of full employment Y_F; not only (as Leijonhufvud [1968] has also emphasized) that disequilibrium between aggregate demand and supply causes a change in output and not price; but also (and this is the distinctively novel feature) that the change in output (and hence income) itself acts as an equilibrating force. That is, if the economy is in a state of excess aggregate supply at (say) the level of output Y_1, then the resulting decline in output, and hence income, will depress supply more than demand and thus eventually bring the economy to equilibrium at Y_0. Or, in terms of the equivalent savings = investment equilibrium condition,

---

7. Though this diagram does not exactly accord with the presentation in chap. 3 of the *General Theory*, it captures its essence; for details, see chap. 5 below. As noted there (p. 129 below), Keynes himself did not provide a diagrammatic exposition of the argument of chap. 3. Fig. 1 has its origin instead in a 1939 article by Samuelson (see Bishop 1948, p. 325, n. 6). There is, however, one difference between the diagram on p. 1115 of Samuelson's article and the present one: in particular, Samuelson's analysis is of an economy in stationary equilibrium, in which by definition there is no net investment; correspondingly, his diagram contains only a consumption function, and not one reflecting the aggregate of consumption and investment expenditures.

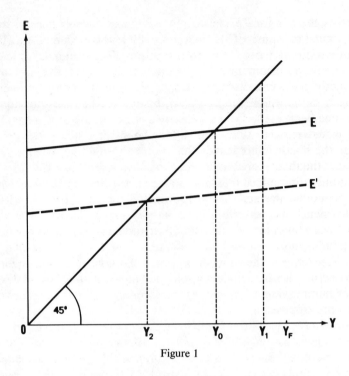

Figure 1

the decline in income will decrease savings and thus eventually eliminate the excess of savings over investment that exists at Y_1. In Keynes' words, "The novelty in my treatment of saving and investment consists, not in my maintaining their necessary aggregate equality, but in the proposition that it is, not the rate of interest, but the level of incomes which (in conjunction with certain other factors) ensures this equality" (1937a, p. 211; cf. also *GT*, p. 31, lines 16–23; p. 179, lines 2–6). In more formal terms (which, like the diagram, Keynes did not use), the theory of effective demand is concerned not only with the mathematical solution of the equilibrium equation $F(Y) = Y$, but with demonstrating the stability of this equilibrium as determined by the dynamic adjustment equation $dY/dt = \Phi[F(Y) - Y]$, where $\Phi' > 0$.[8]

Correspondingly, as Keynes emphasizes in his letter to Harrod and elsewhere, a crucial assumption of his (Keynes') analysis is that the marginal propensity to consume is less than unity, which in turn im-

8. May I add a personal note and say that I am not unaware of the fact that here, as in my discussion of the real-balance effect many years ago, I am attaching crucial significance to the role of a variable in stability analysis; see my *Money, Interest, and Prices* (1965, pp. 176–79).

plies that the marginal propensity to save is greater than zero. For, if the marginal propensity to consume were equal to unity, no equilibrating mechanism would be activated by the decline in output. Specifically, as income (output) decreased, spending would decrease by exactly the same amount, so that any initial difference between aggregate demand and supply would remain unchanged. Alternatively, as income decreased, the initial excess of desired saving over investment would remain unchanged. Thus the system would be unstable. This is the major novel feature of the *General Theory* and its central message: the theory of effective demand as a theory which depends on the equilibrating effect of the decline in output itself to explain why "the economic system may find itself in stable equilibrium with N [employment] at a level below full employment, namely at the level given by the intersection of the aggregate demand function with the aggregate supply function" (*GT*, p. 30).

The foregoing is the essence of the theory of effective demand as presented in "Book I: Introduction" of the *General Theory* under the explicit simplifying assumptions of a constant level of investment (which presupposes a constant rate of interest) and a constant money wage-rate (*GT*, pp. 27–29). But there is obviously more to the *General Theory*. Indeed, after a "digression" from the "main theme" (*GT*, p. 37) in "Book II: Definitions and Ideas" for the purpose of clarifying various concepts, Keynes devotes most of the remainder of the book to an elaboration of the theory of effective demand which (inter alia) is free of these restrictive assumptions. In "Book III: The Propensity to Consume" he elaborates upon the determinants of this component of aggregate demand and also discusses the related multiplier. In "Book IV: The Inducement to Invest" he drops the assumption of a constant level of investment and explains how this level is determined by the marginal-efficiency-of-capital schedule in conjunction with the rate of interest, which rate is determined in turn by the liquidity-preference schedule in conjunction with the quantity of money—with the crucial influence of uncertain expectations on both these schedules being discussed in detail. These uncertainties are a major source of the effectively low interest-elasticity of the first of these schedules, as well as the source of the speculative demand for money, and hence the effectively high (though not infinite) interest-elasticity of the second of them (*GT*, p. 164, lines 21–25; pp. 168–70, 207–9; *KMT*, pp. 103, 111–13). It is to these elasticities that Keynes alludes when he ends "Chapter 12: The State of Long-Term Expectations" with the observation that he is "now somewhat sceptical of the success of a merely monetary policy directed toward influencing the rate of interest . . . since it seems likely that the fluctuations in the market estimation of the marginal efficiency of different types of capital . . . will be too great to be offset by any practicable changes in the rate of interest" (*GT*, p. 164).

Keynes concludes Book IV with a summary chapter (18) entitled "The General Theory of Employment Re-Stated." In substance, though not in form, this chapter (like the diagram on p. 180 of an earlier one) provides a general-equilibrium analysis of the determination (as of a given money-wage rate and nominal quantity of money) of the equilibrium level of national income by the interactions between the commodity (consumption- and investment-goods) and money markets (*GT*, pp. 246–47). The integrated analysis of these two markets is another significant contribution of the *General Theory*, a contribution that Hicks (1937) was subsequently to develop and formalize in his influential *IS–LM* interpretation of the book (*KMT*, pp. 98–101).

Finally, in "Book V: Money-Wages and Prices," Keynes drops the assumption of a constant money-wage rate and applies the theory of effective demand that he had developed in Books I–IV to an analysis (in the first chapter of this Book, "Chapter 19: Changes in Money Wages") of the effects of a decline in this rate. Here Keynes argues that such a decline (which in practice would, because of the resistance of workers, take place only very slowly [*GT*, p. 267; see also ibid., pp. 9, 251, 303]) can increase the level of employment only by first increasing the level of effective demand; that the primary way it can generate such an increase is through its effect in increasing the quantity of money in terms of wage units, thereby decreasing the rate of interest and stimulating investment; that accordingly the policy of attempting to eliminate unemployment by reducing money wages is equivalent to a policy of attempting to do so by increasing the quantity of money at an unchanged wage rate and is accordingly subject to the same limitations as the latter: namely, that a moderate change "may exert an inadequate influence over the long-term rate of interest," while an immoderate one ("even if it were practicable") "may offset its other advantages by its disturbing effect on confidence." Hence his major conclusion—and indeed the negative component of his central message—that "the economic system cannot be made self-adjusting along these lines" (*GT*, pp. 266–67; *KMT*, pp. 95–98). In this way Keynes finally supplies the theoretical basis for his claim in chapter 2 of "Book I: Introduction" that—contrary to the "classical" view—"a willingness on the part of labour to accept lower money-wages is not necessarily a remedy for unemployment," a claim he had promised would be "fully elucidated . . . in Chapter 19" (*GT*, p. 18; see also ibid., p. 9).[9] Implicit in chapter

9. That at many places in chap. 2 Keynes had in mind the analysis to come in chap. 19 is evident by his repeated references to it and its appendix on pp. 7n, 8n, 11, 12n, 13n, and 18. Correspondingly, Keynes begins chap. 19 with an allusion to his earlier discussion of money wages (*GT*, p. 257).

19 is also an explanation of Keynes' enigmatic remark in chapter 2 that "there may exist no expedient by which labour as a whole can reduce its *real* wage to a lower figure by making revised *money* bargains with entrepreneurs" (*GT*, p. 13, italics in original). For if a reduction in money wages does not succeed in affecting the level of effective demand, it will also not affect the level of output, hence the level of labor input, hence the marginal product of labor, and hence (by what Keynes termed "the first classical postulate," to which he adhered throughout the *General Theory* [pp. 5, 17]) the real wage rate (cf. pp. 136, 141–42 below).

Book V also contains "Chapter 21: The Theory of Prices." In "Book I: Introduction," Keynes had stated that "we shall find that the Theory of Prices falls into its proper place as a matter which is subsidiary to our general theory" (*GT*, p. 32). In particular, as we have just seen, the level of effective demand determines the level of employment and hence the real wage rate. For any given money wage rate, then, the price level is determined. In the words of chapter 21, "The general price-level (taking equipment and technique as given) depends partly on the wage-unit and partly on the volume of employment" (*GT*, p. 295). Because he had in this way related his theory to marginal-productivity theory, Keynes felt that his book accomplished another objective, namely the integration of monetary and value theory (*GT*, pp. 292–93). And though he was not completely successful in this respect (see chapter 5 below), I would regard this too as one of the contributions of the *General Theory*.[10]

The last Book of the *General Theory*—"Book VI: Short Notes Suggested by the General Theory"—is, as its title indicates, essentially an appendage to it, one that could have been omitted without affecting the logical integrity of the book as a whole. The Book begins with "Chapter 22: Notes on the Trade Cycle." Here Keynes contends that the cycle is generated by changes in the marginal efficiency of capital—which changes, for reasons discussed in the chapter, "have had cyclical characteristics." He claims no novelty for this interpretation ("these reasons are by no means unfamiliar either in themselves or as explanations of the trade cycle") and explains that the purpose of the chapter is "to link [these reasons] up with the preceding theory" (*GT*, pp. 314–15). Chapter 23 is entitled "Notes on Mercantilism, the Usury Law, Stamped Money and Theories of Under-Consumption"—which title is a further indication that the material of Book VI is not an integral part of the *General Theory*. The last chapter of the Book—and of the book as a whole—is "Chapter 24: Concluding Notes

---

10. Particularly as compared with Keynes' own *Treatise on Money*, in which there is no mention whatever of the marginal concept; cf. *KMT*, pp. 13, 47, 94.

on the Social Philosophy towards Which the General Theory Might Lead." Only to a minor extent, however, is this chapter concerned with the question of short-run, full-employment policy—and in this context Keynes reiterates his skepticism of sole reliance on monetary policy and his corresponding belief "that a somewhat comprehensive socialisation of investment will prove the only means of securing an approximation to full employment" (*GT*, p. 378). Most of the chapter is devoted to the long-run implications of a successful full-employment policy for the accumulation of capital, hence the rate of interest and the distribution of income; for the future of laissez-faire versus state socialism; and for the prospects of war and peace.

From this summary it is clear that the primary concern of the *General Theory* is theory and not policy, though Keynes does make brief use of the theory to explain the necessity for public-works expenditures to combat severe unemployment; that the primary concern of its theory is output (or employment) and not prices; and that the primary concern of its theory of output is the explanation of equilibrium at less-than-full-employment and not cyclical variations in output. The significance of the first of these points has already been indicated (above, pp. 6–7); the significance of the other two will become evident in the lectures which follow.

Another point which is clear from this summary is that, though Keynes refers repeatedly in the *General Theory* to situations of "unemployment equilibrium," he was not using this term in the rigorous sense that nothing in the economy tends to change. On the contrary, it is clear from chapter 19 of the book that the situation he envisaged was one of short-run or temporary equilibrium, in which the existence of unemployment exerts a downward pressure on money wages. But, as Keynes goes on to show in this chapter, even if this pressure were to generate an actual decline in these wages, this would not necessarily lead to an increase in employment. And it is in this sense that a position of unemployment equilibrium exists (cf. also *KMT*, pp. 116–17).

Let me now return to my main argument. You may feel that the analysis of figure 1 is obvious: it even appears on the front covers of some well-known introductory textbooks. But we must put ourselves back forty-five years ago and even longer. To the economist of that time, the very notion of an aggregate-demand curve was strange: for the demand curve that had been drilled into him was one based on an assumption of ceteris paribus; but what could be the meaning of such an assumption—the meaning of "other things equal"—in the case of a demand curve for output as a whole? And it was also strange to conceive of a demand for aggregate output that was in some way different from aggregate income, as if national income expended could somehow differ from national income received. But besides this strangeness—and this is the point I am now emphasizing—there was no perception of the fact that changes in output are themselves an equilibrating factor.

To bring this out more sharply, let me contrast Keynes' discussion in the *General Theory* with the corresponding one of the *Treatise*. In the *General Theory*, a decrease in consumption—or, equivalently, an increase in savings—is represented by a downward shift of the aggregate-demand curve in figure 1 to E'; the resulting decline in output will then cause a corresponding decline in the amount consumed—and in the amount saved, as well—until a new equilibrium is necessarily reached at Y_2 (cf. *GT*, pp. 82–85, 183–84). Contrast this with Keynes' "parable" in the *Treatise* of a simple "banana plantation" economy in an initial position of full-employment equilibrium which is disturbed because (in Keynes' words) "into this Eden there enters a thrift campaign." Making use of the analytical framework of the *Treatise*, Keynes then proceeds to explain that as a result of the increased savings generated by this campaign, entrepreneurs will suffer losses and hence will

> seek to protect themselves by throwing their employees out of work or reducing their wages. But even this will not improve their position, since the spending power of the public will be reduced by just as much as the aggregate costs of production. By however much entrepreneurs reduce wages and however many of their employees they throw out of work, they will continue to make losses so long as the community continues to save in excess of new investment. Thus there will be no position of equilibrium until either (*a*) all production ceases and the entire population starves to death; or (*b*) the thrift campaign is called off or peters out as a result of the growing poverty; or (*c*) investment is stimulated by some means or other so that its cost no longer lags behind the rate of saving (*Treatise* I, pp. 159–60).

In brief, it seems to me that Keynes is (in the terminology he was to adopt in the *General Theory*) implicitly assuming here that the marginal propensity to spend is unity, so that a decline in output cannot reduce the excess of saving over investment and thus cannot act as an equilibrating force. Instead, the decline in output can come to an end, either when it can decline no further, when "all production ceases and the entire population starves to death" (and I cannot help but remark that the unhesitating way in which Keynes lists this "corner solution"—or, as a secretary of mine once rendered it, "coroner solution"—as one of his three alternatives is a revealing indication of his supreme confidence at the time in the analysis of the *Treatise*); or alternatively, the decline might end as the result of some exogenous force that closes the gap between saving and investment—"the thrift campaign is called off," or "investment is stimulated by some means or another."[11] In brief, none of these alternatives indicate that Keynes of the *Treatise* understood that the decline in output itself acts directly as a systematic endogenous equilibrating force.

But, you will undoubtedly ask, what about Keynes' reference to the possibility that equilibrium might be reestablished if "the thrift campaign . . . peters out as a result of growing poverty?" Should this not be taken as an indication of such an understanding? I think not, and this for two reasons: First, it does not seem to me that the language used, "peters out," has the connotation of a systematic force. Second, and far more important, if Keynes had at that time understood that changes in output act as a systematic equilibrating mechanism, he would have sufficed with describing that alternative alone: there would have been no need for listing any additional ones. Or at least he would not have listed the first one, which is a denial of this equilibrating mechanism. In any event, it is significant that in a 1932 allusion to the foregoing passage—by which time Keynes had begun (albeit imperfectly) to take account of the equilibrating effects of changes in output—he refers only to the ultimate equilibrating effect of "the pressure of increasing poverty" and does not refer to any other way in which equilibrium might be reestablished (*JMK* XIII, pp. 386–87, reproduced below on pp. 19–20). And by the time he got to the final draft of the *General Theory*, he concentrated solely on this equilibrating mechanism, which provided him with the "paradox of saving."

This illustrates a basic principle that will guide me in these lectures: that in studying a man's writings we must distinguish between that which was fully integrated into his conceptual framework and that which was not; between the systematic component of his thinking and the random component; between, if you wish, the "signal"—or what I have called the "central message"—the writer wished to convey and the "noise."

Alternatively, in terms of a similar metaphor that I have developed elsewhere, the history of doctrines should be looked upon as an empirical study, with the sample observations being drawn from the universe consisting of the writings and teaching of the economists in question. When I first made that observation some years ago (1969, p. 242), all I meant was that economists who wrote on the history of doctrine

---

11. Actually, in his subsequent analysis in chap. 18 of the *Treatise*, Keynes essentially explains how an increase in saving does generate an endogenous process (namely, a decline in prices, hence a reduction in the "industrial circulation," and hence a reduction in the rate of interest) which stimulates investment. This, however, does not affect my basic contention as presented in the next paragraph.

should support their interpretations with evidence from the relevant texts—and there was a reason for saying so at the time. But in recent years, primarily as a result of my work on the development of Keynes' thought, I have come to look upon the history of doctrines as an empirical science in the broader sense that those of us who engage in it are like econometricians fitting a regression line to a set of empirical observations (points) in order to determine the central tendency of the relationship that exists between the variables in question; so are we trying to pass a regression line through a scholar's work that will represent its central message. Now, precisely because a regression line is a measure of central tendency—that is, an average—there are always points that are not on it; and then the question that faces the econometrician is whether these points are random departures from the line, or whether they reflect a systematic influence that he has not taken account of. The same is true when we pass a regression line through a scholar's work: with the extent depending on the scholar and work in question,[12] there will generally be some passages (especially if it is a book or other long work) that are not (completely) consistent with our interpretation. Then we have to decide what is the true meaning of the work, what is its regression line, and what is a chance phrase, or perhaps even a mistake, whose departure from the regression line should not make us change our view about its central message. And from this viewpoint I feel that Keynes' reference to the possibility that "the thrift campaign . . . peters out as a result of growing poverty" should not lead us to change the foregoing interpretation of the passage in the *Treatise* in which it appears. It is "noise."

I realize that this emphasis on the central message of a work introduces a subjective element into the study of the history of thought. Such an element, however, has always existed: for what student of thought has not chosen to give more weight to certain passages in a scholar's work than to others? Furthermore, to continue with my metaphor, subjective considerations also manifest themselves in ordinary regression analysis. Thus, for example, econometricians to begin with frequently eliminate observations from "special periods" (e.g., wartime, periods of price controls). Similarly, they frequently specify a priori a form for their regression equation that reduces the relative weight of "extreme observations" (e.g., the specification of a

---

12. Less, say, for Hicks' *Value and Capital* (1939), which to the best of my knowledge suffers from only one minor inconsistency—namely, the different definitions of the substitution effect in, respectively, the text and mathematical appendix, an inconsistency which disappears in the limit (Mosak 1942); more, as we shall see in chap. 5 below, for Keynes' *General Theory*. Cf. on all this my contribution to the discussion on pp. 125–26 of Patinkin and Leith (1977).

logarithmic form for the demand function for money in the study of hyperinflation).

I also realize that I have not even attempted to provide a precise definition of "central message." I prefer, however, to wait with such an attempt until my concluding lecture, by which time I hope to have clarified this concept somewhat by means of examples of its opposite: that is, passages from the literature to be studied which in my view (and I hope to persuade you of it as well) do *not* constitute the respective central messages of the writers in question.

I have so far discussed the development of the theory of effective demand as if it had been prompted solely by the discovery of logical deficiencies in the *Treatise*. Actually, as in the development of new theories in the natural sciences, empirical observations also played a role here—even if, because of the nonexperimental nature of economics, a considerably lesser one than in these sciences. Thus it is a commonplace that the *General Theory* was the product of the mass unemployment of the 1930s. But this is a half-truth: for it fails to take account of the fact that the Britain in which Keynes wrote the *Treatise* (unlike the United States and most European countries at that time) was also suffering from a severe and prolonged unemployment. The point, however, is that this unemployment did not constitute an "anomaly" or "puzzle"[13] for the prevailing theory, which explained unemployment as the consequence of too high a wage rate; indeed, this was the explanation Keynes himself advanced in his *Economic Consequences of Mr. Churchill* (1925). Specifically, he explained that the return of Britain to the gold standard in April 1925 at prewar parity had overvalued the pound relative to the existing level of money wages, and it was this that had generated unemployment, first in the export industries and then elsewhere. Thus, in theory, the way to restore full employment was to reduce money wages; but in practice, the resistance of labor made such a policy impossible to carry out, thus making it necessary to adopt alternative policies (*JMK* IX, pp. 208–12, 227–29). And in the *Treatise* (II, pp. 162–65) Keynes repeated this analysis.[14]

In contrast, the unemployment of the 1930s created doubts about the existing theory not only because of the persistence and worsening of unemployment, but because it constituted an anomaly for this theory, and this for two reasons. First, unemployment had become a worldwide phenomenon, and so could not be explained as the result of the specific circumstances of Britain. Second, and this was a point to

13. Cf. Kuhn (1970, chaps. 6–8) and Laudan (1977, chap. 1).
14. As Hutchison (1968, pp. 277–79) has emphasized, other British economists at the time also distinguished between theory and policy when it came to reducing money wages.

which Keynes alluded in the *General Theory* (p. 9), money wages in the early 1930s had fallen sharply in the United States, but to no avail insofar as unemployment was concerned.[15] True, the price level had fallen even more. But this too was part of the anomaly that concerned Keynes: namely, that labor controlled only its money wage and might not have any way of reducing its real wage (*GT*, p. 13). Thus the unemployment of the 1930s was of a kind which the classical theory could not explain and which, therefore, called for a new theory: hence the theory of effective demand. And though this new theory retained the classical inverse relation between real wages and employment, it reversed its causal direction: it was not the real wage rate which determined the level of employment, but the level of employment which determined the real wage rate (*GT*, p. 30).[16]

When did Keynes first formulate his theory of effective demand cum equilibrating effect of changes in output? With the aid of the correspondence and fragments of early drafts of the *General Theory* which have been reproduced in volumes XIII and XXIX of Keynes' *Collected Writings*, and with the aid of student notes of Keynes' lectures, we can now date this on a much firmer basis than heretofore. Thus we already find some indications of this theory in a letter Keynes wrote to Kahn in September 1931 (*JMK* XIII, pp. 373–75); but the argument there is obscure and in any event does not seem to make use of the aforementioned systematic equilibrating mechanism.

A somewhat clearer indication of this mechanism is, however, to be found in a surviving fragment of a mid-1932 draft of the *General Theory* in which Keynes wrote:

> it is natural to expect that, as the earnings of the public [*E*] decline, a point will eventually be reached at which the decline in total expenditure *F*, of both entrepreneurs and public taken together, will cease to be so great as the decline in *E*. For we can, I think, be sure that sooner or later the most virtuous intentions will break down before the pressure of increasing poverty, so that savings will fall off and negative saving will begin to appear in some quarter or another to offset the effect of losses on the expenditure of entrepreneurs. Sooner or later, for example, the determination of the government to

15. Keynes also made this point in his fall 1933 lectures at Cambridge; see the notes on his lecture of October 16, 1933 as recorded by Bryce, Tarshis, and Salant, respectively (cf. n. 18 below).

From 1929 to 1933, money wages (as measured by average hourly earnings) fell in the United States by 28 percent (U.S. Dept. of Commerce, *Historical Statistics of the United States* 1960, p. 92). For further details, see p. 238, n. 27, below.

16. Cf. p. 13 above and pp. 141–42 below. Keynes emphasized this reversal of the classical causal direction even more strongly in a 1933 draft of the book (*JMK* XXIX, pp. 80, 97–99).

pay for the dole out of additional taxation will break down; and even
if it does not, the determination of the taxpayer to economise in his
personal expenditure by the full amount of the additional taxes he
must pay, will weaken. Indeed the mere law of survival must tend in
this direction. . . .

Indeed once we have reached the point at which spending decreases less than earnings decrease with investment stable, the at-
tainment of equilibrium presents no problem. For provided that
spending always increases less than earnings increase and decreases
less than earnings decrease, i.e., provided ΔS and ΔE have the same
sign, and that investment does not change, *any* level of output is a
position of stable equilibrium. For any increase of output will bring
in a retarding factor, since ΔS will be positive and consequently I
being assumed constant, ΔQ will be negative; whilst equally any
decrease of output will bring in a stimulating factor, since ΔS will be
negative and consequently ΔQ positive. [*JMK* XIII, pp. 386–87,
italics in original]

The meaning of the symbols in the second paragraph of this passage is
the same as in the *Treatise;* namely, S = saving, E = factor incomes
(exclusive of abnormal profits), I = investment, and Q = profits, from
which follows the crucial relation (again as in the *Treatise*) $Q = I - S$.
And this points up the most significant aspect of the mid-1932 draft;
namely, that its analytical framework is basically still that of the
Treatise. Indeed, the first paragraph of the foregoing passage, with its
reference to the equilibrating effect of "increasing poverty," clearly
echoes the second of the three alternatives in the passage from the
Treatise which I have quoted earlier. Furthermore, and most important
for our present purposes, the fact that the foregoing mid-1932 passage
states that savings will begin to decline with declining output only after
a certain "pressure of poverty" is created clearly shows that at that
time Keynes had not yet fully recognized what he was later to designate as the "conclusion of vast importance to [his] own thinking"
about the "psychological law that when income increases, the gap
between income and consumption will increase"—at all levels of income.[17]

It is also significant that the mid-1932 draft does not contain any
explicit reference to the aggregate demand function or to its component
consumption and investment functions. Nor do I think that this simply
reflects a failure to state explicitly and formally what was implicitly
understood. For Keynes' contention at the end of the foregoing passage that "once we have reached the point at which spending decreases
less than earnings . . . *any* level of output is a position of stable equilib-

17. These phrases are from Keynes' 1936 letter to Harrod cited on p. 8 above.

rium" shows that he had not yet achieved a full understanding of the basic $C + I = Y$ equilibrium condition that was to constitute his theory of effective demand.

Further indication of the state of Keynes' thinking at the end of 1932 is provided by unique "archaeological" evidence on the chronology of the transition from the *Treatise* to the *General Theory* provided by Robert Bryce's notes on Keynes' lectures during the successive years 1932, 1933, and 1934 and Lorie Tarshis' notes for these years as well as 1935. These notes provide two independent observations on Keynes' thoughts on monetary economics in the fall of 1932, and like the mid-1932 draft of the *General Theory*, both of them show that at that time Keynes' thinking was still largely in the mold of the *Treatise*. The closest thing in these notes to what was to become the theory of effective demand was the following statement by Keynes, as recorded by Lorie Tarshis on October 17, 1932:

> The decision of each individual re extent of disbursements will be affected by amount of income. If at a given level of distribution of income aggregate disbursement would add up to a different total (more) than amount of income—position untenable. Incomes will have to change until the total of income will add to equal disbursement. Every individual disbursement alters individual incomes—I's and D's will change until amount of I's and D's are equal at a particular level.

Similarly, Bryce on that day recorded:

> If at a given level of income individual disbursement added up to more than income the position is untenable and change will be effected to position where aggregate community income equals disbursement, i.e., only rest is where aggregate income is equal to aggregate disbursements, due to effect of individual income on individual disbursements.

But like the mid-1932 draft, no further details are provided on the nature of the equilibrating process, and no explicit reference is made to the aggregate-demand function and its component functions.[18]

And as a final bit of evidence on this point I would like to refer to the

18. I am greatly indebted to Robert Bryce, Lorie Tarshis, and Walter Salant (see below) for making their notes available and permitting me to quote from them.

In *JMK* XXIX (pp. 55–57) there appears a fragment which (on the basis of these notes) Moggridge has identified with Keynes' lecture of November 14, 1932, and which presents a description of the equilibrating role of changes in output. As I have, however, pointed out elsewhere (Patinkin 1980, p. 19), though part of this fragment does appear in Bryce's and Tarshis' notes for that date, the description of the equilibrating mechanism does not. Hence there is no direct evidence that this description was actually included in the lecture of that date.

October 1933 article by Joan Robinson on "The Theory of Money and the Analysis of Output" which (in her words eighteen years later) "gives an outline of Keynes' theory as far as it had got in 1933" (Joan Robinson 1951, p. viii). In this article, Robinson referred to the same revealing passage from the *Treatise* (I, pp. 159–60) that I have cited above and, implicitly making use of the analytical framework of the *Treatise*, quite correctly went on to say:

> [Keynes] points out that if savings exceed investment, consumption goods can only be sold at a loss. Their output will consequently decline until the real income of the population is reduced to such a low level that savings are perforce reduced to equality with investment. But [Keynes] completely overlooks the significance of this discovery, and throws it out in the most casual way without pausing to remark that he has proved that output may be in equilibrium at any number of different levels, and that while there is a natural tendency towards equilibrium between savings and investment (in a very long run), there is no natural tendency towards full employment of the factors of production. [Joan Robinson 1933b, pp. 55–56]

But the article did not refer explicitly to a consumption function, and a fortiori did not explain the crucial role that the less-than-unity marginal propensity to consume played in the equilibrating process. In brief, this article too did not contain the theory of effective demand.

On the basis, however, of the successive "strata" revealed by our archaeological evidence, we can confidently say that Keynes first formulated this theory sometime during 1933, for which year we also have the notes of Walter Salant. For in the lectures which Keynes gave in the fall of that year, we find him saying (according to Lorie Tarshis' notes on November 20, 1933):

> We must assume this—relating peoples' consumption to their incomes. Not universally satisfactory but normally the psychological law is that the ΔC is $<$ the ΔY. The increment of consumption is less than increment of income. When their income increases they don't (over community as a whole) not whole of increase is spent on consumption. . . . This above law is not only necessary for the stability of the system but it also means that if propensity to spend is of such a character that $\Delta C < \Delta Y$ then ΔY can only be positive if ΔI is positive. There are two variables—the propensity to spend—the value of C corresponding to any value of Y—depending not only on Y now but expectations etc. Suppose that state of expectations is given—to every Y there corresponds a C and consequently one must choose that pair of values such that taking account of our given I, $Y = C + I$ holds. If we assume that as Y falls, C falls slower, and as Y rises, C rises at a different rate—there will be a set of values of C and Y to satisfy this.

And much the same thing is to be found in Bryce's corresponding notes. An even more explicit statement was presented by Keynes in a subsequent lecture when he said (according to Robert Bryce's notes[19] from December 4, 1933):

> We have
> $Y = C + I$
> In a given state of the news
> In given w, C is a function of Y. $[C] = \phi_1 (w, Y)$.
> I is a function of w [and the rate of interest, denoted by ρ] $= \phi_2(w, \rho)$
>   i.e. $Y = \phi_1(Y) + \phi_2(\rho)$ when w is given
> Hence it is largely ρ that is important.
> Assume given w.
> Suppose N total number of men employed
> N_1 producing for consumption
> N_2 producing for investment
> $N = N_1 + N_2$
> Assume propensity to spend and to consume given.
> Then $N_1 = f_1(N)$ $N_2 = f_2(\rho)$ (r[ate]. of i[nterest].)
> $N = f_1(N) + f_2(\rho)$.

So it is clear that by that time Keynes had achieved a full understanding of the theory of effective demand.

During the following months Keynes continued to work on his theory until he had developed it into the polished formulation which we find in the mid-1934 draft of the *General Theory,* the surviving fragments of which have been reproduced in *JMK* XIII (pp. 424–56). Indeed, this formulation of the theory of effective demand is in many ways more systematic and mathematically elegant than the one which finally appeared in the *General Theory* (*KMT*, pp. 73–76).

Before going on, let me discuss two pieces of counter evidence to my contention that Keynes first formulated his theory of effective demand in 1933. The first is an oft-cited statement in the Harris Foundation lecture which Keynes gave here at the University of Chicago in June 1931. In this lecture Keynes explained how an excess of savings generates a decline in output, and then went on to say:

19. Lorie Tarshis was apparently absent on this occasion, for his lecture notes for that day carry the legend, "Copied from Bryce's Notes." Salant's notes from this lecture are less complete.

Professor T. K. Rymes of Carleton University (where Bryce's lecture notes are now deposited) has kindly informed me that the third line in the following citation was inserted in pencil after the second line. This makes it clear that w (or the Greek ω, as it might actually be) denotes the "state of the news." I should also observe that in the original notes there is an arrow drawn between the parenthetical phrase "(r. of i.)" in the penultimate line and ρ in the equation which precedes it. As a result of this more careful examination of the handwritten notes, the rendition presented here differs slightly, though not in any substantive way, from the one presented in *KMT* (p. 79, n. 22).

Now there is a reason for expecting an equilibrium point of decline to be reached. A given deficiency of investment causes a given decline of profit. A given decline of profit causes a given decline of output. Unless there is a constantly increasing deficiency of investment, there is eventually reached, therefore, a sufficiently low level of output which represents a kind of spurious equilibrium. [*JMK* XIII, pp. 355–56]

At first sight, this would seem to be an adumbration of the unemployment-equilibrium notion of the *General Theory*.[20] But closer examination of the context in which this paragraph appears indicates that this is not the case. For this context is one in which Keynes is analyzing the forces which generate, not a continuing state of unemployment equilibrium, but the transitory stationary point at the trough of the business cycle. That is, what Keynes is analyzing here is the cause of the eventual elimination of the original excess of saving over investment which generated the slump, and its replacement at the turning point of the cycle by an opposite excess which then begins to generate the recovery.

My main point, however, is that Keynes begins his analysis of the turning point with the following words:

Indeed, let me simplify further, for I should like for a moment to leave the variations in saving out of my argument. I shall assume that saving either varies in the wrong direction (which may, in fact, occur, especially in the early stages of the slump, since the fall in stock-exchange values as compared with the boom may by depreciating the value of people's past savings increase their desire to add to them) or is substantially unchanged, or if it varies in the right direction, so as partly to compensate changes in investment, varies insufficiently (which is likely to be the case except perhaps when the community is, toward the end of a slump, very greatly impoverished indeed). That is to say, I shall concentrate on the variability of the rate of investment. [*JMK* XIII, p. 354]

Keynes then goes on to say, "as soon as output begins to recover" (and Keynes does not really explain why this recovery occurs) "the tide is turned and the decline in fixed investment is partly offset by increased investment in working capital" (ibid., p. 355).

This passage is then followed by the one which I cited at the begin-

20. And this is the way it has been interpreted by Samuelson (1946, p. 330), though not by Klein (1947, pp. 33–36), to whose work Samuelson (1946, p. 315 n) has expressed his general indebtedness. The interpretation which follows agrees in its essentials with that of Klein.

ning of this discussion ("Now there is reason . . ."), and only after-
wards does Keynes drop the assumption that savings are constant and
argue as follows:

> There is also another reason for expecting the decline to reach a
> stopping-point. For I must now qualify my simplifying assumption
> that only the rate of investment changes and that the rate of saving
> remains constant. At first, as I have said, the nervousness engen-
> dered by the slump may actually tend to increase saving. For saving
> is often effected as a safeguard against insecurity. Thus savings may
> decrease when stock markets are soaring and increase when they are
> slumping. Moreover, for the salaried and fixed-income class of the
> community the fall of prices will increase their margin available for
> saving. But as soon as output has declined heavily, strong forces will
> be brought into play in the direction of reducing the net volume of
> saving.
>
> For one thing the unemployed will, in their effort not to allow too
> great a decline in their established standard of life, not only cease to
> save but will probably be responsible for much negative saving by
> living on their own previous savings and those of their friends and
> relations. Much more important, however, than this is likely to be
> the emergence of negative saving on the part of the government,
> whether by diminished payments to sinking funds or by actual bor-
> rowing, as is now the case in the United States. In Great Britain, for
> example, the dole to the unemployed, largely financed by borrow-
> ing, is now at the rate of $500 million a year—equal to about a
> quarter of the country's estimated rate of saving in good times. In
> the United States the Treasury deficit to be financed by borrowing is
> put at $1,000 million. These expenditures are just as good in their
> immediate effects on the situation as would be an equal expenditure
> on capital works; the only difference—and an important one
> enough—is that in the former cases we have nothing to show for it
> afterwards. [*JMK* XIII, p. 356]

All this is far removed from the noncyclical analysis of the *General
Theory,* based exclusively on the fact that an initial decline in investment generates a decrease in output which continues until the systematic downward influence such a decrease exerts on saving brings the
economy to a new equilibrium position in which saving is once again
equal to investment at the new, lower level of the latter. Indeed, though
Keynes' Harris lecture does, in the last passage cited, recognize some
endogenous reaction of saving to the decline in output, the central
message of his lecture is the same as that of the *Treatise:* namely, that
cyclical variations can be analyzed by means of the fundamental equations of price. Nor should this surprise us: for Keynes' Harris lecture

was first and foremost a song of praise to his *Treatise*, which had appeared less than a year before. Thus Keynes began his analysis of the slump in this lecture with a verbal rendition of the fundamental equations and with the accompanying proclamation, "That is my secret, the clue to the scientific explanation of booms and slumps (and of much else as I should claim) which I offer you" (*JMK* XIII, p. 354). Which brings me to observe that, though Keynes alluded to the Bible on more than one occasion in his writings (e.g., the "widow's cruse"), the verse in the Book of Proverbs (27:2), "Let another man praise thee, and not thine own mouth," was apparently not one of his favorites.

The second item which is frequently cited as evidence of an early formulation of the theory of effective demand is Kahn's famous 1931 multiplier article.[21] The accompanying diagram (fig. 2) presents the multiplier *as we teach it today*. An exogenous increase of ΔI. in investment causes the aggregate-demand curve to shift from E to $E + \Delta I$, causing the equilibrium level of national income to increase to $Y_0 + \Delta Y$. Hence the multiplier is

$$\frac{\Delta Y}{\Delta I} = \frac{\Delta Y}{\Delta Y - \Delta C} = \frac{1}{1 - (\Delta C/\Delta Y)} = \frac{1}{1 - MPC},$$

where *MPC* is the marginal propensity to consume.

I said that this is the way we teach the multiplier today; and as such it is clearly a direct implication of the theory of effective demand. But this is *not* the way Richard Kahn first presented the multiplier in his 1931 article. And I am not simply saying that he did not present his analysis in terms of a diagram, but that (and this is the crucial point) he did not present it in the context of a comparative-statics equilibrium analysis of the level of national income. Instead, the multiplier of Kahn's article is the dynamic one, showing in terms of a declining geometric series the sequence of "secondary employments" generated by a once-and-for-all increase in public-works expenditures, and then deriving the multiplier by summing up this infinite series. Correspondingly, the notion of equilibrium is barely mentioned in Kahn's

21. Which appeared in the *Economic Journal* under the title "The Relation of Home Investment to Unemployment." See also Kahn's subsequent exchange with the Danish economist Jens Warming (1932). Because it was the source for Keynes, I am for convenience identifying the origins of the multiplier with Kahn's article. It would not, however, affect my argument if we were instead to follow Hegeland (1954, chap. 1) and identify it with the turn-of-the-century Danish writer Julius Wulff, whose work ultimately influenced Warming. See also Wright (1956) and Topp (1981).

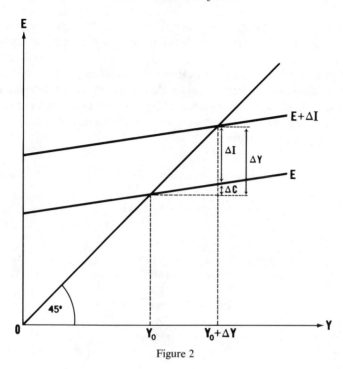

Figure 2

article; indeed it appears only once, in a footnote (p. 12, n. 1)—and even then not with reference to the theory of effective demand.

There is another point that should be emphasized here, and that is the context in which Kahn's article was written. I have already mentioned (above, p. 7) Keynes' advocacy of public works in his 1929 pamphlet *Can Lloyd George Do It?* In this pamphlet Keynes had shown that besides the "primary employment" created by the initial public-works expenditures, there would be additional "indirect employment" created by the subsequent chain of increased expenditures that would be generated. He also contended that, contrary to the so-called Treasury view, the increase in government investment would not be entirely at the expense of private investment, but would itself generate an increase in savings that would enable a net increase in investment. Keynes did not, however, address himself to the question of the quantitative relationship between these two increases. And the major purpose of Kahn's article was to prove (by means of the multiplier formula which he developed) that not only would there be an increase in savings (which increase, significantly enough, he termed an "alleviation"), but that this increase would exactly equal the initial increase in investment (the "aggravation"). This was the central message of Kahn's article, not the development of a theory of effective demand.[22]

The absence of a theory of effective demand from Kahn's article also manifests itself in the fact that he develops his multiplier analysis within the conceptual framework of Keynes' *Treatise*. Indeed, at one point he applies his analysis to the first fundamental equation of the *Treatise* (I, p. 122), namely

$$P = W_1 + \frac{I' - S}{R},$$

where P is the per-unit price of consumption goods, W_1 is their per-unit cost of production, I' is investment evaluated at its cost of production, S is saving, and R is the real output of consumption goods. As a result of Keynes' special definition of income and hence saving, the numerator $I' - S$ then equals total profits in the consumption-goods sector of the economy, so that the quotient $(I' - S)/R$ represents per-unit profits in this sector (see the verbal equation on p. 7 above). In a mechanical way (reminiscent of the mechanical way that Keynes himself had frequently proceeded in the *Treatise* [*KMT*, pp. 51–53]), Kahn then argues that if the supply of consumption goods is completely elastic, so that P and W_1 remain constant as output R increases, then

> however great may be the cost of the investment [I'] that is taking place in road-building, the secondary employment will be such that the total alleviation (*minus* the aggravation) keeps the difference between total savings and total investment [$I' - S$] at a constant amount (or, more accurately, at an amount that varies in direct proportion with the output of consumption-goods [R]).

> But this conclusion—that under certain circumstances employment can be increased without any significant alteration in the difference between savings and investment—does not in the slightest degree invalidate the causal force of Mr. Keynes' argument. The motive force that increases employment is an increase in investment or a reduction in savings. As a concomitant of this increase in employment occur other changes in savings and investment which, partially or wholly, neutralise the effect on the difference between

---

22. Cf. Kahn (1931, pp. 1–3, 8–10). For a detailed discussion of these points see pp. 191–99 below. See also n. 27 below for Kahn's own description of the purposes of his article.

To simplify the task of comparing Kahn's multiplier with Keynes' *General Theory*, I have presented the former as demonstrating that the additional investment would be made possible solely by increased private saving—which accords with Keynes' application of the multiplier in his book. In point of fact, however, Kahn gave at least as much weight in this context to the role of increased government saving and imports. For further details, see pp. 197–99 below.

savings and investment of the change that is the cause of the increased employment. [Kahn 1931, p. 10]

But there is no explicit equilibrium analysis of the determination of the new level of employment.

In this context let me also note that in a letter that Keynes wrote Colin Clark in January 1933 congratulating him on his new book *National Income: 1924–1931* (1932), Keynes went on to describe his use of Clark's data to confirm Kahn's conjecture that the multiplier was about 2 (*JMK* XXIX, pp. 58–59). But Keynes carried out his calculations of the multiplier, not within the framework of what was to become the theory of effective demand of the *General Theory*, but as related in some obscure way to the concepts of the *Treatise* (cf. below, chap. 9, n. 24).

Additional—though indirect—evidence of Kahn's perception of his multiplier article is provided by some correspondence which took place between him and Keynes in the fall of 1931 (*JMK* XIII, pp. 373–75). In the letter which he then wrote to Kahn, Keynes for the first time made explicit use of a savings function and even described the equilibrating effect of changes in output. But Kahn's hesitant comments on Keynes' formulation, and his apologies for being "so useless," are hardly the reactions of a man who has himself already perceived the theory of effective demand.[23]

But over and above all the foregoing evidence that the central message of Kahn's multiplier article was not the theory of effective demand, there is the otherwise inexplicable fact that this theory does not appear in Keynes' writings and lectures more than a year after Kahn's article. And now we know this not only from the notes which Bryce and Tarshis took of Keynes' fall 1932 lectures, but from what are apparently fragments of the notes which Keynes himself had prepared for the lectures he gave in the spring of that year. In these notes Keynes argues that ΔI (an increase in investment) and ΔO (an increase in output) must have the same sign (*JMK* XXIX, p. 37); but he does not make use of Kahn's multiplier article to develop the precise quantitative relation between ΔI and ΔO.

And what is even more significant is that neither did Richard Kahn himself! For *JMK* XXIX now reproduces the hitherto missing memorandum (see *JMK* XIII, p. 376, n. 1) in which Kahn, Joan Robinson, and Austin Robinson presented Keynes with their criticisms of the lecture he had based on the preceding notes. After a brief "Preamble," this memorandum (written in May 1932) begins with the following summary of Keynes' argument:

23. For further details, see *KMT*, pp. 69–70, and Patinkin and Leith (1977, pp. 86–87).

THE FORMAL PROOF

Conditions laid down
 (a) $\Delta E'$ and ΔO have the same sign.
 (b) $\Delta E' - \Delta F$ and $\Delta E'$ have the same sign.
Proof
 $\Delta E' - \Delta F = \Delta I$
 $\therefore \Delta I$ and ΔO have the same sign. [*JMK* XXIX, p. 42, caps and italics in original]

It then proceeds to demonstrate that the foregoing conditions are not necessary, and also criticizes the technical details of Keynes' discussion of "The Exceptional Case," in which I and O do not move in the same direction. But at no point in their memorandum is there even a hint of the fact that in certain circumstances multiplier analysis can be applied to derive an exact quantitative relation between ΔI and ΔO.

Let me finally note that, in contrast to the fall 1932 lectures, those for fall 1933 (as recorded by Bryce and Tarshis) discuss both the theory of effective demand and the multiplier. All of which would seem to suggest that Keynes' recognition of the relationship between the multiplier and the theory of effective demand came simultaneously with—or perhaps even after—his formulation of this theory.[24]

To avoid any possible misunderstanding, let me conclude the discussion of this point by emphasizing that there can be no doubt about the importance of Kahn's 1931 multiplier analysis in the history of the development of macroeconomic theory and in the final version of the *General Theory*.[25] Nor can there be any doubt that, as shown in figure 2 above, Kahn's multiplier formula can be derived directly from the theory of effective demand. Nor do I question Samuelson's recent demonstration[26] that the multiplier equation $\Delta Y = 1/(1 - MPC) \cdot \Delta I$ is logically equivalent to the equilibrium equation of this theory, $F(Y) = Y$. But what I am saying is that this logical relationship was not seen by the protagonists of our drama at the time the article was first published and in the period which immediately followed. And though I am not sure it is relevant, I might add that—to the best of my knowledge— Richard Kahn has never claimed otherwise.[27] I must also emphasize that Samuelson's demonstration does not deal with the relation between the multiplier equation and the stability of the dynamic adjust-

    24. Note also how Keynes distinguishes between these two concepts at the beginning of the excerpt from his 1936 letter to Harrod cited on p. 8 above.
    25. "About half the book is really about it" (letter of Keynes to Beveridge, July 28, 1936 (*JMK* XIV, p. 57).
    26. Which appears in Patinkin and Leith (1977, p. 83).
    27. Cf. Richard Kahn's letter of March 1974 to me, reproduced in Patinkin and Leith (1977, pp. 147–48). In this letter Kahn states that he "regard[s] the main importance of [his] 1931 article as: (1) finally disposing of the 'Treasury view' . . . (2) finally disposing of the idea that the price level is determined by the quantity of money . . . (3) . . . [uninten-

ment equation, $dY/dt = \Phi[F(Y) - Y]$, which is what I have identified as the crucial feature of Keynes' theory of effective demand (see p. 10 above).

This illustrates yet another general principle that will guide me in these lectures: logical equivalence does not imply chronological equivalence; the fact that A implies B does not in turn imply that at the time scholars understood A they also understood B. This is a commonplace of the history of ideas. Indeed—as has frequently been noted—if this principle were not true, then mathematicians would have nothing to discover, for their theorems are implicit in their assumptions.

Illustrations of the foregoing principle also abound in the history of our own discipline. Thus many years ago George Stigler (1941) traced the tortuous and faltering manner in which the full implications of the marginal productivity theory were developed. But the episode that to my mind best illustrates this principle is a more recent one with which we are all familiar—the development of Friedman's permanent-income hypothesis.

As we all know, the essence of this theory is that an individual's current consumption depends not on his current (or "measured") income, but on his wealth or its surrogate, permanent income. Now, in a sense this theory can be said to be expressed already in the book of Genesis, when Joseph—after having made his crop forecast of seven good years to be followed by seven lean ones—advised Pharaoh not to permit the annual consumption of the good years to be determined by the current crop-income of those years, but instead by the permanent income as measured by the expected average annual crop-income over the fourteen-year cycle. In Joseph's own words as they have been cited in the literature, "Gather all the food of those good years that come . . . and that food shall be for store for the land against the seven years of famine"—which analysis and advice Pharaoh rightly acclaimed with the words, "There is none so discreet and wise as thou art!"[28]

If, however, references to more recent economic literature are preferred, then let me remind you that Friedman himself (1957) generously relates his theory to Irving Fisher's 1907 analysis, in his *Rate of Interest*,[29] of the individual maximizing his utility over two periods subject

---

tionally] demonstrating how unsuitable the terminology and assumptions of the *Treatise* were." (On the "Treasury view," see p. 27 above and pp. 192, 197–98 below.)

The outstanding advocate of the contrary view of Kahn's role was Schumpeter, who in his *History of Economic Analysis* (1954, p. 1172) asserted that Kahn's "share in the historic achievement [i.e., the writing of the *General Theory*] cannot have fallen very far short of co-authorship." Unfortunately, and possibly because he did not live to complete his *History* (see ibid., esp. p. 1170, n. 1), Schumpeter did not specify his grounds for this view.

28. Source: Genesis 41:35–39 *plus* literary license.
29. This analysis is essentially repeated in Fisher's later *Theory of Interest* (1930).

to the present value of his income stream, that is, to his wealth. Even more to the point is Hicks' detailed and systematic discussion in his classic *Value and Capital* (1939) of the meaning of income, to which Friedman also refers (1957, p. 10, n. 4); for in this discussion Hicks addressed himself directly to the question of the proper measure of an individual's income during a given period of time and explains why, in a nonstationary economy, "we should not regard the whole of his current receipts as income" (1939, p. 172). Instead, Hicks went on to explain, "the calculation of income consists in finding some sort of *standard* stream of values whose present capitalized value equals the present value of the stream of receipts which is actually in prospect" (ibid., p. 184, italics in original).

But, despite these discussions, the earlier Keynesian literature, and the related econometric studies in particular, all analyzed consumption as a function of current income, with no one (not even, to the best of my knowledge, Hicks) criticizing this procedure. And even after the postwar failure to predict consumption correctly[30] led to the introduction of additional variables into these functions—including lagged income, and even lagged consumption—there was no full understanding of what this meant. Thus, for example, Klein and Goldberger (1955, p. 8) explained their introduction of lagged consumption into the function in terms of their contention that "consumer behavior tends to be repetitive to some extent."

Now "all" that Friedman did was infer from Fisher's analysis that the proper measure of income for use in the consumption function is an estimate of permanent income provided by an average of income over several periods of time—and consumption has never been the same since.

I am sure that all are aware of these aspects of *la condition humaine*. I am sure all of us will empathize with my colleague Nissan Liviatan, who, at one of our departmental seminars a few years ago, quietly replied to a criticism that something he said was a tautology with the words, "Whether or not something is a tautology depends on how fast you think."

Similarly I am sure that each of us has had the experience[31] of saying in the course of his work on a certain problem, "Now why didn't I see that before?"—which means that he did not see it before. If we are fortunate, we say this at a later stage of our work when we indeed achieve that "moment of truth" that enables us to see the deeper

30. Which is a perfect example of an anomaly which has led to the development of a new theory; cf. the references to Kuhn and Laudan in n. 13 above.

31. My own such experience of many years ago—and the one which has provided the introspective basis for this paragraph—has been described in some reminiscences I have published elsewhere (Patinkin 1981, pp. 11, 14). Cf. also pp. 179–80, below.

meaning of what we have done. And if we are less fortunate, we say it only after the priority for seeing it has gone to someone else.

I come now to the last question of this introductory lecture: the time when Keynes actually published his new theory of effective demand. Here I would like first to point out that in the case of the *General Theory* as well as in the earlier *Treatise*, Keynes did not attempt to exploit the relatively long period of preparation that was involved (roughly, five years) in order to publish articles in the leading professional journals on the salient features of his new theories and thus to benefit from their exposure to the criticism of the profession at large before formulating them in final book form. It is true that such a "research strategy" was much less customary at the time Keynes wrote than it became later.[32] But I would conjecture that Keynes' failure to follow such a strategy also reflected his belief that the quintessence of economic knowledge was concentrated in Cambridge, which geographical point need at most be extended to a triangle that would include London and Oxford.[33] So why bother publishing articles in order to benefit from criticism, if the most fruitful criticisms could be reaped more conveniently and efficiently simply by circulating draft manuscripts and galley proofs among his colleagues in this fertile triangle? And I would also conjecture that because of his unbounded faith in this intellectual supremacy, Keynes had no fears that his priority might in the meantime be preempted by some "nontriangular" economist.

But in addition to his role as a professional economist, Keynes was also a publicist; indeed, for some periods of his life (though not the one that now concerns us) it would be more appropriate to say that in addition to being a publicist he was also an economist.[34] So, though they do not for our purpose have the significance of his professional writings (see p. 85 below), let me in this context also examine Keynes' popular writings in the period immediately preceding the *General Theory*, taking due account of the fact that their very nature precluded technical exposition. The most notable of these writings was his March 1933 pamphlet *The Means to Prosperity*, which emphasized the necessity for increasing expenditures as a means of increasing employment and/or prices, and which (explicitly basing itself on Kahn's 1931 article) provided a far more precise description than did *Can Lloyd George Do It?* four years earlier of the multiplier effects of such expenditures (*JMK*

32. Note that it was also not the "strategy" adopted by Marshall, and this too may have influenced Keynes. See Keynes' 1924 memorial to Marshall as reprinted in his *Essays in Biography* (*JMK* X, pp. 179–80).
33. Cf. Harrod (1951, pp. 322–23).
34. Cf. E. Johnson (1974, 1977); cf. also p. xxii above.

IX, p. 339ff.). In the words of this pamphlet:

> How, then, are we to raise prices? It may help us to think clearly, if I proceed by means of a series of very simple, but fundamental propositions.
>
> (1) For commodities as a whole there can be no possible means of raising their prices except by increasing expenditure upon them more rapidly than their supply comes upon the market.
>
> (2) Expenditure can only be increased if the public spend a larger proportion of the incomes they already have, or if their aggregate spending power is increased in some other way.
>
> (3) There are narrow limits to increasing expenditure out of existing incomes—whether by saving less or by increased personal expenditure of a capital nature. . . . It follows, therefore, that we must aim at increasing aggregate spending power. If we can achieve this, it will partly serve to raise prices and partly to increase employment. [*JMK* IX, p. 351]

Thus the main thrust of this passage is on prices: indeed, it appears in a section entitled "The Raising of Prices." In any event, there is no presentation in this pamphlet of the theory of effective demand as such. And in view of the chronology of the development of the *General Theory* documented earlier, we cannot rule out the possibility that this may have simply been a reflection of the fact that Keynes had not yet formulated this theory.

Something closer to this theory appeared a year and a half later in another of Keynes' nonprofessional writings, namely, an article "Poverty in Plenty: Is the Economic System Self-Adjusting?" published in the *Listener* for November 21, 1934.[35] Here Keynes aligns himself with the "heretics"

> who reject the idea that the existing economic system is, in any significant sense, self-adjusting. They believe that the failure of effective demand to reach the full potentialities of supply, in spite of human psychological demand being immensely far from satisfied for the vast majority of individuals, is due to much more fundamental causes. . . .
>
> There is, I am convinced, a fatal flaw in that part of the orthodox reasoning which deals with the theory of what determines the level of effective demand and the volume of aggregate employment; the flaw being largely due to the failure of the classical doctrine to develop a satisfactory theory of the rate of interest.
>
> Put very briefly, the point is something like this. Any individual, if he finds himself with a certain income, will, according to his habits,

---

35. A revised form of this was published under the title "A Self-Adjusting Economic System?" in the *New Republic* of February 20, 1935.

his tastes and his motives towards prudence, spend a portion of it on consumption and the rest he will save. If his income increases, he will almost certainly consume more than before but it is highly probable that he will also save more. That is to say, he will not increase his consumption by the full amount of the increase in his income. Thus if a given national income is less equally divided, or, if the national income increases so that individual incomes are greater than before, the gap between total incomes and the total expenditure on consumption is likely to widen. But incomes can only be generated by producing goods for consumption or by producing goods for use as capital. Thus the gap between total incomes and expenditure on consumption *cannot* be greater than the amount of new capital which it is thought worth while to produce. Consequently, our habit of withholding from consumption an increasing sum as our incomes increase means that it is impossible for our incomes to increase unless either we change our habits so as to consume more or the business world calculates that it is worth while to produce more capital goods. For, failing both these alternatives, the increased employment and output, by which alone increased incomes can be generated, will prove unprofitable and will not persist. [*JMK* XIII, pp. 487, 489–90, italics in original]

And this is the closest Keynes came to publishing his theory of effective demand cum equilibrating mechanism before the *General Theory*. Thus a full statement of the theory appeared for the first time only in the published *General Theory* itself.

My task in the coming lectures is thus clear: to examine the macroeconomic theories of the Stockholm School and of Kalecki with the purpose of determining the extent to which they contain the essential features of the General Theory as described in this lecture; and to carry out this examination while keeping in mind the necessity of distinguishing between the central message and the noise, on the one hand, and between the logical and the chronological, on the other.

2

Anticipations of the General Theory? The Stockholm School

The *General Theory* was published in February 1936. A year later there appeared in the *Economic Journal* (of which Keynes was then editor) Bertil Ohlin's celebrated two-part article, "Some Notes on the Stockholm Theory of Saving and Investment" (1937).[1] This article is best remembered today among English-speaking economists as the source of the fruitful ex ante–ex post distinction of dynamic analysis. But Ohlin's purpose was a much broader one, as indicated by his opening paragraph:

> Owing to a coincidence of circumstances, already at an early stage of the depression Swedish economists [and as becomes clear from the article, the individuals besides himself to whom Ohlin was primarily referring were Erik Lindahl and Gunnar Myrdal] came to deal with the problem of variations in employment, output and

The following draws freely on my "Relation between Keynesian Economics and the 'Stockholm School' " (1978a) and "Some Observations on Ohlin's 1933 Article" (1978b). The first of these papers was also presented at a seminar at the Institute for International Economic Studies in Stockholm in September 1977, on which occasion I benefited greatly from the comments of Bertil Ohlin, Erik Lundberg, and Assar Lindbeck. (Ohlin subsequently published [1978] most of his comments.) Afterward, I continued corresponding with Ohlin on the question until his death in August 1979, though without achieving a meeting of minds. To my deep regret, I did not have the hoped-for opportunity of discussing the final version of this chapter with him. I might, however, note that in this correspondence Ohlin expressed his intention of summarizing his general view on the subject in a paper for *History of Political Economy*. This paper has now appeared posthumously (1981), after having been prepared for publication by Otto Steiger. Section 10 of it largely summarizes points that Ohlin made in our correspondence.

I would also like to express my deepest appreciation to Bent Hansen for the extensive and most helpful discussions I have had with him on the subject of this chapter. Hansen's own views on the Stockholm School are presented in his recent paper (1981).

Though there is some question about the validity of the term "Stockholm School" (see p. 39 below), it continues to be used; for convenience, therefore, I have done so as well.

1. A hitherto unpublished third part of this article has been published posthumously as Appendix III to Ohlin (1981). Excerpts from it were reproduced earlier (together with the relevant correspondence with Keynes) in *JMK* XIV, pp. 186–201.

36

prices by means of a theoretical apparatus rather different from the price theory in economic textbooks. There are surprising similarities as well as striking differences between that apparatus and the conclusions reached in Sweden on the one hand and Mr. Keynes' "General Theory" on the other hand. Hoping that a discussion of two independent attacks on the same set of problems may throw some light on the latter, I intend in this and the succeeding paper to make some observations on these two theories. [Ohlin 1937, p. 87]

And ever since then the question of the relation between the Stockholm School (as Ohlin [1937, p. 92] termed it) and the *General Theory* has been a "perennial of doctrinal history."[2]

As in most debates, two extreme positions can be identified, as well, of course, as a range of intermediate ones. At one extreme is what I shall for convenience call the "Myrdal view." I am not referring to Myrdal's 1933 (p. 370) chiding reference to Keynes' *Treatise* as an example of "the attractive Anglo-Saxon kind of unnecessary originality, which has its roots in certain systematic gaps in the knowledge of the German language on the part of the majority of English economists" (as translated in Myrdal 1939, pp. 8–9); for, though I suffer from the same kind of "gap," I cannot but agree that Myrdal's criticism was well taken, and that the central message of the *Treatise* had been presented many years before by Wicksell (cf. *KMT*, chap. 5).[3] What I am referring to, however, is Myrdal's more recent remark that "the Keynesian revolution . . . was mainly an Anglo-American occurrence. In Sweden, where we grew up in the tradition of Knut Wicksell, Keynes' works were read as interesting and important contributions along a familiar line of thought, but not in any sense as a revolutionary breakthrough" (Myrdal 1972, pp. 4–5).

At the other extreme is what I shall for convenience call the "Cambridge view" and which I can best characterize as stating that ". . . in the beginning" there was the *General Theory,* which developed in complete isolation from intellectual developments in Sweden; and then suddenly, ex post, came Ohlin and claimed that there were some similarities between the *General Theory* and the teachings of some Swedish economists. Let me regretfully note that this extreme view received implicit support from volume XIII (1973) of the Royal Economic Society's new edition of Keynes' *Collected Writings,* the vol-

---

2. So most aptly termed by Gustafsson (1973). Ohlin used the term "Stockholm School" even though Lindahl was then actually at Lund, on the grounds that Lindahl had "worked in Stockholm for many years" (Ohlin 1937, p. 91).
3. Nevertheless, as noted below (pp. 46, 52, 56), Lindahl, Ohlin, Lundberg, and other Swedish economists did make use of the *Treatise* in their work. See also Steiger (1978b, p. 431) and Yohe (1962, p. 277, n. 8).

ume entitled *The General Theory and After: Part I, Preparation*, which
was presented as containing all the relevant materials, including correspondence, which led up to the *General Theory*. For this volume—
which begins with Keynes' work on the *Treatise* in the late 1920s and
ends with the publication of the *General Theory* in February 1936—
does not contain any reference to Swedish economists. I hasten,
though, to add that this misleading impression has in part been corrected by the publication in 1979 of a supplementary volume (*JMK*
XXIX) which includes 1931 correspondence between Keynes and
Ohlin, with reference (inter alia) to the translation of Wicksell's 1898
Interest and Prices (for which project, as Ohlin [1977, pp. 149–50] has
recently recounted, Keynes was the moving spirit), as well as some
1934 correspondence with Lindahl which will be discussed later.[4] And,
of course, we must also remember the famous 1929 Keynes-Ohlin debate on the German transfer problem in which, interestingly enough, it
was Ohlin who stressed that demand was affected by changes in purchasing power, and Keynes who failed to take proper account of this
factor. There were also contacts—not always gratifying to Swedish
economists—that stemmed from Keynes' position as editor of the *Economic Journal*.[5]

I would not, however, want to create the impression that the sides in
this debate have lined up (as they so frequently do in such instances)
along strictly nationalistic lines. Quite the contrary. Thus in his study
of the development of economic theory in the 1930s, the British
economist G. L. S. Shackle concluded that Myrdal had said "in
Swedish in 1931 in very large measure what Keynes said in English in
1936" (Shackle 1967, p. 123; see also pp. 126, 144). And a few years

4. This correspondence was originally reproduced by Steiger (1971); see n. 20 below.
5. Thus Ohlin (1977, pp. 161–62) has also recently recounted how, in the early 1920s,
Keynes rejected a paper that he (Ohlin) had submitted containing the essence of his
subsequently famous factor-proportion theorem. In 1924, Keynes also rejected a paper
by Wicksell on Ricardo; see the recent article by Lars Jonung (1981), who also reproduces the paper in question and the related Keynes-Wicksell correspondence.

In his biography of Wicksell, Torsten Gårdlund (1958, pp. 294–95) has described
Wicksell's visit to wartime England in 1916, the anticipated high point of which was to be
a meeting with Keynes, whom Wicksell regarded as the "keenest theorist" of the Cambridge economists. At the time, however, this regard was not mutual. For (in Gårdlund's
words) Keynes, who was then at the Treasury, "did not in fact have much time to spare
for this foreign colleague whose name meant little to him." So their meeting consisted of
a rushed lunch, the conversation of which Wicksell succeeded in prolonging by walking
Keynes afterward to his barber!

As can be inferred from his role in bringing about the English translation of *Interest
and Prices*, Keynes in later years learned to appreciate Wicksell's contributions. Indeed,
Keynes explicitly based the analysis of his *Treatise on Money* on Wicksell's fundamental
distinction between the natural and market rates of interest and even stated that what he
was trying to say in the *Treatise* was "the same at root as what Wicksell was trying to
say" (*Treatise* I, p. 139, p. 177, n. 3; cf. also *KMT*, chap. 5).

before the appearance of Shackle's study, a Swedish economist, Karl-Gustav Landgren, submitted a doctoral dissertation to the University of Gothenburg whose title (in English translation—the work itself is in Swedish, with an English summary)[6] was *The "New Economics" in Sweden: J. M. Keynes, E. Wigforss, B. Ohlin and the Development 1927–1939* (1960a). The main thesis of this extensively documented study is that the public-works program of the Swedish Social-Democratic government in 1932 was inspired not by the writings of Myrdal and Ohlin, but by the articles Keynes wrote in the *Nation and Athenaeum* from 1924 on, as well as his famous 1929 pamphlet *Can Lloyd George Do It?*—all of which exerted a great influence at the time on Ernst Wigforss, the leading ideologist of the Social-Democratic Party, who was to become the Finance Minister of its 1932 government and thus the man responsible for carrying out this program. Landgren also questioned Ohlin's description of a "Stockholm School" and claimed that the ideas Ohlin presented in his 1937 article as those of this "school" were really ones he himself had developed during 1933 and 1934—in some cases actually as criticism of Lindahl and Myrdal. Similarly, Landgren (1960a, p. 223; cited by Yohe 1978, p. 449) reported that in an interview with him, Alf Johansson—whom Ohlin (1937, p. 91) had listed as a member of this school—stated that "the Stockholm School was . . . an *ex post* construction" of Ohlin. Finally, Landgren contended that Ohlin was actually the only Swedish economist of the early 1930s whose work had a "close affinity" to what Keynes was later to present in his *General Theory;* but that though Ohlin seems to have developed certain of his ideas independently of Keynes, "others can only be explained by the influences which Ohlin, as early as the spring of 1933, derived from the English author."[7]

As might be expected, Landgren's book created quite a stir in Sweden. Thus, immediately after its appearance, the editors of *Ekonomisk Tidskrift* devoted a whole issue (September 1960) to a symposium on this book in which Wigforss himself participated.[8] The latter contended that the Swedish Social-Democratic tradition had been influenced more

6. I have made use in the following of an English translation of this work prepared by Finn Borg (at the time, a student of the Graduate School of Business at the University of Chicago), to whom I am most grateful.

7. Except for the reference to Johansson, this paragraph has been based on pp. 295–97 of Landgren's English summary. Though he rejected this conclusion of Landgren's, Ohlin (1974, p. 893) did agree that he and other Swedish economists in the early 1930s were "stimulated by Keynes' expansionist attitude in 1928–29." Cf. also Ohlin (1981, p. 37).

8. Another participant was Erik Lundberg, on whose contribution see n. 42 below. I have made use in the following of a translation of the major parts of this issue prepared by Moshe Apelblat (at the time, a student at the Hebrew University of Jerusalem), to whom I am grateful.

by English Socialist thought at the beginning of the century than by that
of Keynes and other English Liberals of the 1920s, and that accordingly, even without the contribution of the latter, Swedish Social-
Democratic policy in the 1930s would have been the same (Wigforss
1960, pp. 193–94). Though Landgren (1960b) also participated in the
symposium, he did not address himself to Wigforss' comments. In their
preface to the symposium (p. 159), the editors expressed their hope of
publishing in the subsequent issue further contributions to the symposium by Ohlin, Myrdal, Johansson, Palander, and others—but such
an issue never appeared. And ten years later, Otto Steiger submitted a
doctoral dissertation (in German) to the University of Uppsala which
was a detailed "Anti-Kritik" (1971) of Landgren's work and which was
followed by a further exchange in Swedish between them (1972, 1973;
cited by Uhr 1973, p. 257).[9]

But let me leave aside this debate per se—most of whose aspects (the
intellectual origins of the Swedish Social-Democratic public-works
program of the 1930s, the existence of a Stockholm School) do not bear
directly on the issue which concerns me—and turn directly to this issue
itself: namely, the relation between the theoretical writings of the
Swedish economists and the General Theory. And once again I must
emphasize that I shall be examining these writings only from this narrow viewpoint: I make no attempt to present the theory of the Stockholm School as such.

I start with Knut Wicksell,[10] for though he was no longer alive in
the period which concerns us (he died in 1926 at the age of 75), he was
the father figure of Swedish economics from whom Lindahl, Myrdal,
and Ohlin all claimed intellectual descent. (Thus Ohlin [1937, pp. 91–
92] speaks of the "Wicksell-Myrdal-Lindahl writings.") Wicksell's relevant major works were *Interest and Prices*, which appeared originally
in German in 1898; and volume II of his *Lectures on Political Economy*, devoted to *Money*, which appeared originally in Swedish in
1906, with a second edition appearing in 1911.

9. Fortunately for those of us with language limitations, Landgren's study is supplemented (as already noted) with an English summary. Similarly, Steiger (1976) published
an English article which is an "extension and in part a revision" of that part of his book
which deals with Ohlin. Aspects of the debate have also been surveyed in English by
Winch (1966), Uhr (1973), and the already cited Gustafsson (1973). See also Uhr (1977).
More recently, *History of Political Economy* devoted almost an entire issue (Fall 1978) to
a symposium on Ohlin's 1933 article, on which more below. The earliest exposition in
English of the theory and policy position of the Stockholm School was due to Brinley
Thomas (1936). See also Lerner (1940) and Caplan (1941). I have also made use in the
following of an English translation of parts of Steiger's book prepared by Avraham
Sheshinski-Shani (at the time, a student in the translation program of the Hebrew University), to whom I am indebted.

10. For detailed documentation of the following interpretation, see my *Money, Interest, and Prices* (1956, 1965, suppl. notes E:1 and E:4).

Let me begin at the end: Wicksell was basically a quantity theorist. The problem that troubled him, however, was that the dynamic mechanism of this theory had been spelled out (according to him) only for an economy in which money—which Wicksell defined as gold or other metallic currency—circulated as the main medium of exchange and was held by individuals. In such an economy, a (say) increase in the quantity of money (so defined) generated a direct upward pressure on prices via what we today call the real-balance effect. But, Wicksell asked, how was such a pressure generated in an economy in which most of the money (so defined) accrued not to individuals, but to banks to be held as a reserve against their deposits—in which case there was no real-balance effect? In answer to this question Wicksell formulated his famous "cumulative process," which works as follows: The increased quantity of money (i.e., gold) flows into the reserves of the banking system. The banks, finding themselves with excess reserves, decide to expand their loans and therefore reduce their lending rate. In this way, the "bank rate" or "market rate" falls below the "natural" or "real rate" as determined by the marginal productivity of capital. This induces entrepreneurs to borrow and use the proceeds to increase their demand for investment goods; it also causes a decrease in savings or, what is the same thing, an increase in the demand for consumption goods. Thus the expansion of bank credit—and the resulting expansion in demand deposits, which for Wicksell was an integral part of the process—will generate an increase in "general demand." On the other hand, supply will remain unchanged: for "as a first approximation we are entitled to assume that all production forces are already fully employed" (*Lectures* II, p. 195). Thus "general demand" becomes greater than supply, causing a general rise in both prices and wages. And Wicksell goes on to say:

> This may sound paradoxical, because we have accustomed ourselves, with J. B. Say, to regard goods themselves as reciprocally constituting and limiting the demand for each other. And indeed *ultimately* they do so; here, however, we are concerned with precisely what occurs, *in the first place*, with the middle link in the final exchange of one good against another, which is formed by the demand of money for goods and the supply of goods against money. Any theory of money worthy of the name must be able to show how and why the monetary or pecuniary demand for goods exceeds or falls short of the supply of goods in given conditions. [*Lectures* II, p. 159, italics in original][11]

11. I might note that this passage (inter alia) was cited by Myrdal in some correspondence with Keynes in June 1937, in which he (Myrdal) unsuccessfully tried to convince Keynes that Wicksell had analyzed what happens when saving and investment are not equal (*JMK* XXIX, pp. 259–63). But see n. 14 below.

This rise in prices and wages constitutes a "cumulative process" in the sense that it will continue as long as the "bank rate" lies below the "natural rate": a further rise in prices does not require a further fall in the interest rate (*Interest and Prices*, pp. 93–95). Ultimately, however, the price rise is brought to an end because of the internal drain of bank reserves which it generates, which in turn causes the banks to raise their rate of interest once again to equality with the natural rate.[12] Thus it is by means of this convergent cumulative process that Wicksell extends the quantity theory to an economy with a banking system: that he explains how an increase in the quantity of money in such an economy too ultimately brings it to a new equilibrium position at a higher price level.

That, it seemed to me over twenty-five years ago (Patinkin 1952), and continues to seem to me today, is the central message of Wicksell's *Interest and Prices* and second volume of *Lectures*. And, frankly, it has always been a matter of concern to me—an indication that perhaps I did not fully understand Wicksell—that leading Swedish economists have seen much more, and much that is different, in his writings.[13] Thus, for example, both Myrdal (1939, pp. 5–6, 19–21, 36) and Ohlin (1936, pp. xiii–xiv) see in Wicksell an opponent of the quantity theory. But may I suggest that though Swedish economists should presumably know best about Wicksell, they are also likely to be more susceptible than an outsider like myself to the temptation to rewrite Wicksell in their own image—just as many of those who today call themselves Keynesians have attempted to do with the *General Theory* (see the postscript to chap. 5 below). I am also reassured by the fact that at least one leading Swedish economist, Tord Palander, criticized Myrdal for describing in his book *Monetary Equilibrium* (on which more below) not, as Myrdal claimed, Wicksell's theory itself, but how "Wicksell

12. Note Wicksell's implicit (and implausible) assumption that banks are guided not by their reserve ratio, but by the absolute level of their reserves. This assumption leads Wicksell (in contrast with such well-known quantity theorists as Fisher [1913, pp. 50–53, 162–64], Pigou [1917, pp. 165–66], and Keynes of the *Tract* [p. 63], all of whom generally assumed fixity of the reserve ratio) to view the level of bank deposits as a variable which (for a given absolute level of bank reserves) adjusts itself passively to the demand of business for credit, with the reserve ratio adjusting itself accordingly. The extreme case in which this ratio approaches zero constitutes Wicksell's oft-cited "pure credit economy." Wicksell's view of the passive role of demand deposits would seem to be in part related to his use of the term "money" in the restricted sense of what we today call high-powered money, and to his corresponding interpretation of the quantity theory as referring only to money of this kind. (For specific supporting references to Wicksell's writings, see my *Money, Interest, and Prices* [1965], pp. 588, 592–94.) I might note that generally the Stockholm School followed Wicksell in attributing a passive role to demand deposits; see, e.g., Ohlin (1943).

13. See p. 835, n. 2 and p. 842, n. 3 of my 1952 article; see also my *Money, Interest, and Prices* (1965, p. 588, n. 27, and p. 595, n. 50). See also the next footnote.

ought to have thought 'if he had thought correctly,' and if he had had access to the theoretical apparatus available to Myrdal in 1932 and 1933'' (Palander 1941, pp. 7–8).

In any event, the foregoing discussion makes clear two related points. First, though Wicksell rejected Say's law in the short run and thus recognized that there could exist a difference between aggregate demand and supply, he made use of this difference only to explain a change in prices as distinct from output.[14] Second, Wicksell's famous cumulative process is concerned with such a change in prices; indeed, as we have seen, his analysis of this process was carried out on the explicit assumption that output remains constant at its full-employment level. Surely, then, we cannot find in Wicksell's writings an anticipation of the General Theory. Surely, Myrdal notwithstanding, even someone brought up in the "tradition of Wicksell" would have found much to learn from Keynes of the *General Theory*.

I must emphasize that this concentration on an analysis of the determination of the price level was not unique to Wicksell, but was instead a general characteristic of monetary theory before the *General Theory*. This can be seen from the very titles of the major works of that period. Thus the full title of Wicksell's 1898 work was *Interest and Prices: A Study of the Causes Regulating the Value of Money*. Similarly, the full title of Irving Fisher's classic work on the quantity theory was *The Purchasing Power of Money: Its Determination and Relation to Credit Interest and Crises* (1911), while that of A. C. Pigou on the Cambridge version of this theory was entitled "The Value of Money" (1917). Similarly—and this is evident from their nature as explained in my first lecture—the full name of the fundamental equations of Keynes' *Treatise* was "The Fundamental Equations for the Value of Money."[15]

This does not mean that these economists completely disregarded changes in output. Thus Wicksell discussed them in his "Enigma of Business Cycles" (1907), which he later summarized in his *Lectures* II (pp. 209–14), though not as part of his central message.[16] On the other hand, in Fisher's analysis of the transition period (1911 and 1913, chap. 4), changes in output play a role which, though secondary, are inte-

14. This is not mentioned by either Myrdal (1939, pp. 19–21) or Ohlin (1936, pp. xiii–xiv), both of whom regard Wicksell's rejection of Say's law as one of his basic contributions.

15. Lest we think that this concept of monetary theory was held only by quantity theorists (and Keynes of the *Treatise* was a quantity theorist just like Wicksell [*KMT*, pp. 47–49]), let me note that B. M. Anderson and James L. Laughlin presented their opposition to the quantity theory in books respectively entitled *The Value of Money* (1917) and *Money and Prices* (1919).

16. Wicksell added this summary—and in small print at that—only in the second edition of his book (see translator's note on p. 58 of Wicksell 1907).

grated into his theory. Similarly, Keynes of the *Treatise* (I, pp. 184, 264, 271–75) repeatedly refers to changes in the level of employment and output. But he provides no direct analysis of these changes; instead, his description of what happens to output is derivative from his analysis of price. And in particular, as emphasized in my preceding lecture, there is no analysis of the feedback effect of a change in output. As a corollary to this concentration on the theory of the price level, the objective of the monetary policy advocated by all these writers (including Keynes of the *Treatise*) was also specified in terms of the price level—namely, stabilizing it, with disagreement only about whether the price index chosen for this purpose should be that of consumption goods or of factor services.

With this as a background, let me proceed to an examination of the writings of Erik Lindahl, who was a pupil of Wicksell (Myrdal 1939, pp. 7, 20). What Lindahl regarded as the "more important sections" of his 1930 monograph on *Penningpolitikens medel* [Methods of monetary policy] were translated into English (under his direction) in his *Studies in the Theory of Money and Capital* (1939, p. 9). Significantly enough, the translation of these sections appears under the title "The Rate of Interest and the Price Level." And as in the case of Wicksell, that indeed is the concern of Lindahl's central message: prices, not output. Thus he begins his analysis with the following paragraph:

> In explaining the factors determining changes in the price level, it is convenient to start from the fact that in each period the portion of the total nominal income that is not saved is equal to the total quantities of goods and services consumed during the period, multiplied by their prices. This may be expressed in the form:
>
> $$E(1 - s) = PQ,$$
>
> where E denotes the total nominal income, s the proportion of this income which is saved, P the price level for consumption goods and Q the quantity of such goods in a certain period. [Lindahl (1930) 1939, p. 142]

Some aspects of this paragraph do raise associations with the *General Theory*. This is true, first of all, of Lindahl's use of national income in his equation, a use which befits his role as one of the pioneers of national-income measurement in Sweden (Lindahl et al. 1937). Similarly, the left-hand side of this equation can be interpreted as a consumption function; indeed, at one point in his discussion (p. 174), Lindahl refers to "the propensity to save," though I do not know if the original Swedish wording carries the same connotation. But these similarities to the *General Theory* are superficial: for Lindahl uses his equation to analyze the determination not of output, but of prices, and this remains the case even when he analyzes the effect of a change in the savings ratio ([1930] 1939, pp. 204–8; see also Landgren 1960a, pp. 226–27).

Similarly, though Lindahl does examine the effect of a change in the quantity of consumption goods, Q, on prices, in most of his analysis this change in Q occurs as a result of a changed composition of a given output—a shift from consumption to investment goods caused by a change in the rate of interest—not as a result of a change in total output. At one point, however, Lindahl does assume that there are initially unemployed resources (pp. 176ff.); but he does not analyze how the level of unemployment is determined and merely says that these unemployed resources make it possible for some expansion of output to take place before prices begin to rise. Nor, needless to say, does Lindahl recognize the feedback effect of changes in output. Indeed, when in later years Lindahl wrote a paper "On Keynes' Economic System" (1954), he identified the theoretical novelty of the *General Theory* in much the same way as I have: namely, as "the introduction of the volume of employment and, also, national income as a regulator for the establishment of equilibrium between saving and investment" (Lindahl 1954, p. 167; but see also pp. 170–71).[17]

As an aside, might I note that any complete study of the intellectual interrelationships between Swedish and British economists in the interwar period (which this does not pretend to be) must take account of the fact that not all these interrelationships ran through Keynes. Thus Lindahl prefaces his two chapters on "The Rate of Interest as an Instrument for the Maintenance of an Unchanged Price Level" with the footnote statement that "the reasoning in the following two chapters is similar to that of D. H. Robertson in his outstanding little book *Banking Policy and the Price Level* [1926] where many of the same

17. This paper originated as a lecture which Lindahl gave in Australia in the early 1950s. In a letter to me, Bent Hansen (who was at the time Lindahl's junior colleague at Uppsala) has described the following background to this lecture (letter of August 25, 1978, cited with permission):

> Before Lindahl went to Australia, he discussed with me what to lecture upon. Keynes' *General Theory* came up, and Lindahl rejected the idea because he felt there was nothing new in the *General Theory*. I objected, and Lindahl then started comparing the *Treatise* with his own writings, especially *Penning politikens medel* (1929), which in slightly changed version is one of the chapters in his *Studies in the Theory of Capital and Money* (1939). He felt that *Penning politikens medel* was superior to the *Treatise* (which I did and still do agree with). I pointed out then that the *General Theory* was really something quite different, and he then admitted that he had actually never read it. He read it and was then very impressed. On that occasion he also worked himself through Palander's presentation of Keynes in *Ekonomisk Tidskrift*.

On the article by Palander (1942), see end of this chapter. Hansen's dating of Lindahl's book in this letter is that of its publication for private circulation; the formal publication was a year later, as indicated above (see Hansen 1981, p. 261, n. 3).

problems are discussed" (Lindahl [1930] 1939, p. 199). Similarly, Ohlin has suggested that Lindahl as well as Myrdal and himself might have been influenced by R. G. Hawtrey, and that both he and Myrdal might have been influenced by Kahn.[18] And in the opposite direction we have the influence of Lindahl on Hicks' *Value and Capital* (1939), to which Lerner (1940, p. 586), Caplan (1941), and subsequently Hicks himself (1965, p. 58, n. 2) have referred. Nor should we forget the crucial role Hayek played in the early 1930s in bringing the message of Wicksell to England via Austria (Robbins 1971, pp. 127–29).

Let me conclude this examination of Lindahl's writings by noting that the December 1934 correspondence with Keynes to which I referred earlier (p. 38)[19] provides further confirmation of the nature of the central message of Lindahl's pre–*General Theory* writings: for the main concern of the unpublished note Lindahl sent Keynes at that time— after having visited Cambridge in January of that year—had to do with the determination of prices, and not output. Indeed, in his accompanying letter to Keynes, Lindahl himself relates the argument of his note to the fundamental equations of Keynes' *Treatise* which, as emphasized in my preceding lecture, are concerned with prices.[20, 21]

I turn now to Gunnar Myrdal and will base my discussion primarily on his *Monetary Equilibrium* (1939). In his preface to this book, Myrdal described its evolvement in the following terms:

> The original Swedish text, "Om Penningteoretisk Jämvikt," published in *Ekonomisk Tidskrift, 1931,* was a condensation of a series of lectures on Wicksell's monetary theory given at the Geneva Post Graduate Institute for International Studies and at Stockholm University. A German translation entitled "Der Gleichgewichtsbegriff als Instrument der Geldtheoretischen Analyse" was included in the "Beiträge zur Geldtheorie," a collection of essays edited by Professor Friedrich A. Hayek (Vienna, 1933). The three introductory chapters were added to the German edition and certain sections containing contributions toward the settlement of purely Swedish controversies were omitted. As now published in English, the essay is a translation of the German text without consequential modifications. [Myrdal 1939, pp. v–vi]

18. For Ohlin on Hawtrey's influence, see Steiger (1976, p. 358, n. 24); cf. also Yohe (1978, pp. 449–50). On Kahn's influence, see Ohlin (1981, p. 204).

19. First reproduced in Steiger (1971, pp. 204–13); see also *JMK* XXIX, pp. 122–31.

20. See also what seems to be an implicit reference to this 1934 note in the new essay Lindahl wrote for his *Studies* (1939, p. 66n.).

21. In certain footnotes in Lindahl's essay on *Penningpolitikens medel* (1930), Hansen (1981, pp. 261–63) has found what he interprets as recognition of the possibility of unemployment equilibrium. I do not, however, feel that this interpretation is justified. In any event, Hansen (ibid.) admits that Lindahl did not realize the significance of such an equilibrium position, as witnessed by the fact that the footnotes in question were omitted from the 1939 English translation of this essay (cf. p. 44 above).

This description, however, must be emended in three respects. First, though the volume of *Ekonomisk Tidskrift* in which Myrdal's article appeared is dated 1931, the volume was actually published in 1932 (Palander 1941, p. 2). More specifically, Steiger (1978b, p. 440, n. 23) has told us that "Myrdal's 1932 essay was written in the spring of that year and sent to the printer of *Ekonomisk Tidskrift* in June."[22] Second, Hansen (1981, p. 263, n. 5) has pointed out that there are actually several cross-references between the Swedish and German versions of Myrdal's essay, and that indeed in the opening footnote of the Swedish version Myrdal refers to the "more direct and detailed treatment of the problem which [he] gave" in his then-forthcoming essay in Hayek's volume; correspondingly, Hansen (ibid.) has concluded that "the two versions must have been produced or at least edited simultaneously." I should however note that Ohlin (1981, pp. 199, 201) refers to these two versions in a way which implies that the Swedish version definitely preceded the German one. The third and final emendation is that there are in fact several substantive differences—itemized by Palander (1941, p. 7, n. 3)—between Myrdal's 1933 paper and his 1939 book. Most notably, though Myrdal did make use of the distinction between ex ante and ex post in his 1933 paper, his more systematic presentation of this distinction in chapter 3, sections 9–10 of the book was new to it.[23]

Keeping these facts in mind, let me begin by noting that Myrdal develops the analysis of his book by means of what he calls (1939, p. v; see also pp. 30–32) an "immanent criticism" of Wicksell, by which Myrdal meant that "rather than pioneer with a wholly new approach," he would "project his own ideas within Wicksell's old framework." Thus Myrdal defines the purpose of his analysis in the following terms:

> Wicksell, as is well known, defined the equilibrium position by specifying the level of the "money rate of interest" which brings about monetary equilibrium. This equilibrium interest rate Wicksell calls the "normal rate of interest". . . .
>
> The "normal rate of interest" must now, according to Wicksell, (1) equal the marginal technical productivity of real capital (i.e., the

22. Note Myrdal's reference to "the present time (Spring 1932)" in a passage in the English version (1939, p. 170) that goes back to the Swedish version. (I am indebted to Bent Hansen for confirming this.)

23. According to Ohlin (1977, p. 155), "Myrdal revised and rewrote his presentation in a way which brought these sections on sequence analysis closer to the methods I [Ohlin] used in my report of 1934 [see below] and *Economic Journal* paper of March 1937." Cf. also Ohlin (1978, p. 145; 1981, p. 199) and Steiger (1978b, pp. 425–29). Other sections inserted in Myrdal's book were chap. 4, sec. 15 (last pages); chap. 4, sec. 16; and chap. 5, sec. 16; there was also some material which appeared in the German version but not in the English one (Palander 1941, p. 7, n. 3).

For a behind-the-scenes account of the translation of *Monetary Equilibrium* (in whose preparation, as is obvious from what has just been said, Myrdal took an active part), see the recent recollections of Robert B. Bryce, who was involved in its first stages (Patinkin and Leith 1977, p. 75; cf. also Myrdal's [1939, p. vi] reference to Bryce).

"real" or "natural" rate of interest); (2) equate the supply of and the demand for savings; and, finally, (3) guarantee a stable price level, primarily of consumption goods.

Wicksell assumes that these three criteria for the normal rate of interest are equivalent—i.e., never mutually inconsistent; but he cannot prove it. His formulations are, indeed, too loose and contradictory for this purpose. In the following I will prove that they cannot be identical: Only the first and the second of the equilibrium conditions are even consistent. . . . With respect to the commodity market, however, the fulfilment of these two monetary equilibrium relations means something quite different from an unchanged price level. [1939, pp. 37–38]

(In the chapter he devotes to this last proposition, Myrdal [1939, pp. 131–33] bases it on the argument that an equiproportionate change in all prices and wages will leave Wicksell's first two conditions unaffected.) Myrdal also states that "the main purpose" of his analysis "is to *include anticipations in the monetary system*" (1939, p. 32, italics in original) and criticizes Keynes for having failed to do so in the theoretical part of the *Treatise*.

Myrdal's subsequent detailed analysis of Wicksell's first two propositions (chaps. 4 and 5) seem to be based (like Wicksell's exposition itself; see above, p. 41) on the joint assumptions of price flexibility and full employment (Myrdal 1939, pp. 92, 132–33).[24] It is presumably in this context that Myrdal wrote the following revealing analysis of a "Disturbance of a Monetary Equilibrium by Increased Saving":

The increased saving immediately brings about a rupture of the monetary equilibrium in the capital market; for free capital disposal has increased, but not real investment. A downward Wicksellian process[25] has thus been started.

Furthermore, it is obvious that real investments not only do not increase but must even decrease. For increased savings, defined to mean decreased demand for consumption goods, necessarily bring about some decrease in the prices of consumption goods. This fall in prices must itself tend to lower capital values by influencing anticipations; with the consequence that the profit margin will move in the negative direction, which naturally means that real investments will decline. Equilibrium on the capital market is, therefore, disturbed not only by an increase in free capital disposal but also by a simultaneous decrease of real investment.

A downward Wicksellian process has thus been brought about by

24. I am indebted to Bent Hansen for emphasizing this point in our discussions; see the introductory footnote to this chapter.

25. Which in the present context means a downward movement of the price level, generated by the fact that the money rate has fallen below the real rate.

increased savings, where, paradoxically enough, the *increase* in savings continuously results in a *decrease* of real capital formation. This process does not stop except on these conditions: Either saving is lowered so much that it corresponds to the level of real investment—which means that saving must be reduced as much below its initial level as investment has been reduced by the primary increase in saving—or the rate of interest is lowered and credit conditions are eased to raise capital values and the profit margin enough to induce real investment to regain the level of free capital disposal. [Myrdal 1939, pp. 106–7, italics in original]

Thus a "paradox of saving" exists: but not because of the feedback effect of (money) income on (money) savings, but because the increased savings lowers the profitability of investment; and though the "downward Wicksellian process" might come to an end because "saving is lowered," such a lowering is presented not as the necessary feedback effect of the downward movement in (money) income, but as a chance exogenous event.[26] In brief, there is a striking similarity between this passage and the revealing passage from Keynes' *Treatise* about the "parable of the banana plantation" that I cited in my preceding lecture (above, p. 15).

Only in his subsequent analysis (in chap. 6) of Wicksell's third condition—price stability—does Myrdal for the first time consider the case of price and wage rigidities, and hence unemployment (ibid., pp. 143–44, 151). And it is in this context (ibid., pp. 163–64) that he does (in chap. 7) discuss some aspects of the equilibrating role of changes in output.[27] Thus in a passage which is essentially unchanged from the Swedish and German versions, Myrdal describes as follows the downward Wicksellian movement that is generated in this case by a tightening of credit:

So far the inner mechanics of the depressive process are fairly clear. However, it must now be noted that the total purchasing power of the society, which forms the demand for consumption goods, shrinks significantly less than does the total income. This means, naturally, that total saving is reduced, not only because of the reduction in incomes but also on account of the smaller fraction saved. The political and institutional development of the economy of the countries in an advanced capitalistic stage tends continuously to

26. Though I am not sure of its significance, I should note that this sentence does not appear in the *Ekonomisk Tidskrift* version. It does, however, appear in the German version. (I am indebted to Finn Borg for checking these points.)

27. This point was first made by Steiger (1978b, pp. 429, 440), who cited part of the following passage from Myrdal's *Monetary Equilibrium,* and who also pointed out that it is unchanged from the earlier Swedish and German versions.

increase the importance of these shifts in the use of income during a depressive process.

This tendency may be partially explained by the following considerations. The unemployed workers must live and in view of the ever-growing importance of social ideals, they must not live too badly. The public authority takes its part in several ways. Whether it be that the cost of the care of the unemployed is covered by public loans or by another turn of the tax screw, in so far as this affects saving, in either case it brings about a reduction in total savings, S, and thus also in the free capital disposal, W,[28] available for real investment, compared to the level they would have had if the dole had not been paid. . . . The unemployed also live on their own past savings and those of their relatives, which likewise reduces the quantity W.

Corresponding reasoning holds for the other classes of society. In order not to spoil the chances for raising capital in the future and also on other grounds, industrial firms in general try to keep up their dividend payments, despite the fall in actual earned net income, by entrenching upon reserve funds or anticipating future income. . . .

Even aside from this, the consuming habits of the middle and upper classes are fairly stabilized and resist considerably any change, especially a reduction, of their standards of living. . . . it is these classes above all, which are able to save, and which can now reduce their saving considerably or even live on their capital if their incomes fall. . . . All this brings about a fall in W. . . .

Thus after a credit contraction the business situation can under certain conditions attain quite a fair stability, at least stability for a considerable time, so that the relations fulfil even the equilibrium criterion, $W = R_2$ [i.e., gross savings = gross investment]. The new equilibrium position would be characterized by the following: A largely unchanged price level for consumption goods; capital values which will be sufficiently lower to correspond to the higher interest rate, or more generally, to the tighter credit conditions; somewhat lower wages, particularly in the capital goods industries; some, perhaps quite considerable, unemployment, especially in the capital goods industries; a production volume restricted generally but particularly in the capital goods industries, implying a shorter time structure of production; saving sufficiently reduced to make free capital disposal correspond to real investment, which, according to what has been said, is restricted on the whole and has a less roundabout arrangement of production to maintain. [Myrdal 1939, pp. 164–66, 169]

Though some elements are missing (e.g., the use of a precise multiplier), there are in this passage obvious parallels to Keynes' theory of

28. In present-day terminology, W corresponds more or less to gross savings. Thus, in Myrdal's notation (1939, p. 85), $W = S + D$, where S = "savings proper" (i.e., net savings) and D = anticipated depreciation *less* appreciation.

employment. Nevertheless, I have reservations about regarding it as a basis for the claim that Myrdal was an independent discoverer of the General Theory. First, and most important, if Myrdal had understood the full implications of this passage, he could never have written the earlier passage in *Monetary Equilibrium* that has been cited on pp. 48–49 above. Second, I find in the present passage—and particularly in its explanation of the reduction in savings due to the "unemployed workers"—an echo of the passage from Keynes' 1931 Harris lecture (cited on p. 25 of my preceding lecture) about the possibility of reaching a point of unemployment equilibrium by means (inter alia) of the reduction in savings due to the continued consumption of the unemployed workers living on the dole.[29] And it is in this context that the fact that Myrdal's original paper was written in the spring of 1932 and not in 1931 (see above, p. 47) assumes crucial importance. For Keynes' Harris lecture was published in November 1931,[30] so that it is possible that Myrdal read and was influenced by it before writing his own paper.[31]

My final reservation is that the foregoing passage must be read within its proper context as part of Myrdal's "immanent criticism" of Wicksell's contention that the equating of the money and real interest rates will also achieve equality between savings and investment as well as stability of the price level. More specifically, the passage appears in a chapter entitled "The Indifference Field of Monetary Equilibrium," by which Myrdal means that there is more than one interest rate at which these two additional conditions can be met. This is the main thrust of the passage, and it is noteworthy that the first

29. Thus compare Myrdal's statement in the foregoing passage:

> The unemployed workers must live and in view of the ever-growing importance of social ideals, they must not live too badly. The public authority takes its part in several ways. . . . The unemployed also live on their own past savings and those of their relatives, which likewise reduces the quantity W

with Keynes' statement in his Harris lecture:

> For one thing the unemployed will, in their effort not to allow too great a decline in their established standard of life, not only cease to save but will probably be responsible for much negative savings by living on their own previous savings and those of their friends and relations. Much more important, however, than this is likely to be the emergence of negative saving on the part of the government. [*JMK* IX, p. 356; cited in full on p. 25 above]

30. See back of title page of the book containing the Harris Foundation lectures for 1931.

31. This possibility has also been noted by Steiger (1978b, p. 440). Steiger also reports that in April 1978, Myrdal wrote him a letter commenting on an earlier draft of his (Steiger's) article and stating that he "never read the book [containing the 1931 Harris lecture] then or later, and never heard about it." We must, however, remember that we are dealing here with forty-five-year-old memories of an incident that could not have loomed large at the time. And on the fallibility of such memories (and even those of shorter periods—witness Myrdal's inaccuracies about his own *Monetary Equilibrium* noted on p. 47 above), see chap. 7, n. 10 below.

characteristic of the "new equilibrium position" enumerated in its last paragraph is "a largely unchanged price level for consumption goods" (above, p. 50). This is Myrdal's central message: not the fact that the equilibrium position is one of unemployment.

That Myrdal did not consider the equilibrating role of changes in employment to be his central message also manifests itself in the fact that he did not advert to it again in his subsequent writings, and in his 1934 *Report* on *The Economic Effects of Fiscal Policy* for the Swedish government's Committee on Unemployment in particular.[32] And he a fortiori made no subsequent attempt to develop the ideas of this passage in a more complete and precise manner. Nor was this point taken up by other Swedish economists in subsequent issues of the *Ekonomisk Tidskrift*.[33] It is also significant that, though Palander's lengthy and detailed critique in the 1941 *Ekonomisk Tidskrift* of Myrdal's *Monetary Equilibrium* devotes considerable attention to the case in which prices (including factor prices) are constant and quantities vary (1941, pp. 37–43; cf. also p. 15, n. 14), Palander does not mention Myrdal's reference in this context to the equilibrating role of changes in output. Nor does Brinley Thomas in his survey of Myrdal's writings (1936, pp. 86–102, et passim).

Let me turn now to the writings of Bertil Ohlin. As implied above, both Landgren (1960a, chap. 8) and Steiger (1971, 1976) consider Ohlin's 1933 article "Till frågan om penningteoriens uppläggning"— recently translated in *History of Political Economy* (1978) as "On the Formulation of Monetary Theory"—to be similar to the General Theory. They disagree only on the degree of independent discovery it represented. From my viewpoint, however, Ohlin's 1933 article differs basically from the General Theory. For, like the central message of Keynes' *Treatise*, that of Ohlin's article is the analysis of changes in prices, with the discussion of changes in output being derivative from it. Indeed at several points in his discussion (1933a, pp. 354, 357, 360 [n. 8], 379, 384), Ohlin compares his analysis of price movements with that of Keynes in the *Treatise*, which he includes in what he denotes as the "neo-Wicksellian theory."

32. For details on this committee, see Uhr (1977), pp. 92ff., whose translation of the title of Myrdal's report I have followed here. See also Brinley Thomas (1936, chap. 5) and Hansen (1981, pp. 264ff.). This and the following paragraph of the text owe much to discussions with Bent Hansen.

33. This statement—which must be made with great diffidence (to say the least) by one who cannot read Swedish—is based on (1) a translation by Finn Borg of the titles of the articles in the issues of the *Ekonomisk Tidskrift* for the period 1932–39 and (2) discussions with Bent Hansen of the references in these issues to the writings of Myrdal and Ohlin (a discussion of whose writings follows immediately). I must, however, emphasize that Hansen should not be held responsible for the conclusions I have drawn from these discussions.

At the same time I must emphasize that Ohlin's 1933 article is a decided improvement over the *Treatise*. First, it avoids the mechanical and artificial analysis which was the frequent outcome of the "magic formula mentality" with which Keynes applied his fundamental equations (see *KMT*, chap. 6). Second, and related to the preceding point, Ohlin's 1933 article makes more use than the *Treatise* of the feedback effects of a change in output on aggregate demand. But once again what primarily concerns Ohlin are the consequent effects of the resulting changes in excess demand on prices and hence on the generation of business cycles (1933a, pp. 377, 379, 381). There is no recognition of what I have singled out as the novel central message of the *General Theory:* namely, the equilibrating role of changes in output. And lest I be misunderstood,[34] let me emphasize that my point here is not that Ohlin's analysis should be faulted for having dealt with changes in prices or for being primarily concerned with the dynamics of the business cycles and not with "unemployment equilibrium," but that the dynamic analysis he presents does not take account of the dampening (in the present context of business-cycle analysis, a more appropriate term than "equilibrating") feedback effect of changes in output on the degree of excess supply in the commodity market.

At first glance, the following passage in Ohlin's paper might (as Hans Brems [1978, p. 399] has claimed) seem to contradict this conclusion:

> Imagine that people decide to reduce their saving sharply, so demand for consumers' goods will rise. . . . The decision to reduce saving may not be accompanied by a tightening of credit. If so, investment demand will at first be allowed to go on as usual, assuming an increasing money supply or an increasing velocity of circulation, and the rising investment demand of the consumers' goods industries will eventually bring about an increase in total investment. Total saving, then, is not reduced but on the contrary increased, despite the fact that consumption is up. What makes this possible is expanding output. [Ohlin 1933a, p. 368]

But if we read this passage against the background of the earlier literature, it will be seen that it does not differ fundamentally from Keynes' imprecise contention in *Can Lloyd George Do It?* (1929) that increased investment in public works will generate correspondingly increased savings—in part "by the very prosperity which the new policy will foster" (*JMK* IX, p. 120). Indeed, as I emphasized in my preceding lecture (above, pp. 27–28), one of the major contributions of Richard Kahn's subsequent multiplier article was the rigorous demonstration of this proposition. In brief, I do not believe that Ohlin in the aforemen-

34. Cf. Ohlin 1978; 1981, sec. 10.

tioned passage from his 1933 paper is saying anything more than what
Kahn said in his 1931 multiplier article and its 1932 sequel; and as I
have demonstrated in my preceding lecture, recognition of the multiplier did not constitute recognition of the General Theory.[35] I should
also emphasize that the context in which the foregoing passage appears
is primarily one of the analysis of prices and not output: indeed, the
passage appears in a section entitled "The time sequence of price
changes."

Might I finally note that the concluding section of Ohlin's 1933 article
(pp. 383–84) itself provides conclusive evidence against viewing this
article as an anticipation of the General Theory. For in this section
Ohlin lists five major objectives that he has attempted to accomplish
with the article. The first of these has to do with the definition of
income, and the remaining four with the behavior of prices and the
interest rate. None of them deal with the behavior of output, and correspondingly none even allude to the foregoing passage. Thus by his
"revealed preference" of what is important in his article, Ohlin himself
shows that its central message is not the equilibrating role (or, more
generally, feedback effect) of changes in output. Correspondingly, just
as in the case of Myrdal, this aspect of Ohlin's writings did not stimulate further discussion by other Swedish economists in subsequent
issues of the *Ekonomisk Tidskrift* (see n. 33 above).

The claim that Ohlin was an independent discoverer of the General
Theory has been based at least as much on his 1934 *Report* for the
government Committee on Unemployment (entitled *Monetary Policy,
Public Works, Subsidies and Tariff Policy as Remedies for Unemployment*)[36] as on his 1933 article. Thus in support of this claim, Steiger
(1978b, pp. 439–40) has cited the following analysis of a decrease in
demand which appears in Ohlin's *Report:*

35. I might in this context again refer to Ohlin's statement (1981, p. 204) that both he
and Myrdal "may have been influenced by Kahn's paper in June 1931." On the other
hand, Ohlin may have been influenced by another pioneer of multiplier analysis, Jens
Warming (see chap. 1, n. 21 above), who was his colleague at the University of Copenhagen in the late 1920s (Steiger 1981, p. 184). At the same time I should note that I have not
found any references to Warming in Ohlin's 1933 article or 1934 *Report* (on which see
below).

36. This is the way Ohlin translated the title in some comments he sent me on a
seminar I gave in Stockholm in September 1977 (see the introductory footnote to this
chapter). In these comments, Ohlin designated pp. 12–16, 24–30, 33, 36–40, 42–46, 50–56,
63–65, 69, 74–77, 139–42 of the *Report* as relevant to his claim and emphasized in
particular the importance of pp. 26–28 and 31. In his subsequent published comments
(1978, p. 146), Ohlin referred in particular to pp. 12–14 and 19–23 of his *Report*. At a later
stage of our correspondence, Ohlin kindly provided me with an English translation of pp.
5–37 of his *Report*, carried out by Lewis Taylor of Stockholm under his (Ohlin's) direction. The other pages designated by Ohlin were translated for me by Finn Borg. In an
interview with Landgren (1960a, p. 219, n. 10), Ohlin stated that he had at the time
wanted Brinley Thomas to undertake an English translation of his *Report*, but that the

Since each decrease in demand either decreases prices or quantities sold or both, and so reduces gross incomes, which evokes a tendency to further cutting back of demand, one may well ask, why this deflationary spiral, once it has come well under way, does not continue until everything comes to a standstill. The explanation for why this does not occur should be found to some extent in the fact that the demand for the means of consumption decreases only slowly when it has reached a certain level on the way down, even though the net income should decrease even more. Some people live on their savings, others obtain unemployment compensation financed with loans to cover the deficit in public finances. Above all, persons with fixed wages and income from interest provide a constant element in the demand, which during a period of rapid price decrease as a rule is partly financed through public or private loans. The demand of all of these persons provides income for farmers, retailers etc. and thus to a certain degree of demand on their part. Even if the demand for new real capital is very insignificant, a certain need for reinvestment will always be there; and even if the incomes of the persons who work with the production of such capital are only a fraction of their usual incomes, a certain volume of sales is kept up for these reasons. [Ohlin 1934, p. 33][37]

At the same time, Steiger (1978b, pp. 440–41) has contended that this passage reflects Ohlin's reliance on the Myrdal analysis that has been cited in extenso on pp. 49–50 above. Thus even if this passage should be interpreted as an anticipation of the General Theory, it does not constitute an *independent* anticipation. Furthermore, I deny that it should be so interpreted: for besides the imprecision of its presentation, this passage (like Myrdal's) lacks one of the elements of the General Theory—namely, the multiplier. And what makes this absence all the more significant—an indication that even here Ohlin did not achieve an integrated theory of output—is that subsequently in the *Report*, in his analysis of the impact of public works on employment, Ohlin does discuss the multiplier concept and even refers to Kahn's 1931 article.[38] But over and above these specific points there is the

latter was unable to find the time to do so. Toward the end of his life, Ohlin once again made plans for such a translation, but these were not carried out.

Ohlin himself summarized part of his *Report* in English in part B, secs. 1–8 of his *Economic Journal* paper on the Stockholm School (1937, p. 93, n. 2). See also the discussion of this *Report* in Hansen (1981, p. 274). The *Report* as a whole has been summarized by Brems (1978, pp. 400–409). Unfortunately, Brems has supplemented this summary with exaggerated claims for the *Report* (see Patinkin [1978b, pp. 416–17]; see also the reservations about Brems' claims expressed by Steiger [1978b, pp. 433–35], as well as by Ohlin himself [1981, pp. 212–13]).

37. Translated by Lewis Taylor; see preceding footnote. See also pp. 38–40 of Ohlin's *Report*.

38. See the summary of Ohlin's *Report* in Brems (1978, pp. 405–7).

general one that though the ultimate concern of Ohlin's 1934 *Report* is
unemployment, its central message (like that of his 1933 article) remains the analysis of prices, and not output.[39] I might also note Ohlin's
statement many years later that the 1933 article originated as part of the
1934 *Report*.[40, 41]

A few words must now be said about the work of a then-younger
member of the Stockholm School, Erik Lundberg. Lundberg's dissertation, which appeared as a book entitled *Studies in the Theory of
Economic Expansion* (1937), does indeed contain the essence of the
General Theory. At the same time, the fact that this book appeared a
year after the *General Theory*, that it repeatedly refers to Keynes'
book, and that indeed Lundberg describes the "positive part" of his
book as "an attempt to apply the methods developed by Wicksell and
his followers to the system of explanation formulated by Keynes"
makes it methodologically difficult, if not impossible, to cite it as evidence in a discussion of whether or not the Stockholm School anticipated the *General Theory*.[42, 43]

39. Steiger (1978b, p. 434) also concedes that this is the main thrust of the *Report*. The
references to Keynes' *Treatise* in the *Report* (pp. 16, 28n, 30–31) are another indication
of its concern with prices.
    In a recent article, Lars Jonung (1979) has shown that Swedish macroeconomic policy
in the 1930s was also primarily concerned with prices, and with Wicksell's norm of price
stabilization in particular.
40. "In the spring of 1932 . . . I again started work on my report on *Monetary Policy,
Public Works, Subsidies and Tariffs as Remedies for Unemployment*, the first part of
which was sent to the editor of *Ekonomisk Tidskrift* in February 1933 and published there
a few months later after some not very essential revisions" (Ohlin 1981, p. 198, with the
editor's insertions deleted).
41. Hansen (1981, pp. 264–70) provides a detailed discussion of the final (1935) *Report*
of the Committee on Unemployment (which was drafted by Dag Hammarskjöld, the
secretary of the committee) and claims to find in its first chapter "a simple Keynesian
unemployment equilibrium model" (ibid., p. 264). Without discussing the validity of this
interpretation, let me note that Hansen (ibid.) goes on to say that "nothing like the model
of [this] *Report* can be found elsewhere in the writings of the authors of the Stockholm
School." Furthermore, after a detailed examination of the aforementioned chapter, Hansen (1981, p. 268) concludes that its author "did succeed in formulating a Keynesian
unemployment model but did not succeed in analyzing it."
42. The quotation is from Lundberg's foreword (dated December 1936) to the book. I
might, however, note that in his book Lundberg refers almost as much to the *Treatise* as
to the *General Theory*. In general, Lundberg's book contains far more references to
Keynes than to any other economist. This is not to deny that there is an element of truth
in Schumpeter's statement in his discussion of Lundberg's book that "no work of this
range and depth can, within a single year, be *formed* by an outside reference unless its
author has arrived at somewhat similar conclusions by himself" (Schumpeter 1954, pp.
1173–74, italics in original). But there is at least as much truth in Lundberg's shrewd
observation several years later (1960, p. 197) that "Schumpeter's somewhat exaggerated
praise of my dissertation has its roots in some kind of rivalry with Keynes for the honor
of being the most important political economist of the time. Schumpeter must have
enjoyed using in this way a book by an unknown economist in a remote part of the world
as a means of showing that historically one does not have to regard the essence of the
General Theory as being revolutionarily new." Lundberg's observation appears in his

My final bit of evidence, albeit of a circumstantial nature, is from the detailed exposition and critique of the *General Theory* which Tord Palander—described by Landgren (1960, p. 272) as having been at the time "the foremost authority on Keynes in Sweden," an appraisal that has been confirmed by Bent Hansen—published in the 1942 *Ekonomisk Tidskrift*. In this article, Palander (1942, pp. 233–34) does refer to "Swedish monetary and economic theory discussions of the 1930s," but only in connection with his criticism of Keynes' use of the method of comparative statics, as against the dynamic analysis which characterized these discussions. At no point in the article does Palander even suggest that these discussions contained the General Theory.[44, 45]

My conclusion from the evidence presented in this lecture is that the Stockholm School cannot be credited with the simultaneous discovery of the General Theory. At the same time, the ex ante–ex post analysis which is the hallmark of this school provided the basis for a crucial chapter that was missing from Keynes' exposition of this theory; namely, a chapter analyzing the short-run dynamics of the system. I shall return to this point in my concluding lecture.

---

contribution to the 1960 *Ekonomisk Tidskrift* symposium on Landgren's book and has been cited here from the translation prepared for me by Moshe Apelblat (see n. 8 above). In this contribution, Lundberg did, however, state that "most of my construction of models in Chapter 9 of my book, explaining hypothetical business cycles, was ready and written during the course of 1935" (1960, pp. 197–98). For other aspects of Schumpeter's feeling of rivalry with Keynes, see Patinkin and Leith (1977, pp. 87–89).

43. Another possibly relevant point here is that Lundberg spent 1931–33 in the United States as a Rockefeller fellow, studying at various universities. Correspondingly, the preface to his book (1937, p. vi), contains acknowledgments not only to Lindahl, Myrdal, and other teachers at Stockholm University, but also to "the teachers and fellow-students at these [American] universities." Among them was this University, where Lundberg spent the academic year 1931–32.

44. Hansen's views on Palander were expressed in personal discussions with me; see introductory footnote to this chapter. An indication of the thoroughness of Palander's 1942 article is that he pointed out an error in a formula in chap. 21 ("The Theory of Prices") of the *General Theory* that was noted in the English literature only many years later; see below, chap. 5, n. 32. (I am indebted to Finn Borg for a translation of Palander's article.)

45. Another work of Scandinavian (though not Swedish) origin that is sometimes mentioned in the present context is Ragnar Frisch's "Circulation Planning: Proposal for a National Organization of a Commodity and Service Exchange" (1934). To my mind, however, this article does not really deal with the General Theory and hence is not relevant to the present discussion.

3

Anticipations of the General Theory? Michał Kalecki

The subject of my preceding lecture was a school of individuals who provided intellectual stimulation for one another, a school with an illustrious historical tradition operating in the mainstream of economic thought. In contrast, the subject of my present lecture is a single individual operating in a country, interwar Poland, which from the viewpoint of economic theory (though not from that of other disciplines, such as, e.g., mathematics and logic) was in the backwaters; an individual who, in economic matters, was himself further isolated intellectually by virtue of his being largely an autodidact (Feiwel 1975, p. 48), and whose scientific career was not enhanced by the fact that he was a Jew in a highly anti-Semitic country. For these reasons the achievements of Michał Kalecki, however we may evaluate them, are all the more impressive.[1]

This chapter has been significantly improved, and some inaccuracies in it eliminated, as the result of detailed and provocative comments on an earlier draft of it by Jerzy Osiatyński (editor of the six-volume edition in Polish of Kalecki's *Dzieła* [Works] now in the process of being published) and Kazimierz Laski (formerly of the Central School of Planning and Statistics, Warsaw, where he worked closely with Kalecki during the 1960s; now at the Johannes Kepler University, Linz, Austria), to whom I am much indebted. Needless to say, neither of them is to be held responsible for its conclusions, with which they continue to disagree.

I would also like to thank Marek Belka of the University of Lodz, who first brought it to my attention that Kalecki's *Dzieła* was being published and who sent me a copy of volume 1 of it. Similarly, I am grateful to Henryk Francuz for guiding me through this volume, and to Yossi Ben-Akiva and Barbara Kaminski for translating portions of it.

It was my good fortune to be able to prepare the final draft of this chapter while serving in the fall of 1980 as Wesley C. Mitchell Visiting Research Professor at Columbia University, where I benefited greatly from discussions with Alexander Erlich and Stanislaw Wellisz.

1. A bibliography of Kalecki's writings for the period 1927–63 appears at the end of the *Festschrift* that was published on the occasion of his sixty-fifth birthday (Kowalik et al., 1964). It is reproduced (though without an indication of its source) by Feiwel (1975, pp. 527ff.), who has also supplemented it for the period 1964–72.

58

Again in contrast with the situation that existed with respect to the Stockholm School, there was no personal contact between Keynes and Kalecki in the period before the publication of the *General Theory*. Nor—primarily, though not entirely, because of the language barrier—did either of them exert any intellectual influence over the other during that period. Thus it was not until the beginning of 1937 that there was any correspondence between them (see below, Appendix, p. 96). Similarly, the first work of Kalecki's to which Keynes (1939, pp. 35, 49) referred was the former's 1938 *Econometrica* paper (in English, of course) on the distribution of national income (see p. 101 below). Insofar as Kalecki was concerned, though like most Polish intellectuals in the early 1930s he knew both German and French, he did not begin studying English until 1935, in preparation for going abroad under the Rockefeller fellowship that he had received (see below, Appendix, p. 93). It is however, noteworthy that despite the existence of a 1932 German translation of the *Treatise*, Kalecki (unlike Myrdal and Ohlin) made no reference to this work in his pre–*General Theory* writings. Instead, his only reference to Keynes in these writings occurred in a 1932 article in a Polish socialist review in which he summarized and criticized a public lecture that Keynes gave in February 1932 on "The World's Economic Crisis and the Way of Escape" (1932). Interestingly enough, in this article Kalecki (1932, p. 72) referred to Keynes as "the most serious contemporary bourgeois economist."[2]

Having stressed these contrasts with the Stockholm School, let me note one point of similarity: namely that, like Ohlin, Kalecki advanced his claim to independent discovery of the General Theory shortly after the appearance of Keynes' book. This he did in a long review article (on which more below) which appeared in the fall of 1936 in *Ekonomista*, the professional journal of Poland's economists, published of course in Polish—which explains why his claim (unlike Ohlin's) did not at the time receive any attention in the English-speaking world. A few years later, the claim received some support

2. Similarly, in his application for the aforementioned Rockefeller fellowship, Kalecki listed Keynes as one of the economists (the others were Myrdal and Frisch) he wished to visit. On Kalecki's knowledge of languages, see Osiatyński's editorial note in Kalecki, *Dzieła* [Works], vol. I, p. 431. For examples of Kalecki's references to foreign literature, see the references to a French work by Aftalion and a German one by Tinbergen on, respectively, p. 98, n. 1 and p. 100, n. 3 of Kalecki's 1933 *Próba* (on which more in a moment).

I am indebted to Barbara Kaminski for a translation of Kalecki's 1932 article. According to Osiatyński, Kalecki based his article on the text of Keynes' lecture as reported at length in the Continental press (editorial note in Kalecki, *Dzieła* [Works], vol. 1, pp. 437–38 and personal correspondence). However, the full text of the lecture (which was given as part of the Halley Stewart lectures that year) appeared only later (Keynes 1932).

from Oskar Lange (1939) in an article in a Polish encyclopedia.[3] But Kalecki's claim did not find an echo in the English literature until a decade later in Austin Robinson's wonderful memoir of Keynes, in which Robinson says that "Kalecki was independently approaching the same goal" (1947, p. 58). Kalecki's name, however, is barely mentioned in Schumpeter's *History of Economic Analysis* (1954, pp. 1143–44)—and this despite the fact that, as we have seen in the cases of Kahn and Lundberg (above chap. 1, n. 27 and chap. 2, n. 42), Schumpeter never missed an opportunity to suggest that someone was a co- or independent discoverer of the General Theory. Nor is Kalecki's name mentioned in Roy Harrod's *Life of Keynes* (1951).[4]

Similarly, Kalecki's name does not appear in volume XIII of Keynes' *Collected Writings*, which contains materials relating to the preparation of the *General Theory;* and his name is mentioned only twice in volume XIV, whose materials relate to the subsequent discussion of this book: once in a note from Joan Robinson to Keynes dated October 1936, thanking Keynes for "being kind to [her] Pole" during Kalecki's first visit to Cambridge (*JMK* XIV, p. 140), on which occasion he presented a paper before Keynes' Political Economy Club;[5] and once in a letter from Roy Harrod dated September 1938, where Kalecki's name was included by him in a list of economists working on the problem of business cycles (*JMK* XIV, p. 304). There are also two

3. The article is entitled "The Neoclassical School in Economics." In it Lange traces the teachings of this school through Marshall and the Cambridge economists of the 1930s, including Keynes, then lists several Polish economists whose work in his view bears some similarity to that of the "Cambridge School." Lange then briefly remarks that "a theory of employment, similar to that developed in Cambridge, was independently worked out by M. Kalecki, who on its basis developed his theory of the business cycle" (Lange 1939, p. 68). (Cited by Osiatyński in an editorial note in Kalecki, *Dzieła* [Works], vol. I, p. 453. I am indebted to Osiatyński for bringing this note to my attention and providing me with a translation of it, and to Wellisz for explaining the context of Lange's remark.) However, for reasons that I shall explain below (n. 19), I do not know how seriously or consistently Lange advanced this claim.

4. Once again (see above, chap. 1, n. 27) we should remember that Schumpeter did not live to complete his book; it is also possible that he might not have known of Kalecki's work in Polish. On the other hand, there were writings of Kalecki in English and French (see below) that were available to him.

Most of these references (as well as the one to Klein [1951] which follows) have been obtained from Kowalik (1964, p. 4, n. 4) and Feiwel (1975, pp. 25–26). My interpretation of Schumpeter's bare mention of Kalecki is, however, the opposite of Feiwel's, who lumps Schumpeter with the "economic fraternity" that allegedly did not want to recognize Kalecki's priority (ibid.).

5. See Osiatyński's editorial comment in Kalecki, *Dzieła* [Works], vol. I, p. 515. On the nature of this club, see Harrod (1951, pp. 322–30) and Patinkin and Leith (1977, pp. 48–49, 73–74, et passim); cf. also p. xxii above. Osiatyński adds that Joan Robinson was specially invited to attend this meeting of the club (normally restricted to men) to present Kalecki to its participants. Kalecki's visit took place during the tenure of his Rockefeller Foundation fellowship (see preceding page).

passing references to Kalecki (again, not by Keynes) in volume XXIX, which is a supplement to these two volumes. However, the Polish edition of Kalecki's *Works* reproduces (in Polish translation) a dozen-odd letters that were exchanged between Kalecki and Keynes after the appearance of the *General Theory*, mostly in connection with articles that Kalecki had submitted to Keynes in the latter's capacity as editor of the *Economic Journal*.[6]

The first unequivocal claim for Kalecki in the English literature was advanced at roughly the same time by Lawrence Klein in his 1951 review of Harrod's biography of Keynes and (albeit without details) by Joan Robinson (1952, p. 159). In his review, Klein (1951, pp. 447–48) implicitly criticized Harrod's failure to refer to Kalecki and claimed (on the basis of his reexamination of an article Kalecki had published in the 1935 *Econometrica*, on which more in a moment) that Kalecki had created a system "that contains everything of importance in the Keynesian system" and in some respects is superior to it. On the other hand, Klein himself had barely referred to Kalecki—and even then in a different context—in the original edition of his earlier well-known book, *The Keynesian Revolution* (1947, p. 179). Klein did, however, take advantage of the second edition of this book (1966, pp. 224–25) to add a chapter which, inter alia, reaffirmed his 1951 claims for Kalecki. Similarly, in his contribution to the 1964 Kalecki *Festschrift*, Klein (1964, p. 189) claimed that "the basic ingredients of the Keynesian development were already available in Kalecki's model."

From the 1964 *Festschrift* onward the cause of Kalecki has found increasing support in certain circles. In this *Festschrift*, Joan Robinson provided support for her 1952 statement and declared: "*The General Theory of Employment, Interest and Money* was published in January [*sic*] 1936. Meanwhile, without any contact either way, Michal Kalecki had found the same solution" (J. Robinson 1964, p. 336). And shortly afterward she repeated this claim (as she was to do on several subsequent occasions) in her introduction (1966, p. ix) to a translation of some of Kalecki's essays which appeared under the title *Studies in the Theory of Business Cycles, 1933–1939* (1966).[7] In his own foreword to

6. See Kalecki, *Dzieła* [Works], vol. I, pp. 513–17, 556–59, 564–65, 573–74. I am indebted to Yossi Ben-Akiva for retranslating this correspondence to English. Only part of it bears—and even then tangentially—on the present discussion (see n. 24 below). This part of the correspondence is reproduced in its original English form on pp. 96–102 of the Appendix below. The letter which appears on pp. 573–74 of *Dzieła* [Works], vol. I, has now been reproduced in vol. XXVII of Keynes' *Collected Writings;* for details, see below, p. 96.

7. This introduction in part summarizes and in part reproduces (including the passage just cited) her contribution to the 1964 *Festschrift*. For her subsequent presentations of this claim, see J. Robinson (1971, 1976, 1977). I might here mention that Osiatyński, in an

this book, however, Kalecki himself made no reference to the relation between his work and the *General Theory*, just as he had not done so in his earlier publications in English (see below, n. 21). When, however, three of these same essays were reprinted a few years later in his *Selected Essays on the Dynamics of the Capitalist Economy: 1933–1970* (1971), Kalecki described them "as papers published in 1933, 1934, and 1935 in Polish before Keynes' *General Theory* appeared, and containing, I believe, its essentials" (Kalecki 1971, p. vii). And most recently, a biographer of Kalecki, George Feiwel, has in his book (1975, chap. 2) spoken unequivocally of the "Kalecki-Keynes Revolution," drawing support from the statement in Lawrence Klein's foreword to the book that "Kalecki's greatest achievement, among many, was undoubtedly his complete anticipation of Keynes' *General Theory*" (Klein 1975, p. v). Similar statements have been made by Shackle (1967, p. 127), Eshag (1977a, pp. 1–2), and at one time (albeit in passing) by myself as well.[8] In all these cases the claim is one of independent discovery; no one has suggested that Kalecki influenced Keynes or vice versa.

The main basis for this claim is Kalecki's Polish monograph *Próba teorii koniunktury* [An essay on the theory of the business cycle], which he published in 1933,[9] well before his travels and contacts abroad (above, p. 59). Thus I am once again faced with the problem of being unable to study all the relevant literature in its original language. The problem is, however, much alleviated by two facts: First, the basic contents of Kalecki's 1933 "booklet" (as he, in the passage cited

---

editorial note in vol. I, pp. 515–16 of Kalecki's *Dzieła* [Works], has reproduced (in Polish translation) a letter Joan Robinson wrote to Kalecki in September 1937 which expresses great enthusiasm for his work, but which (it seems to me) does not go so far as to indicate that at the time she attributed to him the independent discovery of the General Theory. Nor—despite her reference in it to Kalecki's work—is there any such indication in her *Introduction to the Theory of Employment* (1937, p. v); instead she (like others at the time—see below) refers only to Kalecki's theory of the cycle (see the preface to the second edition of the book [1969, p. xv]). (I am indebted to Yossi Ben-Akiva for retranslating the aforementioned letter. The original English version of it [with which I was subsequently provided] is reproduced on pp. 94–96 below.)

8. Namely, in a 1974 paper reproduced as chap. 6 below; see in particular p. 169. For other aspects of the similarities and differences between Keynes and Kalecki, see Eshag (1977b). See also McFarlane (1971).

9. Osiatyński (citing Kalecki's reminiscences as transmitted by Tadeusz Kowalik, who wrote the brief biography of Kalecki which appears in the 1964 *Festschrift* for him) relates that at the end of 1932 Kalecki prepared a German translation of this essay for publication, but that these plans came to naught when the potential publisher (who was a socialist) fled Germany to escape from Hitler. Osiatyński also relates that at the beginning of 1933 Kalecki sent a manuscript copy of this translation to Keynes, but that the latter (according to Kalecki's former secretary) returned it with a note which apologetically said that he did not read German (editorial note in Kalecki, *Dzieła* [Works], vol. I, p. 451).

at the end of this paragraph, later termed it) were published before the *General Theory* in the form of two more accessible articles—namely, "A Macrodynamic Theory of Business Cycles," which appeared in the July 1935 *Econometrica*, where it is described (ibid., p. 327) as having been first presented at the 1933 meeting of the Econometric Society in Leiden; and the "Essai d'une théorie du mouvement cyclique des affaires" in the March–April 1935 *Revue d'économie politique*. Second, some twenty-five years later, the essential part of the 1933 essay was translated into English by Kalecki's wife and published in the already mentioned *Studies in the Theory of Business Cycles: 1933–1939* (1966) in a chapter entitled "Outline of a Theory of the Business Cycle." In his foreword to this book, Kalecki gave the following description of the relation between this chapter and his 1933 essay:

> The *Outline of a Theory of the Business Cycle* is the first (and most essential) part of my booklet *An Essay on the Theory of [the] Business Cycle* which was published in 1933. I supplemented this study by a short passage concerning the problem of the money market taken from my *Essai d'une théorie du mouvement cyclique des affaires* published in the French quarterly *Revue d'Economie Politique*, March–April 1935. Apart from this nothing of importance has been added either to this or to other items. [Kalecki 1966, p. 1]

Let me then examine Kalecki's theory as presented in this translated essay, noting that it more or less corresponds to the two 1935 Kalecki articles mentioned in the preceding paragraph. As in the case of the Stockholm School, I must emphasize that my purpose is the narrow one of examining the claim that Kalecki anticipated the General Theory; I am not undertaking an exposition of Kalecki's theory as such.

Kalecki's analytical framework reflects two major influences: Marxian theory on the one hand and national-income accounting (of which Kalecki together with Ludwik Landau were pioneers in Poland) on the other.[10] Thus Kalecki's 1933 booklet begins in a Marxist manner by classifying the members of the economy as capitalists or workers, with the latter being assumed to consume their entire incomes, so that

---

10. On the Marxian influence, see Lange (1939, p. 88; 1959, vol. I, p. 309, n. 35), Klein (1964, p. 189), and Joan Robinson (1964, p. 338; 1966, p. x). On Kalecki and national-income accounting, see Kowalik (1964, pp. 1–2) and Studenski (1958, pp. 475–76). Alexander Erlich has, however, informed me that Kalecki's 1933 booklet was severely criticized by two members of the Polish communist party, Aleksander Rajchman (1933) and Samuel Fogelson, who charged Kalecki both with technical errors and with expressing non-Marxian views. Kalecki wrote a reply (1933c) to Rajchman's criticism, which led to a further sharp exchange between them. See also Osiatyński's comments in Kalecki, *Dzieła* [Works], vol. I, pp. 450, 461, 479–80.

all saving is carried out by the capitalists. In the opening words of Kalecki's essay (in its translated form):

> We shall consider a *closed* economic system, *devoid of trends,* i.e. one which returns to its original state after each cycle. In addition we shall make the following assumptions.
>
> 1. *Gross real profits.* By gross real profits P we understand the aggregate real income of capitalists including depreciation per unit of time consisting of their consumption and saving
>
> (1) $P = C + A$.

Thus C denotes all goods which are consumed by capitalists and A includes—since we abstract from workers' savings or their "capitalist" incomes—all goods which are used in the reproduction and expansion of fixed capital as well as the increase in inventories. In the future A will be referred to as gross accumulation.†

The personal consumption of capitalists is relatively inelastic. Let us assume that C consists of a constant part B_0 and a part which is proportionate to gross profits:

(2) $C = B_0 + \lambda P$

where λ is a small constant.

From equations (1) and (2) we obtain:

$$[a] \quad P = B_0 + \lambda P + A$$

(3)

$$[b] \quad P = \frac{B_0 + A}{1 - \lambda}$$

i.e. the gross real profits P are proportionate to the sum $B_0 + A$ of the constant part of capitalists' consumption B_0 and the gross accumulation A.

The gross accumulation A is according to the above equal to the sum of the production of investment goods and the increase in inventories. *For the sake of simplicity we assume that aggregate inventories remain constant throughout the trade cycle.*

It follows from the above assumptions that the real profits P are proportionate to $B_0 + A$, where B_0 denotes the constant part of the capitalists' consumption, and A the gross accumulation which is equal to the production of investment goods.

---

†The national income is equal on the one hand to the sum of profits and wages, and on the other, to the sum of: (1) the reproduction and expansion of fixed capital and the increase in inventories A; (2) the consumption of capitalists; and (3) the consumption of workers. Since the latter is equal to wages, profits are equal to $C + A$.

[Kalecki 1966, pp. 3–4, with the omission of one footnote, irrelevant for our purposes; italics in original]

Equation (3b) has a familiar look, and I shall return to this point (pp. 70–71, below). Note that Kalecki assumes a closed economy without government savings (i.e., with a balanced budget)—the first explicitly and the second implicitly.[11]

In a precise manner—paying careful attention to the time lags involved—Kalecki then proceeds to distinguish among "three stages . . . in the investment activity": investment orders, I; the resulting production of investment goods, A; and, finally, the resulting delivery of investment goods, D—all per unit of time (ibid., p. 4). He also distinguishes carefully between these flows, on the one hand, and the stock of capital K, on the other. These are related by the fact that the "change [in K] during a given period is equal to the difference between deliveries of new equipment and the volume of productive assets going out of use." The stock of capital is assumed to be at the same level at the end of the cycle as at the beginning, after some "small fluctuations" in the course of the cycle. (In his 1935 *Econometrica* article [p. 340], Kalecki indicates how his analysis can readily be extended to a growing economy.) Kalecki then assumes that investment orders I depend on profitability (as represented by the ratio of profits P to the stock of capital K) and the cost of capital (as represented by the rate of interest i). He also makes (in present-day terminology) the homogeneity assumption that "I is likely to increase in the same proportion as P and K," and accordingly writes his investment function as

$$(4) \qquad \frac{I}{K} = f\left(\frac{P}{K}, i\right),$$

"where f is an increasing function of P/K and a diminishing function of i." He then cites the "known [fact] that the rate of interest rises in the upswing and falls in the downswing" (ibid., p. 8), a fact on which he elaborates in the concluding part of his essay,[12] in order to make the "simplifying assumption" that i is an increasing function of P/K. This is explained in terms of the fact that "the demand for money in circulation increases during the upswing [when P/K is also rising] and falls during the downswing [when P/K is falling]. The rise and fall in the rate of interest follows suit" (ibid., p. 15). (From the context it is clear that the reasoning here is closer to the traditional loanable-funds approach than to Keynes' liquidity-preference one.) This enables Kalecki to rewrite (4) as

11. By virtue of the assumption that total savings equals private (capitalists') savings. In a later version of his theory, Kalecki (1939, p. 117) makes both these assumptions explicit.

12. As Kalecki indicates in the passage from the foreword to his 1966 book cited on p. 63 above, this part was added to the translation of his 1933 booklet from his 1935 French article (pp. 297–98). This discussion also appears in the "Comments" (1936b, sec. 3) that he wrote in reply to Tinbergen (1935) and Frisch and Holme (1935) (see p. 70 below); it does not however appear in Kalecki's original 1935 *Econometrica* article.

(5) $$\frac{I}{K} = F\left(\frac{P}{K}\right) ;$$

and he further assumes that i increases "sufficiently slowly" relative to P/K for $F(\ )$ to be an increasing function of P/K. Substituting from (3b), he then obtains

(6) $$\frac{I}{K} = \phi\left(\frac{B_0 + A}{K}\right) ,$$

which he linearizes as

(7) $$\frac{I}{K} = m\,\frac{B_0 + A}{K} - n ,$$

where m is by assumption positive. Kalecki then states that he will "now show that n must be positive" (ibid., p. 9); he does so, however, only under the additional assumption (for which he gives no economic justification) that $I < mB_0$. For in that case

(8) $$n = \frac{mA + (mB_0 - I)}{K} > \frac{mA}{K} > 0 .$$

He then disregards the fact that this demonstration holds only under the indicated assumption and rewrites (7) as

(9) $$I = m(B_0 + A) - nK ,$$

where both m and n are described as being positive, which equation is his desideratum.

In particular, by making use of the lags in this equation, Kalecki traces out "the mechanism of the trade cycle" in the following terms: Assume that for some reason there is an increase in the production of investment goods, A, which by (9) causes a further increase in investment orders, I. But after a time the resulting increase in capital stock K will, through the negative term nK, exert a depressing effect on I and eventually cause it to diminish. This starts off a downswing which is reversed only after investment orders have fallen below the level needed for replacement of depreciated capital, thus causing a decline in K, and hence (again through the term nK) an eventual upturn in I. I should emphasize that in his 1935 *Econometrica* article (in which the analysis is carried out by means of a differential equation) Kalecki (1935b, p. 335) no longer claims to "show" that n is positive, but instead presents it as "a necessary, though insufficient condition" for the existence of cyclical variations in investment.[13] Unfortunately,

13. Cf. also Kalecki (1936b, p. 359, n. 6).

Kalecki fails to repeat this fact—namely, that his analysis does not *prove* the existence of investment cycles, but instead *assumes* it by virtue of the crucial assumption of a positive *n*—in the 1966 translation of his essay.

In any event, from this cycle in the production of investment goods, Kalecki proceeds to the cycle in aggregate production. But he does not attempt to analyze the latter cycle in a rigorous fashion and instead suffices with the statement that, by equation (3), "gross real profits *P* are . . . an increasing function of the gross accumulation *A*"; and that these profits can also be "expressed as the product of the volume of the aggregate production [say, *Y*] and of profit per unit of output, [*P*/*Y*]," which ratio makes its first appearance at this point in Kalecki's analysis (1966, p. 13)—for up to this point Kalecki had carried out his analysis in terms of profitability as measured by the ratio of profits to capital stock, as in equation (4). In a footnote (corresponding to one in the original Polish essay [1933a, p. 115, n. 8], but which for some reason does not appear at the corresponding point of the *Econometrica* paper [1935b, p. 322]), Kalecki goes on to assume "that aggregate production and profit per unit of output rise or fall together, which is actually the case" (1966, p. 13, n. 4); hence an increase in investment and hence profits generates an increase in output as well. This enables Kalecki to reach the following conclusion, which is also the one reached in his 1935 *Econometrica* article (pp. 342–43):

> The relation between changes in the gross accumulation which is equal to the production of investment goods, and those of the aggregate production materialises in the following way. When production of investment goods rises the aggregate production increases directly *pro tanto*, but in addition there is an increase due to the demand for consumer goods on the part of the workers newly engaged in the investment good industries. The consequent increase in employment in the consumer-good industries leads to a further rise in the demand for consumer goods. The levels of aggregate production and of the profit per unit of output will ultimately rise to such an extent that the increment in real profits is equated to the increment of the production of investment goods.
>
> The account of the process is not yet complete because changes in capitalists' consumption have not been taken into consideration. This consumption *C* is dependent to a certain degree on the aggregate profits *P* and will increase together with the gross accumulation *A* since from the equation (2) and (3) it follows that $C = (B_0 + \lambda A)/(1 - \lambda)$. The increase in capitalists' consumption exerts the same influence as that in the production of investment goods: the production of consumer goods for capitalists expands; this leads to an increase in employment and this raises again the demand for consumer goods

for the workers which causes a further rise in production. *The aggregate production and the profit per unit of output will ultimately rise to such an extent as to assure an increment in real profits equal to that of production of investment goods and capitalists' consumption.* [1966, pp. 13–14, italics in original]

It is on these and similar passages that the claim for Kalecki as an independent, if not prior, discoverer of the General Theory has been based. In particular, the essence of the General Theory has been seen by most of Kalecki's advocates to lie in the proposition that it is the level of investment which determines the level of profits (and hence savings), and not the other way around.[14] Others have gone further and have contended that the italicized sentence at the end of the preceding passage contains the essential point of the General Theory as I have described it: namely, the equilibrating of investment and savings (which for Kalecki is determined by profits) by means of changes in output.[15]

To these claims I have several related reservations. First of all, as demonstrated in my opening lecture (above, pp. 27–28), the proposition that an increase in investment will increase output so as to generate a corresponding increase in savings (which for Kalecki are uniquely related to profits) is not one for which priority can be ascribed to Kalecki, but goes back in a general form at least to Keynes' 1929 *Can Lloyd George Do It?* and in a rigorous one to Kahn's 1931 multiplier article (of which Kalecki was apparently unaware, as witnessed by the absence of any reference to Kahn in Kalecki's pre–*General Theory* writings).[16]

Second, like Kahn, Kalecki seems to me in the preceding passage to be primarily concerned with demonstrating this proposition and not with analyzing the determination of the equilibrium level of output. Kahn's major purpose was, as we have seen, to use this proposition to refute the Treasury view; and Kalecki's was to use it to rigorize the teachings of Marxian economics about what it regarded as two basic and associated features of a capitalist economy: the relation between investment and profits, and the generation of investment cycles. In this connection, let me note that in the first equation in his 1933 essay,

$$P = C + A,$$

14. Cf., e.g., Joan Robinson (1966, pp. viii–ix).
15. This view has been advanced by Laski in his correspondence with me (cited with his permission); see the introductory footnote to this chapter.
16. For another similarity between the analyses of Kalecki and Kahn, see p. 75 below. There are also some differences: thus as noted on p. 28, n. 22 above, Kahn's analysis also took account of the financing of investment by means of increased imports and decreased government deficit, two sources that Kalecki ruled out by assumption (above, p. 65). This difference, however, is of no significance in the present context.

Kalecki uses the symbol A to represent both capitalists' savings and investment[17]—surely an indication (to say the least) that his concern was not with the mechanism by which changes in output equilibrate the independently made savings and investment decisions of a capitalist economy. And this conclusion is only reinforced if one attempts to justify Kalecki's procedure by saying that it reflects his Marxist assumption that capitalists as a class are at one and the same time the savers and investors of the economy.

Third, as can be seen from the foregoing summary of Kalecki's theory, its central message is in any event concerned with the analysis not of output, but of investment. As in my discussion of the Stockholm School (above, pp. 43, 52), let me emphasize that this does not mean that Kalecki was not interested in the level of output and employment. He obviously was. Indeed, in a part of his 1933 *Próba teorii koniunktury* which was not included in the 1966 translation, Kalecki discussed the "applications" of his theory and in this connection made a series of ad hoc assumptions which enabled him to conclude that

$$(10) \qquad Y = q(B_0 + A) + rK,$$

where Y represents output, and q and r are constants.[18] But the very fact that Kalecki did not include this discussion in the 1966 translation of what he designated as the "essential part" of his 1933 essay (above,

17. See the second and third paragraphs of the passage reproduced on p. 64 above. I am indebted to my colleague Yoram Mayshar for this observation.

18. *Próba teorii koniunktury* (1933a, pp. 142–55, esp. pp. 150–52). I am indebted to both Osiatyński and Laski for bringing this part of the essay to my attention, and to Barbara Kaminski for translating it. Kalecki's argument here is as follows, with the notation changed to accord with that used in the 1966 translation (above, p. 64). Start from the identity

$$(a) \qquad \frac{P}{K} = \frac{P}{Y} \cdot \frac{Y}{K},$$

where P/Y is the share of profits in national income and Y/K (states Kalecki) is an index of utilization of capital equipment. Kalecki then assumes that P/Y and Y/K rise and fall together. This implies that P/K and Y/K also rise and fall together. Making use of equation (3b) above, Kalecki then linearizes this relationship as

$$(b) \qquad \frac{Y}{K} = q \frac{B_0 + A}{K} + r,$$

which yields

$$(c) \qquad Y = q(B_0 + A) + rK,$$

as in the text.

Kalecki's resort here as elsewhere in his essay (cf. above, p. 65) to ad hoc assumptions based on casual empiricism brought upon him the criticisms of Kuznets (1939, pp. 805–6) and Lange (1939, p. 285) in their respective reviews of Kalecki's 1939 *Essays in the Theory of Economic Fluctuations,* which contains (in chap. 6) a revised version of his 1933 essay. In another paper which he wrote in 1933, entitled "On Foreign Trade and 'Domestic Exports,' " Kalecki determines output by the even more arbitrary assumption that the share of profits in national income is constant (1933b, p. 18).

p. 63) again shows that the central message of this essay was not the determination of output.

There are other indications that investment, and not output, is the subject of Kalecki's central message. Thus his original Polish booklet (1933a, p. 98) begins with a reference to Aftalion's *Les crises périodiques de surproduction* (1913), whose main thesis was that business cycles are caused by investment cycles generated by the process on which Kalecki elaborated. Again, the empirical estimates with which Kalecki supplements the theoretical analysis of his 1935 *Econometrica* paper (pp. 337–40) refer only to the time path of investment. The major concern of Kalecki's paper with investment behavior also manifests itself in the fact that the comment upon it by Frisch and Holme (1935) was devoted to the nature of the solution of the differential equation that Kalecki had developed to describe this behavior. Similarly, the critique of Kalecki's 1935 paper presented in Tinbergen's survey that year of "Quantitative Business Cycle Theory" concentrated on Kalecki's analysis of investment cycles as being generated by "the production lag and the appearance of K" in the investment function, the latter of which Tinbergen (1935, p. 269) found "questionable." Correspondingly, it was this analysis which concerned Kalecki in the reply (1936b) that he wrote to these two criticisms.

My final reservation is that the subject of the central message of Kalecki's 1933 booklet is in any event cycles and not a state of continued low-level employment. His main conclusions are summarized graphically in the form of sinusoidal curves, in which booms succeed depressions with smooth regularity (1933a, pp. 113, 152; 1966, p. 12). He does not attempt to explain the existence of "unemployment equilibrium"; correspondingly—and with this I return to my main point—there is little if any reference in Kalecki's 1933 essay on the business cycle to the mechanism by which changes in output equilibrate aggregate demand and supply (or, equivalently, savings and investment) at a less-than-full employment level. Nor, let me emphasize, does such a feedback mechanism play a role in the dynamic analysis on which Kalecki bases his theory of the cycle.

This last and crucial point can be demonstrated (and my second reservation thus reaffirmed) by a step-by-step examination of the way Kalecki derives his equation (9), which equation generates his investment cycle (above, p. 66). Though Kalecki does not seem to be aware of it, equation (3a) on p. 64 above is an equilibrium condition: one that determines that level of profits, P, which will enable capitalists to fulfill their plans for both consumption (hence savings) and investment, A. Correspondingly, the solution of (3a), namely

(3b) $$P = \frac{B_0 + A}{1 - \lambda},$$

is (in current terminology) a reduced-form equation which specifies the equilibrium level of P corresponding to any given level of A. (Note that like the corresponding reduced-form equation of the simple Keynesian model—and this is the reason for its aforementioned (p. 65) familiar look—equation (3b) involves a multiplier, which in this case is the reciprocal of 1 *minus* the marginal propensity to consume of capitalists.) Hence when Kalecki substitutes from (3b) into (5) in order to obtain (6) and ultimately (9), he is implicitly assuming that at every point of time in his investment cycle, planned savings and investment per unit of time have—in some unspecified manner—been equilibrated. And this assumption also characterizes Kalecki's analysis of the corresponding cycle in output (see n. 18 above).[19]

I must however add that Kalecki does in effect discuss the Keynesian equilibrating mechanism in a 1935 article published in a Polish semigovernmental weekly magazine devoted to economic commentary and reports, *Polska Gospodarcza* [Economic Poland].[20] This paper, which was translated many years later under the title "The Mechanism of the Business Upswing" (Kalecki 1966, pp. 2, 26–33), contains the

19. Only later did Kalecki (1943, p. 60) realize that his equation (3b) involves a multiplier.

This is a convenient point at which to explain my reservations (above, n. 3) about regarding Lange as an unequivocal supporter of Kalecki's claim to have anticipated the General Theory. Specifically, in contrast with his aforementioned 1939 encyclopedia article, Lange did not advance this claim in his well-known 1938 exposition of Keynes' system. Instead, he mentioned Kalecki's name in this exposition only in connection with his (Lange's) supplementary explanation of how this system is brought to its equilibrium position by a "process of adjustment." Here Lange observed that "if this process of adjustment involves a time lag of a certain kind a cyclical fluctuation, instead of equilibrium, is the result"—and supported this observation with a reference to Kalecki's 1937 article in the *Review of Economic Studies*, on which more below (Lange 1938, p. 175, n. 1).

Nor is there any reference to Kalecki as an anticipator of the General Theory in Lange's long 1941 review of Kalecki's 1939 book of *Essays in the Theory of Economic Fluctuations*. On the other hand, on p. 283 of this review, Lange refers to Kalecki's 1937 article—of which chap. 6 of the book is a revised version—as "a classic of contemporary business-cycle theory." Nor is there any such reference in my lecture notes from the graduate course "Business Cycle Theory" which Lange gave at the University of Chicago in the summer of 1945. After beginning this course with a discussion of Marx and Wicksell, Lange went on to present a detailed exposition of Keynes' theory, stressing that it is an "equilibrium theory." In subsequent lectures, Lange then presented Kalecki's theory as one of two ways (Kaldor's was the other) of dynamizing Keynes' system.

In brief, Lange too seems to have perceived Kalecki's work as providing a theory of cycles, and not of unemployment equilibrium. I might also note that Lange seems to have given at least as much emphasis to the Marxian connection of Kalecki's writings as to the Keynesian; see the references cited in n. 10 above.

20. The masthead of this magazine stated that it was published with the support of the Ministry of Industry and Trade as well as the Ministry of Finance and other government ministries. For this clarification of the nature of *Polska Gospodarcza* I am indebted to Alexander Erlich, who has likened this magazine to the business section of the *New York Times*.

following passage, so strikingly similar to certain passages (e.g., pp. 27, 261) in Keynes' *General Theory:*

A reduction of wages is being recommended as a way to overcome the depression. Now, one of the main features of the capitalist system is the fact that what is to the advantage of a single entrepreneur does not necessarily benefit all entrepreneurs as a class. If one entrepreneur reduces wages he is able *ceteris paribus* to expand production; but once all entrepreneurs do the same thing—the result will be entirely different.

Let us assume that wages have been in fact generally reduced, and likewise taxes as a counterpart of cuts in civil servants' salaries. Now the entrepreneurs owing to the "improved" price-wage relation utilize their equipment to capacity and in consequence unemployment vanishes. Has depression been thus overcome? By no means, as the goods produced have still to be sold. Now, production has risen considerably and as a result of an increase in the price-wage relation the part of production equivalent to profits (including depreciation) of the capitalists (entrepreneurs and rentiers) has grown even more. A precondition for an equilibrium at this new higher level is that this part of production which is not consumed by workers or by civil servants should be acquired by capitalists for their increased profits; in other words, the capitalists must spend immediately all their additional profits on consumption or investment. It is, however, most unlikely that this should in fact happen. Capitalists' consumption changes in general but little in the course of the business cycle. It is true that increased profitability stimulates investment but this stimulus will not work right away since the entrepreneurs will temporise until they are convinced that the higher profitability is going to last. Therefore the immediate effect of increased profits will be an accumulation of money reserves in the hands of entrepreneurs and in the banks. Then, however, the goods which are the equivalent of the increased profits will remain unsold. The accumulating stocks will sound the alarm for a new price reduction of goods which do not find any outlet. Thus the effect of the cost reduction will be cancelled. On balance only a price reduction will have occurred, offsetting the advantage of the cost reduction of the entrepreneurs since unemployment going hand in hand with underutilization of equipment will reappear. [Kalecki [1935c] 1966, pp. 26–27]

But as I have already noted, this theme of "unemployment equilibrium" receives little if any attention in Kalecki's professional writings during the pre–*General Theory* period. And, lest I be misunderstood, let me emphasize that my point here is not that this theme appears in Kalecki's nonprofessional writings, but that it appears *only* there. It is also significant that when in his review article of the *General Theory* (on which more in a moment) Kalecki put forth his claims for priority, he did so entirely on the basis of his 1933 *Próba* and made no mention whatsoever of this 1935 article.

Let me then turn to Kalecki's review article which, as already noted (above, p. 59), appeared in the 1936 *Ekonomista*.[21, 22] Kalecki begins this review by hailing the *General Theory* as a "turning point in the history of economics." At the same time, as the following passage shows, he presents his own claims to priority:[23]

[§4] . . . one could write:

$$Y = f(I) \text{;}$$

where *f* is an increasing function and its "shape" is determined by the size and structure of the capital stock, by the saving habits of capitalists, and by the "tastes" of capitalists and workers. The derivative of the function

$$\frac{dY}{dI} = f'(I)$$

is the so-called Keynesian multiplier. If investment changes from the given level *I* to the given level *I* + Δ*I*, in which Δ*I* is a small in-

---

21. I am greatly indebted to Pearl and Arcadius Kahan for providing me with an English translation of this review. After reading it, I realized that part of the review appeared subsequently in English (though without an indication of its source) as the section entitled "Short-Period Equilibrium" in Kalecki's "Theory of the Business Cycle" (1937, pp. 78–80), which was his first article in English after the publication of the *General Theory*. There are also some similarities to the review in other parts of this article. On the other hand, Kalecki does not repeat in it his claims to priority, and his reluctance as a newly arrived foreigner in the country of Keynes to do so is most understandable.

Feiwel (1975, p. 24) tells us that Kalecki first saw the *General Theory* while visiting Stockholm on his Rockefeller Foundation fellowship. This "Swedish connection" is evident from Kalecki's repeated use of the ex ante–ex post distinction in the course of his review, as well as from his references in it to "Wicksell's cumulative process." Whether or not as a result of his visit to England later in 1936, Kalecki also makes use in the review of marginal analysis, a type of analysis that (to the best of my knowledge) is absent from his earlier writings. (The marginal analysis of the review is included in that part reproduced in Kalecki [1937]; see preceding paragraph of this footnote). In any event, it would seem from the description of Kalecki's program under his Rockefeller Fellowship (see p. 93 of Appendix below) that he wrote the review only after he reached the London School of Economics in April 1936. This conjecture is borne out by Lipiński's (1977, p. 73) statement that Kalecki sent his review to *Ekonomista* "from London."

22. The issue of *Ekonomista* with Kalecki's review article of the *General Theory* carries another review of the book by a leading member of the older generation of Polish economists, Władysław Zawadzki, who during 1932–35 also served as Finance Minister. It would have been interesting to have compared this review with Kalecki's, a task that, because of the language problem, I have not undertaken. Cf., however, Lipiński (1977), p. 73. (Zawadzki was an exponent of general-equilibrium analysis; one of his books, discussing inter alia the work of Walras and Pareto, was published in French [1914], as was a subsequent one on the theory of production [1927].)

23. The first few lines of this passage (viz., those before sec. 5) are more or less the same as the corresponding lines of sec. 3 in Kalecki (1937, p. 80); see n. 21 above.

crease, then the income will change from the level Y to the level $Y +$ $\Delta I \cdot f'(I)$.

§5. Let us consider the contribution of Keynes' theory represented above (in a somewhat different manner than in the original version). We see, first of all, that investments are the factor which determine the short-run equilibrium, and therefore the level of employment and social income at a given moment. This level will determine how much labor power will be absorbed by the existing capital stock.[4] Therefore, the answer to the problem of high or low unemployment and output has to be sought in the analysis of factors which determine the size of investments, the second part of Keynes' theory, which we will review below, represents such an analysis.

In the meantime it is necessary to state that in accordance with the above conclusions it is not savings which determine investments, but on the contrary, investments which determine savings: The equilibrium between the demand for "capital" and the supply of "capital" always exists, because investments always "force" an equal volume of savings.[5] The interest rate cannot be determined by the demand for "capital" and its supply. According to Keynes' concepts other factors determine the level of interest, namely the supply of money and the demand for money (means of payments). If we have, for example, a given quantity of money in circulation and social income rises, the demand for money will increase and the interest rate will increase to such an extent that the same volume of money will be adequate despite the increase in transactions. This is in the most general terms Keynes' theory of the interest rate, which will not be treated in detail.

---

[4]The statement that investments determine the total size of output, I have proved in a manner similar to Keynes in *An Essay on the Theory of the Business Cycle* (Institute of Research on Business Cycles and Prices, Warsaw, 1933), pp. 114–16 [corresponding to pp. 13–14 of Kalecki 1966].

[5]A similar treatment of demand for and supply of capital is provided in *An Essay on the Theory of the Business Cycle* (1933) pp. 117–19 [corresponding to pp. 14–15 (line 12) of Kalecki 1966].

[Kalecki 1936a, pp. 268–69]

What I find noteworthy here is Kalecki's failure to indicate that what he calls the "Keynesian multiplier" was actually (as Keynes himself emphasized) "first introduced into economic theory by Mr. R. F. Kahn in his article on 'The Relation of Home Investment to Unemployment' (*Economic Journal*, June 1931)" (*GT*, p. 113); that Kahn (and after him Keynes) had not sufficed with a general description of the multiplier as $dY/di = f'(I)$, but had demonstrated that it had the form $dY/dI = 1/(1 - MPC)$, thus establishing a precise quantitative relationship between the level of investment and that of output; and that the main message of Kahn's article had been that an increase in investment would generate an equal increase in savings. And I do not think that it is mere chance that Kalecki's mention of these facts would have greatly weakened the implicit claims for priority which he presents in the two footnotes of the preceding passage. Similarly, Kalecki overstates his case when he claims (in the first of these footnotes) that he had proved "in a similar manner to Keynes" that "investments determine the total size of output"; for the passage of his 1933 *Essay* to which he refers (which is essentially the passage reproduced on pp. 67–68 above) does not bring out what is the major analytical contribution of the *General Theory*, namely, the equilibrating role of changes in output.

In general, one gets the impression that Kalecki attempts to play down the importance of Kahn's multiplier. Thus when in his 1937 article "A Theory of the Business Cycle," Kalecki reproduces (inter alia) sec. 4 of his *Ekonomista* review,[24] he adds to it a revealing statement: "income will change from the level Y to the level $Y + \Delta I \cdot f'(I)$. This is the only question the multiplier answers and no other service can be required from it" (1937a, p. 80; cf. with the corresponding passage at the end of sec. 4 of the review, cited on p. 73 above). Similarly, references to Kahn's 1931 article are conspicuously absent from the chapter "Investment and Income" in Kalecki's subsequent book *Essays in the Theory of Economic Fluctuations* (1939, chap. 2).[25] At the beginning of this chapter Kalecki declares that its objective is "to clear up basic questions arising out of the Keynesian theory of the Multiplier" (ibid., p. 42). At no point in this chapter does Kalecki even mention Kahn's name. Nor does he mention it in his 1943 reference to the multiplier noted above (n. 19). And what makes these omissions particularly significant is that Kahn too (1931, pp. 11–12, 17) had carried out his exposition on the assumption that all saving is done by capitalists and none by workers, whereas Keynes of the *General Theory* had not.[26]

24. See preceding footnote. This 1937 article was the subject of some correspondence with Keynes, reproduced in part on pp. 98–100 of the Appendix below.
25. For a letter from Keynes to Kalecki giving his reaction to this book, see pp. 101–2 below.
26. Cf. below, pp. 198–99. There are other indications in this 1939 chapter of an attempt to ignore Kahn's multiplier. Thus while Kalecki presents in it (1939, p. 53) the familiar-looking formula

$$\frac{\Delta Y}{\Delta I} = \frac{1}{1 - \alpha},$$

he derives it not from a consumption function with a marginal propensity to consume of α, but from one which reflects his initial assumption that the consumption of workers equals their income, which is a fixed proportion α of total income Y, while the consumption of capitalists and others is constant at c_0, so that the aggregate consumption function (which Kalecki does not explicitly present) is

Before leaving Kalecki's *Ekonomista* review, let me note that there is, as the following passage from it shows, another conclusion of the *General Theory* for which Kalecki implicitly claims priority:

> In spite of the shortcomings in argumentation, Keynes' statement that the level of nominal wages does not affect, at least directly, the formation of a short-run equilibrium, appears to be correct. In order to prove its probability it would be sufficient to assume that entrepreneurs in their investment activity, do not react *immediately* to the increased profitability resulting from a wage decrease. If they do not increase immediately investments, the short-run equilibrium would remain unchanged and prices will decline in the same ratio as wages. In view of this, the achieved improvement in profitability will appear to be illusory and the reason for an increase in investment will disappear—if after a wage decrease entrepreneurs do not increase immediately investments, they will not increase them subsequently. In such a manner, the change in nominal wages would remain a factor which would not disturb the short-run equilibrium.[6]

---

[6]I pointed out the independence of changes in output from shifts in nominal wages also in the *Essay on the Theory of the Business Cycle* (1933), pp. 145–47.

[Kalecki 1936a, p. 260, italics in the original]

The discussion referred to in this footnote 6 is actually more mechanical than the one in Kalecki's 1935 magazine article cited on p. 72 above; in particular, all that Kalecki essentially says on pp. 145–47 of his 1933 *Essay* is that the present level of investment (hence profits, output, and employment) is completely determined by past investment orders. Thus his criticism of Keynes' "shortcomings in argumentation" notwithstanding, Kalecki's analysis of the impact of a wage decline on the level of output is actually inferior to the detailed analysis of the effect of such a decline (via expectations, possible effect on the balance of trade, interactions with the liquidity-preference function and hence the

---

$$C = c_0 + \alpha Y.$$

Furthermore, when later in his analysis (1939, pp. 62–63) Kalecki drops the assumption of constant capitalists' consumption and instead assumes that their consumption depends positively on their income, $y = (1 - \alpha)Y$, thus attributing to capitalists the consumption function

$$e = \eta(y),$$

he merely concludes that in this case

$$\frac{\Delta Y}{\Delta I} = f'(I) > \frac{1}{1 - \alpha},$$

and does not provide the precise "Kahnian" conclusion that the multiplier is then

$$\frac{\Delta Y}{\Delta I} = \frac{1}{1 - \alpha - (1 - \alpha)\eta'}.$$

rate of interest) which Keynes provides in the chapter of the *General Theory* which he devotes to "Changes in Money Wages" (cf. pp. 12–13 above).[27]

Let me now summarize. In his primary concern with quantities as against prices;[28] in his concentration on national-income magnitudes and functional relations among them; and in his corresponding emphasis on analyzing the relationship between investment and other macroeconomic variables, Kalecki came significantly closer to the General Theory than did the Stockholm School, and this was particularly true of his semipopular 1935 paper "The Mechanism of the Business Upswing." At the same time, I cannot accept such claims as those of Klein that Kalecki's writings before 1936 "created a system that contains everything of importance in the Keynesian system" (1951, p. 447) and that Kalecki should be credited with "the complete anticipation of Keynes' General Theory" (Klein 1975, p. v). Nor can I accept Joan Robinson's contention (1964, p. 336) that Kalecki "found the same solution" as Keynes and that he should be credited with "the independent discovery of what is known as Keynes' theory" (J. Robinson 1977, p. 187). For one thing, Kalecki's theory lacks the integrated character of Keynes' *General Theory* (above, pp. 12–13). It fails to integrate value theory with monetary theory and is indeed devoid of the marginal analysis on which the former is based. And though Kalecki's theory adverts to the simultaneous developments in the money market, it does not present a systematic analysis of the latter and accordingly fails to present an integrated analysis of the commodity and money markets. But my main reason for not considering Kalecki's theory to be an independent development of the General Theory is the one I have already emphasized: namely, that Kalecki's central message has to do not with the forces that generate equilibrium at low levels of output, but with the forces that generate cycles of investment; more

27. We can obtain some insight into Kalecki's treatment of both Keynes' *General Theory* and Kahn's multiplier article from the following recollections of Edward Lipiński, Director of the Warsaw Research Institute on Business Cycles and Prices during the period (namely, the early 1930s) when, as a member of its staff, Kalecki was carrying out the work that has been discussed in this chapter:

> Many people can recall his [Kalecki's] embarrassment on the famous occasion when he was invited to give a course of 15 one-hour lectures at Cambridge: "But I'd have to prepare for it for years," he said. For Kalecki would only expound conclusions which he had arrived at himself. If he referred to the works of other people, it was only in order to rebut them, or more rarely, to indicate that they had a similar opinion to his own. [Lipiński 1977, p. 74]

28. A point duly noted by Tinbergen in his 1935 survey of business cycle theory (p. 270): "Prices . . . , remarkably enough, do not appear in his [Kalecki's] theory." In his "Comments" (1936b, pp. 356–57) on this, however, Kalecki argued that his rate of profits, P/K, actually depended on "the ratio of prices to wages," i.e., on the real wage rate.

specifically, not with the feedback mechanism that equilibrates planned saving and investment via declines in output, but with the cyclical behavior of investment on the implicit assumption that there always exists equality between planned savings and investment.[29]

This is not to deny (and to that extent I agree with Klein and Robinson) that Kalecki's theory enables us to make certain improvements on Keynes'. Thus if on the one hand Kalecki's theory of investment is not (like Keynes à la Fisher) based on the marginal analysis of discounted streams, it on the other hand introduces the stock of capital as a possibly relevant variable—a point which is of particular significance for econometric studies (Klein 1964, p. 190).[30] Again, Kalecki's theory indicates one of the ways of extending the Keynesian system so as to provide a theory of the business cycle. I shall return to these points in my concluding lecture.

Keynes once made a remark about "original works which a fresh scientific mind, not perverted by having read too much of the orthodox stuff, is able to produce from time to time in a half-formed subject like economics" (*Treatise* I, p. 209, n. 1), and I would unhesitatingly place Kalecki's work of 1933–35 in this category. I would, however, add that Kalecki also paid a price for his intellectual isolation—and perhaps part of this price was to come so close to the General Theory and yet not achieve it.

29. For reasons similar to these, I would also reject the claims sometimes advanced that Edward Theiss (1933, 1935) developed the General Theory.

30. I should, however, note that in his chapter on the business cycle, Keynes does take account of this variable and even cites it as one of the factors that generates cyclical variations in investment (*GT*, pp. 317–18; see also ibid., p. 31).

4

Anticipations of the General Theory? Conclusion: The Significance of the Central Message

In concluding that the General Theory cannot properly be considered an instance of multiple discovery, I am (as one can readily gather from the preceding lectures) in a distinct minority among those economists who have concerned themselves with this question. I could, of course, take refuge in one of the sayings of a great teacher of mine at this University, Frank Knight, who upon finding himself in such situations would simply say: "You can be with the majority, or you can be with the right." More seriously, I could point out that I am not completely alone in my views, and that insofar as they relate to the Stockholm School, they are in their broad lines supported by Bent Hansen (1981). But rather than engage in such verbal sparring, I find it more productive to try to analyze the reasons for this difference in conclusions.

In my opening lecture, I emphasized that one cannot meaningfully discuss the question of the multiple discovery of the General Theory unless one first specifies the major analytical innovation of this theory—and this has been the source of some of the differences between my conclusions and those of other writers. Thus some of these writers have not even provided such a specification, while those who have have frequently done so in ways which differ from mine. For example, Joan Robinson has based her claims for Kalecki on a definition of the General Theory which makes no mention of the equilibrating role of changes in output. Thus she writes:

> The main lines of that theory nowadays seem so obvious that it is hard to remember that they did indeed require a revolution in thought. They may be summarized in the propositions that the rate of saving is governed by the rate of investment, that the level of

I have benefited greatly from the penetrating and fruitful comments on earlier drafts of this chapter by Joseph Ben-David, Yehuda Elkana, and especially Robert K. Merton. To all of them I am also indebted for various references to the literature on the sociology of science cited below. Needless to say, responsibility for the views expressed remains solely mine.

79

prices is governed by the level of money wage rates, and that the
level of interest rates is governed by the supply and demand of
money. [Joan Robinson 1966, pp. viii–ix]

And though Lawrence Klein's statement that the General Theory "is
most important as a theory of the determination of the level of aggregate employment and output" (Klein 1951, p. 447) is closer to my
definition, he too fails to emphasize the equilibrating role of changes in
output. Indeed, he admits that Kalecki "did not go into the problem of
unemployment equilibrium and the contrast with classical theory"
(ibid., p. 448).

Different definitions of the General Theory also lie behind some of
the different conclusions about the Stockholm School. Thus Shackle
(1967, chap. 11; 1972, books III and IV; 1974, chap. 3) regards the
"ultimate meaning" of the General Theory to be its analysis of the way
expectations influence behavior in an uncertain world; so it is not surprising that he sees in Myrdal—the father of ex ante–ex post[1]—an
independent discoverer of the General Theory. Again, in the debate
between Landgren and Steiger on Ohlin's 1933 article, the innovation
of the General Theory would seem to have been defined by both of
them as the use of an analysis based on the relation between aggregate
demand and supply—even if the difference between these two magnitudes is assumed to exert its influence in the first instance on prices
(Steiger 1976, p. 344). Correspondingly, one of the major points at issue
between Landgren and Steiger is whether or not Ohlin had read
Keynes' 1933 Means to Prosperity before writing his own 1933
article—and after some detailed detective work, Steiger (1976, pp.
353–54; 1978a) convincingly demonstrates that he (Ohlin) had not. For
me, however, all this is irrelevant: for as I emphasized in my first
lecture (above, pp. 33–34), the Means to Prosperity deals primarily
with the effect of excess aggregate demand on prices; there is no reference in it to what I consider the essential novelty of the General
Theory—namely, the argument that an excess aggregate supply exerts
a direct depressing effect on the level of output, and that the decline in
output itself ultimately eliminates the excess supply and thus brings the
economy to a position of unemployment equilibrium (or, in the context
of business-cycle analysis, the argument that the decline in output
exerts a dampening feedback effect on the dynamic process).[2]

1. On Myrdal's priority with respect to this concept, see Ohlin (1981, p. 200).
2. I should, however, note that Landgren (1960a, p. 191) contends that in these 1933
writings an increase in price implies an increase in output. Even if this is true, it still
leaves these writings without an explicit discussion of the equilibrating role of changes in
output. I should also note that at some points in his book, Landgren (1960a, pp. 175, 183,
254) does distinguish in this context between the influence on prices and output; at the
same time, he seems to consider this distinction to be less crucial than I do (cf. ibid., pp.
178–79).

So in part the difference between my conclusions and those of other writers on this question stems from our differing definitions of the innovative feature and central message of the *General Theory*. The basis for my definition, as well as my reasons for rejecting the alternative ones, have been presented in my opening lecture and need not be repeated here (above, pp. 5–7; but see n. 8 below). I must admit that my definition has sometimes been criticized as too narrow. This may be true. At the same time I must emphasize that if we wish to use a less restrictive definition, we must do so symmetrically for all the claimants to independent discovery, including Keynes himself. In particular, on the basis of my definition, I concluded in my introductory lecture that Keynes discovered the General Theory sometime in 1933 and published it in full only in February 1936, when his book finally appeared. If one wishes to adopt a definition which is less restrictive than mine, then these dates too have to be pushed back. Thus, if it is enough to speak in general terms about aggregate demand and supply, then, as indicated above (pp. 5–7, 41–43), Keynes' 1933 *Means to Prosperity*, Wicksell's 1906 *Lectures*, and perhaps even Malthus' writings almost a century before that constitute the General Theory. Alternatively, if the General Theory can be identified even with an imprecise description of the way a decrease in output decreases saving until it is brought to equality with investment, then Keynes' discovery of it should be dated with his 1931 Harris lecture (above, pp. 23–26). And if the General Theory is the proposition that an increase in investment generates an equal amount of saving, then (as I emphasized in my introductory lecture [above, pp. 27–29]) this theory was first presented in an imprecise form by Keynes in his 1929 *Can Lloyd George Do It?* and was then rigorously developed by Richard Kahn in his celebrated 1931 multiplier article.[3] Indeed, if this is the definition of the General Theory, then there is no point in our whole discussion: for since Kahn's article appeared in the leading scientific journal of the time, the "independent discovery" of this proposition in subsequent years by Ohlin and Kalecki (above, pp. 53–54, 68) can only be regarded as displays of "unnecessary originality" which should be of secondary interest to historians of science.

Differences in definition do not, however, provide a complete explanation of the difference between my conclusions and those of other scholars. Thus I have already noted that, though not exactly the same, Klein's definition of the General Theory is close to mine. Even more to the point is the case of Steiger, who in the context of his more recent contribution to this discussion (1978b, pp. 428–29, 441) has explicitly

---

3. Or, if one prefers to say so, by the earlier Danish writer Julius Wulff; see chap. 1, n. 21 above.

accepted my definition of the innovative feature of the General Theory but has nevertheless rejected my conclusion about Myrdal and Ohlin, claiming that both these writers should be credited with having "anticipated the analytical novelty of the *General Theory*." To explain these differences, I must now take account of the two distinctions emphasized in my introductory lecture: the distinction between the logical and the chronological, and the distinction between the central message a writer wishes to convey and the incidental noise which frequently accompanies it.

Thus it seems to me that the differing conclusions that Klein and I have reached with respect to Kalecki stem in part from our different views about the relation between the logical and the chronological. In particular, Klein's contention that Kalecki "completely anticipated" the *General Theory* is based on his (Klein's) claim to be able to construct from Kalecki's writings a system of equations that is mathematically equivalent to that of the *General Theory*.[4] But even if for the sake of argument[5] this claim is accepted, it does not to my mind mean that Kalecki himself so perceived his system at the time. On the other hand, if we should contend that such a mathematical equivalence justifies the claim that Kalecki independently discovered the General Theory, then (as indicated on p. 30 above) the same claim can be made for Richard Kahn's earlier multiplier article.

But the most significant source of my differences with other scholars is the basic view I have repeatedly propounded in these lectures that a scientist can properly be said to have made a discovery only if it is part of his central message. How is this central message to be identified? Sometimes the author does so explicitly (Keynes in the preface and introduction to the *General Theory* and in correspondence, Ohlin in the conclusion to his 1933 article, Kahn in correspondence). In general, however, the literature that we have been examining does not provide a precise and unambiguous statement of its central message: of the major problem to which it addresses itself and the conclusions it reaches. And in the absence of such a statement I suggest identifying the central message in much the same way that we identify the theme of a movement in a classical symphony: by its being announced early in the movement and by repetition afterward—either exactly or by different combinations of instruments or in different tonal areas. So is the cen-

---

4. See Klein (1964, pp. 188–91, esp. p. 189). Without burdening him with any responsibility for this interpretation of his view, I would like to thank Klein for helpful discussions of this point.

5. Thus it is not clear to me that Klein's formulation of Kalecki's model contains the equivalent of the stable dynamic adjustment equation $dY/dt = \Phi[F(Y) - Y]$, which is what I have defined as the crucial feature of the General Theory (above, p. 10). But this is to raise again the question of the proper definition of this theory.

tral message of a scientific work announced by its presentation early in the work (and frequently in its title) and by repetition, either verbatim or modified in accordance with the circumstances. Let me also emphasize that this announcement must be read in both its "internal" and "external" context (above, pp. 4–5): that is, the context of the state of the literature at the time (including the earlier contributions of the writer in question) and (especially in the social sciences) the context of the events in the real world then impinging on the writer.

Thus, in the context of the policy debates then taking place about the efficacy of public works, as well as Keynes' treatment of this question in his *Can Lloyd George Do It?*, Kahn announces at the beginning of his 1931 article that he will develop a precise formula for the multiplier effect of such works and will show that (contrary to the Treasury view) such works will themselves generate the necessary savings; Lindahl entitles his work "The Rate of Interest and the Price Level"; Myrdal announces that his 1932–33 study is an "immanent criticism" of Wicksell's earlier work, which itself was concerned with the relation between interest and prices in an economy with full employment; Ohlin entitles the successive sections of his 1933 article "The Stability of the Price System," "The Morphology of the Price System," and "An Analysis of Some Price Movements"; Kalecki entitles his 1933 work *An Essay on the Theory of the Business Cycle;* and Keynes entitles his work *The General Theory of Employment Interest and Money* (in brief, everything but prices, which are "subsidiary" to his theory),[6] presents in the introduction to his work a "brief summary of the theory of employment to be worked out in the course of the following chapters" (*GT*, p. 72), and relegates his chapter (22) of "Notes on the Trade Cycle" (a subject not even mentioned in the introduction) to the final part of the book, which as already indicated (above, pp. 13–14) is essentially an appendage to it.

And then there are repetitions. Indeed, the variety of relevant contexts for repeating the respective central messages of the works discussed in these lectures is in some sense greater than that of a symphonic theme: for it includes repetitions not only in the work itself (prices in Ohlin's 1933 article, cycles in Kalecki's *Próba*, unemployment equilibrium in Keynes' *General Theory*), but in other works as well, some of them possibly by other writers. Thus I have in the pre-

6. *General Theory*, p. 32; cf. p. 13 above.
QUESTION: Is one accordingly justified in inferring that my *Money, Interest, and Prices* deals with everything but employment? ANSWER: For obvious reasons, the word "employment" was not included in its title; but that this is part of the central message of the book is made clear in its introduction, which announces that the theory of employment is a "second major theme."

ceding chapters[7] identified the central message of a theoretical work by, *inter alia*, testing for its repetition by the writer in his related work of roughly the same period (Myrdal, Ohlin), in the related empirical studies that he may have carried out (Kalecki), in the part of his work that he chose for translation (Lindahl, Kalecki), and in the part of his work that he chose for presentation in scientific journals and at scientific meetings (Kalecki). And I have also tested for the repetition of the central message in contemporary comments on (Tinbergen and Frisch-and-Holme on Kalecki) or reviews of (Palander of Myrdal) the work in question, and in the writings of contemporaries who were exposed to the work (the messages of Myrdal and Ohlin as reflected in the writings of other Swedish economists in the *Ekonomisk Tidskrift*).

On the basis of these criteria[8] I have in these lectures concluded that

7. And in my 1972 paper reproduced in chap. 6 below (see esp. pp. 166, 169–70, 172, 174–80), in which, however, I had not yet explicitly formulated the notion of a central message. See also the Postscript to chap. 5 below.

8. QUESTION (forcefully put to me by Robert Merton): If these criteria are so precise, why are there different interpretations of the central message of the *General Theory* itself? ANSWER: The criteria are admittedly not that precise, so that (as indicated on p. 17 above) a subjective element is unavoidable. At the same time one should not exaggerate the extent of disagreement about the central message of the *General Theory:* for the prevalent interpretation of this message today, as for the past forty years, is in terms of the theory of effective demand depicted in figure 1 above, of which the interpretation presented in these lectures is only a refinement (above, p. 10). (It is worth noting that Klein's early and well-known study of *The Keynesian Revolution* [1947] also identifies this revolution with the theory of effective demand [ibid., chaps. 2–3, esp. p. 56]. Note too that the standard *IS–LM* interpretation of the *General Theory* which Hicks first presented in 1937 incorporates the theory of effective demand in its *IS* curve. In this connection, see p. 156, n. 45 below for a refutation of some recent attempts to question the validity of this interpretation.)

I also find it significant that the different interpretations of the *General Theory* now being advanced have largely emerged in recent years, after the passage of time has dimmed the memories of the historical context of protracted mass unemployment and deflation in which this book was written, and has also made it easier to accord less attention to its actual text. Correspondingly, it seems to me that those who have advanced these interpretations are really concerned not with the central message of the *General Theory*, but with the attempt to find in this classic work support for their own central messages. For documentation of this statement with respect to Shackle's interpretation (which has also been espoused by Davidson [1974]), see *KMT*, pp. 141–42, Kregel (1976). Hutchison (1978, chap. 7), and (from a different viewpoint) Stohs (1980); see also Samuelson (1946, p. 320) and above, p. 6. For similar documentation with respect to the "Post Keynesian" interpretation of Weintraub, Davidson, and others— making use inter alia of some of the criteria specified here for identifying the central message of a work—see chap. 5 below, and especially its Postscript.

In this connection I must say a few words about Axel Leijonhufvud's influential *On Keynesian Economics and the Economics of Keynes* (1968). This work was originally hailed as a new interpretation of the *General Theory*, and as such was criticized on textual grounds by, for example, Grossman (1972) and Jackman (1974). More recently, Leijonhufvud himself has admitted that his book was about "theoretical problems that were current problems in the early or mid-sixties. . . . What Keynes might have meant etc., was not one of the problems. Doctrine history was not what the book was about" (from pp. i–ii of Leijonhufvud's English foreword to the 1978 Japanese edition of his book).

the respective central messages of the Stockholm School and of Kalecki were not that of the General Theory: that, in brief, the former message was concerned with prices and not output, and that the latter was concerned with investment cycles and not unemployment equilibrium. My point now, however, is not with this conclusion per se, but with the fact that my very emphasis on the central message of a writer is an additional reason for the differences of opinion that have been noted in these lectures. Thus it is significant that in supporting her claim for Kalecki, Joan Robinson (1964, p. 336, bottom) singles out for mention his remarkable 1935 magazine article, "The Mechanism of the Upswing" (above, pp. 71–72), which—because of Kalecki's failure to include its analysis in his scientific writings as well—I have not considered to be part of his central message to the profession (just as I would not so consider a theory which an economist would present in, say, a *Newsweek* column and which did not have a counterpart in his scientific writings). Similarly, I have contended (for the reasons given on pp. 51–52, 55–56 above) that the passages Steiger cites from Myrdal's and Ohlin's writings as presenting the equilibrating role of changes in output were not part of their respective central messages. Indeed, I feel that there may not be much disagreement between Steiger and myself on this point: for that is how I interpret his admission that he "does not mean that he [Ohlin] was able to present this insight in such a precise and elaborated way as Keynes in the *General Theory*" (Steiger 1978b, p. 441).

But, you may ask, why this insistence that a discovery be part of a writer's "central message"? If we are concerned with the question of multiple discovery, is it not enough that a scientist has made a discovery, no matter how incidental it may be to his main work?

To this question I have two answers, and both have to do with the role of science as an institution for the discovery of knowledge. First, I began these lectures with a reference to Merton's analysis (1957) of the importance of recognition of originality (as evidenced by chronological priority) in the reward system of science. Now, in Whitehead's oft-quoted words[9] (1917, p. 127), "To come very near to a true theory and to grasp its precise application, are two very different things, as the history of science teaches us. Everything of importance has been said before by somebody who did not discover it." And if the reward system of science is to function in a productive manner, its rewards must go to the true discoverers.

My second and related answer stems from the view inherent in the sociology of science that "science is public, not private" (Merton

9. See Merton (1968b), p. 1.

1968a, p. 450; see also Merton 1938, p. 219). Science is a cooperative venture of many researchers, and the function of a scientific discovery is not simply to enable an individual scientist to add to his private stock of knowledge, but to stimulate (in Lakatos' [1970, pp. 132ff.; 1978] terms) a new research program on the part of colleagues in his field of inquiry, for only in that way can the full scientific potential of the discovery be efficiently exploited. But the probability that one scientist will stimulate others to devote themselves to a new research program along the lines that he is working is directly related to the extent that he himself is aware of the significance of his work. He is less likely to be able to "sell his product" to his colleagues—or at least (to shift to a normative plane of discourse) he would be unjustified in claiming credit for having sold it to them—if he himself is not convinced of its significance. And this means that his "product" must be part of his central message.

To avoid any possible misunderstanding, let me emphasize that the distinction I am making is not that between chance and intended scientific findings. In particular, I would denote as a discovery even a chance finding, provided its significance was recognized by the researcher in question (e.g., Alexander Fleming and the discovery of penicillin).[10] Nor am I adopting a "productivity-ethics" viewpoint and saying that the "marketplace of science" gives each his due: that if it has not accorded priority to some individual, that alone is evidence that he did not deserve it. I have no doubt that the rewards of science have not always been justly allocated. But I would not cite as examples of such injustices cases in which, after one individual has emphasized and received credit for a scientific discovery, "anticipations" of it are found in passages of earlier works by other individuals who at the time did not consider these passages sufficiently important to incorporate into their central message in order to bring them to the attention of the profession.[11]

Conversely, I would cite as instructive examples of justice being done those "premature discoverers" who despite their emphasis on their respective central messages were at first ignored "because the time was not yet ripe,"[12] but who—when the time did "ripen"—were rewarded with recognition for their priority, and sometimes even with

10. Cf. in this context the interesting study by Barber and Fox of "The Case of the Floppy-Eared Rabbits: An Instance of Serendipity Gained and Serendipity Lost" (1958). Cf. also Barber (1952, pp. 267–71).
11. For a similar view, see Merton's (1968b, pp. 21ff.) discussion of "adumbrations."
12. This expression by itself is of course a tautology. In certain cases, however, it has been endowed with meaning by an analysis of the reasons that may have led to a work's being originally ignored; cf., e.g., Barber (1961), Polanyi (1967), Stent (1972), and the paper by Sandler and Sandler referred to in n. 14 below.

eponymic fame.[13] The classic example is that of Mendel, whose 1865 work on heredity was rediscovered at the end of the century and gave rise to "Mendelism."[14] And in our own discipline we have the well-known examples of Slutsky's (1915) theory of consumer behavior with its "Slutsky equation," rediscovered by Hicks and Allen (1934) as well as by Henry Schultz (1935, pp. 439–40, 443);[15] and of Ramsey's (1928) theory of optimal savings with its "Ramsey solution," in whose rediscovery after World War II Samuelson played a leading role.[16] These examples also suggest that the "premature discoverer" will be rewarded with eponymy too only if his work is rediscovered not too long after the "ripening" of interest in the question—before the name for the (re)discovery has been preempted![17]

To return now to the specific question which concerns us, there can be no doubt that Keynes—with his worldwide reputation, and situated at what was then *the* center of learning in economics—was in an ideal position to communicate his message to the profession as a whole. This fact has been emphasized by, for example, those who have attempted to explain Kalecki's failure to achieve recognition for the discovery of the General Theory by saying that in the early and mid-1930s he was an obscure Polish economist writing in his own language (Feiwel 1975, pp. 23–24, 29). But this cannot be the only reason. For as I have already noted (pp. 63, 70), at the 1933 meetings of the Econometric Society in Leiden, Kalecki had the opportunity of presenting to the profession a paper on what he presumably regarded as the essential points of his 1933 Polish essay, and this paper even drew the attention of two of the then-leading macroeconomists of the world, Jan Tinbergen and Ragnar Frisch. But both of these experts perceived the central message of Kalecki's paper to be (as he himself perceived it) not a theory of unemployment equilibrium, but a theory of the investment cycle. That was the theme that ran through their heads when they left the hall.

---

13. Eponymy: "The practice of affixing the name of the scientist to all or part of what he has found" (Merton 1957, pp. 298–300; see also ibid. for many examples of this practice).

14. Cf. Barber (1961, pp. 544, 547–48, 551). Cf. also the forthcoming paper by Iris and Laurence Sandler on Mendel's discovery and rediscovery.

15. Hicks and Allen became aware of Slutsky's prior discovery only after the publication of their own article; see Allen (1936, p. 120) and Hicks (1939, pp. 19, 309). In a later work, Schultz (1938, p. 38, n. 2) cites Valentino Dominedo (1933) as another rediscoverer of Slutsky.

16. See the references cited in Samuelson (1965, p. 93, n. 1 and p. 94, nn. 3, 4). See also Samuelson and Solow (1956), pp. 261ff. (I am indebted to my colleague Eytan Sheshinski for helpful discussions of this point.)

17. This point has resulted from stimulating discussions with Laurence Sandler, to whom I am indebted. That this condition is not a sufficient one would seem to be suggested by Stephen Stigler's provocative note on eponymy (1980), though there is a need to examine the cases he cites from the view of their respective central messages.

Keynes' advantageous position for making his message heard is even less convincing an explanation of his success vis-à-vis the Stockholm School. After all, Ohlin in 1929 had no difficulty in gaining a worldwide hearing for his difference of opinion with Keynes on the transfer problem. Even more relevant to our present discussion is the significant and rapid impact of the central message of Ohlin's *Interregional and International Trade* (1933) (namely, factor proportions as the explanation of comparative advantage and hence the pattern of trade) on the profession as a whole. I do not underestimate the importance of the fact that these writings appeared in English under prestigious auspices: Ohlin's debate with Keynes in the pages of the *Economic Journal* and his book as a volume in the Harvard Economic Studies.[18] Nevertheless, I contend that if the early-1930s writings of Myrdal and Ohlin in the *Ekonomisk Tidskrift* and in the *Reports* for the government Committee on Unemployment did not have the impact of Keynes' *General Theory*, it was not only because they were written in Swedish and hence not readily accessible to the profession as a whole, but also because their central message was substantively different from that of the *General Theory*. Correspondingly, as noted above (pp. 52, 54), the passages in Myrdal's and Ohlin's writings which have been cited by Steiger and others as constituting independent discovery of the General Theory failed to have an impact not only on the English-speaking part of the profession, but also on the Swedish-speaking, as witnessed by the fact that they did not stimulate further discussion even by Swedish economists in subsequent issues of the *Ekonomisk Tidskrift*.

This has been my main point: The phenomenon for which a desperate world in the early 1930s was searching for an explanation was that of the bewildering and seemingly endless depression that was creating untold misery and threatening its political stability. This was the problem to whose solution Keynes—in contrast with the Stockholm School and Kalecki—devoted his central message: namely, that the state of unemployment equilibrium could be explained by his theory of effective demand, according to which the decline in output itself generates feedback effects which ultimately eliminate the excess of aggregate supply over aggregate demand. I might also note that the fact that this theoretical revolution occurred simultaneously with the revolution in national-income statistics which made possible the quantification of

18. Actually, Ohlin had published his theory of factor proportions a decade before in his doctoral thesis (1924) in Swedish. But language was not the only reason it did not then reach the English-speaking world: for, as indicated above (chap. 2, n. 5), Ohlin has recently recounted how in 1922 he submitted a paper to the *Economic Journal* containing the essence of this theory, only to have it rejected by Keynes who declared that it "amounts to nothing"! (Ohlin 1977, p. 161; cf. also Steiger 1981, pp. 181–82).

Keynes' analytical categories further increased the impact of Keynes' *General Theory* on the profession.[19]

Let me conclude with several observations. First, even if the writings of the Stockholm School and of Kalecki do not constitute the General Theory, they do have (as already noted) points in common, and this is particularly so in the case of Kalecki. Correspondingly, these writings provided important supplements to Keynes' exposition of the theory. In particular, the ex ante–ex post analysis of the Stockholm School was rapidly exploited by the profession to provide an explanation (missing in Keynes' *General Theory*) of the short-run dynamic forces which brought the economy to the equilibrium level of output. In particular, these forces were presented as being generated by the difference between ex ante and ex post (i.e., unplanned) inventory accumulation which causes producers to decrease (increase) their level of output whenever it is above (below) the equilibrium level.[20] Similarly, Kalecki's analysis of the influence of the existing capital stock on investment was rapidly incorporated into the discussions of the investment function, and particularly into the econometric models of the economy which took Keynes' *General Theory* as their point of departure.

My second observation is that the conclusions of this study are not those I expected when I began it: for my expectations then (for the reasons set out in my opening remarks [above, pp. 4–5]) were that I would find that the discovery of the General Theory was indeed, as many have contended, an instance of multiple discovery. Thus, for reasons it is difficult for us today to comprehend—so thoroughly ingrained are we with the conceptual framework of the General Theory—the conceptual framework of the early 1930s had inherent in it certain habits of thought which made the process of achieving the new view of the world expounded by this theory a long and arduous one. What the exact nature of these mental obstacles was I do not fully understand (see, however, pp. 14–15 above). But that

---

19. See chap. 9 below. The implied contrast here is not with Kalecki (whose background in national-income statistics [above, p. 63] led him to use roughly the same analytical categories as Keynes) but with the Stockholm School. Specifically, I feel that the Stockholm School did not succeed in stimulating a fruitful research program even within its own conceptual framework (viz., ex ante–ex post analysis), and that this was largely because there did not at the time exist a commonly accepted method of quantifying its basic analytical concept—the ex ante value of a variable. This situation remained more or less unchanged until Cagan, in his well-known empirical study of hyperinflation (1956), developed and applied the method of adaptive expectations, which method then became a standard fixture of econometric work, though one challenged in recent years by the rational-expectations approach.

20. That Keynes himself did not attach too much importance to this dynamic factor is clear from p. 76 of the *General Theory*.

they did exist is for me indicated by the slowness with which the Cambridge economists themselves progressed from Kahn's 1931 multiplier article to the 1933 discovery of the General Theory (above, pp. 29–30).[21]

Let me also observe that nothing I have said in these lectures should be construed as belittlement of the individuals whose works have been discussed. To take some liberties with Merton's statement (1961, p. 366) that "great scientists will have been repeatedly involved in multiples," let me suggest that it is also the great scientists who are more likely to be involved in alleged or near multiples. Thus that both Myrdal and Ohlin received the Nobel Prize in economics—the former for his work "relating economic analysis to social, demographic and institutional conditions," the latter for his contribution to international-trade theory[22]—is sufficient evidence of their scientific stature. And Kalecki achieved a similar stature not only for his theoretical and empirical work on the investment cycle, but also for his development of the principle of increasing risk and for his work on planning and socialist economics. So my question in these lectures has been whether in addition to these important contributions to our discipline, the foregoing economists can also be credited with the independent discovery of the General Theory.

Nor do I criticize these economists for having claimed to have made such a discovery: for, like many of those who subsequently supported their claims, they too were probably defining the General Theory in a way which differs from mine. They may also have been succumbing to the all-too-human weakness of retroactively giving greater emphasis to points which were not originally part of their central message. After all, who among us has not on occasion felt that the profession has wrongly credited others with what we—with at most "a slight difference of emphasis"—had done before?

Similarly, to the extent that it is meaningful to speculate about such matters, I would not object unduly to the contention that in the course of time these economists would have independently discovered the General Theory—and, again, this is particularly so for Kalecki. But members of our profession more than anyone else should be aware that time has value. It is a commonplace that an essential part of the in-

21. For a general discussion of such mental obstacles in scientific research, see Barber (1961). See also Kuhn's (1962, chap. 7) description of the slowness with which shifts have taken place from one "paradigm" to another. See also Fleck (1935) for a detailed study of the influence of such "thought styles" in a case of medical research. On the other hand, see Polanyi (1967) for a rationalization of the initial resistance of science to completely new ideas.

22. See the respective Nobel Prize citation in the *Scandinavian Journal of Economics* 76 (December 1974), p. 469, and 80 (No. 1, 1978), pp. 62–63.

tangible capital of any society is its stock of scientific knowledge; so it is a matter of significance if an increment to this capital (and to its subsequent yield of fruits) takes place at a time t or $t + \theta$, with the degree of significance increasing with θ. In the long run everything would have been independently discovered by someone else; but students of Keynes need not be reminded that in the long run we are all dead.

Let me also make the obvious comment that if in these lectures I have been able to point out weaknesses in the work of the aforementioned economists, it is only—to paraphrase Newton's famous saying[23]—because I have been able to stand on their shoulders as well as on the shoulders of the generation which succeeded them. What I have learned to appreciate more than anything else as a result of this study is how difficult it is to develop theories which (to quote another of my great teachers at this University, Jacob Viner) are both new and correct. And I can only admire those who succeeded in discovering such theories, as well as those who even came close to doing so.

My final observation—which perhaps should have been my first—is that my conclusion that there was no multiple discovery of the General Theory has been based on a precise (some would say overprecise) definition of the innovative feature of this theory accompanied by a detailed examination of texts which was in turn guided by an emphasis on their respective central messages. The natural question which then arises is whether the other alleged cases of multiple discovery in economics which I listed at the beginning of these lectures (above, p. 4) would stand up under a similar examination, and the immediate answer is that at least some of them would not. Thus, as we all know, Chamberlin (1937, 1951) persistently and quite rightly emphasized that his theory of monopolistic competition differed from Joan Robinson's theory of imperfect competition. Similarly, William Jaffé (1976) recently examined the respective expositions of the marginal-utility theory by Jevons, Menger, and Walras and showed that they "were markedly different and influenced the future course of theoretical model building in fundamentally different ways" (ibid., p. 512). And many years ago I myself showed (1956 and 1965, suppl. notes C:2 and E:1) that there are significant differences between the respective cash-balance approaches of Walras, Wicksell, and the Cambridge School.

Nor should we think that this "dehomogenization" of multiple discoveries upon closer scrutiny is unique to economics or, more generally, to the social sciences. Thus in a detailed study of various allegedly simultaneous technological discoveries, Jacob Schmookler (1966,

---

23. See Merton (1957, p. 303); for the medieval and even classical origins of this saying, see Merton (1965).

chap. 10) showed that there were in fact important differences between them. Similarly, my colleague Yehuda Elkana (1970) demonstrated that the law of conservation of energy—long cited as a standard case of multiple discovery—was strictly speaking not one: "that in the span 1840–1860 different problems were bothering different groups of people in different places, and they came up with different answers. The answers turned out to be related, until finally in the 1860s they proved to be more than related, they turned out to be logically derivable from one another" (ibid., p. 32). And in a comparison of the non-Euclidean geometries invented by Bolyai and Lobachevsky, Petronievics has contended that "Lobachevsky had developed five of the nine salient components of their overlapping conceptions more systematically, more fruitfully, and in more detail."[24]

So let me end with the general conjecture (which I hope will be tested by further case studies) that scientific research is less redundant—and, as a corollary, that the individual scientist is more important—than the by-now familiar long lists of multiple discoveries might lead us to believe (cf. above, p. 4); that upon closer scrutiny there frequently turn out to be significant differences between so-called multiple discoveries; and that even when there are points of similarity, there are significant differences in the extent to which these points were incorporated into the respective central messages of the researchers in question—and hence significant differences in the extent to which they influenced or might have influenced the path of scientific development.

24. Quoted from Merton's (1968b, p. 10) summary of Petronievics' study. Merton (ibid., n. 18) also states that in an earlier study Petronievics reached a similar conclusion with respect to the famous case of the discovery of the theory of evolution by both Charles Darwin and Alfred Russel Wallace. Merton refers to these studies in the course of his remarks on the difficulty of establishing "the degree of similarity between independently developed ideas," particularly in the social sciences with their "typically less precise formulations" (ibid., pp. 9–10).

Appendix

Kalecki and Cambridge: Visits and Correspondence

1. Kalecki's Rockefeller Fellowship

The archives of the Rockefeller Foundation contain the following description (dated February 28, 1936) of Kalecki's fellowship program:[1]

> Business cycle theory, particularly from standpoint of Wicksell's money [*sic*] theory. Will visit a number of Business Cycle Institutes in various European countries but will carry out the main part of his program in the *Scandinavian countries* (*with Prof. G. Myrdal* in *Stockholm* and *Prof. R. Frisch* in *Oslo*) and in England (*Cambridge*) under direction of *Prof. J. M. Keynes* [emphasis in original].

According to the archives, however, most of Kalecki's time in England (which he reached in mid-April 1936, after having spent two-and-a-half months in Sweden, where he met with Myrdal, Ohlin, and Lindahl) was spent at the London School of Economics. Here he "studied the theory of Keynes, taking part in seminars . . . led by Professors Hayek and Robbins. Also contact with Mr. Lerner." After a visit during the summer to Paris and Geneva (where he "had discussions about Keynesian theory and problems of business cycle with Dr. Haberler"), Kalecki returned in September 1936 to London. At this time he "took part in meeting of Econometric Society in Oxford, especially in discussion about Keynesian theory. Also discussed with Mrs Robinson in Cambridge the application of this theory to the long run equilibrium problems and the business cycle." (This was presumably the visit to which Joan Robinson was referring in her October 1936 note to Keynes; see p. 60 above.) Through November 1936, Kalecki continued to take part in seminars at the London School of Economics.

---

1. Cf. p. 59 above. I am indebted to Ralph K. Davidson, deputy director for social sciences, the Rockefeller Foundation, for making this archival material available to me and permitting its publication.

2. Letter of Joan Robinson to Kalecki

In an editorial comment on Kalecki's paper "A Theory of the Business Cycle" in the revised form in which it appears as chapter 6 of his *Essays in the Theory of Economic Fluctuations* (1939),[2] Osiatyński publishes a Polish translation of a letter Joan Robinson wrote to Kalecki in reaction to a draft of this chapter which he had apparently sent her for comments.[3] This letter is reproduced here in its original English form,[4] with the kind permission of Joan Robinson and Osiatyński. Needless to say, Professor Robinson does not agree with my interpretation of it (above, chap. 3, n. 7). I have added some explanations in square brackets and in notes.

Cambridge
September 16 [1937][5]

Dear Mr. Kalecki,
    I have had a glance at your paper,[6] & I will take it away with me & go through it carefully. Meanwhile I cannot delay to tell you what a pleasure it is to me to be arguing with someone who is making an advance upon Keynes instead of endlessly disputing with people who have not understood the elementary points. I am now working on a book[7] in which "Disguised Unemployment" [1936b] will reappear, with a number of essays making applications of the General Theory to various problems (including, international trade). I think you are one of the ten people in Europe who will understand what I am trying to do.
    Your Econometrica article [1935b] makes me ashamed. We ought to have welcomed you long ago as a kindred spirit. Unfortunately mathematics is an insuperable [?] obstacle for me, & I never turned

2. The opening footnote of this chapter (ibid., p. 116, n. 1) describes its genealogy in the following terms:

> This essay is an altered version of the article published in *Review of Economic Studies*, February 1937. The essential ideas in it were developed already in my "Essai d'une Théorie du Mouvement Cyclique des Affaires," *Revue d'Economie Politique*, March–April 1935, and in mathematical form in "A Macrodynamic Theory of the Business Cycle," *Econometrica*, July 1935.

3. This is the way I understand Osiatyński's comments in Kalecki, *Dzieła* [Works], vol. I, pp. 511, 515–16. The draft has apparently not survived. In this context it is worth noting that in the foreword (dated June 1938) to his 1939 book, Kalecki states that he is "very much indebted to Mrs. Joan Robinson, whose comments have enabled [him] to make various improvements" (ibid., p. 7).
4. The original is handwritten.
5. The date "1937" has been inserted on the basis of Osiatyński's comments cited in n. 3 above.
6. That is, the draft of chap. 6.
7. Ultimately published under the title *Essays in the Theory of Employment* (1937).

to the statement at the end.[8] It must be rather annoying for you to
see all this fuss being made over Keynes when so little notice was
taken of your own contribution.

I think it is a pity that you suggest at the beginning of your paper
that you are making an attack on Keynes' system, when your real
object is to fill a gap in it.[9] I think you are wrong that he does not
allow for a "self-winding up" process.[10] He is always talking about
how a movement "feeds on itself", but his treatment is vague &
incomplete, & something on the lines of your paper is needed to give
it precision.

As far as the definitions are concerned I think it is possible to
dispute about them until doomsday because in the nature of this case
no system can be perfect. Keynes' system, as you say, is unrealistic,
but yours is troublesome because marginal prime cost as you define
it is not equal to marginal revenue, or is only equal to it if entrepreneurs are very foolish. It falls short of m[arginal] revenue by some
vague margin corresponding to Keynes m[arginal] user cost.

The idea of marginal disutility of risk-bearing is subject to the
same objection as all utility ideas—that it involves a circular argument.

Why does supply price rise with scale? Because m[arginal] disutility increases. How do you know m[arginal] d[is]u[tility] increases? Because price rises!

However Keynes' method doesn't get out of this difficulty, & it is
one of those awkward points in economic theory that there seems no
way out of. I think the idea of a rising supply curve of risk-bearing
for the individual is very useful, & you might supplement it by a
further rise in the general supply curve due to individual differences
in willingness to take risks. You then get a composite supply curve
exactly analogous with the supply curve of output from land of
differing fertility.

This is only an interim report. I will work through your paper &
you must come up next term a[nd] have another talk.

Yours sincerely,
[signed] Joan Robinson

P.S. I would be interested to have your opinion of my long-period
article.[11] You will find the last section somewhat primitive as I do

8. I think that the reference is to the statement which appears at the end of a section on
the penultimate page of the article and which reads: "*The general level of production and
prices must rise, eventually, so as to provide for an increment of the real profit equal to
the increment of the production of capital goods and of the consumption of capitalists.*"
(Kalecki 1935b, p. 343, italics in original; cf. with the passage cited on p. 68 above).
9. No such "attack" appears in the published version of the chapter, which would
suggest that Kalecki accepted Robinson's point here.
10. Cf. Kalecki's reference in chap. 6 (pp. 143–44) of his 1939 book to the " 'self-
stimulating' process" which his model generates.
11. Presumably, "The Long-Period Theory of Employment" (1936a).

not allow specifically for the "self-winding-up"; but I think my treatment is a necessary stage to take people through. We've got to teach the dog to read bit by bit.

No further correspondence on this point is reproduced by Osiatyński; either there was none or it has not survived.

3. Correspondence between Keynes and Kalecki

The Keynes Papers and the Kalecki Papers between them contain fifteen letters that were exchanged between the two men over the period 1937–44. Almost all of them (and in particular those reproduced below) were first published (in Polish translation) in Jerzy Osiatyński's editorial notes to volume I of Kalecki's *Dzieła* [Works]. One of these letters—a most interesting one from December 1944 in which Keynes expresses his favorable reaction to Kalecki's contribution to the Oxford Institute volume *Economics of Full Employment* (1944)—has now been reproduced in *JMK* XXVII, pp. 381–83. I hope that the rest of the Keynes-Kalecki correspondence will be published in its entirety in future volumes of Keynes' *Collected Writings*.

Relying on this hope, I have largely restricted myself in this Appendix to reproducing those letters—or excerpts thereof—which refer to writings of Kalecki discussed in chap. 3 above. The letters are in their original English form, and I am greatly indebted to Jerzy Osiatyński, Austin Robinson, and Mrs. Ada Kalecki for providing me with photocopies of them and permitting their reproduction here.

The Kalecki letters are reproduced from the originals which he sent to Keynes. Most of these contain handwritten notes which Keynes jotted down in their margins after receipt and which in most cases he subsequently elaborated upon and incorporated in his replies; these marginal notes have not been reproduced here. All of Kalecki's letters—except for the first—are typewritten. Keynes' letters have been reproduced from the typewritten carbon copies he retained. Words or phrases italicized in the following were so emphasized in the original correspondence. As before, my explanatory comments appear in square brackets and in notes.

London, February 4th, 1937[12]

Dear Mr. Keynes,
I beg to send you enclosed my paper "The commodity tax, in-

---

12. The original is handwritten. This seems to have been the first letter that passed between Kalecki and Keynes.

come tax and capital tax in the light of the Keynesian theory"[13] and to ask whether it might be published in the "Economic Journal."
Yours sincerely,
[signed] M. Kalecki

P.S. I tried to do my best as concerns the English but the curve of my "marginal productivity" in this "production" is steeply falling.

[Cambridge,] February 16th, 1937

Dear Kalecki,

I am happy to accept the enclosed, which I find very interesting, for the Economic Journal. The English is not bad, and the corrections required mainly affect the order of the words. The argument would be easier for an English reader to follow if the sentences were somewhat rearranged into our more habitual order. Could you, do you think, pass the article on to some English friend to get him to dictate from it in a more flowing order.

There is only one small suggestion I have to make in the text. I think it would be advisable, in the first part, to make quite explicit your assumption that the consumption of the capitalists is entirely directed to goods other than wage-goods. It is clear to a careful reader that you are assuming this, but since the assumption is a very unrealistic one, it is desirable to make it clearly.

I have been conscious for some time of the relevance of the theory you refer to to the choice between income tax and a capital tax, but I had not myself worked out the conclusions as rigorously as you have done.

I return the article herewith for revision. You are too late for the March Journal and in plenty of time for the June one.
Yours sincerely,
[copy initialed] JMK

London, March 20th, 1937

Dear Mr. Keynes,

I beg to send you the revised version of my paper. The style was corrected by one of my friends according to your kind advice. I also acted on your suggestion to state explicitly that the capitalists consume only goods other than wage-goods in putting the footnote on page 4. I consider there besides the probable effect of this assumption's not being fulfilled.

I enclose the reprint of my paper "A Theory of the Business Cycle"[14] and I should like very much if possible to hear your opinion on it.
Yours sincerely,
[signed] M. Kalecki

13. Subsequently published under the title "A Theory of Commodity, Income, and Capital Taxation" (1937).
14. The reference is to Kalecki's 1937 *Review of Economic Studies* paper.

P.S. I use the opportunity to thank you for the reprint of your article
"The General Theory of Employment."[15]

[Cambridge,] March 30, 1937

Dear Kalecki,

Thank you for the revised version of your article, which I now find
quite clearly written. . . . [Keynes then provides some detailed criticisms of Kalecki's article which concludes with the following paragraph:]

Now my impression is that your assumption about the consumption of capitalists, whilst technically convenient for the particular
method of exposition you have adopted, is not really required to
establish your main conclusions about the effect of various taxes on
output. It is required, on the other hand, to establish your conclusions as to the effect of the taxes on the distribution of real
income between capitalists and workers. The latter, however, is a
matter in which you are only secondarily interested. Will you think
this over? My impression is that your conclusions as to the effect of
taxes on output could be established without such special assumptions. I am inclined to think that the very pretty technique which you
use in the section on short-period equilibrium in your article in the
[1937] Review of Economic Studies[16] would serve your purpose.

You ask me what I think of the above-mentioned article. The first
two sections I like very much. But I am not convinced by the section
on "The Inducement to Invest," particularly pages 84 and 85.

In the second complete paragraph on page 84 you seem to be
assuming not merely that the current rise of prices will have a dis-
proportionate effect on expectations as to future prices, but that
future prices will be expected to rise in exactly the same proportion.
Surely this is an extravagant over-emphasis of the effect of the immediate situation on long-term expectations? It appears to me that it
is only if future prices are expected to rise *in the same proportion* as
present prices that you have established the result that "equilibrium
is not reached and the investment continues to rise."

In the same way on page 85 you point out that the current increase
of wealth does something to diminish the marginal risk. But to
establish your conclusion you appear to be making some quantitative assumption that the effect will be just of the right degree,[17]
which appears to be unjustified. I might mention, in passing, that the
risk relating to prospective profit is already allowed for in my formula for the marginal efficiency of capital.

15. The reference is to Keynes' contribution to the symposium on his book which
appeared in the February 1937 *Quarterly Journal of Economics*.

16. The reference is presumably to Kalecki's diagrammatic analysis on p. 78 of the
article.

17. This is Keynes' handwritten correction of the word "kind" which was originally
typed here. (I am indebted to Donald Moggridge and Judith Allen for this reading of
Keynes' correction.)

In general, therefore, I do not feel that you have sufficiently established the conclusion italicized at the bottom of page 85.[18]

Yours sincerely,
[copy initialed] JMK

April 4, 1937

Dear Mr. Keynes,

Thank you very much for yours of March 30. . . . [After discussing the criticisms Keynes had made in this letter of the article he had submitted to the *Economic Journal,* Kalecki turns to Keynes' criticisms of his *Review of Economic Studies* article:]

May I yet make some remarks on your criticism of my paper in the "Review"? I think that my statement in the second complete paragraph on page 84 you refer to is independent of *how much* expectations improve under the influence of the present rise of prices. I state in this paragraph only that the increase of prices of investment goods which equates the marginal efficiency based on the *initial* state of expectations to the rate of interest, does not create an "equilibrium"; for at the same time expectations improve to some extent and thus investment increases further. I do not deny that this increase may be convergent and then the point A in the Fig. 3 corresponding to this "equilibrium" may be reached without increase of the rate of interest (see the bottom of the page 88); whilst if the reaction of the entrepreneurs to "the present state of affairs" is strong enough full employment will be reached and then the rise in the rate of interest would perform the task of stopping "inflation" and create the "equilibrium" represented by point A.

In any case however, the process of reaching this equilibrium will be in general spread over many τ periods. Thus it is interesting to know what determines the rate of investment decisions *during* the process. I sought [*sic*] of solving this problem by introducing the "principle" of increasing risk and this enabled me to describe the course of reaching point A (Fig. 6).

I think however that the reference to increasing risk (or something like that) is necessary also for adequate explanation of various positions of "equilibrium" (positions in which the rate of investment has no tendency to change). For the facts show the prices of new investment goods are relatively rigid. It follows from the statistics of Mr. Kuznets about gross capital formation that the prices of new investment goods have fallen in U.S.A. between 1929 and 1932 only by 15%. Thus it is clear that the gap between prospective rate of profit and the rate of interest was much lower in the depression than in the prosperity. But then something besides the prices of investment goods is required for the formation of "equilibrium."

You question also my explanation of why it is the *rate* of invest-

18. This conclusion reads, "*the rate of investment decisions is an increasing function of the gap between the prospective rate of profit and the rate of interest.*"

ment decisions which is dependent on the gap between prospective rate of profit and the rate of interest. If in first τ period all capitalists have decided to invest, say, £1.000.000.000 the savings of second τ period will be £1.000.000.000 too. Thus precisely this amount can be freely reinvested in the second τ period—if the gap between prospective rate of profit is the same as in the first τ period—because the investment of *new accumulated capital* does not increase the risk. (The existence of pure rentiers creates some complication but does not affect the argument; if the relation of the net indebtedness of an entrepreneur to his wealth is δ and his saving during a given period s—he can invest without increasing risk the amount $s(1 + \delta)$. The sum of this [*sic*] amounts is $\Sigma s(1 + \delta) = \Sigma s + \Sigma \delta s$ where Σs is the total saving of entrepreneurs and $\Sigma \delta s$ is the total saving of "pure" rentiers, or the sum of amounts to be invested without increasing the risk is the total saving S).

I am very sorry for troubling you with this long discussion.

Yours sincerely,
[signed] M. Kalecki

[Cambridge,] April 22, 1937

Dear Kalecki,

I have your letter of April 4th. We have now got to the point where I must distinguish between what I am entitled to say to you as editor, and my remarks I am moved to make as a private critic. [Keynes then provides comments under both these headings and then turns to Kalecki's discussion in his letter of his *Review of Economic Studies* article:]

One word about pages 4 and 6 of your letter. On page 4[19] your argument seems to me a version of Achilles and the tortoise, and you are telling me at the bottom of the page that even though Achilles does catch the tortoise up, it will only be after many periods have passed by. At the bottom of page 5[20] I feel that you are making too much of a discontinuity between your periods. I quite agree, however, that the amount of unexecuted decisions which the entrepreneurs are ready, so to speak, to have at risk, is an important element in holding up the pace of investment and cannot be neglected. It is only the precision of your conclusion which I was criticising.

Meanwhile I return the article in the hope that you will preface it with a catalogue of your assumptions. For it is not fair to the reader that he should be forced to disentangle them for himself and then wonder whether or not you really are making them.

Yours sincerely,
[copy initialed] JMK

19. The reference is to the paragraph beginning "May I yet make . . ." in Kalecki's letter, and to its third sentence in particular—opposite which Keynes had jotted down "Achilles and the tortoise" (see p. 96 above).

20. The reference is to the paragraph beginning "You question also . . ." in Kalecki's letter.

I do not know whether or not there was any further correspondence on Kalecki's 1937 *Economic Journal* paper; in any event, none has survived. The next letter related to chapter 3 above is the one in which Keynes acknowledged the receipt of the proofs of Kalecki's *Essays in the Theory of Economic Fluctuations* (1939):

King's College,
Cambridge
January 7th, 1939

My dear Kalecki,
Thank you very much indeed for sending me proofs of your book. I have not compared them with the original articles to see how much you have modified them. But I get the impression of immensely improved lucidity. I have found them exceedingly clear and intelligible and most agreeable (and *almost* easy) reading. It will be a most valuable work.

The article which I am writing for the March Journal[21] is mainly concerned with matter you discuss in your first essay.[22] I had been making several references to the [1938] Econometrica version of that, and will now correct these so as to refer to the book. I am also dealing, to a certain extent, with what you discuss in your new essay on Real and Money Wages. But in actual fact, what I am writing does not overlap with that essay nearly so much as the titles suggest. You are considering what happens to real wages when money wages are reduced, so to speak on purpose, other things being equal; whereas I am considering what happens to real wages when there is a change in the output which is what you are dealing with much more in your first essay.

There is, by the way, one small statistical point where perhaps you can help me. On page 14 you mention that according to Bowley the labour share was 41.4 per cent in 1880. In the Table on page 16 you give a figure comparable to more recent figures for 1911. Is it safe to add the 1880 figure to this table, or does that require some modification in order to be comparable?

Yours sincerely,
[signed] J. M. Keynes

In[23] the last essay I don't really [?] follow why the fact that only

21. "Relative Movements of Real Wages and Output" (1939). This was Keynes' reply to Dunlop's (1938) and Tarshis' (1939) empirical criticisms of his statement in the *General Theory* (p. 10) that "the change in real wages associated with a change in money wages, so far from being usually in the same direction, is almost always in the opposite direction."
22. Entitled "The Distribution of National Income."
23. Handwritten postscript. The misprints Keynes lists here remain in the published version of the book, which suggests that Kalecki sent the proofs at too late a stage for any changes to be made in them. Accordingly, I find it difficult to accept Osiatyński's statement (editorial note in Kalecki, *Dzieła* [Works], vol. I, p. 517) that the proofs were sent to

the entrepreneurs save makes the system trendless.

Misprints p. 127 sequencies—delete the *i*
p. 145 cracs (under the diagram)—what is this, it sounds
more Polish than English!

If Kalecki wrote a reply to this letter, it has not survived.

That is all of the surviving Keynes-Kalecki correspondence that refers to writings discussed in chapter 3 above. I cannot however resist the temptation to go beyond the bounds of that chapter and reproduce the following correspondence between Keynes and Kalecki on a subject that has long interested me: namely, what I first called the "Pigou effect" of a declining price level, and subsequently relabeled the "real-balance effect":

[Cambridge,] February 22, 1944

Dear Kalecki,

Looking through your note on Pigou again,[24] the following point occurs to me. Is there anything in it? I offer it to you, for what it is worth, as a possible addition.

On Pigou's assumption, the *real* rate of interest in Irving Fisher's sense would be constantly rising. This would have two effects:

(a) People would save more, and not less, as Pigou assumes.

(b) If the real value of money is constantly increasing, there will be a strong pressure to repay debts. Thus, at the limit, it would become impossible for the banks to keep the stock of money constant except in so far as it was backed by gold.[25] Thus, in effect, Pigou is assuming simultaneously two contradictory hypotheses. And would even the creation of more national debt help, since this would increase personal incomes pari passu?

Yours sincerely,
[copy initialed] K

University of Oxford
Institute of Statistics
28th February 1944

Dear Lord Keynes,

Thank you very much for your letter. May I make the following observations on your points?

(1) Your point on the rising *real* rate of interest is valid only in the

---

Keynes because he was supposed to write a foreword to the book, and that illness prevented his doing so. Nor is there any indication in Keynes' letter that this was the purpose for which the proofs were sent to him.

24. The reference is to Kalecki's "Professor Pigou on the 'Classical Stationary State' " (1944), which was a comment on the article by Pigou (1943) in which the "Pigou effect" was first presented. Both of these articles appeared in the *Economic Journal*.

25. Keynes does not seem to realize that this is precisely the point of Kalecki's note, as the latter makes clear in paragraph (2) of his reply, which follows.

period of adjustment. Once new equilibrium is achieved the wages and prices stop falling. In the *course* of adjustment the factor you mention *will* tend to reduce employment, but an even more important influence in this direction will be exerted by whosesale bankruptcy and the resulting "crisis of confidence" which I mention in my note.

(2) The repayment of bank debts will not affect the situation after the correction I suggest has been introduced: in any case it is only the increase in the real value of *gold* that matters.

(3) If in the initial situation there exists a large National Debt this makes Pigou's adjustment easier because the increase in the real value of the National Debt does mean an increase in the real wealth of firms and persons. (If the interest on Debt is financed by taxation its existence does not affect the aggregate disposable income.[26])

> Yours sincerely,
> [signed] M. Kalecki

> [Cambridge,] March 8, 1944

Dear Kalecki,

I agree that the real rate of interest would not go on rising for ever. But I should have supposed that at the time when it reached its equilibrium level substantially all bank loans would have been paid off. Thus, I do not see how the banking system is going to maintain the quantity of money constant unless it is prepared to issue national debt as a backing for it. Assuming that interest is paid on this out of taxation, it cannot affect the wealth of the community one way or another. Thus, it seems to me that Pigou is in reality depending entirely on the increase in the value of gold.

The whole thing, however, is really too fantastic for words and scarcely worth discussing.

> Yours sincerely,
> [copy initialed] K

It is not clear whether "the whole thing" in this last paragraph refers to the specific point which Keynes raises in these letters or to Pigou's analysis in general. If the latter, then it supports my conjecture that even if Keynes had taken account of the real-balance effect in the *General Theory*, it would not have affected his basic conclusions (*KMT*, p. 110; see also my "Price Flexibility and Full Employment" [1951], p. 281, and *Money, Interest, and Prices*, chap. XIV:1).

---

26. Note Kalecki's view (with which Keynes in the reply which follows concurs) that government debt serviced by taxation is not part of wealth. In the last two decades this question has received increasing attention; thus see, e.g., chap. XII:4 of my *Money, Interest, and Prices* (1965) and Barro (1974).

Bibliography for Part I*

Aftalion, Albert (1913). *Les crises périodiques de surproduction*. Paris: M. Rivière.

Allen, R. G. D. (1936). "Professor Slutsky's Theory of Consumers' Choice." *Review of Economic Studies* 3 (Feb.): 120–29.

Anderson, B. M. (1917). *The Value of Money*. New York: Macmillan.

Barber, Bernard (1952). *Science and the Social Order*. New York: Free Press.

———— (1961). "Resistance by Scientists to Scientific Discovery." *Science* 134 (Sept. 1): 596–602. As reprinted in Barber and Hirsch (1962), pp. 539–56.

Barber, Bernard, and Renée C. Fox (1958). "The Case of the Floppy-Eared Rabbits: An Instance of Serendipity Gained and Serendipity Lost." *American Journal of Sociology* 64 (Sept.): 128–36. As reprinted in Barber and Hirsch (1962), pp 525–38.

Barber, Bernard, and Walter Hirsch, editors (1962). *The Sociology of Science*. New York: Free Press.

Barro, R. J. (1974). "Are Government Bonds Net Wealth?" *Journal of Political Economy* 82 (Nov.–Dec.): 1095–1117.

Bishop, Robert L. (1948). "Alternative Expansionist Fiscal Policies: A Diagrammatic Analysis." In *Income, Employment and Public Policy: Essays in Honor of Alvin H. Hansen*, by L. A. Metzler *et al.* New York: W. W. Norton, pp. 317–40.

Blaug, Mark (1976). "Kuhn versus Lakatos *or* Paradigms versus Research Programmes in the History of Economics." In *Method and Appraisal in Economics*, edited by S. Latsis (Cambridge: Cambridge University Press), pp. 149–80.

———— (1978). *Economic Theory in Retrospect*. 3rd edition. Cambridge: Cambridge University Press.

Brems, Hans (1978). "What Was New in Ohlin's 1933–34 Macroeconomics?" *History of Political Economy* 10 (Fall): 398–412.

---

* Reprinted or translated works are cited in the text by year of original publication; the page references to such works in the text are, however, to the pages of the reprint or translation in question.

Bronfenbrenner, Martin (1971). "The 'Structure of Revolutions' in Economic Thought." *History of Political Economy* 3 (Spring): 136–51.

Cagan, Phillip (1956). "The Monetary Dynamics of Hyperinflation." In *Studies in the Quantity Theory of Money,* edited by Milton Friedman (Chicago: University of Chicago Press): 25–117.

Cannan, Edwin (1893). *A History of the Theories of Production and Distribution in English Political Economy from 1776 to 1848.* London: Percival.

Caplan, Benjamin (1941). "Some Swedish Stepping Stones in Economic Theory: A Comment." *Canadian Journal of Economics and Political Science* 7 (Nov.): 559–62.

Chamberlin, Edward H. (1933). *The Theory of Monopolistic Competition.* Cambridge, Mass.: Harvard University Press.

—— (1937). "Monopolistic or Imperfect Competition?" *Quarterly Journal of Economics* 51 (Aug.): 557–80.

—— (1951). "Monopolistic Competition Revisited." *Economica* 18 (Nov.): 343–62.

Clark, Colin (1932). *The National Income: 1924–1931.* London: Macmillan.

Davidson, Paul (1972). *Money and the Real World.* London: Macmillan.

Davis, J. Ronnie (1971). *The New Economics and the Old Economists.* Ames, Iowa: Iowa State University Press.

Dominedo, Valentino (1933). "Considerazioni intorno alla teoria della domanda." *Giornale degli economisti e rivista di statistica* 73: (January) 30–48, (November) 765–807.

Dunlop, John T. (1938). "The Movement of Real and Money Wage Rates." *Economic Journal* 48 (Sept.): 413–34.

Elkana, Yehuda (1970). "The Conservation of Energy: A Case of Simultaneous Discovery?" *Archives Internationales d'Histoire des Sciences* 90–91 (Jan.–Juin): 31–60.

Eshag, Eprime (1977a). Introduction to Special Issue of Michal Kalecki Memorial Lectures. *Oxford Bulletin of Economics and Statistics* 39 (Feb.): 1–6.

—— (1977b). "Kalecki's Political Economy: A Comparison with Keynes." *Oxford Bulletin of Economics and Statistics* 39 (Feb.): 79–86.

Feiwel, George R. (1975). *The Intellectual Capital of Michał Kalecki.* Knoxville, Tenn.: University of Tennessee Press.

Fisher, Irving (1907). *The Rate of Interest.* New York: Macmillan.

—— (1911). *The Purchasing Power of Money.* New York: Macmillan.

—— (1913). *The Purchasing Power of Money.* Revised edition, New York: Macmillan. Reprinted, New York: Augustus M. Kelley, 1963. (Date of edition as given in reprint is incorrect).

—— (1930). *The Theory of Interest.* New York: Macmillan. Reprinted, New York: Kelley and Millman, 1954.

Fleck, Ludwik (1935). *Genesis and Development of a Scientific Fact.* Translated from the original German by Fred Bradley and Thaddeus J. Trenn. Chicago: University of Chicago Press, 1979.

Friedman, Milton (1957). *A Theory of the Consumption Function.* Princeton: Princeton University Press, for the National Bureau of Economic Research.

Frisch, Ragnar (1934). "Circulation Planning: Proposal for a National Organization of a Commodity and Service Exchange." *Econometrica* 2: (July) 258–336, (Oct.) 422–35.

Frisch, Ragnar, and H. Holme (1935). "The Characteristic Solutions of a Mixed Difference and Differential Equation Occurring in Economic Dynamics." *Econometrica* 3 (April): 225–39.

Gårdlund, Torsten (1958). *The Life of Knut Wicksell.* Stockholm: Almqvist and Wiksell.

Garvy, George (1975). "Keynes and the Economic Activists of Pre-Hitler Germany." *Journal of Political Economy* 83 (March/April): 391–405.

Gelting, Jørgen H. (1975). "Origins of the Balanced-Budget-Multiplier Theorem: V. Some Observations on the Financing of Public Activity." *History of Political Economy* 7 (Spring): 36–42.

Grossman, Herschel I. (1972). "Was Keynes a 'Keynesian'? A Review Article." *Journal of Economic Literature* 10 (March): 26–30.

Gustafsson, Bo (1973). "A Perennial of Doctrinal History: Keynes and 'The Stockholm School'." *Economy and History* 16: 114–28.

Haavelmo, Trygve (1945). "Multiplier Effects of a Balanced Budget." *Econometrica* 13 (October): 311–18.

——— (1946). "Multiplier Effects of a Balanced Budget: Reply." *Econometrica* 14 (April): 156–58.

Hansen, Alvin (1951). *Business Cycles and National Income.* New York: W. W. Norton.

Hansen, Bent (1975). "Origins of the Balanced-Budget-Multiplier Theorem: IV. Introduction to Jørgen Gelting's 'Some Observations on the Financing of Public Activity.'" *History of Political Economy* 7 (Spring): 32–35.

——— (1981). "Unemployment, Keynes, and the Stockholm School." *History of Political Economy* 13 (Summer): 256–77.

Harris Memorial Foundation (1931). *Unemployment as a World Problem.* Edited by Quincy Wright. Chicago: University of Chicago Press.

Harrod, R. F. (1937). "Mr. Keynes and Traditional Theory" *Econometrica* 5 (January): 74–86. As reprinted in Lekachman (1964): 124–52.

——— (1951). *The Life of John Maynard Keynes.* London: Macmillan. Reprinted, New York: Augustus M. Kelley, 1969.

Hegeland, Hugo (1954). *The Multiplier Theory.* Lund: C. W. K. Gleerup.

Hicks, J. R. (1937). "Mr. Keynes and the 'Classics'; A Suggested Interpretation." *Econometrica* 5 (April): 147–59. As reprinted in *Readings in the Theory of Income Distribution,* selected by a committee of the American Economic Association (Philadelphia: Blakiston, for the American Economic Association, 1946), pp. 461–76.

——— (1939). *Value and Capital.* Oxford: Clarendon Press.

——— (1965). *Capital and Growth.* Oxford: Oxford University Press.

Hicks, J. R., and R. G. D. Allen (1934). "A Reconsideration of the Theory of Value." *Economica* 1: (Feb.) 52–76, (May) 196–219.

Hutchison, T. W. (1953). *A Review of Economic Doctrines 1870–1929.* Oxford: Clarendon Press.

——— (1968). *Economics and Economic Policy in Britain 1946–1966: Some Aspects of Their Inter-Relations.* London: George Allen and Unwin.

——— (1978). *On Revolutions and Progress in Economic Knowledge.* Cambridge: Cambridge University Press.

Jackman, Richard (1974). "Keynes and Leijonhufvud." *Oxford Economic Papers* 26 (July): 259–72.

Jaffé, William (1976). "Menger, Jevons and Walras De-Homogenized." *Economic Inquiry* 14 (Dec.): 511–24.

Johannsen, Nicholas A. J. (1908). *A Neglected Point in Connection with Crises.* New York: Bankers Publishing Co. Reprinted, New York: Augustus M. Kelley, 1971.

Johnson, Elizabeth S. (1974). "Keynes: Scientist or Politician?" *Journal of Political Economy* 82 (Jan./Feb.): 99–111. As reprinted in Johnson and Johnson (1978), pp. 7–29.

——— (1977). "Keynes as a Literary Craftsman." In Patinkin and Leith (1977), pp. 90–97. As reprinted in Johnson and Johnson (1978), pp. 30–37.

Johnson, Elizabeth S., and Harry G. Johnson (1978). *The Shadow of Keynes: Understanding Keynes, Cambridge and Keynesian Economics.* Chicago: University of Chicago Press.

Jonung, Lars (1979). "Knut Wicksell's Norm of Price Stabilization and Swedish Monetary Policy in the 1930's." *Journal of Monetary Economics* 5 (October): 459–96.

——— (1981). "Ricardo on Machinery and the Present Unemployment: An Unpublished Manuscript by Knut Wicksell." *Economic Journal* 91 (March): 195–205.

Kahn, R. F. (1931). "The Relation of Home Investment to Unemployment." *Economic Journal* 41 (June): 173–98. As reprinted in Kahn (1972), pp. 1–27.

——— (1932). "The Financing of Public Works: A Note." *Economic Journal* 42 (Sept.): 492–95.

——— (1972). *Selected Essays on Employment and Growth.* Cambridge: Cambridge University Press.

Kalecki, Michał (1932). "Przewidywania p. Keynesa" [Mr. Keynes' predictions]. *Przegląd Socjalistyczny* [Socialist review] 2 (nr. 6). As reprinted in Kalecki (1979), pp. 72–74. (Published under the cryptonym "H. Br.").

——— (1933a). *Próba teorii koniunktury* [An essay on the theory of the business cycle]. Warsaw: Institute of Research on Business Cycles and Prices. As reprinted in Kalecki (1979) pp. 95–157.

——— (1933b). "O handlu zagranicznym i 'eksporcie wewnetrznym' " *Ekonomista* 33 (No. 3): 27–35. Reprinted in Kalecki (1979), pp. 199–209. As translated by Ada Kalecki under the title "On Foreign Trade and 'Domestic Exports' " in Kalecki (1966), pp. 16–25.

——— (1933c). "Odpowiedź na 'Uwagi krytyczne o jednej z matematycznych teorii koniunktury' Aleksandra Rajchmana" ["Critical comments on one of the mathematical theories of the business cycle" by Aleksander Rajchman: a rejoinder.] *Kwartalnik Statystyczny* [Statistical quarterly] 10 (No. 4): 497–502. As reprinted in Kalecki (1979), pp. 158–69.

——— (1935a). "Essai d'une théorie du mouvement cyclique des affaires." *Revue d'économie politique* 2 (March/April): 285–305.

——— (1935b). "A Macrodynamic Theory of Business Cycles." *Econometrica* 3 (July): 327–44.

——— (1935c). "Istota poprawy koniunkturalnej." *Polska Gospodarcza* [Economic Poland] 43: 1320–24. Reprinted in Kalecki (1979), pp. 225–32. As translated by Ada Kalecki under the title "The Mechanism of the Business Upswing" in Kalecki (1966), pp. 26–33.

——— (1936a). "Parę uwag o teorii Keynesa" [Some remarks on Keynes' theory]. *Ekonomista* 36 (No. 3): 18–26. As reprinted in Kalecki (1979), pp. 263–73.

——— (1936b). "Comments on the Macrodynamic Theory of Business Cycles." *Econometrica* 4 (Oct.): 356–60.

——— (1937a). "A Theory of the Business Cycle." *Review of Economic Studies* 4 (Feb.): 77–97.

——— (1937b). "A Theory of Commodity, Income and Capital Taxation." *Economic Journal* 47 (Sept.): 444–50. As reprinted in Kalecki (1971), pp. 35–42.

——— (1938). "The Determinants of Distribution of the National Income." *Econometrica* 6 (April 1938): 97–112.

——— (1939). *Essays in the Theory of Economic Fluctuations*. London: Allen and Unwin.

——— (1943). *Studies in Economic Dynamics*. London: Allen and Unwin.

——— (1944). "Professor Pigou on 'The Classical Stationary State': A Comment." *Economic Journal* 54 (April): 131–32.

——— (1946). "Three Ways to Full Employment." In Oxford University Institute of Statistics, *The Economics of Full Employment* (Oxford: Basil Blackwell), pp. 39–58.

——— (1966). *Studies in the Theory of Business Cycles: 1933–1939*. Translated from the original Polish by Ada Kalecki. Oxford: Basil Blackwell.

——— (1971). *Selected Essays on the Dynamics of the Capitalist Economy: 1933–1970*. Cambridge : Cambridge University Press.

——— (1979). *Kapitalizm: Koniunktura i zatrudnienie. Dzieła*, tom 1 [Capitalism: business cycles and employment. Works, Vol. I]. Edited by Jerzy Osiatyński. Warsaw: Państwowe Wydawnictwo Ekonomiczne [State Publishers for Economics] for Polska Akademia Nauk [Polish Academy of Sciences].

———. See also T. Kowalik *et al.*, *Festschrift* volume.

Keynes, John Maynard (1921). *A Treatise on Probability*. As reprinted in Keynes, *Collected Writings*, Vol. VIII.

——— (1923). *A Tract on Monetary Reform*. As reprinted in Keynes, *Collected Writings*, Vol. IV.

——— (1924). "Alfred Marshall 1842–1924." *Economic Journal* 34 (Sept.): 311–72. As reprinted in Keynes, *Collected Writings*, Vol. X, pp. 161–231. (See Keynes [1933b]).

——— (1925). *The Economic Consequences of Mr. Churchill*. As reprinted in Keynes, *Collected Writings*, Vol. IX, pp. 207–30.

—— (1929a). "The German Transfer Problem." *Economic Journal* 39 (March): 1–7. As reprinted in *Readings in the Theory of International Trade,* selected by a committee of the American Economic Association (Philadelphia: Blakiston, for the American Economic Association, 1949), pp. 161–69.

—— (1929b). "The Reparation Problem: A Rejoinder." *Economic Journal* 39 (July): 179–82.

—— (1930). *A Treatise on Money,* Vol. I: *The Pure Theory of Money.* As reprinted in Keynes, *Collected Writings,* Vol. V.

—— (1930). *A Treatise on Money,* Vol. II: *The Applied Theory of Money.* As reprinted in Keynes, *Collected Writings,* Vol. VI.

—— (1931a). "An Economic Analysis of Unemployment." In Harris Memorial Foundation (1931), pp. 3–42. As reprinted in Keynes, *Collected Writings,* Vol. XIII, pp. 343–67.

—— (1931b). *Essays in Persuasion.* As reprinted with additions in Keynes, *Collected Writings,* Vol. IX.

—— (1932). "The World's Economic Crisis and the Way of Escape." In Arthur Salter *et al., The World's Economic Crisis and the Way of Escape* pp. 69–88. London: Allen and Unwin. As reprinted in Keynes, *Collected Writings,* Vol. XXI, pp. 50–62. (Halley Stewart Lecture).

—— (1933a). *The Means to Prosperity.* As reprinted in Keynes, *Collected Writings,* Vol. IX, pp. 335–66.

—— (1933b). *Essays in Biography.* As reprinted with additions in Keynes, *Collected Writings,* Vol. X.

—— (1934). "Poverty in Plenty: Is the Economic System Self-Adjusting?" *Listener* 12 (Nov. 21): 850–51. As reprinted in Keynes, *Collected Writings,* Vol. XIII, pp. 485–92.

—— (1935). "A Self-Adjusting Economic System?" *New Republic* 82 (Feb. 20): 35–37.

—— (1936). *The General Theory of Employment Interest and Money.* As reprinted in Keynes, *Collected Writings,* Vol. VII.

—— (1937a). "Alternative Theories of the Rate of Interest." *Economic Journal* 47 (June): 241–52. As reprinted in Keynes, *Collected Writings,* Vol. XIV, pp. 201–15.

—— (1937b). "The General Theory of Employment." *Quarterly Journal of Economics* 51 (February): 209–23. As reprinted in Keynes, *Collected Writings,* Vol. XIV, pp. 109–23.

—— (1939). "Relative Movements of Real Wages and Output." *Economic Journal* 49 (March): 34–51. As reprinted in Keynes, *Collected Writings,* Vol. VII, pp. 394–412.

——. *The General Theory and After: Part I, Preparation.* Edited by Donald Moggridge. Vol. XIII of Keynes, *Collected Writings.*

——. *The General Theory and After: Part II, Defence and Development.* Edited by Donald Moggridge. Vol. XIV of Keynes, *Collected Writings.*

——. *Activities 1922–1929: The Return to Gold and Industrial Policy.* Edited by Donald Moggridge. Vol. XIX of Keynes, *Collected Writings* (in two parts).

——. *Activities 1931–1939: World Crises and Policies in Britain and America.* Edited by Donald Moggridge. Vol. XXI of Keynes, *Collected Writings.*

——. *Activities 1940–1946: Shaping the Post-War World: Employment and Commodities.* Edited by Donald Moggridge. Vol. XXVII of Keynes, *Collected Writings.*

——. *The General Theory and After: A Supplement.* Edited by Donald Moggridge. Vol. XXIX of Keynes, *Collected Writings.*

——. *Collected Writings.* 30 volumes planned. Published to date: Vols. I–VI (1971), Vols. VII–VIII (1973), Vols. IX–X (1972), Vols. XIII–XIV (1973), Vols. XV–XVI (1971), Vols. XVII–XVIII (1978), Vols. XIX–XX (1981), Vol. XXI (1982), Vol. XXII (1978), Vols. XXIII–XXIV (1979), Vols. XXV–XXVII (1980), Vol. XXIX (1979). London: Macmillan, for the Royal Economic Society.

Keynes, John Maynard, and Hubert Henderson (1929). *Can Lloyd George Do It?: An Examination of the Liberal Pledge.* As reprinted in Keynes, *Collected Writings,* Vol. IX, pp. 86–125.

Klein, Lawrence (1947). *The Keynesian Revolution.* New York: Macmillan.

—— (1951). "The Life of John Maynard Keynes." *Journal of Political Economy* 59 (Oct.): 443–51.

—— (1964). "The Role of Econometrics in Socialist Economics." In Kowalik *et al.* (1964), pp. 181–91.

—— (1966). *The Keynesian Revolution.* Revised edition. New York: Macmillan.

—— (1975). Foreword to Feiwel (1975).

Klein, Lawrence, and A. S. Goldberger (1955). *An Econometric Model of the United States 1929–1952.* Amsterdam: North-Holland.

Knight, Frank (1921). *Risk, Uncertainty and Profit.* New York: Houghton Mifflin.

Kowalik, T. (1964). "Biography of Michał Kalecki." In Kowalik *et al.* (1964), pp. 1–12.

Kowalik, T., et al. (1964). *Problems of Economic Dynamics and Planning: Essays in Honour of Michał Kalecki.* Warsaw: Polish Scientific Publishers.

Kregel, J. A. (1976). "Economic Methodology in the Face of Uncertainty: The Modelling Methods of Keynes and the Post-Keynesians." *Economic Journal* 86 (June): 209–25.

Kuhn, Thomas S. (1962). *The Structure of Scientific Revolutions.* Chicago: University of Chicago Press, 1962.

—— (1970). *The Structure of Scientific Revolutions.* Second enlarged edition, Chicago: University of Chicago Press.

Kuznets, Simon (1939). Review of *Essays in the Theory of Economic Fluctuations,* by Michal Kalecki. *American Economic Review* 29 (Dec.): 804–06.

Lakatos, Imre (1970). "Falsification and the Methodology of Scientific Research Programmes." In Lakatos and Musgrave (1970), pp. 91–196.

—— (1978). "Science and Pseudoscience." In Lakatos, *The Methodology of Scientific Research Programmes: Philosophical Papers.* Vol. I. Edited by John Worrall and Gregory Currie. Cambridge: Cambridge University Press, pp. 1–7.

Lakatos, Imre, and Alan Musgrave, editors (1970). *Criticism and the Growth of Knowledge.* Cambridge: Cambridge University Press.

Landgren, Karl-Gustav (1960a). *Den 'nya ekonomien' i Sverige: J. M. Keynes,*

E. Wigforss, B. Ohlin och utvecklingen 1927–1939 [The "new economics" in Sweden: J. M. Keynes, E. Wigforss, B. Ohlin and the development 1927–1939]. Stockholm: Almqvist and Wiksell. (Includes English summary).

——— (1960b). "Replikskifte kring Landgrens bok" [Some comments on Landgren's book]. *Ekonomisk Tidskrift* 62 (Sept.): 212–14.

——— (1972). "Bakgrunden till 1930— talets krispolitik: Ett genmäle till Otto Steiger" [The background of the recovery policies of the 1930s: a reply to Otto Steiger]. *Arkiv för studier i arbetarrörelsens historia* [Archive for the study of the history of the labor movement] 2 (May): 96–107.

Lange, Oskar (1938). "The Rate of Interest and the Optimum Propensity to Consume." *Economica* 5 (February): 12–32. As reprinted in *Readings in Business Cycle Theory,* selected by a committee of the American Economic Association (Philadelphia: Blakiston, for the American Economic Association, 1944), pp. 169–92.

——— (1939). "Neoklasyczna szkoła w ekonomii" [The neoclassical school of economics]. In *Encyklopedii Nauk Politycznych,* Vol. IV. Warszawa: Instytut Wydawniczy, Biblioteka Polska, pp. 23–35. As reprinted in Lange, *Dzieła* [Works], Vol. III, edited by Tadeusz Kowalik. Warsaw: Państwowe Wydawnictwo Ekonomiczne [State Publishers for Economics] for Polska Akademia Nauk [Polish Academy of Sciences], 1975, pp. 64–92.

——— (1941). Review of *Essays in the Theory of Economic Fluctuations,* by Michal Kalecki. *Journal of Political Economy* 49 (April): 279–85.

——— (1959). *Political Economy.* Vol. I.: *General Problems.* Translated from the original Polish by A. H. Walker. Oxford: Pergamon Press, 1963.

Laudan, Larry (1977). *Progress and Its Problems.* Berkeley: University of California Press.

Laughlin, James L. (1919). *Money and Prices.* New York: Charles Scribner's Sons.

Leijonhufvud, Axel (1968). *On Keynesian Economics and the Economics of Keynes.* New York: Oxford University Press.

——— (1978). Foreword to the Japanese edition of Leijonhufvud (1968). Tokyo: Toyo Keizai Shinposha.

Lekachman, Robert, editor (1964). *Keynes' General Theory: Reports of Three Decades.* New York: St. Martin's Press.

Lerner, Abba P. (1933). "Factor Prices and International Trade." *Economica* 19 (Feb. 1952): 1–15. As reprinted in Lerner (1953), pp. 67–84. (Paper originally written in 1933).

———. (1936). "The General Theory." *International Labour Review* 34 (Oct.): 435–54. As reprinted in Lekachman (1964), pp. 203–22.

——— (1940). "Some Swedish Stepping Stones in Economic Theory." *Canadian Journal of Economics and Political Science* 6 (Nov.): 574–91. As reprinted in Lerner (1953), pp. 215–41.

——— (1953). *Essays in Economic Analysis.* London: Macmillan.

Lindahl, Erik (1930). *Penningpolitikens Medel* [The methods of monetary policy]. Lund: Forlagsaktiebolagets i Malmö Boktryckeri. (Published for private circulation in 1929).

——— (1939). *Studies in the Theory of Money and Capital.* London: Allen and Unwin.

―――― (1954). "On Keynes' Economic System." *Economic Record* 30: (May) pp. 19–32, (Nov.) 159–71.
Lindahl, Erik, Einar Dahlgren, and Karin Kock (1937). *National Income of Sweden 1861–1930,* 2 Vols. Institute for Social Services of Stockholm University. London: P. S. King and Son.
Lipiński, Edward (1977). "Michal Kalecki." *Oxford Bulletin of Economics and Statistics* 39 (Feb.): 69–78.
Lundberg, Erik (1937). *Studies in the Theory of Economic Expansion.* London: P. S. King and Son.
―――― (1960). "Om att begripa Keynes och att förstå andra" [To comprehend Keynes and to understand others] *Ekonomisk Tidskrift* 62 (Sept.): 195–205.
Marget, Arthur William (1931). "Léon Walras and the 'Cash-Balance Approach' to the Problem of the Value of Money." *Journal of Political Economy* 39 (Oct.): 569–600.
McFarlane, B. J. (1971). "Michal Kalecki's Economics: An Appreciation." *Economic Record* 47 (March): 93–105.
Merton, Robert K. (1938). *Science, Technology and Society in Seventeenth-Century England.* In *OSIRIS: Studies on the History and Philosophy of Science, and on the History of Learning and Culture.* Edited by George Sarton. Bruges, Belgium: St. Catherine Press. Reprinted, New York: Howard Fertig, 1970.
―――― (1957). "Priorities in Scientific Discovery." *American Sociological Review* 22 (Dec.): 635–59. As reprinted in Merton (1973), pp. 286–324.
―――― (1961). "Singletons and Multiples in Science." In *Proceedings of the American Philosophical Society* 105 (Oct.): 470–86. As reprinted in Merton (1973), pp. 343–70.
―――― (1965). *On the Shoulders of Giants: A Shandean Postscript.* New York: Harcourt, Brace & World.
―――― (1968a). "The Matthew Effect in Science." *Science* 159 (Jan. 5): 56–63. As reprinted in Merton (1973), pp. 439–59.
―――― (1968b). *Social Theory and Social Structure.* Enlarged edition. New York: Free Press.
―――― (1973). *The Sociology of Science: Theoretical and Empirical Investigations.* Edited and Introduction by Norman W. Storer. Chicago: University of Chicago Press.
Mill, John Stuart (1848). *Principles of Political Economy.* Edited by W. A. Ashley. London: Longman Green, 1909.
Mosak, J. L. (1942). "On the Interpretation of the Fundamental Equation of Value Theory." In *Studies in Mathematical Economics and Econometrics: In Memory of Henry Schultz,* edited by Oscar Lange et al. (Chicago: University of Chicago Press): 69–74.
Mummery, A. F., and J. A. Hobson (1889). *The Physiology of Industry.* London: John Murray.
Myrdal, Gunnar (1931). "Om penningteoretisk jämvikt" [On monetary equilibrium]. *Ekonomisk Tidskrift* 33 (No. 5–6): 191–302.
―――― (1933). "Der Gleichgewichtsbegriff als Instrument der geldtheoretischen Analyse." In *Beiträge zur Geldtheorie,* edited by Friedrich A. Hayek (Wien: Julius Springer), pp. 365–485.

—— (1934). [*Report*]. *Finanspolitikens Ekonomiska Verkningar* [The economic effects of fiscal policy]. Stockholm: Kungl. Boktryckeriet. (For further bibliographical details, see listing under Government Publications.)

—— (1939). *Monetary Equilibrium*. London: W. Hodge.

—— (1972). *Against the Stream: Critical Essays in Economics*. New York: Pantheon.

Ohlin, Bertil (1924). *Handelns teori* [The theory of trade]. Stockholm: P. A. Norstedt & Söner (Ohlin's Ph.D. thesis).

—— (1929a). "Transfer Difficulties, Real and Imagined." *Economic Journal* 39 (June): 172–78. As reprinted in *Readings in the Theory of International Trade*, selected by a committee of the American Economic Association (Philadelphia: Blakiston, for the American Economic Association, 1949), pp. 170–78.

—— (1929b). "Mr. Keynes' Views on the Transfer Problem: A Rejoinder." *Economic Journal* 39 (Sept.): 400–04.

—— (1933a). "Till frågan om penningteoriens uppläggning." *Ekonomisk Tidsskrift* 35 (No. 2): 45–81. As translated under the title "On the Formulation of Monetary Theory" by Hans J. Brems and William P. Yohe. *History of Political Economy* 10 (Fall 1978): 353–88.

—— (1933b). *Interregional and International Trade*. Cambridge, Mass.: Harvard University Press.

—— (1934). [*Report*]. *Penningpolitik, Offentliga Arbeten, Subventioner och Tullar Som Medel Mot Arbetslöshet* [Monetary policy, public works, subsidies and tariff policy as remedies for unemployment]. Stockholm: Kungl. Boktryckeriet. (For further bibliographical details, see listing under Government Publications.)

—— (1936). Introduction to English translation of Wicksell, *Interest and Prices* (London: Macmillan).

—— (1937). "Some Notes on the Stockholm Theory of Saving and Investment." *Economic Journal* 47: (March) 53–69, (June) 221–40. As reprinted in *Readings in Business Cycle Theory*, selected by a committee of the American Economic Association (Philadelphia: Blakiston, for the American Economic Association, 1944), pp. 87–130.

—— (1943). "Stockholmsskolan kontra kvantitetsteorien." *Ekonomisk Tidsskrift* 45 (March): 27–46. As translated under the title "The Stockholm School Versus the Quantity Theory," by William P. Yohe. *International Economic Papers* 10 (1960), pp. 132–46.

—— (1974). "On the Slow Development of the 'Total Demand' Idea in Economic Theory: Reflections in Connection with Dr. Oppenheimer's Note." *Journal of Economic Literature* 12 (Sept.): 888–96.

—— (1977). "Some Comments on Keynesianism and the Swedish Theory of Expansion Before 1935." In Patinkin and Leith (1977), pp. 149–65.

—— (1978). "Keynesian Economics and the Stockholm School, A Comment on Patinkin's Paper." *Scandinavian Journal of Economics* 80 (No. 2): 144–47.

—— (1981). "Stockholm and Cambridge: Four Papers on the Monetary and Employment Theory of the 1930s." Posthumously edited by O. Steiger. *History of Political Economy* 13 (Summer): 189–255.

Palander, Tord (1941). "Om 'Stockholmsskolans' begrepp och metoder." *Ekon-*

omisk Tidskrift 43 (March): 88–143. As translated under the title "On the Concepts and Methods of the 'Stockholm School,' " by R. S. Stedman. *International Economic Papers* 3 (1953): 5–57.

—— (1942). "Keynes' allmänna teori" [Keynes' General Theory]. *Ekonomisk Tidskrift* 44 (Dec.): 233–71.

Patinkin, Don (1948). "Price Flexibility and Full Employment." *American Economic Review* 38 (Sept.): 543–64.

—— (1951). "Price Flexibility and Full Employment." In *Readings in Monetary Theory*, selected by a committee of the American Economic Association (Philadelphia: Blakiston, for the American Economic Association), pp. 252–83. (Revised version of Patinkin [1948].)

—— (1952). "Wicksell's 'Cumulative Process'." *Economic Journal* 62 (Dec.): 835–47.

—— (1956). *Money, Interest, and Prices*. Evanston, Ill.: Row, Peterson.

—— (1965). *Money, Interest, and Prices*. 2nd edition. New York: Harper and Row.

—— (1969). "The Chicago Tradition, the Quantity Theory, and Friedman." *Journal of Money, Credit and Banking* 1 (Feb.): 46–70. As reprinted in Patinkin (1981), pp. 241–64.

—— (1976). *Keynes' Monetary Thought: A Study of Its Development*. Durham, N.C.: Duke University Press.

—— (1977). "The Process of Writing the *General Theory*: A Critical Survey." In Patinkin and Leith (1977), pp. 3–24.

—— (1978a). "On the Relation between Keynesian Economics and the 'Stockholm School'." *Scandinavian Journal of Economics* 80 (No. 2): 135–43.

—— (1978b). "Some Observations on Ohlin's 1933 Article." *History of Political Economy* 10 (Autumn): 413–18.

—— (1980). "New Materials on the Development of Keynes' Monetary Thought." *History of Political Economy* 12 (Spring): 1–28.

—— (1981). *Essays On and In the Chicago Tradition*. Durham, N.C.: Duke University Press.

Patinkin, Don, and J. Clark Leith, editors (1977). *Keynes, Cambridge and the General Theory : The Process of Criticism and Discussion Connected with the Development of the General Theory*. London: Macmillan.

Pigou, A. C. (1917). "The Value of Money." *Quarterly Journal of Economics* 32 (Nov.): 38–65. As reprinted in *Readings in Monetary Theory*, selected by a committee of the American Economic Association (Philadelphia: Blakiston, for the American Economic Association, 1951), pp. 162–83.

—— (1943). "The Classical Stationary State." *Economic Journal* 53 (December): 343–51.

Polanyi, Michael (1967). "The Growth of Science in Society." *Minerva* 4 (Summer): 533–45.

Rajchman, Aleksander (1933). "Uwagi krytyczne o jednej z matematycznych teorj 'konjunktury' " [Critical comments on one of the mathematical theories of the "business cycle"]. *Kwartalnik Statystyczny* [Statistical quarterly] 10 (No. 2, 3): 325–37.

Ramsey, Frank P. (1928). "A Mathematical Theory of Saving." *Economic Journal* 38 (Dec.): 543–59. As reprinted in *Readings in Welfare Economics*, selected by a committee of the American Economic Association (Homewood, Ill.: Richard D. Irwin, for the American Economic Association, 1969), pp. 619–33.

Robbins, Lionel (1971). *Autobiography of an Economist*. London: Macmillan.

Robertson, D. H. (1926). *Banking Policy and the Price Level*. London: P. S. King and Son.

Robinson, E. A. G. (1947). "John Maynard Keynes 1883–1946." *Economic Journal* 57 (March): 1–68. As reprinted in Lekachman (1964), pp. 13–86.

Robinson, Joan (1933a). *The Economics of Imperfect Competition*. London: Macmillan.

——— (1933b). "The Theory of Money and the Analysis of Output." *Review of Economic Studies* 1 (Oct.): 22–26. As reprinted in J. Robinson, *Collected Economic Papers*, Vol. 1, pp. 52–58.

——— (1936a). "The Long-Period Theory of Employment." *Zeitschrift für Nationalökonomie* 7 (March): 74–93. As reprinted with minor revisions in Robinson (1937b), pp. 75–100.

——— (1936b). "Disguised Unemployment." *Economic Journal* 46 (June): 225–37. As reprinted with minor revisions in Robinson (1937b), pp. 60–74.

——— (1937a). *Introduction to the Theory of Employment*. London: Macmillan.

——— (1937b). *Essays in the Theory of Employment*. Oxford: Basil Blackwell.

——— (1951). Preface to J. Robinson, *Collected Economic Papers*, Vol. I.

——— (1952). *The Rate of Interest: And Other Essays*. London: Macmillan.

——— (1964). "Kalecki and Keynes." In Kowalik *et al.* (1964), pp. 335–42.

——— (1966). Introduction to Kalecki (1966).

——— (1969). *Introduction to the Theory of Employment*. 2nd edition. London: Macmillan.

——— (1971). "Michal Kalecki." *Cambridge Review* 93 (October 22): 1–3. As reprinted in J. Robinson, *Collected Economic Papers*, Vol. IV, pp. 87–91.

——— (1976). "Michal Kalecki: A Neglected Prophet." *New York Review of Books* 23 (March 4): 28–30.

——— (1977). "Michal Kalecki on the Economics of Capitalism." *Oxford Bulletin of Economics and Statistics* 39 (February): 7–17. As reprinted in J. Robinson, *Collected Economic Papers*, Vol. V, pp. 184–96.

——— *Collected Economic Papers*, Vol. I (1951), Vol. II (1960), Vol. III (1965), Vols. IV–V and General Index (1980). Oxford: Basil Blackwell.

Roll, Erich (1939). *A History of Economic Thought*. New York: Prentice-Hall, Inc.

Salant, Walter S. (1975). "Origins of the Balanced-Budget-Multiplier Theorem: I. Introduction to William A. Salant's 'Taxes, the Multiplier and the Inflationary Gap.' " *History of Political Economy* 7 (Spring): 3–18.

Salant, William A. (1975a). "Origins of the Balanced-Budget-Multiplier Theorem: II. Taxes, the Multiplier, and the Inflationary Gap." *History of Political Economy* 7 (Spring): 19–27.

——— (1975b). "Origins of the Balanced-Budget-Multiplier Theorem: III. The

Balanced Budget Multiplier as the Sum of an Infinite Series." *History of Political Economy* 7 (Spring): 28–31.

Samuelson, Paul A. (1939). "A Synthesis of the Principle of Acceleration and the Multiplier." *Journal of Political Economy* 47 (Dec.): 786–97. As reprinted in Samuelson, *Collected Scientific Papers*, Vol. II, pp. 1111–22.

——— (1946). "Lord Keynes and the General Theory." *Econometrica* 14 (July): 187–200. As reprinted in Lekachman (1964), pp. 315–31.

——— (1948). "International Trade and the Equalisation of Factor Prices." *Economic Journal* 58 (June): 163–84. As reprinted in Samuelson, *Collected Scientific Papers*, Vol. II, pp. 847–68.

——— (1949). "International Factor-Price Equalisation Once Again." *Economic Journal* 59 (June): 181–97. As reprinted in Samuelson, *Collected Scientific Papers*, Vol. II, pp. 869–97.

——— (1965). "A Catenary Turnpike Theorem Involving Consumption and the Golden Rule." *American Economic Review* 55 (June): 486–96. As reprinted in Samuelson, *Collected Scientific Papers*, Vol. III, pp. 93–103.

——— (1975). "Origins of the Balanced-Budget-Multiplier Theorem: VI. The Balanced-Budget Multiplier: A Case Study in the Sociology and Psychology of Scientific Discovery." *History of Political Economy* 7 (Spring): 43–55. As reprinted in Samuelson, *Collected Scientific Papers*, Vol. IV, pp. 841–53.

——— *The Collected Scientific Papers of Paul A. Samuelson.* Vols. I–II (1966), edited by Joseph E. Stiglitz; Vol. III (1972), edited by Robert C. Merton; Vol. IV (1977), edited by Hiroaki Nagatani and Kate Crowley. Cambridge, Mass.: M. I. T. Press.

Samuelson, Paul A., and Robert M. Solow (1956). "A Complete Capital Model Involving Heterogeneous Capital Goods." *Quarterly Journal of Economics* 70 (Nov.): 537–62. As reprinted in Samuelson, *Collected Scientific Papers*, Vol. I, pp. 261–86.

Sandler, Iris, and Laurence Sandler. "A Speculation on a Conceptual Ambiguity That Resulted in the Neglect of Mendel's Paper," forthcoming.

Schmookler, Jacob (1966). *Invention and Growth.* Cambridge, Mass.: Harvard University Press.

Schultz, Henry (1935). "Interrelations of Demand, Price, and Income." *Journal of Political Economy* 43 (Aug.): 433–81.

——— (1938). *The Theory and Measurement of Demand.* Chicago: University of Chicago Press.

Schumpeter, Joseph A. (1954). *A History of Economic Analysis.* New York: Oxford University Press.

Shackle, G. L. S. (1967). *The Years of High Theory: Invention and Tradition in Economic Thought.* Cambridge: Cambridge University Press.

——— (1972). *Epistemics & Economics: A Critique of Doctrines.* Cambridge: Cambridge University Press.

——— (1974). *Keynesian Kaleidics: The Evolution of a General Political Economy.* Edinburgh: Edinburgh University Press.

Shapere, Dudley (1964). "The Structure of Scientific Revolutions." *Philosophical Review* 73 (July): 383–94.

Slutsky, Eugen E. (1915). "Sulla teoria del bilancio del consumatore." *Giornale degli economisti e rivista di statistica* 51 (July): 1–26. As translated under the title "On the Theory of the Budget of the Consumer" by Olga Regusa in *Readings in Price Theory,* selected by a committee of the American Economic Association (Chicago: Richard D. Irwin, for the American Economic Association, 1952), pp. 27–56.

Steiger, Otto (1971). *Studien zur Entstehung der Neuen Wirtschaftslehre in Schweden: Eine Anti-Kritik.* Berlin: Duncker & Humblot.

——— (1972). "Till frågan om den nya ekonomiska politikens tillomst i Sverige" [On the question of the origins of the new economic policy in Sweden]. *Arkiv för studier i arbetarrörelsens historia* [Archive for the study of the history of the labor movement] No. 1 (Jan.): 4–28.

——— (1973). "Bakgrunden till 1930—talets socialdemokratiska krispolitik: Ett tyvärr ganska långt svar på Karl-Gustav Landgrens genmäle [The background of the Social Democratic recovery policies of the 1930s: an answer to Karl-Gustav Landgren's reply]. *Arkiv för studier i arbetarrörelsens historia* [Archive for the study of the history of the labor movement] No. 4 (Sept.): 67–83.

——— (1976). "Bertil Ohlin and the Origins of the Keynesian Revolution." *History of Political Economy* 8 (Fall): 341–66.

——— (1978a). "Substantive Changes in the Final Version of Ohlin's 1933 Paper." *History of Political Economy* 10 (Fall): 389–97.

——— (1978b). "Prelude to the Theory of a Monetary Economy: Origins and Significance of Ohlin's 1933 Approach to Monetary Theory." *History of Political Economy* 10 (Fall): 420–46.

——— (1981). "Bertil Ohlin, 1899–1979." *History of Political Economy* 13 (Summer): 179–88.

Stein, Herbert (1969). *The Fiscal Revolution in America.* Chicago: University of Chicago Press.

Stent, Gunther S. (1972). "Prematurity and Uniqueness in Scientific Discovery." *Scientific American* 227 (Dec.): 84–93.

Stigler, George J. (1941). *Production and Distribution Theories.* New York: Macmillan.

——— (1980). "Merton on Multiples, Denied and Affirmed." In *Science and Social Structure: A Festschrift for Robert K. Merton,* edited by Thomas F. Gieryn. *Transactions of The New York Academy of Sciences,* Series II, Vol. 39: 147–57.

Stigler, Stephen M. (1980). "Stigler's Law of Eponymy." In *Science and Social Structure: A Festschrift for Robert K. Merton,* edited by Thomas F. Gieryn. *Transactions of The New York Academy of Sciences,* Series II, Vol. 39: 147–57.

Stohs, Mark (1980). " 'Uncertainty' in Keynes' *General Theory.*" *History of Political Economy* 12 (Fall): 372–82.

Studenski, Paul (1958). *The Income of Nations.* New York: New York University Press.

Tarshis, Lorie (1939). "Changes in Real and Money Wages." *Economic Journal* 49 (March): 150–54.

Theiss, Edward (1933). "A Quantitative Theory of Industrial Fluctuations

Caused by the Capitalistic Technique of Production." *Journal of Political Economy* 41 (June): 334–49.

———— (1935). "Dynamics of Saving and Investment." *Econometrica* 3 (April): 213–24.

Thomas, Brinley (1936). *Monetary Policy and Crises: A Study of Swedish Experience*. London: G. Routledge and Sons.

Tinbergen, Jan (1935). "Annual Survey: Suggestions on Quantitative Business Cycle Theory." *Econometrica* 3 (July): 241–308.

Topp, Niels-Henrik (1981). "The Multiplier Theory in Denmark 1896–1932." *History of Political Economy* 13 (Winter): 824–45.

Toulmin, Stephen (1972). *Human Understanding*. Princeton: Princeton University Press.

Uhr, Carl G. (1973). "The Emergence of the 'New Economics' in Sweden: A Review of a Study by Otto Steiger." *History of Political Economy* 5 (Spring): 243–60.

———— (1977). "Economists and Policymaking 1930–1936: Sweden's Experience." *History of Political Economy* 9 (Spring): 89–121.

Warming, Jens (1932). "International Difficulties Arising Out of the Financing of Public Works During Depressions." *Economic Journal* 42 (June): 211–24.

Whitehead, A. N. (1917). *The Organisation of Thought: Educational and Scientific*. London: Williams and Norgate. Reprinted, Westport, Conn.: Greenwood Press, 1974.

Wicksell, Knut (1898). *Interest and Prices*. Translated from the original German by R. F. Kahn. London: Macmillan, 1936.

———— (1906). *Lectures on Political Economy*. Vol II: *Money*. Translated from the original Swedish by E. Classen, edited by L. Robbins. London: Routledge, 1935. (Second Swedish edition, 1911; English translation from posthumous 1938 Swedish edition, edited by Emil Sommarin).

———— (1907). "Krisernas Gata." *Statsøkonomisk Tidsskrift* 21: 225–84. As translated under the title "The Enigma of Business Cycles" by C. G. Uhr. *International Economic Papers* 3 (1953): 58–74.

Wicksell, Knut. See also Jonung (1981).

Wigforss, Ernst (1960). "Den nya ekonomiska politiken" [The new economic policy]. *Ekonomisk Tidsskrift* 62 (Sept.): 185–94.

Winch, Donald (1966). "The Keynesian Revolution in Sweden." *Journal of Political Economy* 74 (April): 168–76.

———— (1969). *Economics and Policy: A Historical Study*. London: Hodder and Stoughton.

Wright, A. Ll. (1956). "The Genesis of the Multiplier Theory." *Oxford Economic Papers* (new series) 8 (June): 181–93.

Wright, Quincy. See Harris Memorial Foundation.

Yohe, William P. (1962). "A Note on Some Lesser-Known Works of Erik Lindahl." *Canadian Journal of Economics and Political Science* 28 (May): 274–80.

———— (1978). "Ohlin's 1933 Reformulation of Monetary Policy." *History of Political Economy* 10 (Fall): 447–53.

Zawadzki,Władysław (1914). *Les mathématiques appliquées à l'économie po-litique*. Paris: M. Rivière.
—— (1927). *Esquisse d'une théorie de la production*. Paris: M. Rivière.
—— (1936). "Nowa teoria pieniądza Keynesa" [Keynes' new monetary theory] *Ekonomista* 36 (No. 3): 68–84.

Government Publications

Statens Offentliga Utredningar. [Official reports of the government] 1934:1. Arbetslöshetsutredningens [Committee on unemployment]. Betänkande II, Bilagor, Band 2. G. Myrdal, *Finanspolitikens Ekonomiska Verkningar* [The economic effects of fiscal policy]. Stockholm: Kungl. Boktryckeriet.
Statens Offentliga Utredningar. [Official reports of the government] 1934:12. Arbetslöshetsutredningens [Committee on unemployment]. Betänkande II, Bilagor, Band 4. B. Ohlin, *Penningpolitik, Offentliga Arbeten, Subventioner och Tullar som Medel Mot Arbetslöshet* [Monetary policy, public works, subsidies and tariff policy as remedies for unemployment]. Stockholm: Kungl. Boktryckeriet.
Statens Offentliga Utredningar. [Official reports of the government] 1935:6. Arbetslöshetsutredningens [Committee on unemployment]. Betänkande II, Bilagor, Band 2. *Åtgärder Mot Arbetslöshet* [Policies for dealing with un-employment]. Stockholm: Kungl. Boktryckeriet. (Final report of the Com-mittee on Unemployment, drafted by Dag Hammarskjold, Secretary of the Committee).
U.S. Bureau of the Census (1960). *Historical Statistics of the United States, Colonial Times to 1957*. Washington D.C.: Government Printing Office.

Unpublished Sources

Bryce, Robert B. Notes on Keynes' lectures at Cambridge, Autumn term 1932, 1933, and 1934. Handwritten notes deposited at Carleton University, Ottawa. Typewritten version (with some inaccuracies) filed in the Keynes Papers (see below).
Michał Kalecki Papers. In possession of Mrs. Ada Kalecki, Warsaw.
J. M. Keynes Papers. Deposited in the Marshall Library, Cambridge, England.
Patinkin, Don. Notes on Oskar Lange's course on "Business Cycle Theory" at the University of Chicago, Summer 1945. Handwritten notes in Patinkin's possession.
Rockefeller Foundation. Archives.
Salant, Walter. Notes on Keynes' lectures at Cambridge, Autumn term 1934. Handwritten notes in Salant's possession.
Tarshis, Lorie. Notes on Keynes' lectures at Cambridge, Autumn term 1932, 1933, 1934, and 1935. Handwritten notes in Tarshis' possession.

II The Theory of Effective Demand

5

A Critique of Keynes' Theory of Effective Demand

1. Keynes' chapter 3, "The Principle of Effective Demand" is at one and the same time the most important and the most obscure chapter in the *General Theory:* most important, because, as emphasized above (pp. 8–11), the theory it presents constitutes the major innovation of the book; most obscure, as the following crucial passages from this chapter readily indicate:

> It is sometimes convenient, when we are looking at it from the entrepreneur's standpoint, to call the aggregate income (i.e., factor cost *plus* profit) resulting from a given amount of employment the *proceeds* of that employment. On the other hand, the aggregate supply price[1] of the output of a given amount of employment is the expectation of proceeds which will just make it worth the while of the entrepreneurs to give that employment.[2]
>
> It follows that in a given situation of technique, resources and factor cost per unit of employment, the amount of employment, both in each individual firm and industry and in the aggregate, depends on the amount of the proceeds which the entrepreneurs expect to receive from the corresponding output. For entrepreneurs will endeavor to fix the amount of employment at the level which they expect to maximise the excess of the proceeds over the factor cost.

This chapter is based on two separate though related papers respectively presented at the meetings of the Western Economic Association in June 1978 and at the University of Chicago Graduate School of Business in November 1978. The chapter is a further development—and in part a correction—of the critique of Keynes' theory of effective demand which appears in chapter 9 of *KMT*. It draws freely on the discussion there and in Patinkin (1979).

I am indebted to Giora Hanoch, Aviah Spivack, and Peter Howitt for helpful comments. I have also benefited from the comments of participants in the Money and Banking Workshops at the University of Chicago and at the University of Western Ontario. My thanks also to Clark Nardinelli for technical assistance.

This chapter concentrates on Keynes' theory of effective demand as presented in "Book I: Introduction" of the *General Theory;* it does not deal with the elaboration of this theory in the subsequent parts of the book (cf. above, pp. 11–14).

Let Z be the aggregate supply price of the output from employing
N men, the relationship between Z and N being written $Z = \phi(N)$,
which can be called the *aggregate supply function*. Similarly, let D
be the proceeds which entrepreneurs expect to receive from the
employment of N men, the relationship between D and N being
written $D = f(N)$, which can be called the *aggregate demand function*.

Now if for a given value of N the expected proceeds are greater
than the aggregate supply price, i.e., if D is greater than Z, there will
be an incentive to entrepreneurs to increase employment beyond N
and, if necessary, to raise costs by competing with one another for
the factors of production, up to the value of N for which Z has
become equal to D. Thus the volume of employment is given by the
point of intersection between the aggregate demand function and the
aggregate supply function; for it is at this point that the entrepreneurs' expectation of profits will be maximised. The value of D at
the point of the aggregate demand function, where it is intersected
by the aggregate supply function, will be called *the effective demand*.

---

1. Not to be confused (*vide infra*) with the supply price of a unit of output in the
ordinary sense of this term.

2. The reader will observe that I am deducting the user cost both from the *proceeds*
and from the *aggregate supply price* of a given volume of output, so that both these
terms are to be interpreted *net* of user cost. . . .

[*GT*, pp. 24–25, italics in original]

A few pages on, Keynes repeats this argument in the following words:

Thus, given the propensity to consume and the rate of new investment, there will be only one level of employment consistent with
equilibrium; since any other level will lead to inequality between the
aggregate supply price of output as a whole and its aggregate demand price. This level cannot be *greater* than full employment, i.e.,
the real wage cannot be less than the marginal disutility of labour.
But there is no reason in general for expecting it to be *equal* to full
employment. [*GT*, p. 28, italics in original]

In a later chapter, Keynes again writes:

Furthermore, the *effective demand* is simply the aggregate income
(or proceeds) which the entrepreneurs expect to receive, inclusive of
the incomes which they will hand on to the other factors of production, from the amount of current employment which they decide to
give. The aggregate demand function relates various hypothetical
quantities of employment to the proceeds which their outputs are
expected to yield; and the effective demand is the point on the

aggregate demand function which becomes effective because, taken in conjunction with the conditions of supply, it corresponds to the level of employment which maximises the entrepreneur's expectation of profit. [*GT*, p. 55, italics in original]

From these passages it is clear that Keynes uses the terms "proceeds" and "aggregate demand price" interchangeably. It is also clear that the aggregate demand function represents the proceeds entrepreneurs *expect* to receive. At other points in the *General Theory* (pp. 29–30, 96, 120, 125–27), Keynes specifies the form of this function as having a positive, less-than-unity, and declining slope, representing the corresponding properties of the marginal propensity to consume.

In contrast, neither in these passages nor (with one exception)[1] elsewhere in the *General Theory* does Keynes provide any detailed information about the nature of the aggregate supply price and the corresponding function. It is reasonable to assume that Keynes visualized this function as being positively sloped (cf., e.g., *GT*, p. 300); but there are no further indications of its assumed properties. Furthermore, no explanation is given of the crucial though ambiguous phrase "just make it worthwhile" (*GT*, p. 24) which Keynes uses to define the aggregate supply price. And a similar ambiguity marks Keynes' later derivation of the aggregate supply function of the economy as a whole from

the aggregate supply function for a given firm (and similarly for a given industry or for industry as a whole) [which] is given by

$$Z_r = \phi_r(N_r),$$

where Z_r is the proceeds (net of user cost) the expectation of which will induce a level of employment N_r. [*GT*, p. 44]

Once again, the crucial phrase "which will induce" is not explained.

More specifically, Keynes' formulation of his analysis in terms of "demand price" and "supply price,"[2] as well as his use of the phrase

---

1. See section 5 below.
2. The distinction between these two prices was essentially also the basis of the "fundamental equations" of Keynes' earlier *Treatise*. Thus in the first of these equations, written in the form

$$P = W_1 + \frac{Q_1}{R}$$

(*Treatise* I, p. 124), P represents demand price (a term which on occasion Keynes used in the *Treatise*; cf., e.g., vol. I, pp. 186, 189), W_1 represents cost of production or (making allowance for the absence of marginal analysis in the *Treatise*) supply price (a term which, however, does not appear in the *Treatise*), while Q_1/R represents per-unit profits. And a similar statement holds for the second fundamental equation. (For further details on the nature of these equations, see *KMT*, pp. 33–36. See also p. 7 above.)

"just make it worthwhile" in connection with the latter, reflect his desire to pattern his analysis after that of Marshall's value theory; that is the implicit message of the first footnote in the passage from pp. 24–25 cited above (p. 124). But whereas Marshall makes it clear that his "supply price" represents the marginal costs that have to be covered in order for the firm to find it "just worthwhile" to produce a certain quantity *instead of a slightly smaller one* (cf., e.g., *Principles,* pp. 345, 373–74), Keynes in the foregoing passages leaves it ambiguous whether his "supply price" represents such costs or whether it represents the variable costs that have to be covered in order for the firm to find it "just worthwhile" to produce a certain quantity *or nothing at all.* Now, it is true that at other points in the *General Theory* (e.g., p. 67) Keynes explicitly equates the supply price with marginal cost. The question, however, is whether he did so consistently throughout his book; and as we shall see in the course of the following discussion (see especially pp. 147–49), there are good grounds for suspecting that he did not.

There are two other problematic aspects of Keynes' attempt in these passages to pattern his discussion after Marshall's value theory. The first is that Marshall's representative firm in a competitive industry does not—and indeed, by definition, cannot—perceive the demand curve for the industry as a whole. Instead it is confronted in the market by a given demand price. In contrast, as we have seen from the foregoing passages, Keynes' firms do somehow perceive the aggregate demand curve. Furthermore, Keynes' assumption that the aggregate demand curve represents entrepreneurs' expectations involves him not only in a deviation from Marshallian analysis, but in a logical contradiction: for it implies that at (say) the level of employment N_1 in figure 3,[3] entrepreneurs are at one and the same time expecting two different per-unit prices: that corresponding to the aggregate supply price N_1T, which caused them in the first place to employ N_1 men; and that corresponding to the aggregate demand price N_1W.[4] Alternatively stated, if entrepreneurs expect the per-unit price, and hence (by the assumption

---

3. The aggregate supply curve in this diagram is drawn only for illustrative purposes; no significance should be attached to its specific form.

4. See the passage from pp. 24–25 of the *General Theory* cited on p. 124 above. This "double expectation" is even more manifest in Keynes' discussion with Dennis Robertson of the presentation of the theory of effective demand in the early proofs of the *General Theory* (February 1935). In this discussion, Keynes explained to Robertson that

> D is the sale proceeds for which it is expected that the output from employing N men can be *sold. D'* is the sale proceeds the expectation of which will cause the output from employing N men to be *produced.* It is simply the age-old supply function. (*JMK* XIV, pp. 512–13, italics in original)

(D' in these proofs represented supply price, i.e., what Keynes was to denote by Z in the final version of the *General Theory;* see *JMK* XIV, pp. 370–71.)

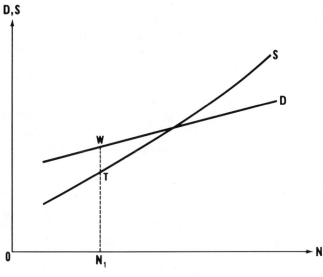

Figure 3

of a constant money-wage which, for simplicity, Keynes temporarily [*GT*, p. 27] makes in his chap. 3) real wage rate corresponding to the aggregate demand price N_1W, then they should have employed more than the N_1 men appropriate for the lower real wage rate corresponding to the aggregate supply price N_1T.

The second, and related, problematic aspect is Keynes' statement that ''the point of intersection between the aggregate demand function and aggregate supply function . . . [is the point at which] the entrepreneurs' expectation of profits will be maximised'' (*GT*, p. 25)—which has no counterpart in Marshallian price theory. In particular, if the representative firm should produce (say) q_1 in figure 4, it will find itself receiving the per-unit demand price p_1, exceeding its supply price p_2. The excess of the former (= marginal revenue) over the latter (= marginal cost) will lead the firm to expand output, and this process will continue until equilibrium position C (at which marginal revenue = marginal cost) is reached (*Principles*, p. 345). Note, however, that total profits at this position—with the industry producing q_0 and receiving a price of p_0—are not necessarily greater than at the disequilibrium position where it produced q_1 and received p_1. Indeed, if the demand curve is inelastic over the segment AC, total profits will necessarily be smaller: for total industry receipts will have declined, while total costs will have risen. Nevertheless, the forces of competition will bring the representative firm, and hence the industry, to equilibrium point C.

Similarly, there are problems in understanding the nature of the

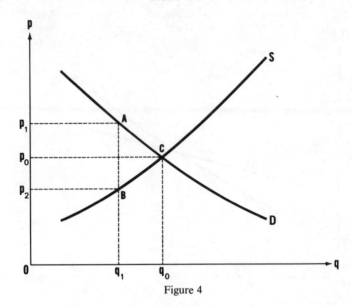

Figure 4

dynamic forces which Keynes conceived as causing the entrepreneurs to (say) expand output. For whereas in the foregoing passage from pp. 24–25 of the *General Theory* Keynes explains these forces in terms of the excess of aggregate demand $D = f(N)$ over aggregate supply $Z = \phi(N)$, in his discussion of the implications of Say's law, he describes an expansion that takes place even in the absence of such an excess. In Keynes' words:

> On classical theory, according to which $D = \phi(N)$ for *all* values of N, the volume of employment is in neutral equilibrium for all values of N less than its maximum value; so that the forces of competition between entrepreneurs may be expected to push it to this maximum value. Only at this point, on the classical theory, can there be stable equilibrium.[5] [*GT*, p. 29, italics in original]

But no explanation is given of the "forces of competition" which "push" entrepreneurs to the "maximum" (i.e., full employment) value of N even though "$D = \phi(N)$ for *all* values of N."

5. In a later (October 1937) correspondence with Kaldor on a different question, Keynes admitted he had the "habit" of using the term "neutral equilibrium" when he meant "unstable equilibrium" (*JMK*, XIV, p. 242). Strictly speaking, however, the less-than-maximum values of N in this passage do not represent unstable equilibria: for even in the absence of an external shock, the economy will (according to Keynes) systematically move away from them until it reaches full employment. So perhaps Marshall's or Hicks' (1939, pp. 122–23) "temporary equilibrium" would be a better term by which to describe these values, though this too might not correspond to the original use of the term.

2. Before attempting to clarify these issues, let me note two additional features of Keynes' presentation of his theory of effective demand which are undoubtedly strange to the present-day reader.

There is, first of all, Keynes' exasperating failure to make use of diagrammatic analysis. How much pain and paper would have been saved by a diagram depicting the "point of intersection between the aggregate demand function and the aggregate supply function" (*GT*, p. 25)! But for some reason Keynes was averse to the use of diagrammatic analysis[6]—and this despite the fruitful precedent of his teacher Marshall. Thus there is no analytical diagram in either the *Tract on Monetary Reform* (1923) or the *Treatise on Money* (1930); and the only one in the *General Theory*—which occurs in the course of Keynes' discussion of the classical theory of interest—is (as Keynes acknowledges) one Roy Harrod suggested to him (*GT*, p. 180n).

The second strange (for today) feature is Keynes' presentation of his theory in terms of employment N instead of real national income Y (or, in Keynes' terms, national income in wage units, Y_w). In his chapter 4, "The Choice of Units," Keynes makes it clear that his choice of N is a deliberate one reflecting his methodological objections to Y on the grounds (so he contended) that

> the community's output of goods and services is a non-homogeneous complex which cannot be measured, strictly speaking, except in certain special cases, as for example when all the items of one output are included in the same proportions in another output. [*GT*, p. 38]

And he concluded his discussion with the famous passage:

> To say that net output to-day is greater, but the price-level lower, than ten years ago or one year ago, is a proposition of a similar character to the statement that Queen Victoria was a better queen but not a happier woman than Queen Elizabeth—a proposition not without meaning and not without interest, but unsuitable as material for the differential calculus. [*GT*, p. 40]

Keynes recognized that labor too was nonhomogeneous; but he claimed that this problem could be dealt with by regarding individuals

---

6. Similarly, to judge from student notes that have survived, Keynes made practically no use of diagrams in his lectures. Thus Lorie Tarshis' notes from the years 1932–36 contain only one diagram; Robert Bryce's notes from 1932–35 contain three; and Walter Salant's notes from 1933, none. Furthermore, none of these diagrams occur in the lecture notes dealing with the theory of effective demand. (For information on the nature of these notes, see p. 21 above.)

I might also mention here Colin Clark's January 1933 correspondence with Keynes on empirical estimates of the multiplier, in which Clark wrote: "I enclose also the relevant data, because I know you fight shy of diagrams" (*JMK* XXIX, p. 62). For further details, see chap. 9, n. 24 below.

"as contributing to the supply of labour, in proportion to their re-
muneration" (*GT*, p. 42). He failed to realize, however, that this
procedure—namely, weighting quantities by base-period prices—is
essentially the same one used in measuring real national income.

I suspect that Keynes' procedure here was also influenced by the
fact that at the time he wrote the *General Theory*, national-income
estimates had not yet become the household concept that they are
today; indeed, there did not then even exist official estimates of British
national income.[7] In contrast, ever since the early 1920s, current official estimates of British employment—or rather unemployment, as measured by the "Number of Insured Persons Recorded as Unemployed"—were being published in the *Ministry of Labour Gazette*.[8]
Furthermore, it was the level of employment—the chronically
low level that had existed ever since the mid-1920s and had dropped
disastrously lower in the early 1930s—which Keynes saw as the
major problem to be explained by his *General Theory*. At the same
time I would conjecture that had current estimates of British national
income been available then instead of only after the outbreak of World
War II, Keynes would have formulated his theory of effective demand
in terms of this variable, probably as measured in wage units. Thus, at
later points in the *General Theory* Keynes expresses his consumption
function not in terms of N (as he had in chap. 3, especially pp. 28–29),
but in terms of Y_w (cf. ibid., pp. 114–15). Similarly, in his chapter 18,
"The General Theory of Employment Re-stated," Keynes specifies his
"dependent variables [as] the volume of employment and the national
income (or national dividend) measured in wage units" (*GT*, p. 245; cf.
also p. 247). And when a few years later, in his *How to Pay for the War*
(1940), Keynes applied the analytical framework of the *General Theory*
to problems of wartime finance, he did so entirely in terms of national
income (*JMK* IX, pp. 381ff.).

3. From the passages cited in Section 1 above, it is clear that Keynes
intended to derive his aggregate supply function from the principle of
profit maximization. The ambiguities in those passages, however, raise
the question whether he succeeded in doing so correctly. To provide a
convenient frame of reference for examining this question, let me first
rigorously derive an aggregate supply function from the standard prin-

7. For details, see pp. 244–46 below. As indicated there, neither did official United
States national-income estimates begin to appear until early 1935, by which time the
General Theory had already reached the proof stage. Official British estimates began only
in 1941.
8. Cf., e.g., the table on pp. 176–77 of the May 1929 *Gazette*, which provides the
estimates for the preceding month. Note Keynes' reference to these estimates in *Can
Lloyd George Do It?* (1929; *JMK* IX, p. 92). For further details, see p. 194 below.

ciple of profit maximization. Accordingly, let the production function be

$$(1) \qquad\qquad Y = \psi(N),$$

so that the labor-demand function is

$$(2) \qquad\qquad w/p = \psi'(N),$$

where $\psi'(N)$ is the marginal product of labor. This function can be more conveniently written in the inverse form as

$$(3) \qquad\qquad N^d = \psi'^{-1}(w/p) \equiv G(w/p).$$

Substituting from (3) into (1) then yields the aggregate supply function

$$(4) \qquad\qquad Y^s = \psi[G(w/p)].^9$$

In money terms, this becomes

$$(5) \qquad\qquad pY^s = p\psi[G(w/p)].$$

And over the past years there have been several writers who have presented a diagrammatic derivation equivalent to the foregoing analytic one, and who have contended that pY^s is what Keynes meant by his aggregate supply price Z.[10]

Now, if this contention is to be taken literally, it cannot be accepted: for neither in the *General Theory*, nor in the materials connected with its preparation that have been reproduced in *JMK* XIII, nor in the student notes from Keynes' lectures at the time[11] is this derivation to be found. And this is a fortiori the case for the complicated diagrammatic analysis in terms of which the aforementioned writers have presented their interpretation. Furthermore, the foregoing derivation attributes to Keynes an involved chain of complicated mathematical reasoning which is entirely out of keeping with his usual analytical style (*KMT*, p. 93; see also ibid., pp. 8, 21–25).

9. Up to this point, the development is that of chaps. IX:3 and XIII:2 of my *Money, Interest, and Prices* (1956, 1965), which did not attribute this function to the *General Theory*.

10. See especially Weintraub (1958, pp. 24–30; 1961, p. 36), who has been followed on this by Davidson and Smolensky (1964, pp. 118–28), and, more recently, Roberts (1978, sec. 1). The procedure of these writers is to assume a fixed value of w, and then—for different values of p—to determine the corresponding values of N^d from a labor-demand curve representing (3), which values are applied to a total production curve representing (1) to determine the corresponding values of Y^s. The corresponding products of p and Y^s are then plotted against the relevant values of N to yield an aggregate supply function. See also Wells (1960, 1962, 1974), who, however, apparently does not believe that Keynes actually thought in terms of the derivation (1)–(3) (Wells 1960, pp. 540–41).

11. Cf. n. 6 above. These lecture notes are as obscure on the subject of the aggregate supply function as is the final version of the *General Theory*.

There is, however, another level at which this discussion can be carried out. On previous occasions (see above, pp. 16–17), I have emphasized that the study of history of doctrine should be looked upon as an empirical study, with the universe from which the relevant empirical evidence is drawn consisting of the writings and teachings of the economists in question. If so, we can attempt to explain our observations from this universe by means of an "as if" hypothesis. That is, let us see if the discussions of the aggregate supply function in the *General Theory* can be explained by the hypothesis that Keynes wrote them "as if" he had derived this function from equations (1)–(5).

For this purpose it will be more convenient to express aggregate supply not in money terms, but in wage units and as a function of N.[12] The production function in wage units is

$$(6) \qquad Y_w = \frac{p\psi(N)}{w} .$$

Upon substitution from profit maximizing condition (2), this becomes the aggregate supply function

$$(7) \qquad Z_w = \frac{\psi(N)}{\psi'(N)} ,$$

whose slope is accordingly

$$(8) \qquad \frac{dZ_w}{dN} = 1 - \frac{\psi(N)\psi''(N)}{[\psi'(N)]^2} > 1 ,$$

where use has been made of the assumption of diminishing marginal productivity, that is, $\psi''(N) < 0$. Define profits in wage units as

$$(9) \qquad \pi_w = \frac{pY - wN}{w} = Y_w - N$$

and differentiate with respect to N to yield

$$(10) \qquad \frac{d\pi_w}{dN} = \frac{dY_w}{dN} - 1 .$$

Restricting ourselves to profit maximizing situations and making use of (8), this becomes

$$(11) \qquad \frac{d\pi_w}{dN} = \frac{dZ_w}{dN} - 1 = - \frac{\psi(N)\psi''(N)}{[\psi'(N)]^2} > 0 ,$$

which is, of course, the second term on the right-hand side of (8).

---

12. Such a function has been attributed to Keynes by Marty (1961). The latter has also derived various properties of this function, though not the ones which concern us in what follows.

In graphic terms, equation (11) represents the familiar fact that as the input of labor increases along the negatively sloped labor-demand curve of figure 5 from (say) N_1 to N_2, the "triangle" representing profits increases from ABC to ADE. Hence the crosshatched area $BCDE$ in this diagram corresponds to the right-hand side of (11).[13]

Thus the economic interpretation of equation (8) is that a unit increase in the input of labor carried out in accordance with the principle of profit maximization will generate increased receipts which will be large enough to cover the marginal cost of the labor (by definition, equal to 1 in wage units) as well as to make a positive addition to profits. This is the meaning of the fact that the aggregate supply curve (7) must have a greater-than-unitary slope.

On the other hand, nothing can be said about the convexity or concavity of this curve: this depends on the third derivative of the produc-

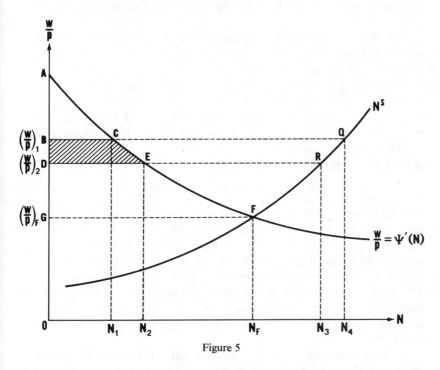

Figure 5

13. Note, however, that area of the triangle is measured in output units and not wage-units; that is, the triangle actually represents

$$\pi_p = (pY - wN)/p = Y - (w/p)N.$$

But since

$$\pi_w = \pi_p (p/w) ,$$

and since along the demand curve p/w increases with N, there is a positive monotonic relationship between π_w and π_p.

tion function, $\psi'''(N)$, which in turn determines the rate at which profits increase as N increases.

To make this more concrete, consider the case where the production function is of the Cobb-Douglas form

(12) $$Y = AN^\alpha \, ,$$

where A and α are constants with $A > 0$ and (by the assumption of diminishing returns) $0 < \alpha < 1$. Substituting in (7) we obtain the aggregate supply function

(13) $$Z_w = \frac{AN^\alpha}{\alpha AN^{\alpha-1}} = \frac{1}{\alpha} N \, ,$$

depicted in figure 6 by the radius-vector with the greater-than-unity slope.[14] By construction, *every* point on this aggregate supply curve is a point of maximum profits—for the real wage rate to which it corresponds.

Since labor is assumed to be the only variable input, the 45° radius vector in figure 6 represents total variable costs (or in Keynes' terminology, total prime cost)[15] in wage units, and is thus labeled. Correspondingly the vertical distance between these two radius-vectors represents profits in wage units: thus profits generated by the labor input (say) N_1 are equal to TU, which (in accordance with fig. 5) increase to RS at (say) the labor input N_2. In accordance with the property of a Cobb-Douglas function, the share of wages in the total value of output at both these inputs is constant and equal to

$$\alpha = N_1 U / N_1 T = N_2 S / N_2 R \, .$$

Assume now that the aggregate demand curve is represented in figure 6 by $D_w = {}^1 f(N)$. Then the "effective demand"—that is, "the value of D_w at the point of the aggregate demand function, where it is intersected by the aggregate supply function"[16] equals OA. The corresponding levels of employment and profits are, respectively, N_1 and TU. From figure 5 we see that the corresponding real wage rate that firms pay is $(w/p)_1$, which exceeds the rate (measuring their marginal disutility) upon which workers insist in order to supply that volume of labor.

Assume now that the aggregate demand function shifts upward to $D_w = {}^2 f(N)$. Then effective demand increases to OB, employment to

14. The vertical portion of this curve should for the moment be ignored.

15. See *GT*, p. 53, keeping in mind that user cost is being neglected (*GT*, p. 24, n. 2, cited on p. 124 above).

16. *GT*, p. 25 (cited on p. 124 above), with D replaced by D_w to make it consistent with the discussion here.

N_2, and profits to SR, while the real wage rate falls to $(w/p)_2$. Finally, if aggregate demand should shift upward to $D_w = {}^3f(N)$, effective demand would increase to OC and employment to N_F, at which level firms pay a real wage rate $(w/p)_F$ equal to that on which workers insist. This accordingly is the level of full employment: for employment cannot exceed this level, inasmuch as the real wage firms would then be willing to pay is less than the one on which workers would insist as commensurate with their marginal disutility. Correspondingly, the aggregate supply function becomes vertical at N_F.

Note finally that on the simplifying assumption of a constant money-wage rate (see p. 138 below), the foregoing analysis also determines the absolute price level. Thus if the money-wage rate is constant at w_0, then the foregoing real wage rates $(w_0/p)_1 > (w_0/p)_2 > (w_0/p)_F$ correspond, respectively, to the absolute price levels (say) $p_1 < p_2 < p_3$.

4. Let us now see to what extent the foregoing account accords with Keynes' exposition in the *General Theory*.

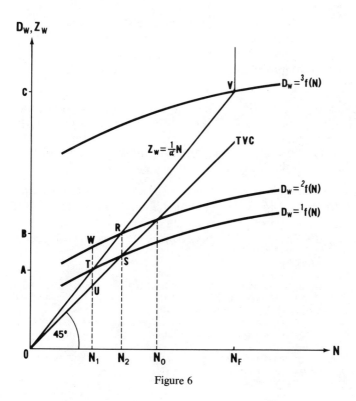

Figure 6

I start (as so many other students of Keynes' writings have started)[17] by emphasizing the basic consistency of the foregoing with Keynes' emphasis in chapter 2 of the *General Theory* that while he rejects the "second postulate" of the "classical theory of employment" (namely, that "the utility of the wage when a given volume of labor is employed is equal to the marginal disutility of that amount of employment"), he accepts the first one (namely, that the "wage is equal to the marginal product of labor") (*GT*, p. 5, italics removed; see also pp. 17–18). And since Keynes also accepts the classical law of diminishing returns,[18] this implies his acceptance of the following:

> In a given state of organisation, equipment and technique, the real wage earned by a unit of labour has a unique (inverse) correlation with the volume of employment. Thus *if* employment increases, then, in the short period, the reward per unit of labour in terms of wage-goods must, in general, decline and profits increase. [*GT*, p. 17, italics in original]

What I find particularly significant here—and particularly suggestive of figure 5 above—is Keynes' reference to the fact that an increase in employment generates not only a decline in real wages, but also an increase in profits. Indeed, Keynes attaches a long footnote here, demonstrating this increase by means of a numerical example.[19]

Figure 5 also provides a simple interpretation of the involved definition of "involuntary unemployment" Keynes gives in chapter 2, namely:

> Men are involuntarily unemployed if, in the event of a small rise in the price of wage-goods relatively to the money-wage, both the aggregate supply of labour willing to work for the current money-wage and the aggregate demand for it at that wage would be greater than the existing volume of employment. [*GT*, p. 15][20]

Specifically, all this definition means is that involuntary unemployment exists if the economy is on the demand curve for labor leftward of the point of intersection F. For at such a point (say, C in fig. 5) a rise in p, reducing the real wage to, say, $(w/p)_2$, will leave both the amounts

---

17. Cf., e.g., Modigliani (1944, sec. 2); Klein (1947, pp. 74–75).

18. Keynes' major reason for assuming this law to operate, however, is not the usual one (i.e., the changing proportion of labor to capital), but the fact that "as output increases, a given firm has to bring in labour which is less and less efficient" (*GT*, p. 42, see esp. n. 1). Indeed, on p. 295 he states that if laborers are "homogeneous and interchangeable in their efficiency to produce what is wanted," then constant returns would prevail.

19. Here is another instance where Keynes' exposition could have been much simplified by the use of a diagram; cf. p. 129 above.

20. In the original, the entire sentence is italicized.

supplied (N_3) and demanded (N_2) of labor greater than the existing volume of employment (N_1). (Note that the decrease in the amount of labor supplied caused by the decreased real wage [represented by the movement from Q to R on the supply curve in fig. 5] is regarded by Keynes as "voluntary unemployment" [*GT*, pp. 6, 15].) In contrast, if at point F there should be a further rise in p and hence a decline in w/p, it would not be true that the "supply of labour willing to work would be greater than the existing volume of employment," N_F. Hence N_F represents the point of full employment.

Let me now digress briefly to make two related observations. First, the reason Keynes generates the foregoing decline in the real wage rate by means, not of a decline in the money wage, but of an increase in the price level is related to his earlier oft-cited assumption that "Whilst workers will usually resist a reduction of money-wages, it is not their practice to withdraw their labour whenever there is a rise in the price of wage-goods" (*GT*, p. 9). On the basis of this statement, it is frequently contended that Keynes assumed that workers suffer from "money illusion." In the strict sense of the term, however, this is not the case. Indeed, immediately after the foregoing statement Keynes himself explicitly rejects the contention "sometimes" made that this behavior is "illogical" (*GT*, p. 9). And he refers the reader at this point to his discussion a few pages later where he explains that workers

> who consent to a reduction of money-wages relatively to others, will suffer a *relative* reduction in real wages, which is a sufficient justification for them to resist it. On the other hand it would be impracticable to resist every reduction of real wages, due to a change in the purchasing-power of money which affects all workers alike. [*GT*, p. 14, italics in original]

In brief, Keynes assumes that the labor supply function of workers in a given industry depends not only on their real wage, but on real wages in other industries as well. And I do not think I am reading too much meaning into Keynes if I interpret him as essentially making a distinction akin to that of current business-cycle theory (see Lucas 1973) and assuming that workers resist a reduction in their money wage because they do not know to what extent it is specific to their industry, and to what extent it is part of a reduction in the general wage level (cf. also *GT*, p. 267).[21] Correspondingly, if workers in a given industry were to

21. Peter Howitt has pointed out to me that this observation has already been made by Axel Leijonhufvud: see Alchian (1970, p. 44, n. 27). This theme—of the crucial distinction between effecting a wage reduction in one industry and effecting one in the economy as a whole—appears already (with respect to the export industry) in Keynes' *Economic Consequences of Mr. Churchill* (1925; *JMK* IX, pp. 211, 227–29). It also appears in the *Treatise:* for details, see *KMT*, pp. 122–23.

know with certainty that the latter were the case, they would react in the same way as to a "rise in the price of wage-goods." And this is the true meaning of absence of money illusion.

My second observation is that chapter 2 is contained in Book I of the *General Theory,* entitled "Introduction" (cf. p. 11, above). Correspondingly, the assumption of this chapter "that labour is not prepared to work for a lower money-wage" is made only "for the moment" (*GT*, p. 8). Indeed, on the following page Keynes stresses the implausibility of the assertion that "unemployment in the United States in 1932 was due . . . to labour obstinately refusing to accept a reduction of money-wages" (*GT*, p. 9)—an obvious allusion to the sharp decline (28 percent) that had taken place in United States money wages from 1929 to 1933 at the same time that unemployment grew to unprecedented levels (cf. above, p. 19, n. 15).

The temporary nature of this assumption is also indicated in the "brief summary of the theory of employment" which Keynes goes on to present in chapter 3, which is also part of Book I. Here Keynes assumes that

> the money-wage and other factor costs are constant per unit of labour employed. But this simplification, with which we shall dispense later, is introduced solely to facilitate the exposition. The essential character of the argument is precisely the same whether or not money-wages, etc., are liable to change. [*GT*, p. 27]

And, indeed, this assumption is dispensed with in chapter 19, appropriately entitled "Changes in Money Wages." Thus the many contentions to the contrary notwithstanding, the analysis of the *General Theory* as a whole does not depend on the assumption of absolutely rigid money wages. Needless to say, this does not mean that Keynes went to the opposite extreme of assuming wages to be perfectly flexible. Instead, Keynes' view of the real world was that "moderate changes in employment are not associated with very great changes in money-wages" (*GT*, p. 251). At the same time, Keynes emphasizes that there exists an "asymmetry" between the respective degrees of upward and downward wage flexibility: that, in particular, "workers, are disposed to resist a reduction in their money-rewards, and that there is no corresponding motive to resist an increase" (*GT*, p. 303).

Let me now return to my main argument and indicate some additional passages in the *General Theory* which accord with the story about figures 5 and 6 that has been told in the preceding section. There is, first of all, the passage from p. 28 of chapter 3 that has been cited on p. 124 above. And a little later on Keynes writes

> Thus the volume of employment is not determined by the marginal disutility of labour measured in terms of real wages, except in so far

as the supply of labour available at a given real wage sets a *maximum* level to employment. The propensity to consume and the rate of new investment determine between them the volume of employment, and the volume of employment is uniquely related to a given level of real wages—not the other way round. If the propensity to consume and the rate of new investment result in a deficient effective demand, the actual level of employment will fall short of the supply of labour potentially available at the existing real wage, and the equilibrium real wage will be *greater* than the marginal disutility of the equilibrium level of employment. [*GT*, p. 30, italics in original]

Similarly revealing are several passages in Keynes' chapter 21, "The Employment Function." This function relates the level of employment to the different levels of effective demand (in terms of wage units) generated by shifts in the aggregate demand function caused (say) by "changes in the rate of investment" (*GT*, p. 281). Thus points *T*, *R*, and *V* in figure 6 above are points on the employment function. Clearly, they are also points on the aggregate supply function; indeed, Keynes states that the employment function is the inverse of the aggregate supply function defined in wage units (*GT*, p. 280). Keynes then goes on to say:

Now, in so far as the classical theory assumes that real wages are always equal to the marginal disutility of labour and that the latter increases when employment increases, so that the labour supply will fall off, *cet. par.*, if real wages are reduced, it is assuming that in practice it is impossible to increase expenditure in terms of wage-units. . . .

Moreover, it would in this event, be impossible to increase employment by increasing expenditure in terms of money; for money-wages would rise proportionally to the increased money expenditure so that there would be no increase of expenditure in terms of wage-units and consequently no increase in employment. But if the classical assumption does not hold good, it will be possible to increase employment by increasing expenditure in terms of money until real wages have fallen to equality with the marginal disutility of labour, at which point there will, by definition, be full employment. [*GT*, p. 284]

And a few pages later he writes:

We have shown that when effective demand is deficient there is under-employment of labour in the same sense that there are men unemployed who would be willing to work at less than the existing real wage. Consequently, as effective demand increases, employment increases, though at a real wage equal to or less than the existing one, until a point comes at which there is no surplus of labour available at the then existing real wage; i.e., no more men (or hours of labour) available unless money-wages rise (from this point onwards) *faster* than prices. The next problem is to consider what will happen if, when this point has been reached, expenditure still continues to increase.

Up to this point the decreasing return from applying more labour to a given capital equipment has been offset by the acquiescence of labour in a diminishing real wage. But after this point a unit of labour would require the inducement of the equivalent of an increased quantity of product [i.e., increased real wage], whereas the yield from applying a further unit would be a diminished quantity of product. The conditions of strict equilibrium require, therefore, that wages and prices, and consequently profits also, should all rise in the same proportion as expenditure, the "real" position, including the volume of output and employment, being left unchanged in all respects. We have reached, that is to say, a situation in which the crude quantity theory of money (interpreting "velocity" to mean "income-velocity") is fully satisfied; for output does not alter and prices rise in exact proportion to *MV*. [*GT*, p. 289, italics in original]

Both here and in the preceding passage, Keynes' interpretation of the classical position is that since full employment prevails, an increase in aggregate demand in money terms cannot cause an increase in output and hence in employment; it follows that the marginal product of labour and hence the real wage rate also remain unchanged; but since the increase in money demand has generated an upward movement of prices, this means that the money-wage rate must rise in the same proportion as prices.

The argument in the second paragraph of this last passage is apparently the "further develop[ment] in chapter 21" to which Keynes refers the reader in the concluding paragraph of his chapter 15 on liquidity preference, in which he states:

For purposes of the real world it is a great fault in the quantity theory that it does not distinguish between changes in prices which are a function of changes in output, and those which are a function of changes in the wage-unit. [*GT*, p. 209]

In particular, the distinction which Keynes draws here is that between a (say) increase in prices accompanying an increase in output which, because of the diminishing returns which it generates, causes an increase in per-unit costs of production even with an unchanged wage-unit; and an increase in prices accompanying an (equiproportionate) increase in the wage-unit, output remaining unchanged. The increase in aggregate demand at full employment described in the passage just cited from chapter 21 is clearly an example of the latter. On the other hand, an increase in aggregate demand under conditions of unemployment might generate a price increase for both reasons: for in an adumbration of the Phillips-curve analysis, Keynes assumes that "the wage-unit will tend to rise before full employment has been reached" (*GT*, p. 296; see also ibid., pp. 173, 249, 253, 301). In such a case prices will obviously rise more than proportionately to the wage-unit, for the increase in employment is necessarily accompanied by a decrease in the real wage rate.[22]

The story about figures 5 and 6 also provides a simple interpretation of Keynes' oft-cited delphic pronouncement in chapter 2 of the *General Theory* that:

> In assuming that the wage bargain determines the real wage the classical school have slipt in an illicit assumption. For there may be *no* method available to labour as a whole whereby it can bring the wage-goods equivalent of the general level of money-wages into conformity with the marginal disutility of the current volume of employment. There may exist no expedient by which labour as a whole can reduce its *real* wage to a given figure by making revised *money* bargains with the entrepreneurs. This will be our contention. We shall endeavour to show that primarily it is certain other forces which determine the general level of real wages. [*GT*, p. 13, italics in original]

Now, the way a reduction in money wages might increase aggregate demand and hence employment through its prior effect on the real quantity of money and hence (through the liquidity-preference equation) on the rate of interest is analyzed by Keynes in his chapter 19, "Changes in Money-Wages," to which he repeatedly refers in chapter 2. But in chapter 19 Keynes also stresses the adverse expectations that might be generated by a wage reduction. Thus one can conceive of circumstances in which such expectations might be sufficiently strong to prevent the reduction in the money-wage rate from having any net effect on aggregate demand, hence on equilibrium output, and hence on employment. It follows that in such circumstances the reduction in the money-wage rate will not affect the real wage rate. This interpretation

22. That Keynes consistently assumed the real wage rate to decline as employment, and hence output, increased along his employment (or aggregate supply) function has rightly been emphasized by Weintraub (1958, pp. 31–32, 35; 1961, p. 36). See also Davidson and Smolensky (1964, p. 123). At one time (see *KMT*, p. 91, n. 13) I thought that the passage on pp. 248–49 of the *General Theory* was an exception to this rule. Subsequent discussions with David L. Roberts, however, convinced me that I was wrong: for details, see Patinkin (1979, p. 168, n. 14).

I might note that Keynes' emphasis on the distinction between a change in the price level relative to money wages and an equiproportionate change in the two echoes one of the major themes of his *Treatise* (cf., e.g., vol. I, p. 171), though in a different context: for the *Treatise* does not make use of the law of diminishing marginal productivity, or for that matter of any marginal notion (*KMT*, pp. 13, 94).

receives support from Keynes' statement (in the passage already cited on p. 139 above) that:

> The propensity to consume and the rate of new investment determine between them the volume of employment, and the volume of employment is uniquely related to a given level of real wages—not the other way round. [*GT*, p. 30]

It is, however, characteristic of Keynes' analysis in the *General Theory* that he does not specify the dynamic market mechanism involved in the preceding case. In terms of figures 5 and 6, under the assumption that aggregate demand is represented by $D_w = {}^1 f(N)$, so that the economy is initially at equilibrium position T, Keynes does not trace through the dynamic process by which a decline in the money wage rate generates an initial decline in the real wage rate from $(w/p)_1$ to $(w/p)_2$, which increases the level of employment from N_1 to N_2 with a corresponding increase in output, which then generates an excess of aggregate supply over aggregate demand (assumed in accordance with the preceding paragraph to remain unaffected by the wage decline), thus bringing the price level down until the initial real wage $(w/p)_1$ and corresponding level of employment N_1 are restored.

The story that has been told above about figures 5 and 6 also provides part of the answer to the puzzle that has been noted on p. 128 above in connection with Keynes' discussion of Say's law. Under the assumption of this law, the aggregate demand curve in figure 6 would coincide with the aggregate supply curve "for *all* values of N" (*GT*, pp. 25–26, italics in original). Nevertheless, the exact value of N that obtains in the economy is not a matter of indifference to entrepreneurs: for the larger this value, the greater (as we have seen in fig. 5) their profits. Thus the "forces of competition between entrepreneurs may be expected to push it [i.e., N] to this maximum value [i.e., N_F]" (*GT*, p. 29, cited in full on p. 128 above).

Note once again Keynes' failure to specify the exact nature of the dynamic market mechanism—that is, "the forces of competition"—which brings this result about. Furthermore, in the present case the "forces of competition" must first operate not "between entrepreneurs," but between unemployed workers, causing them to reduce their money (and hence real) wage and thus stimulate an increase in the amount of labour demanded and hence output supplied. But in contrast with the preceding case, Say's law assures that this increased output will be matched by an increased demand, so that the economy will continue to expand in this way until the full-employment level N_F is reached.

5. So much for the points of accord between the story of figures 5 and 6 and that of the *General Theory*, points that for the most part have been

stressed in many interpretations of the *General Theory* since its appearance. I turn now to two hitherto overlooked points of inconsistency.

The first such point has already been indicated above (p. 127). If, following Keynes, the aggregate demand curve (say, $D_w = {}^2f(N)$ in fig. 6) is assumed to be perceived by entrepreneurs as a whole and to represent their expected proceeds, then its intersection with the aggregate supply curve at point R is not (as Keynes contended) the point at which "entrepreneurs' expectations of profits will be maximised" (*GT*, p. 25).[23] Indeed, relative to other attainable points on this aggregate demand function, it is (in terms of wage units) the point of minimum profits! For no matter what the form of the aggregate supply function in figure 6, the total-variable-cost curve (under the assumption that labor is the only factor of production) has a unitary slope; on the other hand, the aggregate demand curve is assumed to have a less-than-unitary slope. Hence the further the level of employment falls below N_2 in figure 6, the greater the excess of proceeds over costs, and hence the greater the profits.

By making what I would consider to be relatively minor changes in Keynes' exposition, we can however remove this inconsistency between it and the analysis of figure 6. In particular, let us (in proper analogy to the Marshallian demand curve) assume that the aggregate demand curve is *not* perceived by entrepreneurs; and let us accordingly describe this curve as representing not "the proceeds which entrepreneurs expect," but (as in current expositions of Keynesian theory) the total consumption and investment expenditures which households and firms respectively plan to make at different levels of employment and hence income. The analysis would then proceed to point out that if entrepreneurs were to employ (say) N_1 men, they (the entrepreneurs) would find themselves with actual aggregate proceeds, N_1W, in excess of the aggregate supply price, N_1T, which they had expected to prevail when they decided to employ N_1 men; hence with actual per-unit market price greater than marginal cost; hence with an incentive to expand output in the attempt to increase profits—and that this dynamic process (which involves a declining per-unit demand price and, on the assumption of a constant money wage, rising per-unit supply price) would continue until the economy reaches equilibrium point R on figure 6, where aggregate demand and supply prices are equal: that is, where, for the representative competitive firm, market price equals marginal cost. Thus from the viewpoint of such a firm, R is a point of maximum profits in the sense that the firm has no profit incentive to depart from it.

---

23. Cited in full on p. 124 above; see also the passage cited there from *GT*, p. 55.

In brief, it seems that in the aforementioned passages, Keynes did not distinguish properly between propositions which are valid for the representative firm operating under conditions of perfect competition and those valid for firms as a whole, operating as one unit. A related possibility is that Keynes confused the valid proposition that, for the competitive representative firm, *every* point on the aggregate supply curve is a point of maximum profits—for the real wage to which it corresponds; and the invalid proposition that the point of intersection of the supply curve with the demand curve marks the *maximum maximorum*. Yet another possibility is that the source of Keynes' confusion may have been his basic proposition that "if employment increases . . . profits increase" (*GT*, p. 17; see above, p. 136)—which may have led him into believing that expanding employment to the limit set by aggregate demand generates the maximum attainable profit. The fallacy in this line of reasoning lies in the failure to realize that the foregoing proposition describes what happens to profits if (in terms of figure 6) entrepreneurial receipts are measured by the aggregate supply curve; as we have just seen, it does not describe what happens if these receipts are measured (as they should be) by the aggregate demand curve. More precisely, only in the case of Say's law—which implies the identity of these two curves—is this line of reasoning correct (cf. above, p. 142).

Note finally that if Keynes' theory of effective demand is interpreted as being concerned *solely* with equilibrium points, then the puzzle of his referring to such a point as one of "maximum profits" is only deepened. For to any (normally shaped) pair of aggregate demand and supply curves there corresponds only one equilibrium point—so that the whole notion of "maximum" becomes meaningless. In brief, according to this interpretation, Keynes' theory of effective demand is not concerned with any other (disequilibrium) points with which profits at the equilibrium point could be compared.

The second point of inconsistency between Keynes' presentation in the *General Theory* and the analysis of section 3 above is a much more serious one. In particular, on the one occasion in the *General Theory* that Keynes specified the form of the aggregate supply function, he did so in a way which identified it not with the profit-maximizing supply curve $Z_w = (1/\alpha)N$ in figure 6, but with the 45° radius-vector representing total variable costs. In Keynes' words:

> For example, let us take $Z_w = \phi(N)$, or alternatively $Z = W\phi(N)$ as the aggregate supply function (where W is the wage-unit and $WZ_w = Z$). Then, since the proceeds of the marginal product is equal to the marginal factor-cost $[\Delta N]$ at every point on the aggregate supply curve, we have $\Delta N = \Delta A_w - \Delta U_w = \Delta Z_w = \Delta\phi(N)$, that is to say

$\phi'(N)=1$; provided that factor cost bears a constant ratio to wage cost, and that the aggregate supply function for each firm (the number of which is assumed to be constant) is independent of the number of men employed in other industries, so that the terms of the above equation, which hold good for each individual entrepreneur, can be summed for the entrepreneurs as a whole. This means that, if wages are constant and other factor costs are a constant proportion of the wages-bill, the aggregate supply function is linear with a slope given by the reciprocal of the money-wage. [*GT*, p. 55, n. 2]

The analysis of section 3 above not only demonstrates the invalidity of Keynes' description of the supply curve as having a constant unitary slope, but also suggests that the immediate cause of Keynes' error was his failure to distinguish between the supply function and the production function. More specifically, under conditions of perfect competition it is of course true that (in the words of the footnote) "the proceeds of the marginal product is equal to the marginal factor-cost at every point on the aggregate supply curve": indeed, this is an alternative statement of the above-mentioned fact that every point on the aggregate supply curve is one of maximum profits. But the proper mathematical formulation of Keynes' statement is not (as he would have it) $\Delta N = \Delta \phi(N)$, but

$$(14) \qquad \Delta N = \frac{p}{w} \Delta \psi(N) \, ,$$

where as before $\psi(N)$ and $\phi(N)$ represent the aggregate production and supply functions, respectively. Alternatively, in terms of equation (2) above translated into wage units, the proper formulation of Keynes' footnote statement is

$$(15) \qquad \frac{p}{w} \psi'(N) = 1 \, .$$

Thus it is not the slope of the aggregate supply function which is unity at every one of its points, but the slope (measured at each point in the wage unit corresponding to it) of the production function.

Was Keynes' implicit, erroneous identification of the production and supply functions transitory or permanent? Was it a chance error of this footnote or a systematic component of his thinking? The evidence is not clear, but I think the latter alternative is closer to the truth. Thus in the mid-1934 draft of the *General Theory*, Keynes defined the "employment function" $D_w = F(N)$—which was to evolve into the aggregate supply function of the final draft[24]—and stated that it shows how

24. See *KMT*, p. 74, n. 14.

"an effective demand equal to D_w leads to N units of labour being employed" (*JMK* XIII, p. 440). Again, in the 1935 lecture on Keynes' theory in which, with the master's blessings, Robert B. Bryce brought the gospel to the London School of Economics—"the nearest concentration of heathen available from Cambridge," as he was to put it many years later[25]—he simply defined the "supply function of consumption goods" as the function which "will relate the quantity of labour which will be employed in making consumption goods, N_1, to the expenditure on consumption goods, C"—and gave a corresponding definition of the supply function of investment goods.[26] Thus in both instances we seem to have a description of a technological relationship between an input of labor and an output (albeit in value terms) of goods.

Be that as it may, there is another aspect of Keynes' error in the foregoing footnote which is more likely to have constituted a systematic, and not chance, component of his thinking. I am referring to its implicit identification of the aggregate supply curve with the total-variable-cost curve. For as I have suggested elsewhere (*KMT*, pp. 86, 91–92), this identification would seem to represent the vestigial influence of Keynes' way of thinking in the *Treatise*, in which there is no reference to profit maximization and marginal analysis, and instead the basic analytical categories of the system (as expressed in the famous "fundamental equations") are per-unit demand price, on the one hand, and per-unit variable costs, on the other; correspondingly, it is the very existence of a difference between these two—that is, the very existence of profits, in contradistinction to the desire to maximize them—which provides the motive force of the system of the *Treatise*. In a similar fashion, Keynes of the *General Theory* may have assumed that the motive force of the system was provided by the difference between the aggregate demand price (i.e., total proceeds) and aggregate supply price defined as total variable costs, without realizing that this assumption was inconsistent with the marginal analysis which it was his declared objective to apply in that book.

I have on an earlier occasion (Patinkin 1979, p. 171) noted that evidence in support of this conjecture is provided (inter alia) by the third set of proofs of the *General Theory* (dating from 1935), in which Keynes refers to the "supply price" not as something related to marginal costs, but as "the aggregate cost of production" (*JMK* XIV, pp. 370, 374; on the dating, see ibid., p. 351). And now additional striking evidence has become available from some newly discovered fragments of certain draft chapters of the *General Theory* which Moggridge has

25. See Bryce 1977, p. 40.
26. Bryce 1935, p. 132; for Keynes' blessings, see his letter to Bryce as reproduced in Patinkin and Leith (1977, pp. 127–28).

dated as having been written at various times during 1933.[27] For in one of them we find the following passage, with its pregnant reference to the *Treatise:*

If over any period the aggregate expenditure is approximately equal to the costs which have been incurred on output which has been finished during that period, the firms will have made in the aggregate neither gain nor loss, the losses of individual firms being exactly balanced by the gains of other firms. Thus assuming the firms to be similar in their response to a given expectation of gain or loss (a simplification which we shall remove in later chapters), there will be no tendency, apart from time-lags in changing over from one job to another, for the aggregate of employment to change. . . .

But if the aggregate expenditure varies in a different manner from aggregate costs, then the diminished incentive to employment in one direction will not be exactly balanced by an increased incentive to employment in another direction. If aggregate expenditure increases relatively to aggregate costs, there will be, on balance, a greater incentive to employment than before; and if aggregate expenditure decreases relatively to aggregate costs, there will be a diminished incentive to employment. Thus fluctuations in employment will primarily depend on fluctuations in aggregate expenditure relatively to aggregate costs.

. . . In my *Treatise on Money* the equality of savings and investment, as there defined, was a condition equivalent to the equality of aggregate expenditure and aggregate costs, but I failed to point out that this by itself provided only for neutral equilibrium and not for, what one might call, optimum equilibrium.[28] [*JMK* XXIX, pp. 90–92]

In brief, Keynes of this passage essentially treats the aggregate variable cost curve as if it were the aggregate supply curve.[29]

Similarly, in another fragment from this draft we find the following passage:

The law of production in an entrepreneur economy can be stated as follows. A process of production will not be started up, unless the money proceeds expected from the sale of the output are at least equal to the money costs which could be avoided by not starting up the process. [*JMK* XXIX, p. 78]

27. Though I have reservations about the dating of some of this material (cf. Patinkin 1980, pp. 18–19), I shall for convenience accept it in what follows. For my present purpose, it suffices that these were early drafts of the book.
28. By which, as is clear from the context, Keynes meant equilibrium at full employment. Cf. also Keynes' use in the *General Theory* (p. 164) of "optimum rate of investment" to describe that rate that generates full employment.
29. Cf. also the ambiguous passages in the same vein from this and other 1933 drafts on pp. 64 (lines 26–29), 80 (lines 5–8), and 98 (lines 13–14) of *JMK* XXIX.

Now, this passage as such is correct: as between producing a certain amount and not producing at all, entrepreneurs will choose not to produce at all if they cannot at least cover their variable costs (cf. p. 126 above). But, significantly enough, the passage does not go on to indicate that another "law of production in an entrepreneur economy" is that once variable costs are covered, entrepreneurial decisions are governed by marginal costs.

This is not to say that elsewhere in this draft Keynes did not recognize the role of marginal costs. Thus at a slightly later point he wrote:

> Each firm calculates the prospective selling prices of its output and its variable cost in respect of output on various possible scales of production. Its variable cost per unit is not, as a rule, constant for all volumes of output but increases as output increases. Output is then pushed to the point at which the prospective selling price no longer exceeds the marginal variable cost. In this way the volume of output, and hence the volume of employment, is determined. [*JMK* XXIX, p. 98]

But the very fact that within a few pages of the same draft Keynes could present two such different analyses of the determination of the equilibrium level of employment—one in terms of a comparison between "aggregate expenditure" and "aggregate costs," which corresponds to a comparison between price and average cost, and one in terms of a comparison between price and "marginal variable cost"—is itself evidence that he did not at this time have a full and precise understanding of the difference between these two kinds of cost.

This is also the impression created by other passages in the newly discovered 1933 fragments. Specifically, these fragments contain such statements as:

> For small changes in price [P] and output [O] we have . . . $P\Delta O = W\Delta N$ [where W = money wage rate and N = employment], i.e., the value of the marginal product is equal to its variable cost. . . . [*JMK* XXIX, p. 72]

> The classical theory makes the fundamental assumptions, (1) that the value of the marginal unit of output is equal to the variable cost of producing it (value and cost being measured in the same unit), and (2) that the marginal utility of output is equal to the marginal disutility of effort. [*JMK* XXIX, p. 101]

Now, if these statements are interpreted in accordance with the strict rules of grammar, they are correct: for if (in the first passage) we relate "its variable cost" to the antecedent "marginal product," then we have "the variable cost of the marginal product," which is, of course, the marginal cost. And a similar statement holds for the second passage. But I think it less likely that Keynes was engaging in grammatical acrobatics on the brink of error than that he was simply failing to distinguish properly between marginal and variable.

But the most significant passage in these 1933 drafts is one in which Keynes does distinguish between marginal and variable costs, only to express his preference for the latter as an explanation of entrepreneurial behavior in the real world. In Keynes' words:

> Above all, however, we are basing our conclusions about employment on the proper criterion, namely whether it is expected to *pay* a firm in possession of a capital equipment to spend money on incurring variable costs; i.e., whether the result of spending money on employment and of selling the output is expected to result in a larger net sum of money at the end of the accounting period than if the money had been retained. Other criteria, such as the relation between the real output which a given employment will yield and the disutility or real cost of that employment, *or the relation between the real wages of a given employment and the amount of its marginal output*, are not appropriate to the actual nature of business decisions in a world in which prices are subject to change during an accounting period, such changes being themselves a function *inter alia* of the amount of investment during the period. [*JMK* XXIX, p. 66, second set of italics added]

In brief, unlike the position he was to take in the final version of the *General Theory* (pp. 5, 17–18), Keynes in this passage rejected not only the ''second postulate'' of the ''classical theory of employment,'' but the first one as well (cf. p. 136 above). And this is what may have lain behind his identification of the aggregate supply curve with the aggregate variable cost curve.[30]

Let me conclude this discussion of Keynes' aggregate supply curve with the following two observations. First, there can be no doubt that at the time he wrote the various 1933 drafts of the *General Theory*, Keynes was not completely clear in his mind about certain aspects of price theory, and about this curve in particular. This brings me to my second point: for the 1933 draft was just that—a draft; and who of us would wish to be judged by rough early drafts of what we ultimately publish! My justification for doing so in this case, however, is that at at least one point where the aggregate supply curve is discussed in the

---

30. Note that the foregoing passage is not quite an adumbration of the ''full-cost'' principle, for the passage refers only to variable costs. It is interesting that several years after the publication of the *General Theory*—in his 1939 reply to Dunlop and Tarshis (see above, p. 101, n. 21)—Keynes again expressed doubts about the extent to which actual business decisions were based on the marginal principle, this time with respect to pricing policy (Keynes 1939, p. 407; I am indebted to Martin Weitzman for bringing this passage to my attention).

final version of the *General Theory*, we find what seems to be a continued manifestation of a basic error of this early draft—and I am of course referring to that footnote on p. 55 which describes the supply curve in a way that is identical with the variable-cost curve; while at other points where the supply curve is discussed, we find not a refined and precise presentation of it, but an obscure one—and I am of course referring to the passage from chapter 3 of the *General Theory* with which I began this discussion (above, pp. 123–24).

And that is my main point: that the obscurity with which the aggregate supply curve is presented in the *General Theory* is a sign not of profundity, but of obscurity: not, as some would have us believe, of a deep underlying analytical framework in which everything falls into place, but of the same confusions and imprecisions which manifested themselves in the 1933 drafts of the book and which continued to live on in Keynes' mind furtively, below the surface, through the final version as well.

6. If Keynes' presentation of his theory of effective demand is guilty of such basic errors, how is it that this has received little if any attention until now? And, in particular, how is it that these errors were not caught in the careful prepublication scrutiny to which Richard Kahn and Joan Robinson, surely experts in price theory, subjected the successive proofs of the *General Theory?*

To these most natural questions I suggest the following answers. First, the errors are not that basic. Second, in some sense, these errors were implicitly noted in the early Keynesian literature. And, third, these are not the only technical errors which were not caught by the prepublication critics of the *General Theory*.

Let me elaborate on these points, in reverse order. Kahn and Robinson did undoubtedly apprehend various technical errors in the earlier drafts of the *General Theory;* indeed, it may well be that it was due in part to their criticisms that the more blatant errors of the 1933 draft do not appear in the final version. At the same time, there are technical errors which escaped even their attention and, in some cases, the attention of many postpublication critics of the *General Theory* as well. I am referring to the incorrect description of the ordinary supply curve, which was caught only after the first printing of the *General Theory;*[31] the incorrect elasticity formula used to analyze the implications of the quantity theory, which was not noted until six years after publication,

---

31. Bottom of p. 44. In the second and third proofs of the book, as well as in its first printing, the term representing user costs was omitted; this was corrected in subsequent printings. See *JMK* XIV, pp. 390–91. See also the 1936 correspondence with Hugh Townshend, a former pupil of Keynes, who brought this omission to Keynes' attention after the book was first published (*JMK* XXIX, pp. 243–44).

and which was then twice independently rediscovered, after another fourteen years and twenty-six years, respectively;[32] and in the incorrect description of the relation between changes in the size of the multiplier and changes in the marginal propensity to consume which, to the best of my knowledge, has not been pointed out before.[33]

Furthermore, there is a special reason why Kahn and Robinson might not have been able to catch the errors in the description of the aggregate supply curve upon which I have dwelt in this chapter: for significantly enough, both the footnote description of the aggregate supply curve on p. 55 of the *General Theory* and the statement on p. 25 that profits are maximized at the point of intersection of the aggregate demand and supply curves appear for the first time in the published version of the *General Theory*. So these errors could not have been caught in the proof stage by the keen eyes of Kahn and Robinson for the simple reason that these errors were not then present![34]

Insofar as the lack of attention to these passages in the earlier Keynesian literature is concerned, I feel that this may actually have reflected its awareness of their problematic nature and resulting "revealed preference" for ignoring them.[35] An even more telling indication of this "revealed preference" is that this literature not only ignored these problematic passages, but rapidly replaced them by the

---

32. See *GT*, p. 305 (line 5), which presents and then applies an incorrect formula, while at the same time referring to the correct formula which appears on p. 285 (line 3 from bottom). This error was first pointed out by Palander (1942), as cited by Borch (1969). As Jacob Frenkel has pointed out to me, it was subsequently noted independently by Bronfenbrenner (1956, p. 107, n. 1) and Naylor (1968, pp. 172–73). The error has been noted in the new edition of the *General Theory* (p. 385) that was published as *JMK* VII.

33. In a footnote to his discussion of the multiplier (*GT*, p. 126, n. 2), Keynes defines the fraction

$$\frac{\Delta Y}{Y} \bigg/ \frac{\Delta I}{I} = \frac{\Delta Y}{Y} \cdot \frac{Y - C}{\Delta Y - \Delta C} = \left(1 - \frac{C}{Y}\right) \bigg/ \left(1 - \frac{dC}{dY}\right)$$

(which I shall designate as Q) and then goes on to say:

As wealth increases dC/dY diminishes, but C/Y also diminishes. Thus the fraction increases or diminishes according as consumption increases or diminishes in a smaller or greater proportion than income.

It can, however, readily be shown that

$$\text{sign} \frac{dQ}{dY} = \text{sign} \left[\left(1 - \frac{dC}{dY}\right) \frac{C}{Y^2} (1 - \eta_{CY}) + \left(1 - \frac{C}{Y}\right) \frac{d^2C}{dY^2}\right],$$

where η_{CY} is the income elasticity of consumption. Under Keynes' assumptions in the text to which this footnote is attached (namely, $C/Y < 1$, $dC/dY < 1$, $d^2C/dY^2 < 0$), the second term in the square brackets is negative; hence, Keynes to the contrary, $\eta_{CY} < 1$ does not imply sign $dQ/dY > 0$. Note too that the additional assumption that Keynes makes in the footnote just cited, namely, $d(C/Y)/dY < 0$, actually implies $\eta_{CY} < 1$—and it is also not clear if Keynes realized this.

34. This can be seen from an examination of the relevant proofs as reproduced in *JMK* XIV, pp. 370–71, 398–418.

35. For further details, see pp. 156–57 below.

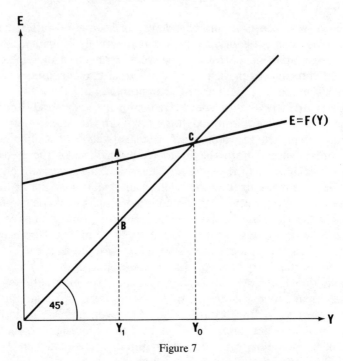

Figure 7

analysis depicted in the familiar diagonal-cross diagram of figure 7. The 45° line in this diagram can properly be identified as the aggregate supply curve—provided notice is taken (though, admittedly, it generally was not)[36] that every point on this line corresponds to a different real wage rate: namely, that rate corresponding to the marginal product of the labor input necessary to produce the output in question. The point of intersection between this curve and the aggregate demand curve is not described in this literature as one at which profits are maximized relative to other attainable points. And the dynamic market forces which bring the economy to this point from (say) the level Y_1 are described in terms, not of the excess of "aggregate demand price" over "aggregate supply price," but of the unplanned drawing down of inventories.[37]

36. As has been properly emphasized by Sidney Weintraub (1958, pp. 31–32, 35; 1961, p. 36); see also Davidson and Smolensky (1964, p. 123). See also the discussion and accompanying diagrams in chaps. IX:3 and XIII:2 of my *Money, Interest, and Prices* (1956, 1965).

37. Though Keynes did at one point in the *General Theory* recognize the possible influence of such a dynamic force, he did so only as a footnote concession to Hawtrey (*GT*, p. 51n), and at a later point also stated that "Mr. Hawtrey has not convinced me that this is the factor to stress" (*GT*, p. 76). I might also note that this footnote concession appeared already in the first proofs of the *General Theory*. Correspondingly, the comment to which Keynes refers in it was made by Hawtrey not on the *General Theory* (which he did not see before the proof stage), but on the *Treatise*. For details, see *JMK* XIV, p. 398 and *KMT*, pp. 54, 60.

Finally, insofar as the significance of the errors is concerned, errors that can be "corrected" by simply revising or disregarding two or three brief passages in an entire book (especially when one is a footnote inserted at the "last minute") cannot be that basic. More generally, the importance of an error in a book must be judged relative to its central message. And with this I return to the theme of my introductory lecture (above, pp. 8–11: the central message of the *General Theory* is the theory of effective demand cum equilibrating effect of changes in output generated by discrepancies between aggregate demand and supply; and the force of that message is not significantly weakened by the existence of technical errors or ambiguities about the exact nature of these curves and of the related dynamic process. Alternatively, in terms of a metaphor I have used before (above, pp. 16–17), these errors are minor deviations from the regression line that represents the central message of the *General Theory*.

Postscript: A Plea for Common Sense

It is a well-known fact that Orthodox Jews keep their heads covered, especially on religious occasions. Yet the Five Books of Moses—whence all commandments originate—contain no reference to this practice. Nothing daunted, generations of Talmudic students have (in one of the classic in-jokes of the rabbinical seminaries) found the necessary scriptural basis for this practice in the verse of Genesis which reads: "And Jacob went out from Beersheba and went toward Haran" (Genesis 28:10). Now, goes the argument, a good Jew like Jacob would obviously not go out bareheaded! Here, then, is scriptural proof that one must keep one's head covered.

I am afraid that "Jacob's principle" (if I may coin a phrase) has guided some modern-day Keynesians who, starting from the Weintraub-Davidson interpretation of Keynes' theory of effective de-

This postscript is an abridged and slightly revised version of my article "Keynes' Aggregate Supply Function: A Plea for Common Sense," *History of Political Economy* 10 (Winter 1978): 577–96. This started out as a reply to Roberts (1978) but went on to deal with general issues as well. Only the portions dealing with such issues have been reproduced here.

Without holding them in any way responsible, I would like to thank Stanley Fischer, Jacob Frenkel, Edi Karni, Ephraim Kleiman, and Nehemiah Shiff for comments on earlier drafts of the original article. I would also like to express my appreciation to my research assistants, Avraham Kamara and Peter Spiro, for their efficient help.

Most of the work on the original article was carried out while I was serving as a Fellow of the Institute for Advanced Studies at the Hebrew University of Jerusalem. Financial aid was received from a Ford Foundation grant, administered by the Maurice Falk Institute for Economic Research in Israel. The article was completed with the aid of NSF Grant no. SOC77–12212 while serving during 1977–78 as Ford Foundation Visiting Research Professor at the University of Chicago. I am greatly indebted to all these institutions.

mand,[38] have taken it as axiomatic that Keynes could not have been so "incompetent a theorist" as to have been guilty of the kind of errors and confusions that have been documented above; correspondingly, in the face of the evidence,[39] they have contended that Keynes was "one universally acclaimed to be Marshallian in method" and that he accordingly provided in the *General Theory* "a logical consistent framework for aggregate demand and supply analysis."[40] The Weintraub-Davidson interpretation also contends that Keynes' aggregate supply function is a basic component of the *General Theory*, and that because it fails to present it as such, the standard version of the Keynesian system (viz., the *IS-LM* analysis which Hicks presented in his classic 1937 article "Mr. Keynes and the 'Classics' ") also fails egregiously to represent what Keynes really meant.

Actually, one who aspires to be a historian of ideas might be well advised to eschew Jacob's principle almost entirely; at least he should be careful to apply it from a proper historical perspective. For the history of ideas is in large part the history of the false starts, errors, and confusions that have generally attended the emergence of new ideas; correspondingly, it is the history of the slow process by which ideas that were initially considered complicated and difficult to understand ultimately became clarified and frequently even commonplace. And

38. For references, see n. 10 above.

39. In fairness, I should point out that this did not then include the new evidence from the materials of *JMK* XXIX presented on pp. 146–49 above.

40. The three quotations in this sentence are respectively from Roberts (1978, pp. 550, 575); Tuchscherer (1979, p. 104, n. 11); and Roberts (1978, p. 576). Both of these writers reaffirm the Weintraub-Davidson interpretation of Keynes' theory of effective demand. In the aforementioned footnote, Tuchscherer also says that "although there is no explicit evidence establishing Keynes' utilization of the standard micro techniques employed above, I am firmly convinced that he proceeded along these lines." See also n. 4 on p. 100 of Tuchscherer's article. I might in this context also mention the views of Harcourt (1977), Froyen (1978), Wells (1978), and Marty (1979), all of whom have effectively contended that since it is analytically incorrect to define the aggregate supply curve as identical with the total-variable-cost curve, Keynes could not have so defined it. In a related manner, some of the foregoing writers have, in the attempt to support their contention that Keynes correctly derived his aggregate supply function from marginal analysis, cited various statements of Keynes which merely indicate his intention to do so. I might also note that it is a mark of their lack of concern with the actual text of the *General Theory* that, despite their voluminous writings on Keynes' aggregate supply curve, neither Weintraub nor Davidson has ever referred to Keynes' own description of this curve (so much at variance with theirs) contained in n. 2 on p. 55 of the *General Theory* (see above, pp. 144–45). (For details of a similar lack of concern by Minsky, see Patinkin [1978, p. 582, n. 12].) It is also indicative of Weintraub's approach to the *General Theory* that when he recently referred to the article (1979) in which I first presented the criticisms of his interpretation that appear in this chapter, he did not address himself to the substantive points involved, but sufficed with the statement that "just as the Good Book lends itself to diverse interpretations by theologians so . . . [are there] different perceptions of Keynes' Great Book" (Weintraub 1980, p. 79).

what better example could there be than Keynes' own originally strange and difficult theory of effective demand, which has by now long since become standard fare for any introductory textbook in economics.

It should accordingly be obvious that whether or not an error is sufficiently serious to justify castigating its perpetrator as "incompetent" depends crucially on the stage of development of the idea in question at which it was committed. Thus, for example, no one would consider citing Jacob Viner's famous complaint in his pioneering 1931 article "Cost Curves and Supply Curves" (about the stubborn draftsman who refused to draw the long-run average-cost curve as one passing through the minimum points of all the short-run curves, and not lying above any of them) as grounds for calling Viner an "incompetent theorist." In subsequent reprints of this article, Viner deliberately left this error uncorrected so as to provide "pleasure" to "future teachers and students" (Viner 1952, p. 227); he might well have added that it also provided a valuable object lesson to historians of economic thought.

Indeed, it is a lesson that is particularly appropriate to apply to the present discussion; for the major point at issue is whether in those early days Keynes too might not on occasion have erred with respect to the proper relationship between average and marginal (cf. pp. 146–49 above). And to reinforce my contention that he might have, let me again note that—as any competent graduate student *today* can readily demonstrate—on at least one occasion in the *General Theory*, Keynes was guilty of a cognate error.[41] Let me also note (if further proof is needed) that by the "revealed preference" of the problems they chose to write about, Viner was more interested in the precise analysis of the relation between average and marginal than was Keynes; indeed, by the testimony of Joan Robinson herself (1969, p. xi), "Keynes was not much interested in the theory of imperfect competition" that she was developing in the early 1930s in what constituted the second revolution that was going on in Cambridge at that time.[42] And let me finally express the view that Viner was a more careful and precise scholar

41. Namely, in his description of the relation between changes in the size of the multiplier and changes in the marginal propensity to consume; see n. 33 above.

42. See also Austin Robinson's similar testimony in Patinkin and Leith (1977, p. 79). More generally, Joan Robinson (1963, p. 79) has written: "Keynes himself was not interested in the theory of relative prices. Gerald Shove used to say that Maynard had never spent the twenty minutes necessary to understand the theory of value." (Gerald Shove was a colleague of Keynes' at Cambridge whose "central interests were at that time in the rethinking of Marshallian value theory" [Austin Robinson 1977, p. 28].) In a letter to me, Richard Kahn has also attributed such a remark to Shove.

than Keynes.[43] So for all these reasons I feel that if Viner could have then made an "obvious" error with respect to the proper relationship between average and marginal, so too could have Keynes.

Let me also place Keynes' aggregate supply function in its proper perspective and again note that, contrary to the Weintraub-Davidson contention, neither Keynes nor his contemporaries attached major importance to this function.[44] Thus in his detailed letter of August 1936 to Roy Harrod on a draft of the latter's review article on the *General Theory* (cited on p. 8, above), Keynes lists what are to his mind the three major components of this book. These are the theory of aggregate demand, with particular emphasis on the assumption of a marginal propensity to consume of less than unity; the theory of liquidity preference; and the theory of the marginal efficiency of capital. The theory of the aggregate supply function is notable by its absence.

Similarly, in his correspondence with Hicks on the latter's "Mr. Keynes and the 'Classics' " (1937), Keynes wrote that he "found it very interesting and really [had] next to nothing to say by way of criticism." Nor did the criticisms Keynes did have to make refer either to Hicks' failure to mention the aggregate supply curve or to his *IS–LM* representation of the *General Theory* (*JMK* XIV, p. 79).[45]

Furthermore, in the two years following the publication of the *General Theory,* the book was also honored with review articles by Ralph Hawtrey, D. G. Champernowne, W. B. Reddaway, Abba Lerner, A. C. Pigou, Jacob Viner, Dennis Robertson, Wassily Leontief, and Frank Taussig. Except for Robertson, none of these even referred to the aggregate supply function. Furthermore, in the correspondence and/or formal replies which Keynes carried on with almost every one of the foregoing individuals, he made no complaint of this omission; and

43. The reader should be warned that I was a student of Viner's; nevertheless, I think my comparison is an objective one. I think it is also relevant in this context to remind the reader of the serious errors in the *Treatise* (e.g., the alleged "widow's cruse fallacy" and the tautological nature of the so-called "fundamental equations") for which Keynes' contemporaries criticized him (for references, see *KMT,* pp. 54–55). Similarly relevant are Keynes' somewhat less than scholarly estimates of the multiplier in the *General Theory;* for details, see pp. 234–36 below.

44. Cf. pp. 151–52 above. Needless to say, this conclusion implies nothing about the question as to whether or not an aggregate supply function *should* play an important role in macroeconomic analysis; see end of this Postscript.

45. In recent years, much has been made in some quarters (cf., e.g., Weintraub 1976, pp. 618, 624–26) of some actually mild reservations that Hicks (1974, pp. 6–7) has expressed about his *IS–LM* interpretation. Without commenting on these reservations as such, let me observe that what Hicks has written now, more than thirty-five years later, cannot change the basic fact that his 1937 article represented his interpretation of the *General Theory* at the time of its appearance—and that Keynes accepted this interpretation. Correspondingly, regardless of the weight attached to Hicks' recent reservations, they are of no relevance for the interpretation of what Keynes himself meant in the *General Theory*.

though in his correspondence with Robertson Keynes did refer to the latter's discussion of the aggregate supply function (*JMK* XIV, p. 89), he did not do so in his published reply.[46]

In this context, I might finally refer to Joan Robinson's *Introduction to the Theory of Employment* (1937), which was designed (so its foreword tells us) "to provide a simplified account of the main principles of the Theory of Employment," to which Keynes expressed no objection (*JMK* XIV, p. 149), and which does not discuss the aggregate supply function as such.[47] Indeed, in some circles today this book would be denounced as an early example of the "bastard Keynesian paradigm."

As a final observation on the perspective from which we should approach Keynes' discussion of his aggregate supply function, let me note that this discussion is a confused one in the operational sense that it has given rise to almost as many interpretations as there have been interpreters. Thus Dillard, Hansen, and de Jong before Weintraub, and Davidson, Wells, and Millar after him, have each in their own and frequently differing ways explained the "true meaning" of this curve.[48] Indeed, almost a decade after Keynes' death, Ralph Hawtrey and Dennis Robertson—each of whom had had the benefit of intensive personal discussions with Keynes both before and after the publication of the *General Theory*—were still carrying out an argument in the pages of the *Economic Journal* about what Keynes really meant by this function.[49] In the light of these facts, I find it difficult even to understand the meaning of someone's contending today that he knows precisely what Keynes meant by the aggregate supply function of the *General Theory*. As this chapter has shown, Keynes himself did not.

This postscript is headed by the word "plea"—and my plea is a twofold one prompted by the character of much of the vast literature that has grown up over the past quarter-century on the question of Keynes' aggregate supply function. My first plea is the obvious (though

46. For detailed references to the material cited in this paragraph, see *KMT*, chap. 13. The relevant correspondence with Lerner appears in *JMK* XXIX, pp. 212–15.

47. All that we do find is a brief reference to the fact that in the initial stages of the revival, when there is "surplus plant," supply will be "elastic" in the sense of increasing without generating much of a price increase (Robinson 1937, p. 48).

48. For references, see *KMT*, p. 84, n. 2. For my own early misguided participation in this discussion, see ibid., p. 84, n. 3 and p. 91, n. 12.

49. Hawtrey (1954, 1956) and Robertson (1955, 1956). See also Hawtrey's discussions with Keynes as recorded in *JMK* XIII, pp. 567–68 and *JMK* XIV, pp. 31–32; and Robertson's discussions as recorded in *JMK* XIII, pp. 497–98, 512–14, 520 and in *JMK* XIV, pp. 89, 96. I might note that the aforementioned argument in the course of which Hawtrey wrote was accompanied by an intensive correspondence in the course of which Hawtrey wrote to Robertson: "I still do not think that your version of what Keynes meant is reconcilable with what he wrote" (cited from the Hawtrey Papers with the kind permission of Donald Moggridge, Hawtrey's literary executor).

in the present context, unfortunately necessary) one that any study in
the history of ideas should be based on a careful examination of the
relevant texts and documents, as well as on the understanding that the
history of ideas is in large part the history of the errors and inaccuracies
that inevitably accompany the search for new scientific truths. My
second plea starts from the fact that in macroeconomic theory, as in
any other field of our discipline, there is always room for further developments: room for correcting past errors and deficiencies, and room
for extending the analysis to new problems. Accordingly, it is only
natural for some macroeconomists today to be concerned with correcting deficiencies in the analysis of aggregate supply; others, with
extending the analysis of uncertainty; and still others, with developing
a theory of market disequilibrium. But let the economists who wish to
make their contributions to such developments have the courage to cut
the umbilical cord to Keynes: let them have the courage to say what
they wish to say on these problems without invoking the alleged authority of Keynes. In this way they would be doing a service both to
Keynes and to the development of macroeconomic theory: for they
would permit the study of Keynes' thought to concern itself not with
what Keynes might have said or should have said about current
theoretical questions, but with what he actually did say; and they
would permit their attempts to improve upon the current state of macroeconomic theory to be judged substantively, on their own merits,
without confusing the issue with arguments about "what Keynes really
meant." Surely it is no accident that the most fruitful contributions to
the theory of aggregate supply during the past decade have not attempted to find support in chapter and verse of the General Theory.[50]

50. I am referring to the work on the microeconomic foundations of the Phillips curve,
the nature of implicit labor contracts, the effects of incomplete information, and the like.
   For further discussion of the interpretations of the General Theory alluded to in this
paragraph, see chap. 4, n. 8 above.

Bibliography for Part II*

Alchian, Armen A. (1970). "Information Costs, Pricing, and Resource Unemployment." In *Microeconomic Foundations of Employment and Inflation Theory*, E. Phelps *et al.* (New York: W. W. Norton), pp. 27–52.

Borch, Karl (1969). "Another Note on Keynesian Mathematics." *Economic Journal* 79 (March): 182–83.

Bronfenbrenner, Martin (1956). "An Elasticity of Inflation." *Metroeconomica* 8 (August): 107–17.

Bryce, Robert B. (1935). "An Introduction to a Monetary Theory of Employment." In Patinkin and Leith (1977), pp. 128–45.

——— (1977). "Keynes as Seen by His Students in the 1930s." In Patinkin and Leith (1977), pp. 39–43.

Davidson, Paul, and Eugene Smolensky (1964). *Aggregate Supply and Demand Analysis*. New York: Harper and Row.

Froyen, Richard (1978). Review of *Keynes' Monetary Thought*, by D. Patinkin. *Journal of Monetary Economics* 4 (Jan.): 147–50.

Harcourt, G. C. (1977). Review of *Keynes' Monetary Thought*, by D. Patinkin. *Economic Record* 3 (Dec.): 565–69.

Hawtrey, R. G. (1954). "Keynes and Supply Functions." *Economic Journal* 64 (Dec.): 834–39.

——— (1956). "Keynes and Supply Functions." *Economic Journal* 66 (Sept.): 482–84.

Hicks, J. R. (1937). "Mr. Keynes and the 'Classics'; A Suggested Interpretation." *Econometrica* 5 (April): 147–59. As reprinted in *Readings in the Theory of Income Distribution*, selected by a committee of the American Economic Association (Philadelphia: Blakiston, for the American Economic Association, 1946), pp. 461–76.

——— (1939). *Value and Capital*. Oxford: Clarendon Press.

——— (1974). *The Crisis in Keynesian Economics*. New York: Basic Books.

---

* Reprinted or translated works are cited in the text by year of original publication; the page references to such works in the text are, however, to the pages of the reprint or translation in question.

159

Keynes, John Maynard (1923). *A Tract on Monetary Reform.* As reprinted in Keynes, *Collected Writings,* Vol. IV.

––––– (1925). *The Economic Consequences of Mr. Churchill.* As reprinted in Keynes, *Collected Writings,* Vol. IX, pp. 207–30.

––––– (1930). *A Treatise on Money, Vol. I: The Pure Theory of Money.* As reprinted in Keynes, *Collected Writings,* Vol. V.

––––– (1930). *A Treatise on Money, Vol. II: The Applied Theory of Money.* As reprinted in Keynes, *Collected Writings,* Vol. VI.

––––– (1931). *Essays in Persuasion.* As reprinted with additions in Keynes, *Collected Writings,* Vol. IX.

––––– (1936). *The General Theory of Employment Interest and Money.* As reprinted in Keynes, *Collected Writings,* Vol. VII.

––––– (1939). "Relative Movements of Real Wages and Output." *Economic Journal* 49 (March): 34–51. As reprinted in Keynes, *Collected Writings,* Vol. VII, pp. 394–412.

––––– (1940). *How to Pay for the War.* As reprinted in Keynes, *Collected Writings,* Vol. IX, pp. 367–439.

–––––. *The General Theory and After: Part I, Preparation.* Edited by Donald Moggridge. Vol. XIII of Keynes, *Collected Writings.*

–––––. *The General Theory and After: Part II, Defence and Development.* Edited by Donald Moggridge. Vol. XIV of Keynes, *Collected Writings.*

–––––. *The General Theory and After: A Supplement.* Edited by Donald Moggridge. Vol. XXIX of Keynes, *Collected Writings.*

–––––. *Collected Writings.* 30 volumes planned. Published to date: Vols. I–VI (1971), Vols. VII–VIII (1973), Vols. IX–X (1972), Vols. XIII–XIV (1973), Vols. XV–XVI (1971), Vols. XVII–XVIII (1978), Vols. XIX–XX (1981), Vol. XXI (1982), Vol. XXII (1978), Vols. XXIII–XXIV (1979), Vols. XXV–XXVII (1980), Vol. XXIX (1979). London: Macmillan, for the Royal Economic Society.

Keynes, John Maynard, and Hubert Henderson (1929). *Can Lloyd George Do It?: An Examination of the Liberal Pledge.* As reprinted in Keynes, *Collected Writings,* Vol. IX, pp. 86–125.

Klein, Lawrence (1947). *The Keynesian Revolution.* New York: Macmillan.

––––– (1966). *The Keynesian Revolution.* Revised edition. New York: Macmillan.

Lucas, Robert E., Jr. (1973). "Some International Evidence on Output-Inflation Tradeoffs." *American Economic Review* 63 (June): 326–34.

Marshall, Alfred (1920). *Principles of Economics.* 8th edition. London: Macmillan.

Marty, Alvin (1961). "A Geometrical Exposition of the Keynesian Supply Function." *Economic Journal* 71 (Sept.): 560–65.

––––– (1979). Review of *Keynes' Monetary Thought,* by D. Patinkin. *Journal of Money, Credit, and Banking* 11 (Feb.): 124–26.

Modigliani, Franco (1944). "Liquidity Preference and the Theory of Interest and Money." *Econometrica* 12 (Jan.): 45–88. As reprinted in *Readings in Monetary Theory,* selected by a committee of the American Economic Association (Philadelphia: Blakiston, for the American Economic Association, 1951), pp. 186–240.

Naylor, Thomas H. (1968). "A Note on Keynesian Mathematics." *Economic Journal* 78 (March): 172–73.

Palander, Tord (1942). "Keynes' allmänna teori" [Keynes' General Theory]. *Ekonomisk Tidskrift* 44 (Dec.): 233–71.

Patinkin, Don (1956). *Money, Interest, and Prices.* Evanston, Ill.: Row, Peterson.

——— (1965). *Money, Interest, and Prices.* 2nd edition. New York: Harper and Row.

——— (1976). *Keynes' Monetary Thought: A Study of Its Development.* Durham, N.C.: Duke University Press.

——— (1978). "Keynes' Aggregate.Supply Function: A Plea for Common Sense." *History of Political Economy* 10 (Winter): 577–96.

——— (1979). "A Study of Keynes' Theory of Effective Demand." *Economic Inquiry* 17 (April): 155–76.

——— (1980). "New Materials on the Development of Keynes' Monetary Thought." *History of Political Economy* 12 (Spring): 1–28.

Patinkin, Don, and J. Clark Leith, editors (1977). *Keynes, Cambridge and the General Theory: The Process of Criticism and Discussion Connected with the Development of the General Theory.* London: Macmillan.

Roberts, David L. (1978). "Patinkin, Keynes, and Aggregate Demand and Supply Analysis." *History of Political Economy* 10 (Winter): 549–76.

Robertson, D. H. (1955). "Keynes and Supply Functions." *Economic Journal* 65 (Sept.): 474–78.

——— (1956). "Keynes and Supply Functions." *Economic Journal* 66 (Sept.): 484–87.

Robinson, E. A. G. (1977). "Keynes and His Cambridge Colleagues." In Patinkin and Leith (1977), pp. 25–38.

Robinson, Joan (1937). *Introduction to the Theory of Employment.* London: Macmillan.

——— (1963). *Economic Philosophy.* Chicago: Aldine.

——— (1969). *Introduction to the Theory of Employment.* 2nd edition. London: Macmillan.

Tuchscherer, Thomas (1979). "Keynes' Model and the Keynesians: A Synthesis." *Journal of Post Keynesian Economics* 1 (Summer): 96–109.

Viner, Jacob (1931). "Cost Curves and Supply Curves." *Zeitschrift für Nationalökonomie* 3 (Sept.): 23–46. As reprinted in *Readings in Price Theory,* selected by a committee of the American Economic Association (Chicago: Richard D. Irwin, for the American Economic Association, 1952), pp. 198–226.

——— (1952). "Cost Curves and Supply Curves: Supplementary Note." In *Readings in Price Theory,* selected by a committee of the American Economic Association (Chicago: Richard D. Irwin, for the American Economic Association), pp. 227–32.

Weintraub, Sidney (1958). *An Approach to the Theory of Income Distribution.* Philadelphia: Chilton.

——— (1961). *Classical Keynesianism, Monetary Theory and the Price Level.* Philadelphia: Chilton.

——— (1976). "Revision and Recantation in Hicksian Economics: A Review

Article." *Journal of Economic Issues* 10 (Sept.): 618–27.
—— (1980). "Comment on Aggregate Demand and Price Level Diagrammatics." *Journal of Post Keynesian Economics* 3 (Fall): 79–87.
Wells, Paul (1960). "Keynes' Aggregate Supply Function: A Suggested Interpretation." *Economic Journal* 70 (Sept.): 536–42.
—— (1962). "Aggregate Supply and Demand: An Explanation of Chapter III of the *General Theory.*" *Canadian Journal of Economics and Political Science* 28 (Nov.): 585–90.
—— (1974). "Keynes' Employment Function." *History of Political Economy* 6 (Summer): 158–62.
—— (1978). "In Review of Keynes." *Cambridge Journal of Economics* 2 (No. 3): 315–25.

Serial Publications

The Economist.
[Great Britain]. *Ministry of Labour Gazette.*

Unpublished Sources

Bryce, Robert B. Notes on Keynes' lectures at Cambridge, Autumn term 1932, 1933, and 1934. Handwritten notes deposited at Carleton University, Ottawa. Typewritten version (with some inaccuracies) filed in the Keynes Papers (see below).
R. G. Hawtrey Papers. Deposited in the Archive Centre of Churchill College, Cambridge, England. File reference: HTRY 10/78
J. M. Keynes Papers. Deposited in the Marshall Library, Cambridge, England.
Salant, Walter. Notes on Keynes' lectures at Cambridge, Autumn term 1934. Handwritten notes in Salant's possession.
Tarshis, Lorie. Notes on Keynes' lectures at Cambridge, Autumn term 1932, 1933, 1934, and 1935. Handwritten notes in Tarshis' possession.

III Monetary Theory and Policy

6

Keynesian Monetary Theory and the Cambridge School

I am indeed honored to be invited here this evening to present the Sir Dennis Robertson lecture. I still remember with pleasure my first—and, to my regret, only—meeting with Robertson some twenty years ago, as well as the discussions we continued to carry on by correspondence in subsequent years. And I find it particularly appropriate that my subject for this lecture deals with the very school of which Robertson himself was such an illustrious member.

Let me, then, turn to my subject. The monetarist revival of the last decade and more has been accompanied, especially in recent years, by a renewed interest in the nature of the quantity theory before Keynes. In this connection it seems to me that present-day adherents of this theory have claimed too much for it—and correspondingly, too little for the Keynesian theory.[1]

The exaggerated claims for the quantity theory have expressed themselves in the attempt (especially by Milton Friedman [1970, p. 202]) to present Keynes' monetary theory not as a new theory, but as a variation on the Cambridge cash-balance theory. It is this contention

Reprinted by permission from H. G. Johnson and A. R. Nobay, eds., *Issues in Monetary Economics* (Oxford: Oxford University Press, 1974), pp. 3–30. This was the proceedings volume of the 1972 Money Study Group Conference in Bournemouth, England. Some material which now appears elsewhere in this book has been deleted, with resulting changes in the section numbers. Some minor stylistic changes have also been made.

I am very grateful to Stanley Fischer for helpful comments on an earlier draft. I am also indebted to Lord Robbins for illuminating discussions of various points dealt with here.

I wish to thank Allan Drazen and Akiva Offenbacher for their assistance. I am also indebted to the Central Research Fund of the Hebrew University of Jerusalem, and to the Israel Academy of Sciences and Humanities for research grants to cover the costs of technical assistance.

The reader is asked to keep in mind that this paper was delivered as the opening address of a conference—and to excuse various facetious remarks. A shorter version of the paper has been previously published in the *Banca Nazionale del Lavoro Quarterly Review*, 25 (June 1972): 138–58.

1. In what follows, I shall make free use of Patinkin (1969, 1972a, b).

that I shall here examine—and, on the basis of this examination, reject. And lest I be misunderstood (though there is really no reason that I should), I should like to emphasize at the outset that this examination should not be interpreted as a criticism of the Cambridge School. For I would certainly consider it unjustified to criticize these economists for not having fully understood and integrated into their thinking what we have succeeded in learning only in the course of the subsequent development of Keynesian monetary theory. My criticism is only of those who make exaggerated claims for the Cambridge economists.

Before embarking on this examination, I would like to say a few words about my general approach to doctrinal history, which is certainly not an unusual one. This approach can be succinctly summarized by the statement that isolated passages do not a theory make. Instead, one of our major concerns in the study of the history of theory is the determination of the extent to which ideas expressed at various points in a work are integrated into—and hence are really part of—its main theoretical framework. And this accordingly will be my major concern this evening.

Another point I should clarify at the outset is my use of the terms "quantity theory" and "Keynesian theory." By the first of these I mean, quite pragmatically, the monetary theory expounded at the end of the nineteenth century and through the late 1920s by Irving Fisher in the United States and by the Cambridge School (Marshall, Pigou, Robertson, Lavington—and the younger Keynes) in this country.

By "Keynesian monetary theory" I mean the one developed in the *General Theory* and the literature to which it gave rise—though I should note that the aspect of the theory that is my primary concern here (namely, the treatment of money from the viewpoint of the choice of an optimum portfolio) is in some respects more precisely developed in Keynes' *Treatise on Money* (I, pp. 31–32, 127–31, 222–30) and Hicks' "Suggestion for Simplifying the Theory of Money (1935)."[2] Insofar as the later development is concerned, I have in mind in particular the work of James Tobin and his colleagues. And in a still, small voice I add: and Milton Friedman too. A small voice—because I do not want right at the beginning of this conference to run the risk of setting off a violent argument. Nor do I want to offend the man who is really responsible for my being here this evening; for surely you would not have brought me all the way from Israel to speak on this antiquarian subject in a conference devoted to such currently pressing matters as European monetary integration, commercial bank behavior, and

---

2. Shackle (1967, pp. 222–27), however, claims that there are important differences between these two treatments.

British monetary policy in the 1970s, were it not for the reawakened interest in the doctrinal history of the quantity theory that has been sparked in recent years by Friedman's repeated and provocative assertions about its alleged nature.

By the foregoing definition of the quantity theory, I obviously do not mean to imply that Fisher and the Cambridge School are coterminous with the quantity theory. Indeed, at the same time that they were doing their work, Léon Walras in Switzerland was developing his version of the quantity theory in terms of the *encaisse désirée;* and Knut Wicksell in Sweden (whom I continue to regard—by virtue of his own repeated declarations—as a quantity theorist [see p. 41 above]) was making his invaluable contribution to our understanding of the way the quantity theory manifests itself through the interest-rate mechanism in an economy with a banking system.

But since neither Walras nor Wicksell had the sense to write in English, the sad fact—that many years ago prompted Myrdal's (1939, p. 8) chiding remark about "the attractive Anglo-Saxon kind of unnecessary originality"—the sad fact is that Wicksell's work, for instance, did not become known in this country until the mid-1920s. Furthermore, if I make the proper inference from Keynes' *Treatise* (I, pp. 167, 175–78, and esp. p. 178, n. 2), the development of Keynes' thinking even then was not influenced by Wicksell. For this reason the work of Walras and Wicksell has no bearing on the question that concerns us, namely, the relationship of Keynesian monetary theory as here defined to the quantity theory that Keynes knew and, indeed, at one time helped to develop.

I would like to emphasize one further point: what interests me now is monetary theory, not monetary policy. These represent two different spheres of discourse. And whatever the relationship between the two, it is clearly not a one-to-one correspondence: different policy recommendations can emanate from the same conceptual theoretical framework; and different frameworks can lead to the same policy recommendations.

Some of the clearest examples of this can be taken from the monetary field itself. Thus those of us who studied at Chicago under Henry Simons did not need the conceptual framework of the *General Theory* to advocate government deficits to combat depressions; for quite independently of Keynes—and, indeed, before the *General Theory*—Simons taught this to his students on the basis of the conceptual framework embodied in Fisher's $MV = PT$. Indeed, Simons taught us not to suffer patiently those conventional souls who continued to preach the righteous orthodoxy of a balanced budget even in the face of mass unemployment.

I might digress for a moment to note that Simons was far from being a voice in the wilderness at that time in the United States—and that there were then also similar voices here in England. Thus in a most remarkable passage in a work systematically based on the quantity theory, Pigou (1933, p. 213) made the distinction that only Keynesians are supposed to make between the efficacy of monetary policy in countering expansionary forces in the economy by raising the bank rate sufficiently and the limitations of monetary policy in countering "a contraction in aggregate money income" by lowering this rate. For though it is "always possible for the Central Bank, by open market operations, to force out money into balances held by the public . . . there may be *no* positive rate of money interest that will avail to get this money used." (A "liquidity trap" at zero interest!) In such circumstances, Pigou continued, a purely monetary policy is "bound to fail. If, however, at the same time that the banking system keeps money cheap, the government adopts a policy of public works, the risk of failure is greatly reduced."[3]

Thus both quantity theorists and Keynesians—each from their own conceptual framework—advocated policies of combating unemployment by public-works expenditures and/or deficit financing. Conversely (and once again I must speak in a small voice), the common conceptual framework of most monetary theorists today—Friedman as well as Tobin—is (as I shall argue this evening) the Keynesian one; but this has clearly not precluded the emergence from this framework of quite different policy recommendations, based both on different political philosophies and on different interpretations of the empirical findings.

(As an aside, I might quite frankly note that what generates in me a great deal of skepticism about the state of our discipline is the high positive correlation between the policy views of a researcher [or, what is worse, of his thesis director] and his empirical findings. I will begin to believe in economics as a science when out of Yale there comes an empirical Ph.D. thesis demonstrating the supremacy of monetary policy in some historical episode, and out of Chicago, one demonstrating the supremacy of fiscal policy.)

In any event, the examples of Simons, Pigou, and others have led me to suspect that the real Keynesian Revolution took place not in the sphere of economic policy (where changes were already occurring in

3. Italics in original. Actually, this passage is not as Keynesian as it sounds: for Pigou presents his argument in the Wicksellian terms of the effect of such public-works expenditure on the difference between the actual bank rate and the "proper" one [cf. pp. 207–8 below]. At the same time, he does recognize that a decrease in public-works expenditures "directly contracts to [the?] real demand for labor" (Pigou 1933, pp. 213–14, esp. n. 1).

the early 1930s), but in that of economic theory. I suspect that the real change wrought by Keynes' *General Theory* was in the conceptual framework from which we viewed the problems of employment, interest, and money. But that is a question that I shall defer for discussion on another occasion.[4]

1. The Novelty of Keynesian Monetary Theory: Stocks and Flows

Let me return to our main question. Consider the familiar representation of the Keynesian model in terms of a simultaneous analysis of the markets for commodities and money. I think that everyone would agree that the conceptual framework of effective demand that Keynes developed to analyze equilibrium in the commodity market was indeed a new one (leaving aside the case of Kalecki and perhaps one or two other possible precursors).[5] The question is whether the same can be said for the conceptual framework of liquidity preference that Keynes developed to analyze equilibrium in the money market. In order to answer that question, we must first clarify what we mean by a "new theory."

Clearly, every theory advanced at one point in time has some antecedents in earlier theories. Nevertheless, there are stages in the development of a science where, by consensus, a "new" theory is said to develop. And one of the major questions discussed by philosophers and historians of science are the characteristics which justify calling a theory "new" (see Kuhn 1970; Agassi 1968; and Stigler 1955). Some related questions that I have already alluded to are the difference between "the asides" referring to an idea in the antecedent theories, as compared with its "systematic development" in the "new theory"; and the difference between "mentioning an idea in passing" or "as an aside," as compared with "integrating it into one's thinking."

By their very nature, questions of this type are not susceptible of hard-and-fast answers. The general type of answer that has on occasion been given, and that I would like to give here, is that a theory is "new"

---

4. I might, however, note that I find support for the foregoing view in Winch's study (1969) of English economic thought and policy in the 1920s and early 1930s, and in Davis' corresponding study (1971) for the United States. See also Hutchison (1953, chap 24; 1968, appendix). [See pp. 6–11 above].

5. [In view of my rejection in chapter 3 above of the claim that Kalecki anticipated the General Theory, let me note that I have deliberately left this parenthetical remark unchanged to serve as an example of the uncritical way this claim has frequently been accepted: for at the time I made the remark, I had only the most cursory knowledge of Kalecki's writings, based entirely on my dim memories of what I had read as a graduate student more than twenty-five years before.]

if it deals in a different manner with one of the central concepts of the science. Similarly, it is "new" if it stimulates concentrated research along hitherto neglected directions.

Now, that does not take us very far, for it has merely replaced the mystery of "new" by that of "central" and "neglected." Still I think it can help us on the present question of the novelty of Keynesian monetary theory.

To begin with, I think we are all agreed that one of the central distinctions of economic theory is that between stocks and flows. Correspondingly, what I would consider to be one of the hallmarks of Keynesian monetary theory is the sharp distinction it draws between the two sets of decisions an individual has to make: the decision as to the forms in which to hold his stock of wealth at a given instant of time, and particularly the amount to be held in money; and the decision as to the rate at which to add to this wealth over time—that is, the decision as to the flows of savings and investment.

The Keynesian approach has led to the development of the theory of the demand for money as part of a general theory of the choice of an optimum portfolio of assets. Correspondingly, the emphasis of this theory is on the optimal relationship between the stock of money and the stocks of other assets, as influenced primarily by the alternative rates of return available on these assets. Other determinants of this demand are the total wealth of the individual (which defines the wealth restraint that must be satisfied by the portfolio) and the flow of income (which is the major determinant of the transactions demand for money).[6]

All agree that this conceptual framework is quite different from that of Fisher. The question is whether it is also different from that of the Cambridge School. (I might incidentally note that the sharp contrast that is traditionally drawn between the "mechanical" Fisher and the "behavioristic" Cambridge economists is, in my opinion, largely a Cantabrigian tale; but the discussion of that question too must be deferred to another occasion, though see Patinkin [1965, pp. 167, 599].) Let me, then, contrast the foregoing conceptual framework with that of the Cambridge School, and with that of Keynes of the *Tract on Monetary Reform* (1923) in particular.

There is no doubt that Keynes of the *General Theory* is at one with Keynes of the *Tract* in taking as his point of departure the individual's demand for money holdings. Thus in his exposition in the *Tract* (which

6. This approach has received its most formal development at the hands of James Tobin (1955, 1963, 1969) and, more recently, Duncan Foley and Miguel Sidrauski (1971). The individual in this development is conceived as making his optimizing decisions while being subject to a wealth (stock) restraint as well as an income (flow) restraint. See also Gurley and Shaw (1960).

he explicitly based on Marshall [1923] and Pigou [1917]), Keynes wrote that the demand for real "purchasing power" in the form of money holdings depends

> partly on the wealth of the community, partly on its habits. Its habits are fixed by its estimation of the extra convenience of having more cash in hand as compared with the advantages to be got from spending the cash or investing it. The point of equilibrium is reached where the estimated advantages of keeping more cash in hand compared with those of spending or investing it about balance. The matter cannot be summed up better than in the words of Dr. Marshall. [*Tract*, p. 64]

And here Keynes quotes at length from Marshall's well-known discussion in his *Money, Credit and Commerce* (1923, pp. 44–45)—which goes back to much earlier statements—about "the fraction of their income which people find it worth while to keep in the form of currency," as well as Marshall's example of an economy whose inhabitants "find it just worth their while to keep by them on the average ready-purchasing power to the extent of a tenth part of their annual income, together with a fiftieth part of their property."[7] Keynes also notes, when referring to Marshall's discussion of the antecedents of this approach in the writings of Petty and others, that "in modern conditions the normal proportion of the circulation [of money] to this national income seems to be somewhere between a tenth and a fifteenth" (*Tract*, p. 64, n. 1).

Actually, the clearest statement of the Cambridge approach—though one that Keynes does not cite, possibly because he was restricting himself to the writings of his teachers, as distinct from his contemporaries—is that of Lavington,[8] who also based himself on Marshall. After discussing "the general principle on which an individual distributes his resources among their various uses," Lavington wrote:

---

7. These passages are cited at length and further discussed in the Appendix to this chapter, pp. 181–83 below.

8. Frederick Lavington (1881–1927) began his university studies (at Cambridge) relatively late (in 1908) after eleven years' service in a bank. He began his academic career at Cambridge in 1918, after a further period in administrative work. This late start—as well as his illness and early death—undoubtedly helps explain why his role in the development of Cambridge monetary thought was less than it otherwise would have been. But I suspect that an at least equally important factor was Lavington's self-effacing outlook on his own work as reflected in his favorite saying that "It's all in Marshall, if you'll only take the trouble to dig it out." Cf. the obituaries of Lavington by H[arold] W[right] and C. R. F[ay] in the September 1927 *Economic Journal*. (I am indebted to Lord Robbins for the identification of Harold Wright, and for the information that Wright was the author of the Cambridge Economic Handbook, *Population* [1923].)

Resources devoted to consumption supply an income of immediate satisfaction; those held as a stock of currency yield a return of convenience and security; those devoted to investment in the narrower sense of the term yield a return in the form of interest. In so far therefore as his judgment gives effect to his self-interest, the quantity of resources which he holds in the form of money will be such that the unit of resources which is just and only just worth while holding in this form yields him a return of convenience and security equal to the yield of satisfaction derived from the marginal unit spent on consumables, and equal also to the net rate of interest. [1921, p. 30; the reference to Marshall is on p. 27]

I might note that no such passage appears in the first (1922) edition of Dennis Robertson's celebrated little volume on *Money* in the Cambridge Economic Handbooks series. But Robertson did introduce such a passage in the 1928 (pp. 38–39) and subsequent editions of this book.

At first sight, these passages seem to indicate that the conceptual approach of the Cambridge School did not differ much from that of the later Keynesian monetary theory. What I shall now show, however, is that this is not the case: First of all, there are some substantive differences in the description of the optimum portfolio—though less so with respect to Lavington than the others. Second, and more important, the Cambridge economists did not recognize the full implications of the optimum-portfolio approach to monetary theory; they did not really integrate it into their thinking. In particular, as I shall show in the next section, they failed to take account of the implications of this approach at the appropriate points in their discussions.

By my first point I mean that Cambridge monetary theory did not draw the sharp and basic distinction Keynesian theory draws between stocks and flows, and sometimes it even indiscriminately interchanged "wealth" and "income." Thus, it is not clear from the foregoing passages whether the Cambridge economists conceived of the individual as holding a quantity of money that is optimum with reference to his stocks of other assets, or optimum with reference to his income, or optimum with reference to some combination of the two.

To prevent any misunderstanding, I must emphasize that in actual fact the individual's holdings of money should be optimum with respect to both his wealth and his income. This, after all, is the view implicit in Keynes' liquidity-preference function $L_1(Y) + L_2(r)$—and explicit in the presentation of the demand for money by Tobin (1955, p. 208; 1969) and Foley and Sidrauski (1971, pp. 30–31). My point is, however, that some Cambridge economists (Pigou, Robertson, and possibly Lavington) expressed the demand for money as a function of income—without referring at all to wealth; and that even those who did refer to both wealth and income (Marshall and Keynes of the *Tract*) did so in a way that does not reveal awareness of the basically different roles these magnitudes play in determining the demand for money: namely, that tangible wealth is the variable that constitutes the total budget restraint on the holding of assets, including money—so that an increase in wealth generally results in increased holdings of all assets; whereas income is one of the relevant variables explaining the (transactions) demand for money in a portfolio of a given size, so that an increase in income increases the demand for money, at the expense of other assets.

To make this criticism more concrete, consider the basic passages from Marshall's *Money, Credit and Commerce* that Keynes cites in the *Tract* as an expression of his position too (above, p. 171). At one and the same time these consecutive passages present a theory of people's demand for money as a "fraction of their income" and as "a tenth part of their annual income, together with a fiftieth part of their property." It is inconceivable to me that Marshall and Keynes of that time could have understood the full implications of the distinction between stocks and flows (and of the corresponding distinction between wealth and income), and yet that Marshall could have juxtaposed two such different descriptions of the demand for money—and that, even more so, Keynes could have cited them without comment.[9]

As further evidence on this point, consider Marshall's statement that the "relation between the volume of this currency and the general level of prices may be changed permanently by changes in . . . population and wealth, which change the aggregate income" (1923, p. 45). Marshall is clearly assuming here that an increase in wealth increases the demand for money only by first increasing the subsequent flow of income, and hence the transaction needs for money; there is no awareness here of the possibility that an increase in wealth may directly increase the demand for money as one of the assets in which form this wealth is held. In brief, if in modern monetary theory we sometimes use (permanent) income as a proxy for wealth, here Marshall is using wealth as a proxy for income.

Significantly enough, my criticism on this point would seem to be related to one that Keynes of the *Treatise* makes of the Cambridge School, including explicitly Keynes of the *Tract:* namely, that the

9. For further discussion of this point, see the Appendix to this chapter, pp. 182–84. This failure of neoclassical economists to distinguish sharply between wealth and income may be related to the corresponding absence of a sharp distinction in the writings of the classical economists (and of Smith and Ricardo in particular), for whom capital (i.e., wealth) was last year's crop carried over to the current year.

Cambridge equation $P = kR/M$—in which R (for "resources") represents "the current income of the community"—can explain the demand for income (or demand) deposits, which are held for transactions needs; however, contends Keynes, it does not explain the demand for savings (or time) deposits. This demand, too, can be said to depend on the "resources" of the individuals; "but 'resources' in this connection ought not be interpreted, as it is interpreted by Professor Pigou, as being identical with current *income*" (*Treatise* I, pp. 207–8, italics in original).

I wish I could go on to say that Keynes explicitly states here that "resources" in this connection should be interpreted as wealth. Unfortunately for me, he does not; but that this is what he meant is, I think, quite clear from Keynes' analysis earlier in the *Treatise* of the holding of saving deposits, in which he explicitly relates these holdings to the individual's total wealth, and not to the "current increment" to this wealth (*Treatise* I, p. 127).

I must admit that Keynes' criticism here does not apply to Lavington, who explicitly stated that part of the demand for money that is held as a contingency reserve changes "in some measure independently of the volume of payments" (1921, p. 33). On the other hand, Lavington—unlike Keynes of the *Treatise* (I, pp. 127–29)—does not relate this contingency reserve to the individual's wealth; nor does he relate its magnitude to the price of the securities that can be held as an alternative. Instead, Lavington speaks only in general terms of the magnitude of this reserve being "regulated largely by the general level of confidence" (1921, p. 33). It is also significant that Lavington himself considers his description of the demand for money as a contingency reserve to be "rather different from (though not inconsistent with) that laid down by the Quantity theory" (1921, p. 32). Finally, it is noteworthy that though Robertson (1933, pp. 92–93) defends the Cambridge equation against Keynes' criticisms here, he (Robertson), too, makes no mention of Lavington in this context.[10]

2. The Novelty of Keynesian Monetary Theory: The Recognition of the Implications of the Optimum-Portfolio Approach

The preceding discussion has explicated the distinction between Keynes and the Cambridge School that is reflected in their respective treatments of stocks and flows. A related distinction manifests itself in the already noted fact that despite its description of an optimum portfolio, the Cambridge School did not realize the full implications of

10. For further details, see the Appendix to this chapter, pp. 185–88.

the portfolio approach to monetary theory. Conversely, it is the systematic application of this approach that is the hallmark of Keynesian monetary theory.

This distinction reflects itself, first of all, in the way these two approaches analyze the effects of a monetary increase on the economy. Keynesian theory analyzes the initial impact of this increase on the balance sheet of the individual: it emphasizes that in order to persuade the public to hold a portfolio with such an increased stock of money, the rates of return on the other assets in this portfolio must fall. That is, stock equilibrium can be achieved now only at lower rates of return on these other assets. This decline in interest and other rates of return then increases the demand for the flow of consumption and (primarily) investment goods, thus disturbing the equilibrium in the commodity-flow markets, and thus causing an increase in output and/or prices (depending on the state of unemployment).

In brief, Keynesian theory analyzes the initial impact of a monetary increase in terms of the substitution effects it generates. I am sure that it will come as no surprise to anyone if I say that Keynesian economics is to be criticized for this concentration on the substitution effects, to the exclusion of the possible wealth—or real-balance—effect. For though there are indeed cases in which monetary changes do not generate a wealth effect (namely, some open-market operations),[11] there are other cases (namely, monetary changes generated by deficit financing) in which they do.

On the other hand, I cannot think of a case in which a monetary change generates only a wealth effect and not a substitution effect. And it is the fact that the Cambridge School nevertheless frequently analyzed a monetary change precisely in this way that distinguishes it so sharply from the later Keynesian economics.

Ironically enough, this distinction is clearest from a passage by Keynes himself in the *Tract* (p. 62) that reads as follows: "When people find themselves with more cash than they require . . . , they get rid of the surplus by buying goods or investments, or by leaving it for a bank to employ, or, possibly, by increasing their hoarded reserves" (see also Keynes 1911). Thus Keynes here conceives of the individual as directly using his "cash surplus" to increase his "hoarded reserves," and makes no mention whatsoever of the variation in interest required to induce him to do so.[12] In this way Keynes fails to realize

11. Cf. Patinkin (1965, chap. XII:4, esp. p. 294, n. 23).
12. I am indebted to Dr. Luigi Ceriani, editor of the *Banca Nazionale del Lavoro Quarterly Review,* for pointing out an error in my original discussion of this passage. In that discussion I interpreted "investments" as "investment goods"—whereas it should have been clear from Keynes' use of "investments" in other parts of the *Tract* (pp. 4–6, 12, and passim) that what he meant by the term is *financial* investment—i.e., the purchase of securities of various kinds.

the full implications of his own description (cited above) of "equilibrium [as being] reached where the estimated advantages of keeping more cash in hand compared with those of spending or investing it about balance" (*Tract*, p. 64).

He does not recognize the fact (that he was later to emphasize so systematically in the *General Theory*) that the monetary increase will disturb the foregoing balance at the margin—and that the individual's holdings of money and other assets can accordingly be in equilibrium once again only at a lower rate of interest.

The absence of appropriate references in the Cambridge literature to the dependence of the demand for money on interest is of great significance in the present discussion, not because such a dependence is necessarily of empirical importance, but because the recognition of such a dependence seems to me to constitute a critical and unambiguous indicator of whether the Cambridge economists really understood the analytical apparatus they described. Let me then provide some additional instances in which their writings fail to indicate such a recognition.

Thus, despite what I have said above, Cambridge economists did indeed assign an important role to changes in the rate of interest in their analysis of the effects of a monetary increase. But the way they discussed this role is itself evidence of how different their conceptual framework really was from that of the Keynesians. In particular, Marshall, Pigou, the younger Keynes, and other quantity theorists all analyzed the effects of a monetary increase that reflected itself in the first instance in an increase in bank reserves. Indeed, this was the major case they considered. They argued that the resulting excess reserves would lead to an increased desire on the part of banks to make loans, hence to a decrease in the rate of interest[13] (Wicksell's "money rate" or "bank rate," though the Cambridge economists did not describe it in these terms), hence to increased borrowings, hence to increased demand for goods by the borrowers, and hence to a rise in prices.

Now, the interesting aspect of this description of the adjustment process is that none of these Cambridge economists even alluded to the fact—implicit in their analyses of the demand for money cited above—that the changes in the rate of interest would affect not only the amount of the public's borrowing, but also the quantity of money it chooses to hold.

13. This can be interpreted as reflecting the optimum-portfolio adjustment of the banks; but the Cambridge economists did not present such an interpretation—nor should they be expected to have done so. Once again, however, Lavington (1921, pp. 30–31) is something of an exception; see the Appendix to this chapter, pp. 185–87.

A similar picture emerges when we consider the instances—unfortunately, few—in which Cambridge economists supplemented their theoretical monetary analysis with empirical investigations. Thus Pigou (1929, pp. 163–72) tried to apply to British data for the period 1878–1914 the same techniques used by Carl Snyder (1924) in his study of the equation of exchange for the United States. Pigou concludes from the data that the higher price level of 1914 as compared with 1878 was the result of a higher velocity of circulation at that time (1914). Now, what is interesting about Pigou's discussion is that he does refer to the possibility that velocity increased because of an increase in the rate change of the price level (by Pigou's data [ibid., p. 392]—though he does not explicitly refer to them—prices had been *falling* before 1878, and had remained *constant* in the period 1912–14, which could have explained part of the higher velocity in the latter period). On the other hand, Pigou does not refer to the possible effect of changes in the rate of interest on velocity (though it must be conceded that the yield on consols in 1914 [3.3 percent] was only slightly higher than in 1878 [3.2 percent] [Mitchell and Deane 1962, p. 455]). Thus the evidence here is ambiguous.

The situation with reference to Keynes is clearer. In his *Tract* (p. 67), Keynes compares the data for prices and money supply in October 1920 with those for October 1922—and concludes that his k (which equals the Cambridge KT in the equation $M = KPT$) increased significantly during this period. Now, Keynes does mention (though as the effect of the increase in k, and not as its cause) the sharp (33 percent) decline in the price level during this period. On the other hand, he does not cite as a possible explanatory factor the fact that the yield on consols fell from 5.3 percent in 1920 to 4.4 percent in 1922—or that the maximum rate on three-month bills fell from 6.5 percent in 1920 to 2.7 percent in 1922. Of course, one might say that in accordance with Fisher's distinction between nominal and real rate of interest, this decline in nominal interest reflected in part the fact—which Keynes did mention—that the price level was declining. But it would be carrying things too far to try in this way to justify Keynes' failure even to mention the rate of interest in this context.

Furthermore, in his immediately following discussion about the ways to stabilize k' (i.e., the real value of the demand for current deposits), Keynes states that "a tendency of k' to increase may be somewhat counteracted by lowering the bank-rate, because easy lending diminishes the advantage of keeping a margin for contingencies in cash" (*Tract*, p. 68). Now this sentence can be interpreted as reflecting the effect on the demand for money of the more ready availability of money substitutes like easy credit facilities. But however it is interpreted it will not yield a reaffirmation of the contention that, ceteris paribus, lowering the rate of interest causes an increase in k—and hence in the real amount of money demanded.

I might note that Pigou and Keynes are representative of what seems to have been a systematic tendency of quantity theorists to explain observed variations in the velocity of circulation in terms not of the rate of interest, but of variations in the rate of change of prices (Patinkin 1972a). Keynes' procedure on this score is particularly enigmatic; for in his description of the post–World War I inflations in his *Tract* (pp. 40ff.), he provides a precise analysis of the influence of a high rate of increase of prices in causing the public to develop "economizing habits" with reference to its demand for money; yet in his systematic presentation of the Cambridge demand for money he does not mention this factor at all, but does analyze the influence of the rate of interest (ibid.,·pp. 64ff.). In this discrepancy, too, I see additional evidence of the failure of the Cambridge economists to integrate the different elements of their monetary theory into their thinking [but see *KMT*, pp. 11–12].

A similar difference characterizes Pigou's analysis of the trade cycle (1929). Changes in the velocity of circulation play an important role in this analysis, but they are never related to the concurrent changes taking place (according to Pigou) in the rate of interest. Instead, the changes in velocity are attributed solely to the anticipation of price changes—and to changes in "confidence." A similar statement holds for Lavington's analysis (1922). As an aside, I might also note that the emphasis that both these writers placed on "confidence" makes it clear that—in contrast with Friedman's "reformulated quantity theory" (1956, p. 16)—they did not think of velocity, and hence the demand for money as a stable function of stipulated economic variables.

I would like to conclude this examination of the Cambridge literature with another indication of its failure to realize the full implication of its conceptual framework. It seems to me that if an economist has a full understanding of the portfolio approach to monetary theory, then one of the natural questions he will be led to ask is about the effects on the rates of returns of the various assets of a shift in tastes with reference to the forms in which individuals wish to hold their assets (of which Keynes' shift in liquidity preference is the archetype). It should be emphasized that such a shift will affect the rate of interest (and rates of return in general) even under conditions of full employment and perfectly flexible prices.[14] Correspondingly, the complete absence from the Cambridge literature of an analysis of such a shift in taste—in contrast with the attention paid to the effects of a shift in tastes with

14. See Patinkin (1965), chap. X:4.

respect to the desired level of K—is to me clear evidence that the Cambridge quantity theorists did not really approach monetary problems from the viewpoint of an optimally composed portfolio of assets.

3. Concluding Remarks

My conclusion from the evidence presented here is that the conceptual framework of the Cambridge School was not really the Keynesian one described in the opening section of this paper: namely, a framework that conceives of the individual as deciding on the amount of his money holdings as a component of a portfolio of assets that is optimally composed with reference to the alternative rates of return available on these assets; a framework that (in contrast with the Cambridge School) distinguishes between the initial *stock* (or balance-sheet) adjustments generated by a monetary change, and the subsequent effect on the demand for *flows* of commodities of the changes in rates in interest generated by these adjustments.

One indication of this fact is the failure of the Cambridge School to analyze the effects on the equilibrium rate of interest of a shift in the tastes of the individual with reference to the desired asset-composition of his portfolio. Another indication is that despite the fact that the Cambridge School referred to the influence of the rate of interest on the demand for money, it did not really integrate this influence into its thinking: it did not call it into use in explaining observed variations of the velocity of circulation; nor did it cite it as a factor in its theoretical explanations of variations of the velocity of circulation over the trade cycle.

It is because of these differences from the Cambridge School that the Keynesian theory of liquidity preference can properly be considered a "new theory"—one that makes it impossible for us today to approach monetary problems without taking account of these factors.[15]

I would like to end with some personal reminiscences that I hope will support this interpretation of the Cambridge School—though I am sure that for some it will merely be an indication of my prejudices.

There is some effrontery in claiming that although scholars described a certain analytical apparatus, they did not really understand its full implications. I dare nevertheless to advance this contention not only because of what I feel to be the convincing evidence presented here, but also on the basis of my own recollections of how I, too, failed at

---

15. It is for these reasons that I cannot accept the contrary conclusions of Eshag (1963), pp. 62–68.

one time to see these implications. For though my studies of economics at Chicago began some years after the appearance of the *General Theory*, I was educated in the analytical spirit of the quantity theory that prevailed there. Hence, even though we also studied the *General Theory*, I know that I did not think then in terms of the sharp Keynesian distinction between stock and flow equilibrium. I know that my instinctive way of thinking of monetary influences at that time was directly from the increase in the stock of money to the increase in the demand for the flow of commodities—without the aid of any intervening portfolio-adjustment substitution effects. I know that I thought of a change in the velocity of circulation solely in terms of a change in tastes as to the desired proportion between the stock of money and the flow of expenditure on current commodities; not in terms of the consequence of a change in tastes as to the desired proportion between the stock of money and the stocks of other assets in a portfolio of a given size.

Knowing these things about the workings of my own mind, I hope I will not be considered presumptuous if I interpret the detailed evidence from the writings of the Cambridge economists that I have here presented as evidence that they too were subject to a similar failure to see what is so clear to us today—as a result of the changes wrought by Keynesian monetary theory.

Appendix

The Textual Sources

The passages from Marshall's *Money, Credit and Commerce* (1923, pp. 44–45) referred to on p. 171 above are reproduced here, together with the relevant footnote:

> To give definiteness to this notion, let us suppose that the inhabitants of a country, taken one with another (and including therefore all varieties of character and of occupation) find it just worth their while to keep by them on the average ready purchasing power to the extent of a tenth part of their annual income, together with a fiftieth part of their property; then the aggregate value of the currency of the country will tend to be equal to the sum of these amounts. . . .
>
> Thus the position is this. In every state of society there is some fraction of their income which people find it worth while to keep in the form of currency; it may be a fifth, or a tenth, or a twentieth. A large command of resources in the form of currency renders their business easy and smooth, and puts them at an advantage in bargaining; but, on the other hand, it locks up in a barren form resources that might yield an income of gratification if invested, say, in extra furniture; or a money income if invested in extra machinery or cattle. . . . But, whatever the state of society, there is a certain volume of their resources which people of different classes, taken one with another, care to keep in the form of currency; and, if everything else remains the same, then there is this direct relation between the volume of currency and the level of prices, that, if one is increased by ten per cent, the other also will be increased by ten per cent. Of course, the less the proportion of their resources which people care to keep in the form of currency, the lower will be the aggregate value of the currency, that is, the higher will prices be with a given volume of currency.
>
> This relation between the volume of the currency and the general level of prices may be changed permanently by changes in, first, population and wealth, which change the aggregate income; secondly, by the growth of credit agencies, which substitute other

181

means of payment for currency; thirdly, by changes in the methods of transport, production, and business generally, which affect the number of hands through which commodities pass in the processes of making and dealing, and it may be temporarily modified by fluctuations of general commercial confidence and activity.*

---

*The above statement is reproduced from my answers to Questions 11,759–11,761 put by the Indian Currency Committee in 1899. In fact a considerable part of the present discussion of the problems of money and credit may be found in my answers to Questions 11,757–11,850 put by that Committee: and my answers to Questions 9,623–10,014 and 10,121–10,126 put by the Gold and Silver Commission in 1887–88.

In his memoir on Marshall, Keynes writes:

We must regret still more Marshall's postponement of the publication of his *Theory of Money* until extreme old age, when time had deprived his ideas of freshness and .his exposition of sting and strength. . . . His theories were not expounded in a systematic form until the appearance of *Money, Credit and Commerce* in 1923. By this date nearly all his main ideas had found expression in the works of others. He had passed his eightieth year; his strength was no longer equal to much more than piecing together earlier fragments; and its jejune treatment, carefully avoiding difficulties and complications, yields the mere shadow of what he had had it in him to bring forth twenty or (better) thirty years earlier. [*JMK* X, pp. 189–90]

It does not take any expertise in textual criticism to see how the passage cited here from *Money, Credit and Commerce* reflects such "piecing together." In particular, the first paragraph of this passage—in which the demand for money is expressed as "a tenth part of their annual income, together with a fiftieth part of their property"—clearly presents a different theory of the demand for money than does the second paragraph, which refers only to the "fraction of their income which people find it worth while to keep in the form of currency." This difference is a reflection of the fact that the second and third[1] paragraphs in the passage cited essentially reproduce Marshall's 1899 testimony before the Indian Currency Committee (reproduced in Marshall 1926, pp. 267–69) to which he refers in the first sentence of the footnote he attached to this passage. And this tes-

---

1. The reader is reminded of the discussion on p. 173 above emphasizing that the allusion in this paragraph to the influences of changes in wealth on the demand for money visualizes this effect not as a direct one, but as an indirect one exerted through the influence on this demand of the increase in income generated by the increase in wealth.

timony essentially goes back to an unpublished manuscript that Marshall wrote around 1871.[2]

On the other hand, the first paragraph in this passage does not appear in any of Marshall's various testimonies as reprinted in his *Official Papers;* nor, to the best of my knowledge, does it appear in any of his published works; nor, finally, does it appear in the unpublished manuscript for 1871 just mentioned. Thus it may have been written at the time Marshall was preparing his *Money, Credit and Commerce.*

In view of the circumstances under which Marshall wrote his *Money, Credit and Commerce* (as described by Keynes), it may be that one should not attach too much importance to the fact that in this book Marshall described the demand for money in two different ways. But this cannot explain why Keynes in his *Tract* (p. 64) cites the foregoing passages from *Money, Credit and Commerce* at length—and makes no comment that would indicate his realization of the fact that from the stock-flow viewpoint there are indeed two different descriptions here.

In addition to the foregoing passages that he cites from Marshall, Keynes also describes this demand repeatedly (*Tract,* pp. 62, 64, and passim) by the statement that the demand of individuals for money "depends partly on their wealth, partly on their habits." As the reader can verify, this statement does not appear in the above-cited passages from *Money, Credit and Commerce.* It does, however, appear in one of the memoranda that Marshall submitted in 1887 to the Gold and Silver Commission in which he states that "the volume of the business in each country which requires the use of coin [is] determined by each country's wealth and habits" (Marshall 1926, p. 177).

In this material we also find another example of the failure of Marshall to distinguish sharply between wealth and income in this context:

> Assuming the habits of business to remain unchanged, the amount of coin which a person finds it convenient to carry about, taking one with another, depends upon his general *wealth*. A shopkeeper with an *income* of £1,000 a year would be likely to use a great deal more

2. See the thirteenth and fourteenth pages of this manuscript, which is to be found in the Marshall Library of Economics in Cambridge. I am indebted to the senior assistant librarian of the library and to Professor Robin Matthews for providing me with a photocopy of the manuscript. This manuscript is referred to by Keynes in his memorial essay on Marshall (*JMK* X, p. 190).

[This manuscript has now been published in *The Early Economic Writings of Alfred Marshall* (1975). The passage referred to here—in which Marshall supposes that an individual's demand for money is "one tenth of his yearly income"—appears in vol. 1, p. 168 of this book. It is worth noting that on the page before that Marshall refers to the "portion of a man's wealth" which he keeps in the form of money, so that this early manuscript too is marked by a failure to make a precise distinction between income and wealth.]

gold than an architect with the same *income*, but if prices rose generally so that the money income of each increased 10 percent, and the expenditure of each in every direction increased also 10 percent, then (their habits of business remaining unchanged) each of them would, I believe, keep 10 percent more money in his purse. [1926, p. 43, italics added]

The passages cited in the text above from Pigou's "Value of Money" (1917, pp. 164–67) are the following—where once again the relevant footnote has been reproduced:

There is thus constituted at any given moment a definite demand schedule for titles to legal-tender money. Let R be the total resources, expressed in terms of wheat, that are enjoyed by the community (other than its bankers) whose position is being investigated; k the proportion of these resources that it chooses to keep in the form of titles to legal tender; M the number of units of legal tender, and P the value, or price, per unit of these titles in terms of wheat. Then the demand schedule just described is represented by the equation $P = kR/M$. When k and R are taken as constant, this is, of course, the equation of a rectangular hyperbola.

. . . consider the variable k. When the aggregate wheat value of the community's resources is given, the quantity of wheat value kept in the form of titles to legal tender is determined by the *proportion* of his resources that the average man chooses to keep in that form. This proportion depends upon the convenience obtained and the risk avoided through the possession of such titles, by the loss of real income involved through the diversion to this use of resources that might have been devoted to the production of future commodities, and by the satisfaction that might be obtained by consuming resources immediately and not investing them at all. These three uses, the production of convenience and security, the production of commodities, and direct consumption, are rival to one another. For our present purpose, the use of immediate consumption need not be particularly considered. Its presence mitigates, but never does more than mitigate, the effect of the principal causes with which we have to deal. Practically, the critical question for a business man—and the same class of question has to be asked by everybody—is, as Professor Carver well observes: "will it pay better to have one more dollar in his cash drawer and one less on his shelves, or will it pay better to have one less dollar in his cash drawer and one more on his shelves."*

American Economic Association Papers (1905), p. 131.

Incidentally, I think that this was the first appearance in print of the Cambridge equation.

In view of Lavington's distinctive contributions to the Cambridge School, I should like to cite at length from chapter 6 of his *English Capital Market* (1921):

In a modern community each person with resources at his disposal needs some means by which he can employ these resources in order to obtain goods from other parties, to pay his dues to the State and to meet more uncertain demands to which he may be exposed. . . . Each therefore will find it convenient to hold a part of his resources in the form of a stock of something which, being generally acceptable and easily transferable, serves as general purchasing power and may be readily passed from hand to hand as a means of making payments.

He will of course have to forego interest upon the resources which he invests in this particular form of a stock of money, but he will obtain instead facilities for making payments, which may be expressed as a return of convenience and security. His stock yields him an income of convenience, for it reduces the cost and trouble of effecting his current payments; and it yields him an income of security, for it reduces his risks of not being able readily to make payments arising from contingencies which he cannot fully foresee. The investment of resources in the form of a stock of money which facilitates the making of payments is then in no way peculiar; it corresponds to the investment by a merchant in the office furniture which facilitates the dispatch of business, to the investment of the farmer in agricultural implements which facilitate the cultivation of his land, and indeed to investment generally.

Such being the *nature* of an individual's demand for money, we have now to consider the causes governing its *amount*. In order to do so, let us first state the general principle on which an individual distributes his resources among their various uses, and then pass on to consider the causes determining the amount which he invests in this particular use—money.

This general principle is familiar enough. As a person extends the application of resources in any particular use, the yield from each successive unit of resources so applied satisfies a less and less urgent need. Accordingly he presses their employment in each use up to that point where in his judgment the marginal yield is equal all round; for if this yield differed as between any two uses it would pay him to transfer resources from one to the other. Resources devoted to consumption supply an income of immediate satisfaction; those held as a stock of currency yield a return of convenience and security; those devoted to investment in the narrower sense of the term yield a return in the form of interest. In so far therefore as his judgment gives effect to his self-interest, the quantity of resources which he holds in the form of money will be such that the unit of resources which is just and only just worth while holding in this form yields him a return of convenience and security equal to the yield of satisfaction derived from the marginal unit spent on consumables, and equal also to the net rate of interest.

The distinction between the yield of convenience and security brings out the consideration that the stock of money held by a business man serves not only to effect his current payments but also as a first line of defense against the uncertain events of the future. . . .

If we arrange a business man's investments in order of their marketability, we may regard his resources as distributed among a series of uses ranging from his stock of the supremely acceptable thing, money, up to his investments in the permanent plant from which he draws his main money income. This arrangement conveniently illustrates the essential similarity between the distribution of resources by a business man and the distribution effected by a bank, where the two main consideration, the need to meet current and contingent demands and the need to earn a profit, are shown in clearer contrast. . . .

Even in normal circumstances, therefore, the size of the stock of money held by a business man depends partly on the volume of his current transactions, partly on his individual business outlook. . . .

These considerations lead to a definition of the demand for money rather different from (though not inconsistent with) that laid down by the Quantity theory. In that theory the demand for money during the year is taken to be the aggregate of goods (and services) exchanged against money during that period. . . . Can this total, the volume of payments to be effected, be properly regarded as forming the demand for money? This question must be answered in the light of the considerations which have just been noticed. . . .

. . . In order to carry through his payments quickly and conveniently each person holds a part of his resources in the form of a stock of money. The size of that part of this stock which he holds to carry through current transactions depends directly upon the volume of his payments; . . . But the size of that part of this stock which he holds as a first line of defense against emergencies depends less directly upon the volume of his payments; it depends upon his *estimate* of contingent payments, and consequently varies with his state of mind, or, more concretely, with the business outlook. . . . It seems reasonable, therefore, to regard this latter part of the aggregate money stock as a reserve whose size is regulated largely by the general level of confidence—a reservoir from which money flows into active circulation when times are good, and into which money flows from active circulation when times are bad. . . . Accordingly it seems that theory is brought into closer relation with the facts when we recognize that part of the demand for money arises from the need to make provision against contingent payments, and that this part of the demand fluctuates in response to changes in the general condition of confidence in some measure independently of the volume of payments. [1921, pp. 29–33, italics in original]

In its clear distinction between the two incentives for holding money—and in its explicit statement that that part held as a contingency reserve changes "in some measure independently of the volume of payment"—this striking passage is, to the best of my knowledge, unique in the Cambridge literature. I find it accordingly significant that Lavington himself considers this description of the demand for money to be "rather different from (though not inconsistent with) that laid down by the Quantity theory."

As noted above (p. 172), there is no discussion of the relative advantages of holding different assets in the first (1922) edition of Robertson's book *Money*. In the 1928 and later editions, however, Robertson wrote that

> . . . taking the country as a whole at any given time, we can express its demand for money—that is, the real value of its money supply—as a proportion of its real national income. . . .
>
> On what then does the magnitude of this proportion depend? It depends on the one hand, as has been said, on the convenience and sense of security derived from the possession of a pool of money, and on the other, on the strength of the alternative attractions of increased consumption, or lucrative investment in trade capital or in Government or industrial stocks, against which these advantages have to be weighed up. Thus the magnitude of the demand for money, like that of the demand for bread, turns out to be the result of a process of individual weighing-up of competing advantages *at the margin*. [1928, pp. 38–39, italics in original; the same passage appears on pp. 36–37 of the 1948 edition]

Keynes' criticism in the *Treatise* of Pigou's presentation of the Cambridge equation, $P = kR/M$ (cited on pp. 173–74 above), is as follows:

> The introduction of the factor R, the current income of the community, suggests that variation in this is one of the two or three most important direct influences on the demand for cash resources. In the case of the income-deposits this seems to me to be true. But the significance of R is much diminished when we are dealing, not with the income-deposits in isolation, but with the total deposits. Indeed the chief inconvenience of the "Cambridge" quantity equation really lies in its applying to the total deposits considerations which are primarily relevant only to the income-deposits, and in its tackling the problem as though the same sort of considerations which govern the income-deposits also govern the total deposits [i.e., income-deposits *plus* savings deposits—or in United States terminology, demand deposits *plus* time deposits]. . . .
>
> The prominence given to k, namely the proportion of the bank-deposits to the community's *income*, is misleading when it is extended beyond the income-deposits. The emphasis which this method lays on the point that the amount of real balances held is

determined by the comparative advantages of holding resources in cash and in alternative forms, so that a change in k will be attributable to a change in these comparative advantages, is useful and instructive. But "resources" in this connection ought not to be interpreted, as it is interpreted by Prof. Pigou, as being identical with current *income*. [*Treatise* I, pp. 207–8, italics in original]

I might note that even though Robertson defends the Cambridge equation against Keynes' criticisms here, he does not question Keynes' interpretation of Pigou's term "resources" as "income." Robertson's not very convincing answer to Keynes is as follows:

It is of course true (as is recognized in Marshall's own illustration of the "Cambridge" theory) that many people will have other quantities than their income in mind (for instance, their capital or their business turnover) in deciding upon their monetary requirements. But from the fact that their money stock is not exclusively *determined* as a proportion of their income, it does not follow that it cannot usefully be *expressed* as such a proportion; still less that the real value of the whole community's total money stock cannot usefully be expressed (as in the equation $M/P = KR$) in terms of the constituents of real income or output. For the whole of M is *potentially* expendable against output, and if in any period of time more or less of it were to be so expended than was previously the case, P would alter. It is of the utmost importance that under certain conditions money which has been imprisoned in what Mr. Keynes calls the "savings deposits" and "business deposits" may seep out, raise the aggregate of incomes and "income deposits," and drive up P. Such a change is represented in the "Cambridge" approach by a diminution of K: it would not be represented by any change in a symbol which stood for the proportion borne to R by the real value of "income deposits" alone. [1933, pp. 92–93, italics in original]

I presume that what Robertson had in mind in his reference to "Marshall's own illustration of the 'Cambridge' theory" is Marshall's discussion in the first paragraph of the citation from *Money, Credit and Commerce* (1923, p. 44) reproduced at the beginning of this Appendix. In any event, as already noted above (p. 174), it is puzzling that Robertson does not refer here to the far more substantive discussion in Lavington (1921, pp. 32–33) cited above in this Appendix (last three paragraphs of the passage cited).

7

Keynes and the Multiplier

I sincerely appreciate the invitation of the Money Study Group to participate in this conference in memory of Harry Johnson; for, in addition to my general relationship with him, it was Harry who first brought me to a conference of this group over five years ago.[1]

Nor is it an accident that I have chosen to speak today on an aspect of Keynes' work, for this was a subject that was central to Harry's interest. Thus on more than one occasion in his unfortunately short lifetime he was called upon by the profession to deliver his considered judgment on the nature of Keynes' contribution. Most notable in this context was Harry Johnson's invited lecture at the December 1960 meetings of the American Economic Association, "The *General Theory* after Twenty-five Years."

This much-reprinted paper also provides an excellent example of the incisive literary style, broad perspective, and highly developed critical judgment which characterized Harry's work. Thus Harry interpreted the *General Theory* not as an isolated book, but against the background of Keynes' earlier *Treatise* and of the general Marshallian tradition. Nor did he hesitate to criticize various aspects of the *General Theory*. And he was even more critical (and this was a recurrent theme of many of his subsequent writings on Keynes[2]) of

Reprinted by permission from the *Manchester School* 45 (September 1978): 209–23. This was a special issue containing the proceedings of a conference of the Money Study Group in memory of Harry Johnson held in April 1978 at Manchester University. The last third of the original article contained material that appears elsewhere in this book, and so has been deleted. As indicated, however, other material has been added at the end. Some minor changes have also been made at other points.

This paper was written while I was serving as Ford Foundation Visiting Research Professor at the University of Chicago. I would like to acknowledge the aid received from NSF grant no. SOC77–12212. My thanks too to my research assistant, Clark Nardinelli, and to Mrs. Myrna Lane for typing this paper through its various drafts. The paper draws freely on my *Keynes' Monetary Thought* (1976).

1. [On which occasion the paper reproduced in the preceding chapter was presented.]
2. Most of these have been reproduced in the collection of essays by Elizabeth and Harry Johnson entitled *The Shadow of Keynes* (1978).

the hardening of certain of Keynes's conclusions into rigid dogmas in the hands of his disciples—notably the hardening of his legitimate criticisms of the quantity theory into militant opposition to any form of quantity theory reasoning, and the hardening of his opinion that monetary policy might be ineffective in combating a collapse of the marginal efficiency of capital into the conflicting dogmas (*a*) that monetary restriction is dangerous because it might precipitate such a collapse, (*b*) that monetary restriction is useless because it will have a negligible effect on effective demand. Part of it is that for obvious reasons Keynesians have tended to be politically left of center, a position associated with distrust of central bankers—particularly in England, due to the part the Bank of England played in the restoration of the gold standard and the downfall of the second Labor Government. Much of it is simply that the "vulgar Keynesians" seized on the simplest and most striking version of the Keynesian system—autonomous investment and the multiplier—as the essence of it, ignoring the monetary analysis as an irrelevant complication. [1961, p. 145]

In the light of some of the things that have recently been written about the relationship between Harry and Chicago monetarism, it is worth noting that these views were expressed by him a relatively short time after he had come to Chicago. So to my mind they provide further support for David Laidler's contention in his paper for this conference[3] that Harry's shift toward a more monetaristic approach to macroeconomics began before his arrival at Chicago.

Despite the somewhat disparaging reference to the multiplier at the end of the passage just cited, it is clear that Harry considered the multiplier to be a central feature of the *General Theory*. In his words:

The contribution of the *General Theory* to modern economics is certainly not Keynes's specific model of income determination, for not only is his consumption function too simple but his theory of investment is incomplete and has to be extended to make it usable. Rather, the contribution lies in the general nature of Keynes's approach to the problem of income and employment. In the first place, he concentrated attention on the expenditure-income and income-expenditure relationships, which are much easier to understand and apply than the quantity theory relationships and which provide, in the multiplier analysis, a key to dynamic processes of change. [1961, p. 144]

And again:

The novel and intriguing element in the theory was the propensity to consume, together with its *alter ego*, that inexhaustibly versatile mechanical toy, the multiplier. [1961, p. 140]

3. "Harry Johnson as a Macroeconomist" (1982).

And it is of the evolution of this "toy" that I wish to speak today.

Let me begin by noting that the general notion of the multiplier—by which I mean the notion that an initial increase (or decrease) in expenditures has a multiple effect on total expenditures—goes back at least to the nineteenth century. Thus in his monograph *The Multiplier Theory* (1954, pp. 1–3), Hugo Hegeland finds references to this notion in the intensive debate about Say's law which took place in the second quarter of that century, and in the writings of Bagehot at the end of its third quarter.

The notion—and even the term "multiplying principle"—appeared clearly in Nicholas Johannsen's 1908 book, *A Neglected Point in Connection with Crises* (pp. 43ff.), in the context of explaining the cumulative effects of the downswing of the cycle. Though Keynes did not discuss this "principle" in his *Treatise*, he did refer to Johannsen as one of those "amateur American economists (cranks some might say)" (*TM* II, p. 90). But Johannsen's work was at the time considered sufficiently important to be referred to several times in Wesley Mitchell's classic 1913 work on *Business Cycles* (pp. 18–19, 389, 580–81) as well as in his later *Business Cycles: The Problem and Its Setting* (1927, p. 25n). And it apparently also influenced J. A. Hobson's *Industrial System* (1910, p. 302; cited by Coppock 1953, p. 56, n. 5).

In contrast with the *Treatise*, the *General Theory* does, of course, discuss the multiplier; on the other hand, it does not refer to Johannsen! Instead, as we all know, the discussion in the *General Theory* (chap. 10) is based on Richard Kahn's celebrated 1931 article "The Relation of Home Investment to Unemployment." At the time he wrote the first version of this article, Kahn—who had been tutored by Keynes at Cambridge only a few years before—was acting as joint secretary of the Committee of Economists, of which Keynes was chairman.[4] This was a subcommittee of the Economic Advisory Council, on which more in a moment.

Actually, though, Keynes' relation to the multiplier—albeit without use of that term—dates back at least to the May 1929 pamphlet *Can Lloyd George Do It? An Examination of the Liberal Pledge* that he wrote with Hubert Henderson. This pamphlet was written in connection with the 1929 election campaign which was then under way, and in which the Liberal Party, with Lloyd George at its head, had pledged itself to reduce the heavy unemployment that had prevailed in Britain since the return to the gold standard in 1925 by undertaking a program of public works.

By its own description (*JMK* IX, p. 87), *Can Lloyd George Do It?*

---

4. Cf. Howson and Winch (1977, pp. 48–49), [I have taken advantage of this reprinting to correct a minor error of fact which appeared here in the original article.]

was written as a supplement to the Liberal Party pamphlet *We Can Conquer Unemployment* which had appeared two months before. This in turn was based on the famous "Yellow Book" of the Liberal Party—*Britain's Industrial Future* (1928)—which had set out the program of the Liberal Party in detail, and in whose writing Keynes had played a prominent role (Harrod 1951, pp. 329–93). *We Can Conquer Unemployment* had provoked an official response from the government in the form of its *Memoranda on Certain Proposals Relating to Unemployment* (1929, Cmd. 3331). In addition to criticizing details of the Liberal Party public-works program, this famous (or infamous, depending on one's viewpoint) White Paper advanced the general contention that:

> Apart from its financial reactions, a big programme of State-aided public works has a disturbing effect upon the general industrial position. If it is a long programme with continuity of work promised to the personnel, it draws off labour which would otherwise find employment, though perhaps with less regularity, in normal industry, without being able to ensure replacement. . . . [Cmd. 3331, p. 10]

This was an expression of what had become enshrined as the "Treasury view," according to which expenditures on public works would simply divert investment from the private to the government sector and hence would not generate a net increase in employment. This "view" was the subject of intensive debates at the time (Hutchison 1953, pp. 416–17, 421); and it is a discouraging reflection on the state of our discipline to note that in recent years, half-a-century later, this issue is again being hotly debated—this time, under the heading of "crowding-out effect."

After devoting the first five chapters of *Can Lloyd George Do It?* to the British economic situation and the nature of the Liberal program, Keynes and Henderson turned their attention in chapter 6 to the specific question, "How Much Employment Will the Liberal Plan Provide?" They began the first section of this chapter with an estimate of the amount of employment that would be directly generated by (say) £1,000,000 of expenditures on road building (*JMK* IX, pp. 103–4), then went on (in sec. 2) to emphasize the importance of the "indirect employment" that would also be generated. In Keynes' words:[5]

> There is nothing fanciful or fine-spun about the proposition that the construction of roads entails a demand for road materials, which

5. Chapters and sections of the original publication are respectively indicated by roman and arabic numbers in the form as reprinted in *JMK* IX. According to Harrod (1951, p. 395), Keynes was the major author of *Can Lloyd George Do It?* Accordingly, I shall for convenience refer henceforth only to him in this connection.

entails a demand for labour and also for other commodities, which, in their turn, entail a demand for labour. Such reactions are of the very essence of the industrial process.Why, the first step towards a right understanding of the economic world is to realise how far-reaching such reactions are, to appreciate how vast is the range of trades and occupations which contribute to the production of the commonest commodities. That a demand for a suit of clothes implies a demand for cloth; that a demand for cloth implies a demand for yarns and tops, and so for wool; that the services of farmers, merchants, engineers, miners, transport workers, clerks, are all involved—this is the A B C of economic science. . . .

Generally speaking, the indirect employment which schemes of capital expenditure would entail is far larger than the direct employment. This fact is one of the strongest arguments for pressing forward with such schemes; for it means that the greater part of the employment they would provide would be spread far and wide over the industries of the country. But the fact that the indirect employment would be spread far and wide does not mean that it is in the least doubtful or illusory. On the contrary, it is calculable within fairly precise limits. [*JMK* IX, pp. 105–6]

Let me immediately emphasize that this is not what we now call the multiplier: for there is nothing in this description to imply that the total expansion in the economy will exceed the initial expenditure of £1,000,000. In terms of present-day input-output analysis, what the foregoing passage describes is how an increase in road building as a component of the final-bill-of-goods percolates through the system of interindustry relations to yield a total increase in the demand for labor as one of the primary inputs of the economy. But there is no reference in this passage to the subsequent increase in the consumption component of the final-bill-of-goods generated by the increased labor income and to the consequent further increase in the demand for labor—and that is the critical feedback assumption of the multiplier.

Such a feedback effect is however alluded to in section 3 of chapter 6 of *Can Lloyd George Do It?*, which begins as follows:

But this is not the whole of the story. In addition to the indirect employment with which we have been dealing, a policy of development would promote employment in other ways. The fact that many workpeople who are now unemployed would be receiving wages instead of unemployment pay would mean an increase in effective purchasing power which would give a general stimulus to trade. Moreover, the greater trade activity would make for further trade activity; for the forces of prosperity, like those of trade depression, work with a cumulative effect. When trade is slack there is a tendency to postpone placing orders, a reluctance to lay in stocks, a general hesitation to go forward or take risks. When, on the other hand, the wheels of trade begin to move briskly the opposite set of forces comes into play, a mood favorable to enterprise and capital extensions spreads through the business community, and the expansion of trade gains accordingly a gathering momentum.

It is not possible to measure effects of this character with any sort of precision, and little or no account of them is, therefore, taken in *We Cán Conquer Unemployment*. But, in our opinion, these effects are of immense importance . . . [*JMK* IX, pp. 106–7]

Here, then, among other things, is the idea of the multiplier; but note that for Keynes at that time its effects could not be measured "with any sort of precision."

Let me digress for a moment and note that Keynes' analysis of an increase of £1,000,000 of government expenditures in terms of its effects on employment and not national product was simply due to the fact that there were as yet no official current national-income estimates in Britain.[6] In contrast, ever since the early 1920s, current official estimates of British employment (or rather unemployment, as measured by the "Number of Insured Persons Recorded as Unemployed") had been published in the *Ministry of Labour Gazette*. Indeed, Keynes referred to them at an earlier point in *Can Lloyd George Do It?* (*JMK* IX, p. 92). Furthermore, it was employment—the chronically low level of employment that had existed ever since the mid-1920s—which was Keynes' primary concern in this pamphlet.

To complete his case for public works expenditures, Keynes had to deal with the "Treasury view." Accordingly he began chapter 9 of *Can Lloyd George Do It?* with the following statement:

The objection which is raised more frequently perhaps, than any other, is that money raised by the state for financing productive schemes must diminish *pro tanto* the supply of capital available for ordinary industry. If this is true, a policy of national development will not really increase employment. It will merely substitute employment on State schemes for ordinary employment.

This was the contention of the Chancellor of the Exchequer[7] in his budget speech.

"It is the orthodox Treasury dogma, steadfastly held," he told the House of Commons, "that whatever might be the political or social advantages, very little additional employment and no permanent additional employment, can, in fact, and as a general rule, be created by State borrowing and State expenditure." Some State expenditure he concluded, is inevitable, and even wise and right for its own sake, *but not as a cure for unemployment.*

6. For details, see pp. 244–46 below.
7. Who was none other than Winston Churchill.

In relation to the actual facts of today, this argument is, we believe, quite without foundation. [*JMK* IX, p. 115, italics in original]

And Keynes then proceeded with an analysis of the different ways the
new investment would generate new savings, which he summarized in
the following words:

> Here, then, is our answer. The savings which Mr. Lloyd George's
> schemes will employ will be diverted, not from financing other cap-
> ital equipment, but [1] partly from financing unemployment. [2] A
> further part will come from the savings which now run to waste
> through lack of adequate credit. [3] Something will be provided by
> the very prosperity which the new policy will foster. [4] And the
> balance will be found by a reduction of foreign lending.
>
> The whole of the labour of the unemployed is available to increase
> the national wealth. It is crazy to believe that we shall ruin ourselves
> financially by trying to find means for using it and that "Safety
> First" lies in continuing to maintain men in idleness.
>
> It is precisely *with* our unemployed productive resources that we
> shall make the new investments. [*JMK* IX, p. 120, italics in original;
> bracketed numbers added]

By the first of these four ways, Keynes had in mind the reduction in
government expenditure (and hence in its deficit) made possible by the
removal from the dole of those men who now find employment. The
second way must be understood within the conceptual framework of
the *Treatise*, on which Keynes was then working, and in which savings
and investment were not necessarily equal (*TM* I, pp. 113–14, 132). The
third way is the most interesting of all from the viewpoint of Keynes'
later writings (see above, pp. 9–10), for it contains a hint of a feedback
mechanism by which greater prosperity generates greater savings
(though I must admit that in contrast with the other three ways described here, this one is not discussed at an earlier point in chapter 9 of
Can Lloyd George Do It? and is mentioned only in the foregoing summary paragraph). Note, however, the absence of a demonstration that
savings not only increase in these four ways, but do so to the full extent
necessary for financing the additional government investment.

The next episode in the story of the multiplier took place at the
Economic Advisory Council. This council has been established by the
newly elected Labor government in January 1930 for the purpose of
advising it on the serious economic problems which confronted the
country, foremost among which was that of unemployment. As might
be expected, Keynes played a leading, if not dominating, role on this
council. It operated with a small junior staff which included Colin
Clark, who had been recruited by G. D. H. Cole (also a member of the
council), whose student Clark had been at Oxford (Howson and Winch

1977, p. 25).[8] In May 1930, Keynes and Cole recommended that the staff of the council prepare an estimate of the direct and indirect effects on employment of the maximum feasible expansion of exports. Accordingly, a month later Colin Clark submitted a mimeographed three-page memorandum titled "Export Trade in Relation to Unemployment"[9] which assumed that exports could expand by £100 million and then addressed itself to the following questions:

> It is required firstly to estimate the employment which would be directly available in the actual manufacture of the volume of goods in question. Secondly, an estimate is required of the number of workers who would be employed in transportation, merchanting and other non-industrial work in connection with this assumed increase in trade. Thirdly, arises the question of the possible improvement in the general demand for food, clothing, amusements, etc., consequent upon the re-employment of workers in the exporting industries and also the psychological effect of a considerable increase in the export figures.

Simple estimates were then presented of the first two items, with an allowance being made "for the imported raw materials incorporated in the value of British exports." Clark then stated:

> There finally remains the consideration of the third point, as to what might be called the "repercussive" effects of any considerable increase in the export trade. It will be seen at once that any crude method of calculation, such as assuming a further rise in employment owing to the spending in the home market of any given proportion of the earnings of the re-employed workers in the export trades, would lead to assuming an infinite series of beneficial repercussions. This clearly might misrepresent the case; on the other hand we cannot deny the possibility of beneficial repercussions. The limiting factors, however, are obscure and economic theory cannot state the possibilities with precision.

This, then, was the state of the art in May 1930: except among adherents of the Treasury view, there was no doubt that the multiplier (which term was not yet in use) was greater than unity; but the theoretical question to which no satisfactory answer had yet been formulated was, why was it not infinity?[10] Alternatively, in terms of the

---

8. [Clark (1977) has recently written a memoir of his experiences as an economist during the early 1930s, including those at the Economic Advisory Council.]

9. Referred to by Howson and Winch (1977, p. 36n).

10. This is the way I understand Clark's reference to "an infinite series of beneficial repercussions." However, in his discussion of this paper at the conference, John Flemming pointed out that as a graduate of the physical sciences (Clark's degree was in chemistry), Clark must have surely known that the sum of an infinite series was not necessarily infinite. Thus Clark might have simply meant that he did not not know how to provide a precise mathematical description of the "infinite series of beneficial

question Sir Austin Robinson recalls having asked in the early 1920s,[11] if somebody spends an additional pound, why does it not just keep on being spent by successive recipients until it puts all the unemployed back to work?

And now the stage was set for Richard Kahn's multiplier article. The first version of this (which I have unfortunately not succeeded in seeing) was completed in September 1930 as a memorandum for the Committee of Economists of the Economic Advisory Council (Kahn 1972, p. vii; *JMK* XIII, p. 340, n. 3; Howson and Winch 1977, pp. 48–49). In the published version, Kahn made use of the notion (though not the term) of the marginal propensities to import and save, respectively, and (assuming these to be greater than zero) showed that the infinite series of "beneficial repercussions" (Kahn 1931, p. 1) could then be expressed as a convergent geometric series. It was only if these propensities were both zero that "one man put to work on the roads would then place all the remainder of the unemployed into secondary employment" (Kahn 1931, pp. 13, 18–19).[12]

The sum of the series in the usual, convergent case yielded (in Kahn's terms) "the ratio of secondary to primary employment"— which, of course, is one less than the multiplier (a term which Kahn did not use). Relying on (unspecified) data with which Colin Clark had supplied him, Kahn then provided estimates of this ratio in Britain under various assumptions as to the values of the different marginal propensities. Kahn felt that the most plausible estimate was a ratio slightly greater than 0.75—corresponding to a multiplier of 1.75 (Kahn 1931, pp. 13–15).

However, Kahn's purpose was not only to provide the precise formula of a finite multiplier, but also to demonstrate that the funds to

---

repercussions"—and hence obviously could not sum it up. I find it difficult to accept this alternative interpretation: for if Clark had in mind "an infinite series of beneficial repercussions" which converged to a finite magnitude, why should he have thought that "this clearly might misrepresent the case" and, even more so, that "the limiting factors . . . are obscure"?

[In Part I above I have on several occasions expressed (sometimes implicitly) unwillingness to accept the present-day recollection of various individuals as definitive evidence of events which occurred thirty or forty years ago (cf. the references to Ohlin, Myrdal and Joan Robinson on, respectively, pp. 36 (introductory footnote), 51 (n. 31), and 94 above). A conversation I had with Colin Clark in July 1978 about his 1930 memorandum—and which with his characteristic candor he has gallantly consented to my reproducing here—provides an excellent example of the pitfalls involved in such recollections. In particular, in that conversation I asked Colin Clark which of the two interpretations of what he had in mind in the aforementioned passage from this memorandum, mine or Flemming's, was correct—and he unhesitatingly replied that Flemming's was. But as we continued with our conversation, Clark suddenly remarked that he actually had no recollection of ever having written the 1930 memorandum!]

11. See his contribution to the discussion recorded in Patinkin and Leith (1977, p. 82).

12. Unfortunately, Kahn does not indicate the source of this expression.

finance the increased employment would necessarily be forthcoming, thus refuting the Treasury view.[13] This he did in two alternative ways:[14] first, by summing up the geometric series of "leakages"[15] into imports and savings corresponding to the "repercussions" and showing that this sum equaled the initial "cost of investment" in the public works; second, by making use of "Mr. Meade's relation,"[16] which Kahn (1931, p. 17) rendered as

cost of [additional] investment =
    saving on dole + increase in excess of imports
    over exports + increase in unspent profits.

[By "saving on dole" Kahn meant the first of the sources of additional savings that Keynes had pointed out in his *Can Lloyd George Do It?* (above, p. 195). By "increase in unspent profits" he meant "that part of the increase in profits that is devoted neither to home-produced consumption-goods nor to imported goods" (Kahn 1931, p. 17). Thus, in present-day terms, "Mr. Meade's relation" is simply the national-income identity

increase in investment = decrease in government deficit
    + increase in import surplus + increase in private savings,

where (by Kahn's assumption) the increase in private savings comes solely out of profits. Thus Kahn assumed that all additional wage income generated by the "secondary employment" is consumed.[17] In any event, Kahn seems to have given more weight to the first two of his sources for financing the additional investment than to the third. Indeed, Warming (1932, p. 214) subsequently accused him of concentrating solely on the leakage into imports, a charge Kahn (1932, p. 492) firmly denied, saying that his original article "is crammed with

---

13. In some recent reminiscences, Kahn has again stated that one of the main purposes of his 1931 article was "finally disposing of the 'Treasury view' " (see his 1974 letter to me as reproduced in Patinkin and Leith [1977, p. 147]). [See also p. 30, n. 27 above.]
    14. I am indebted to Michael Danes of Queen Mary College for pointing this out at the conference.
    15. A term which Kahn first used only in a later, 1933 article; see also *JMK* XIII, p. 414.
    16. At the time Kahn was working on this article, James Meade was visiting for a year at Cambridge from Oxford, and Kahn had many discussions with him on these questions.
    17. This has recently been pointed out by Cain (1979, pp. 110–11), who refers in this context to pp. 11–14 of Kahn's article (pp. 184–85 of the original *Economic Journal* version). (The evidence from "Mr. Meade's relation" is even clearer on this point.) Cain goes on to infer from this that Kahn (as contrasted with the Danish economist Warming) did not at the time really have the notion of a savings function. This inference, however, seems to me to be unwarranted, for after all Kahn did relate the amount of "unspent profits" to the total of such profits: namely, the former was assumed to be a constant proportion of the latter (Kahn 1931, pp. 14–17).

references to 'the saving on the dole' and to 'the increase in unspent profits.' "[18]

In his chapter in the *General Theory* entitled "The Marginal Propensity to Consume and the Multiplier," Keynes cites Kahn's 1931 article as the place where "the conception of the multiplier was first introduced into economic theory" (*GT*, p. 113). The essential role that the multiplier plays in the *General Theory* is attested to by Keynes' declaration to Beveridge, shortly after its publication, that "about half the book is really about it" (*JMK* XIV, p. 57). There are, however, differences of emphasis between Kahn's multiplier and Keynes'. Thus, for reasons that I have elsewhere explained (*KMT*, pp. 13, 16, 136), Keynes' analysis in the *General Theory* for the most part assumes a closed economy; correspondingly, though Keynes does discuss the leakage into imports in this chapter (*GT*, pp. 120–22), he is not too much concerned with it. Furthermore, for reasons I do not understand, he no longer refers to "saving on the dole." Nor does he in this chapter distinguish between the marginal propensities of wage-earners and profit recipients.[19] Thus it is only the aggregate savings—or consumption—function that concerns Keynes. Correspondingly, he describes the economy in terms of a single marginal propensity to consume and then shows that the multiplier is simply $1/(1 - MPC)$ (*GT*, pp. 115 and 126, n. 2).][20]

Let me conclude this paper by noting that there are two further aspects of the multiplier which deserve attention: first, the relation between Kahn's multiplier analysis and the discovery of the *General Theory;* second, Keynes' empirical estimates of the multiplier. These aspects are respectively discussed in chapter 1 above (pp. 26–31) and in chapter 9 below (pp. 234–37).[21]

18. Cf. again Cain (1979, pp. 113–14).

19. Though he had made such a distinction in his 1933 *Means to Prosperity,* where he had assumed a higher marginal propensity to consume for wage earners (*JMK* IX, p. 343).

20. This simplified formula may in part have been motivated by Keynes' attempt in the *General Theory* to present an estimate of the multiplier based on national-income data, for at the time such data existed at best only for aggregates. In this connection it should be noted that Keynes' first attempt to construct such an estimate occurred in 1933. For further discussion of these points, see pp. 234–37 below.

21. [The concluding paragraphs of the original article more or less reproduced the material just referred to; see introductory footnote to this chapter.]

8

The Development of Keynes' Policy Thinking

Since my concern in this paper is with economic policy, I must begin with a brief description of the economic situation in Britain during the period in question, 1920–35. Figure 8 shows that significant unemployment prevailed throughout the 1920s and, as a result of the Great Depression in the United States, became even more severe in the beginning of the 1930s. But despite this continued unemployment, the nominal wage rate in Britain declined very slowly, and this together with the sharper decline in the price level meant that the real wage rate actually rose. This should be contrasted with the situation in the United States, where the nominal wage rate declined sharply, but not as sharply as the price level, so that there too there was an increase in the real wage rate, though much less so than in Britain (see below, p. 238, n. 27).

There are two additional crucial events of the period, and both have to do with the gold standard. The first was Britain's return to this standard at prewar parity in April 1925, a decision that, according to Keynes (1925), created deflationary pressures and hence a worsening of the unemployment. The second event was Britain's departure from gold in September 1931, which was followed by the collapse of the international gold standard as a whole.

You will note that in my description of the economic developments

Presidential Address delivered at the first meeting of the Israel Economic Association in Jerusalem in April 1976. The paper appeared originally in Hebrew in the proceedings volume of these meetings, *Iyunim Be-kalkalah* [Studies in economics], edited by Nadav Halevi and Yaakov Kop (Jerusalem: The Israel Economic Association and the Maurice Falk Institute for Economic Research in Israel, 1976), pp. 1–10. The following is a slightly modified form of the English version of the paper which was subsequently published in *Theory for Economic Efficiency: Essays in Honor of Abba P. Lerner*, edited by H. I. Greenfield et al. (Cambridge, Mass.: M.I.T. Press, 1979), pp. 151–66. Reprinted with permission. The discussion of the *General Theory* at the end has been expanded, and a few minor changes have been made in the earlier parts.

This paper draws freely on the material in chapter 12 of my monograph *Keynes' Monetary Thought* (1976). It is part of a larger study undertaken at the Maurice Falk Institute for Economic Research in Israel and financed in part by a grant from the Ford Foundation, received through the Israel Foundation Trustees.

of this period I have not made use of what would seem to be the most relevant macroeconomic statistics for this purpose: national-income statistics. The reason is simple: my desire is to present the economic picture as it was seen by the economists and policymakers of the period, and official annual national-income statistics were not then available. Indeed they did not become available in Britain until World War II, several years after their appearance in the United States. Similarly I have not presented any figures on the money supply, for, surprising as it may seem, such data were not published in Britain until the early 1960s, a full quarter-century after they began to be published in the United States (cf. below, pp. 244–46 and p. 255 n. 55).

Against this background I will discuss the puzzle (for it is one) of the changes in Keynes' thought as represented in his major monetary writings of the interwar period: the *Tract on Monetary Reform* (December 1923), the *Treatise on Money* (October 1930), and last and, of course, most important, the *General Theory* (February 1936). In his first book, Keynes recapitulated the quantity theory of money as he had inherited it from his teachers at Cambridge, Alfred Marshall and A. C. Pigou. In his second book, Keynes developed what he presented in his preface as a "novel" theory (*TM* I, p. xvii), which took the form of his famous fundamental equations. And in his third book he developed the $C + I + G = Y$ macroeconomic theory, which we continue to teach today.

A central problem that concerned Keynes in all three of these books was unemployment. As I have already noted, Britain suffered from unemployment in the two years that preceded the publication of the *Tract*. It continued to prevail throughout the five years that Keynes was writing the *Treatise*, and even more seriously throughout the five years that he was writing the *General Theory*. A common characteristic of all three of these books is Keynes' opposition to attempts to combat unemployment by reducing the nominal wage rate. At the same time, it seems to me that there is a difference between the *Treatise* and the *General Theory* on this point, for my impression is that in the *Treatise*, Keynes believed that such a reduction could theoretically help but practically could not be carried out; whereas in the *General Theory*, he opposed it on theoretical grounds as well. In part this difference may have stemmed from the fact that Keynes in 1930 was writing under the influence of the inflexibility of British money wages in the years that had preceded, whereas in 1936 he also had before him the United States experience of the sharp reduction in money wages during 1929–33 that had not succeeded in solving the unemployment problem (note Keynes' allusion to this experience on p. 9 of the *General Theory*).

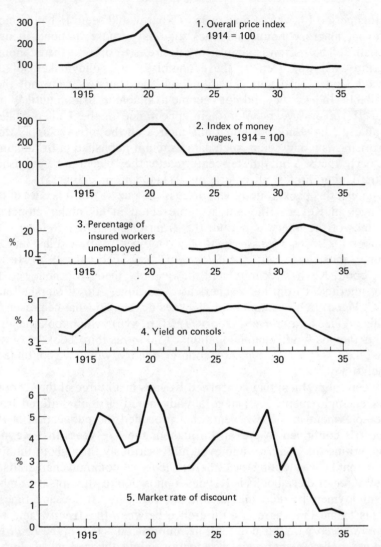

Figure 8. Major economic developments in the United Kingdom, 1913–35. From Mitchell and Deane (1962): chart 1, pp. 474–75; chart 2, pp. 344–45; chart 3, p. 67; chart 4, p. 455; chart 5, p. 460.

I will not, however, discuss this question further here, for what interests me is not the similarity between these two books but the difference between them with respect to the policies they advocated to reduce unemployment. The commonly accepted view is that whereas in the *Treatise* Keynes advocated the use of monetary policy, in the *General Theory* he advocated fiscal policy instead. By the latter I obviously mean a policy that makes use of variations in the level of government expenditures and/or tax receipts to affect macroeconomic behavior. But to avoid any possible misunderstandings, I must emphasize that the meaning of "monetary policy" in this context does not correspond to its meaning today: for under the influence of Milton Friedman, this term has come to denote a macroeconomic policy that makes use of variations in the money supply; when applied to Keynes of the *Treatise*, however, it denotes a central-bank policy that attempts to affect macroeconomic behavior by variations in the rate of interest. Indeed, as I have already noted, at the time Keynes wrote there did not even exist official statistics on the money supply. Correspondingly, when in his *Treatise* Keynes wished to provide an empirical description of the changes in the supply of money in Britain, he had to construct the estimates himself (*Treatise* II, chap. 23).

This is the accepted version of the change in Keynes' policy views. And though in its broad lines it is correct, it does not properly describe what was in fact a much more complex development. The simplest and most concrete indication of this fact is that Keynes' advocacy of public-works expenditures preceded the *General Theory* by many years. In particular, he had already advocated such expenditures in 1929 in his famous tract *Can Lloyd George Do It?* which he wrote with Hubert Henderson in support of the Liberal party's platform in the British elections of that year. Here Keynes advocated "a positive policy of national development" (*JMK* IX, p. 86) as a necessary one for solving the serious problem of unemployment that then beset the country. Indeed he even went on to say that public-works expenditures would achieve this purpose not only because of the "direct employment" that they provided, but also because of the "indirect employment" generated by the need to supply the necessary raw materials and the like for these works. And yet further employment would be generated by the fact that "many workpeople who are now unemployed would be receiving wages instead of unemployment pay [and this] would mean an increase in effective purchasing power which would give a general stimulus to trade. Moreover, the greater trade activity would make for further trade activity; for the forces of prosperity, like those of trade depression, work with a cumulative effect" (*JMK* IX, p. 106). In brief, the beginnings of the multiplier, but that is another story.[1] What concerns me instead is the following question: Did Keynes advocate fiscal policy in 1929, change his mind and advocate monetary policy in his 1930 *Treatise*, and then change his mind once again in his 1936 *General Theory?*

1. [Which has been told in the preceding chapter.]

Merely to describe such a quick double-reversal is enough to indicate its implausibility. This is particularly true in light of the well-known fact that Keynes spent several years writing and rewriting the *Treatise* and was indeed so engaged at the very time that he wrote *Can Lloyd George Do It?* Correspondingly one must ask why the strong advocacy of public works that characterizes the latter is not reflected in the *Treatise*.

One might contend that Keynes changed his mind about public works at too late a stage in the writing of the *Treatise* to reflect it there and that, indeed, this advocacy was one of the things he had in mind in his preface to the *Treatise* when he said that were he to write the book again, he would do it differently. In my opinion, however, this can at best explain only a very small part of the puzzle, for it does not fit in with what is now known about the chronology of the writing of the *Treatise*. In particular, Keynes wrote *Can Lloyd George Do It?* in May 1929, whereas in August 1929 we find him writing his publisher that a one-volume edition of the *Treatise* was more or less ready in proof, but that he had come to the realization that he must "embark upon a somewhat drastic rewriting" (*JMK* XIII, pp. 117–18; *KMT*, p. 78). And, indeed, as a result of this "rewriting" the book expanded to two volumes, which appeared only after another fourteen months. We also know that at the time that Keynes advocated public works in his "private evidence" before the Macmillan Committee in February 1930 (on which more below), he was still working on the proofs of the *Treatise*. It is clear, therefore, that even after May 1929, Keynes had the opportunity to introduce changes into the *Treatise*, had he so desired. And so the puzzle of the apparent inconsistency between Keynes of *Can Lloyd George Do It?* and Keynes of the *Treatise* remains.

As a preliminary to solving this puzzle, let me add two more pieces of background information—two characteristics of Keynes that are essential to our story. The first is that Keynes did not live in the world of academe. He was not a professor. Indeed, in the interwar period he was not even a university lecturer. For Keynes first achieved fame not as a professional economist but as a publicist. In particular his sweeping criticism of the Versailles Treaty in his 1919 book, *The Economic Consequences of the Peace*, turned him overnight into a worldwide figure. And from then on Keynes devoted a good part of his time to journalistic activities, which throughout the interwar period were his main source of income (E. Johnson 1977, pp. 30–32). During this time Keynes was also extremely active in the political sphere. He not only wrote political tracts, but also advised prime ministers and ministers of finance—sometimes informally, sometimes even formally. Thus Keynes was the central figure of three major government committees which, each in its own way, were charged with dealing with the problem of unemployment: the Macmillan Committee (1929–31), the Economic Advisory Council (1930–39), and its related Committee of Economists (1930).[2]

The second of Keynes' characteristics that I would like to emphasize is that, with the exception of his largely descriptive *Indian Currency and Finance* (1913), the *Treatise* was his first scholarly work in economics. Indeed it seems to me that after Keynes in the 1920s had won world acclaim as a public figure, he attempted by means of the *Treatise* to win similar acclaim as a professional economist. This was to be his magnum opus that would firmly establish his reputation in the academic world as a whole. And when Keynes first published the *Treatise,* there was no doubt in his mind that he had accomplished this purpose. This is evident from his very choice of the term "fundamental equations" to denote what he considered to be the book's primary theoretical contribution. Similarly his faith in the significance of the *Treatise* is exemplified by the fact that to provide Ralph Hawtrey with what Keynes thought would be a proper basis for his (Hawtrey's) testimony before the Macmillan Committee, Keynes supplied him with a set of proofs of the book (*JMK* XIII, p. 126). At roughly the same time (May 1930), Keynes also wrote to the governor of the Bank of England that he based his analysis of the *Treatise* on the "difficult theoretical proposition" embodied in his fundamental equations, and went on to say that it was "very important that a competent decision should be reached whether it [the proposition] is true or false. I can only say that I am ready to have my head chopped off if it is false" (cited by Howson and Winch 1977, p. 48). And a year later, in June 1931, Keynes participated in the Harris Foundation lectures in Chicago on "Unemployment as a World Problem" and presented a paper that was essentially a song of praise to the *Treatise* (cf. pp. 25–26 above).

I have elaborated on this background material because it seems to me that it contains half the answer to our puzzle. For let us turn to the relevant pages of the *Treatise*, namely those of chapter 37 of volume II, *The Applied Theory of Money.* Here we find what at first appears to be an unqualified advocacy of monetary policy in the form of compensatory central-bank variations of the interest rate. Thus Keynes writes that if a given reduction in this rate does not suffice to establish full employment, the central bank need only continue vigorously with yet further reductions:

> circumstances can arise when, for a time, the natural rate of interest
> falls so low that there is a very wide and quite unusual gap between

2. For further details, see pp. 195–97 above.

the ideas of borrowers and of lenders in the market on long-term. . . . How is it possible in such circumstances, we may reasonably ask, to keep the market rate and the natural rate of long-term interest at an equality with one another, *unless we impose on the central bank the duty of purchasing bonds up to a price far beyond what it considers to be the long-period norm.* [*Treatise* II, p. 334, italics in original]

So how surprising it is to find Keynes, just one page later, referring to "the insuperable limitation on the power of skilled monetary management to avoid booms and depressions" that has its source in "international complications"; more specifically, in a gold-standard world, reduction of the interest rate by one central bank acting in isolation will lead to the outflow of gold and hence to a dangerous loss of international reserves.

But for this too Keynes has a solution, international cooperation: that is, cooperation among all the central banks of the world to lower their rates of interest together. But what if such cooperation cannot be achieved? Then, and only then, does Keynes mention public works. In brief, when all else fails, when it is impossible to carry out a monetary policy of reducing the rate of interest, only then is Keynes ready to advocate public works as a means of combating unemployment.[3] In Keynes' words:

Finally, there remains in reserve a weapon by which a country can partially rescue itself when its international disequilibrium is involving it in severe unemployment. In such an event open-market operations by the central bank intended to bring down the market rate of interest and stimulate investment may, by misadventure, stimulate foreign lending instead and so provoke an outward flow of gold on a larger scale than it can afford. In such a case it is not sufficient for the central authority to stand ready to lend—for the money may flow into the wrong hands—it must also stand ready to borrow. In other words, the Government must itself promote a programme of domestic investment. It may be a choice between employing labour to create capital wealth, which will yield less than the market rate of interest, or not employing it at all. If this is the position, the national interest, both immediate and prospective, will be promoted by choosing the first alternative. But if foreign borrowers are ready and eager, it will be impossible in a competitive open market to bring the rate down to the level appropriate to domestic investment. Thus the desired result can only be obtained through some method by which, in effect, the Government subsidises approved types of domestic investment or itself directs domestic schemes of capital development.

3. This is the central point of the illuminating article by Moggridge and Howson (1974).

About the application of this method to the position of Great Britain in 1929–30 I have written much elsewhere, and need not enlarge on it here. Assuming that it was not practicable, at least for a time, to bring costs down relatively to costs abroad sufficiently to increase the foreign balance by a large amount, then a policy of subsidising home investment by promoting (say) 3 per cent schemes of national development was a valid means of increasing both employment today and the national wealth hereafter. The only alternative remedy of immediate applicability, in such circumstances, was to subsidise foreign investment by the exclusion of foreign imports, so that the failure of increased exports to raise the foreign balance to the equilibrium level might be made good by diminishing the volume of imports. [*Treatise* II, 337–38]

On the other hand, for a country in the position of the United States—whose relatively small degree of dependence on international trade and finance made it less subject to the dangers of "international complications"—Keynes continues to advocate monetary policy as the means for dealing with the problem of unemployment (*Treatise* II, p. 336, n. 1).[4]

What is particularly interesting for our present purposes is Keynes' reference at the beginning of the second paragraph of this passage to the fact that he has "written much elsewhere" about his support of public-works expenditures for Britain at that time, undoubtedly an allusion to *Can Lloyd George Do It?* And, indeed, if we go back and read this tract more carefully, we will find that there too, at the end (*JMK* IX, pp. 118–19), Keynes explains that in the situation that then prevailed in Britain, one could not combat unemployment by reducing the rate of interest: for whereas Britain at that time was suffering from serious unemployment, the United States was in the midst of a great boom, which the Federal Reserve was attempting to keep under control by raising the rate of interest. Correspondingly, Keynes in *Can Lloyd George Do It?* contended that a reduction in the rate of interest in Britain would simply generate an outflow of capital and a consequent dangerous loss of gold reserves (*JMK* IX, pp. 118, 123–24).

There is one further point that is relevant here: note how in the foregoing passage from the *Treatise* (and similar passages can be found in *Can Lloyd George Do It?* [*JMK* IX, pp. 118–19]), Keynes presented public-works expenditures not as we would today (that is, not as an increase in the government component of aggregate demand that di-

4. [This differential policy position—interest rate reductions for the United States and public works for Britain—was repeatedly stressed by Keynes in his contributions to the round-table discussions at the 1931 Harris Foundation lectures; for details, see my "Keynes and Chicago" (1979, pp. 292–93).]

rectly increases employment), but—in accordance with the analytical framework of the *Treatise*—as a reduction in the rate of interest. The crucial point is that it is not a uniform reduction but a discriminatory one, which reduces the rate of interest to a certain domestic borrower (the government) who will use the funds to finance public works at home, and which keeps the rate at its originally high level with respect to any potential foreign borrower, who would (if induced to borrow by a lower rate of interest) simply cause an outflow of gold.

Let me also note in passing that, in both *Can Lloyd George Do It?* and the *Treatise*, Keynes overlooked the gold outflow that is generated by an expansionary development in the economy, whether due to monetary or fiscal policy. For such an expansion causes an increase in imports and hence a deficit on current account. It is as if in Keynes' mind gold flows were generated in the balance of payments only by changes on capital account, and not by those on current account. This is a puzzling point that deserves further study. In any event, this is the same "blind spot" that characterized Keynes' position in the famous German-reparations debate that he was carrying on at roughly the same time (1929) with Ohlin. For in that debate, too, Keynes effectively ignored the influence on the demand for imports of the change in "buying power" generated by the reparations, whereas Ohlin assigned this influence a crucial role.[5]

Thus, to return to our main question, there is no real contradiction between the *Treatise* and *Can Lloyd George Do It?* In both, Keynes advocated a reduction in the rate of interest as a means of increasing employment; and in both he said that if restrictions imposed by the international gold standard render it impossible to make much of a reduction, then the government should instead carry out public-works expenditures. But whereas in the *Treatise* the primary message is the advocacy of interest-rate policy—with public-works expenditures barely mentioned as a special case—in *Can Lloyd George Do It?* the opposite is true: the primary message is the advocacy of public-works expenditures, with only some passing remarks at the end to explain why interest-rate reductions are not feasible. And it seems to me that this difference in emphasis is a reflection of what I have described above about the different roles that Keynes was simultaneously playing during this period of his life.

More specifically, in the *Treatise*, Keynes was the distinguished man of science, presenting to the world as a whole the definitive work on money, the work in which he revealed the secret of the fundamental equations. Correspondingly the policy he emphasized in that book is

5. See Keynes (1929 a,b) and Ohlin (1929 a,b). For further details, see *KMT*, pp. 129–31.

the one based on the universal truth embodied in these equations: a policy for all people and for all times. For that reason it is also a policy with a universal orientation: in principle the way to stabilize an economy is by means of monetary policy, and if perchance a specific economy is prevented by "international complications" from carrying out the interest-rate reductions called for by this policy, then the appropriate solution is "international cooperation."

But even in the *Treatise*, Keynes could not forget that in addition to his role as a scientific economist of international repute, he was also Britain's leading independent political economist with a singular influence on the formulation of its economic policy. Hence, even in a *Treatise* addressed to the world as a whole, he could not escape the responsibility of saying something relevant to contemporary British problems. For that purpose he could not make do with an ineffective appeal for "international cooperation" as a means of solving these problems. Correspondingly, in a small voice—as if out of a sense of obligation—he included at the end of the *Treatise* the passage cited above about the public-works expenditures. On the other hand, Keynes' role in *Can Lloyd George Do It?* was exactly the opposite: here he was participating in a strictly domestic debate about the proper policy to pursue at that moment of time; hence only the existing British situation was of concern to the audience he was addressing.

Much the same pattern characterizes the "private evidence"—or, in effect, series of seminars—that Keynes gave before the Macmillan Committee in February and March 1930. Here, in a manner which reminds me of Cyrano de Bergerac's recital of the ten different ways of reaching the moon, Keynes described eight different ways of increasing employment. He did indeed begin his evidence with an exposition of the basic interest-rate policy of the *Treatise*, but he hastened to explain that because of the danger of loss of gold reserves, that policy could not be used in the existing British situation. Correspondingly, Keynes then proceeded to a detailed discussion of seven "alternative remedies," dwelling in particular on his "favourite remedy," public-works expenditures. And only at the very end—as lip service to a measure that would in principle be most desirable but that in practice was unattainable—did Keynes mention the possibility of international monetary cooperation as a way of avoiding loss of gold reserves (*JMK* XX, pp. 38–157, esp. pp. 71, 79–80, 94–95, 125–48, 150–52).

An additional bit of evidence on this point comes from the last sentence of the previously cited *Treatise* passage, where Keynes referred cryptically to "the only alternative remedy . . . to subsidise foreign investment by the exclusion of foreign imports." I can understand this sentence only as a veiled suggestion to stimulate employment by imposing a tariff on imports. For it is well known that at this time Keynes—to the consternation and even wrath of his academic colleagues—began to consider the possibility of abandoning the century-old British doctrine of free trade and advocating a tariff instead. Indeed, this was one of the possible remedies that he presented in his evidence before the Macmillan Committee, though at that time he added the reservation that he had not yet reached "a clear-cut opinion as to where the balance of advantage" lay between the long-run advantages of free trade and the short-run advantages of the stimulus to employment that a tariff would provide.[6] In any event Keynes' reference to this "remedy" in the *Treatise* is noticeably less explicit than in his evidence before the Macmillan Committee; indeed, it seems to me that in the aforementioned sentence in the *Treatise* he even deliberately avoided the use of the term "tariff." In my view all this is simply a reflection of the fact that tariffs are a highly nationalistic measure and hence have no proper place in a *Treatise* written for the world as a whole. Correspondingly, Keynes restricted himself in this book to a bare hint at the possibility of imposing them.

I cannot conclude my discussion of this point without returning to a question I raised with reference to *Can Lloyd George Do It?* Is it reasonable to expect Keynes' discussion before the Macmillan Committee about the possibility of imposing a tariff to be fully reflected in the *Treatise?* For the publication of books takes time, and so is it not possible that Keynes' testimony before the committee came at too late a stage to affect the final version of the *Treatise?* But just as my question is similar to the one I asked above, so is my answer: From the materials published in *JMK* XIII, we know that at the same time that Keynes was testifying before the Macmillan Committee (February and March 1930), he was also engaged in correcting the proofs of the *Treatise (JMK* XIII, pp. 123–32, XX, p. 87; see also *KMT*, p. 134). Thus it would appear that, if Keynes had really wanted to, he could have modified the discussion of the *Treatise* to reflect his testimony before the Macmillan Committee; or, at the very least, he could have made explicit use of the term "tariff."

Britain's departure from the gold standard in September 1931 caused a basic change in the framework of its economic policy by freeing the Bank of England from the restrictions on its interest-rate policy that have been repeatedly mentioned above: for in the years immediately following the devaluation of sterling, Britain was effectively on a floating exchange rate and hence had no need for international gold re-

---

6. *JMK*, XX, p. 120. Keynes did not come out publicly in favor of tariffs until March 1931. For details, see Howson and Winch (1977), pp. 57–58; see also Winch (1969), pp. 150–51.

serves. And, indeed, in accordance with this fact, Keynes (immediately after the 1931 devaluation) advocated a reduction in the rate of interest, thus laying the basis for the well-known "cheap-money" policy of subsequent years (Moggridge and Howson 1974, pp. 237–38). Correspondingly, as figure 8 shows, the long-run rate of interest steadily declined during those years.

Despite this decline, however (and this is also brought out by the diagram), the level of unemployment remained very high in Britain, with roughly 20 percent of the labor force out of work. As a result of this development, a fundamental change took place in Keynes' policy views. In particular, despite the fact that interest-rate reductions were no longer limited by the international gold standard, Keynes nevertheless came to the conclusion that such reductions would not suffice to eliminate unemployment, so that it would also be necessary to carry out public-works expenditures. In other words, Keynes at this phase supported public works not because of the "international complications" that would be generated by continued reductions in the rate of interest, but because such reductions would not be adequate to the task. This shift in view was already reflected in Keynes' contribution to the 1931 Halley Stewart lecture in which, shortly after Britain's abandonment of the gold standard, he said:

> I am not confident, however, that on this occasion the cheap money phase will be sufficient by itself to bring about an adequate recovery of new investment. Cheap money means that the riskless, or supposedly riskless, rate of interest will be low. But actual enterprise always involves some degree of risk. It may still be the case that the lender, with his confidence shattered by his experiences, will continue to ask for new enterprise rates of interest which the borrower cannot expect to earn. Indeed this was already the case in the moderately cheap money phase which preceded the financial crisis of last autumn.
>
> If this proves to be so, there will be no means of escape from prolonged and perhaps interminable depression except by direct State intervention to promote and subsidize new investment. Formerly there was no expenditure out of the proceeds of borrowing, which it was thought proper for the State to incur, except war. In the past, therefore, we have not infrequently had to wait for a war to terminate a major depression. I hope that in the future we shall not adhere to this purist financial attitude, and that we shall be ready to spend on the enterprises of peace what the financial maxims of the past would only allow us to spend on the devastations of war. At any rate I predict with an assured confidence that the only way out is for us to discover *some* object which is admitted even by the deadheads to be a legitimate excuse for largely increasing the expenditure of someone on something! [*JMK* XXI, p. 60, italics in original]

This changed view was expressed even more vigorously in Keynes' later *Means to Prosperity* (1933), where he stated that if a state of employment has existed for a prolonged period, then even after the central bank has reduced the

> long-term rate of interest [to a level which] is low for all reasonably sound borrowers . . . it is unlikely that private enterprise will, on its own initiative, undertake new loan-expenditure on a sufficient scale. Business enterprise will not seek to expand until *after* profits have begun to recover. Increased working capital will not be required until *after* output is increasing. Moreover, in modern communities a very large proportion of our *normal* programmes of loan-expenditure are undertaken by public and semi-public bodies. The new loan-expenditure which trade and industry require in a year is comparatively small even in good times. Building, transport, and public utilities are responsible at all times for a very large proportion of current loan-expenditure.
>
> Thus the first step has to be taken on the initiative of public authority; and it probably has to be on a large scale and organised with determination, if it is to be sufficient to break the vicious circle and to stem the progressive deterioration, as firm after firm throws up the sponge and ceases to produce at a loss in the seemingly vain hope that perseverance will be rewarded.
>
> Some cynics, who have followed the argument thus far, conclude that nothing except a war can bring a major slump to its conclusion. For hitherto war has been the only object of governmental loan-expenditure on a large scale which governments have considered respectable. In all the issues of peace they are timid, over-cautious, half-hearted, without perseverance or determination, thinking of a loan as a liability and not as a link in the transformation of the community's surplus resources, which will otherwise be wasted, into useful capital assets.
>
> I hope that her government will show that Great Britain can be energetic even in the tasks of peace. It should not be difficult to perceive that 100,000 houses are a national asset and 1 million unemployed men a national liability. [*JMK* IX, pp. 353–55, italics in original]

Let me turn finally to the *General Theory*. In contrast with the *Treatise* (whose first volume, *The Pure Theory of Money*, is accompanied by a second one, *The Applied Theory of Money*, the latter half of which is largely devoted to problems of policy), the *General Theory* is concerned almost exclusively with pure theory and contains only brief, passing discussions of policy (see pp. 6–7, 13–14 above; see also *KMT*, pp. 12–19). On these occasions—as the following well-known passages show—Keynes repeated the view of his *Means to Prosperity* that the problem of unemployment could not be solved by monetary policy alone, but that a program of government investment was necessary:

> For my own part I am now somewhat sceptical of the success of a merely monetary policy directed towards influencing the rate of interest. I expect to see the State, which is in a position to calculate the marginal efficiency of capital-goods on long views and on the basis of the general social advantage, taking an ever greater responsibility for directly organising investment; since it seems likely that the fluctuations in the market estimation of the marginal efficiency of different types of capital, calculated on the principles I have described above, will be too great to be offset by any practicable changes in the rate of interest. [*GT*, p. 164]

> Furthermore, it seems unlikely that the influence of banking policy on the rate of interest will be sufficient by itself to determine an optimum rate of investment. I conceive, therefore, that a somewhat comprehensive socialisation of investment will prove the only means of securing an approximation to full employment; though this need not exclude all manner of compromises and of devices by which public authority will cooperate with private initiative. But beyond this no obvious case is made out for a system of State Socialism which would embrace most of the economic life of the community. It is not the ownership of the instruments of production which it is important for the State to assume. If the State is able to determine the aggregate amount of resources devoted to augmenting the instruments and the basic rate of reward to those who own them, it will have accomplished all that is necessary. Moreover, the necessary measures of socialisation can be introduced gradually and without a break in the general traditions of society. [*GT*, p. 378]

My conclusion from all this is that the change in Keynes' policy views between the *Treatise* and the *General Theory* stemmed less from the transition from the fundamental equations to the $C + I + G = Y$ equation than from British economic developments in the quinquennium between the appearance of these two books. For, as we have seen, Keynes advocated public-works expenditures for the purpose of combating unemployment even in the *Treatise,* albeit as a second-best policy to be carried out in special circumstances. And what brought him to advocate such expenditures as a necessary policy for this purpose was the experience of five additional years of deep depression in the face of a continuously declining rate of interest.

Let me conclude with a more general lesson that can be learned from all this. Let us be skeptical of the optimistic belief that changes in views about economic policy are the direct consequence of developments in economic theory. And a prime example of the simplism of this belief is provided by the story I have just told, for clearly Keynes began to give greater stress to a policy of public-works expenditures even before he perfected the macroeconomic analysis that was to provide the theoretical underpinning for this policy. It was like the Children of Israel at the foot of Mount Sinai, waiting to receive the Tablets of the Law from the hands of Moses, and proclaiming "We shall do," even before they had said "We shall listen."

Postscript: After the General Theory

Without undertaking the detailed study the question deserves, let me note that in the years after the *General Theory,* Keynes continued to advocate public-works expenditures as a necessary component (in addition to low interest rates) of a full-employment policy. Thus in a letter to *The Times* in December 1937 he wrote: "Public loan expenditure is not, of course, the only way, and not necessarily the best way, to increase employment. Nor is it always sufficiently effective to overcome other adverse influences. . . . But public loan policy remains vitally significant, partly because it is the most controllable element in the situation, and partly because, in the modern world, a very large proportion of domestic investment necessarily depends on the policy of Government Departments, local authorities, public boards, and semi-public corporations, such as the railways" (*JMK* XXI, p. 430). And in a letter to President Roosevelt in February 1938, Keynes attributed the United States recession of 1937 in part to the fact that "public works and other investments aided by government funds and guaranties . . . have been greatly curtailed" (*JMK* XXI, p. 435).

With the approach of war, Keynes became engrossed in problems of war finance. But in 1943 he began to concern himself also with postwar problems and wrote a memorandum on "The Long-Term Problem of Full Employment" advocating a program in which "two-thirds or three-quarters of total investment is carried out or can be influenced by public or semi-public bodies" (*JMK* XXVII, p. 322). And in reply to a comment on it by James Meade, he wrote (letter of May 27, 1943): "It is quite true that a fluctuating volume of public works at short notice is a clumsy form of cure and not likely to be completely successful. On the other hand, if the bulk of investment is under public or semi-public control and we go in for a stable long-term programme, serious fluctuations are enormously less likely to occur" (*JMK* XXVII, p. 326). Similar views were expressed by Keynes in a note on postwar employment written February 1944 (*JMK* XXVII, p. 365, point 5) and in a letter to Beveridge in December 1944 (ibid., p. 381).

Bibliography for Part III*

Agassi, Joseph (1968). "The Novelty of Popper's Philosophy of Science." *International Philosophical Quarterly* 8 (Sept.): 442–63.

Cain, Neville (1979). "Cambridge and Its Revolution: A Perspective on the Multiplier and Effective Demand." *Economic Record* 55 (June): 108–17.

Clark, Colin (1930). "Calculations Regarding Possible Expansion in Certain Export Trades." (For further details, see listing under Unpublished Sources).

———— (1977). "The 'Golden' Age of the Great Economists: Keynes, Robbins et al. in 1930." *Encounter* 48 (June): 80–90.

Coppock, D. J. (1953). "A Reconsideration of Hobson's Theory of Unemployment." *The Manchester School* 21 (Jan.): 1–21.

Davis, J. Ronnie (1971). *The New Economics and the Old Economists.* Ames, Iowa: Iowa State University Press.

Eshag, Eprime (1963). *From Marshall to Keynes: An Essay on the Monetary Theory of the Cambridge School.* Oxford: Blackwell.

F[ay], C. R. (1927). "[Obituary of] Frederick Lavington." *Economic Journal* 37 (Sept.): 504–05.

Foley, D. K., and M. Sidrauski (1971). *Monetary and Fiscal Policy in a Growing Economy.* New York: Macmillan.

Friedman, Milton (1956). "The Quantity Theory of Money—A Restatement." In *Studies in the Quantity Theory of Money,* edited by M. Friedman (Chicago: University of Chicago Press), pp. 3–21.

———— (1970). "A Theoretical Framework for Monetary Analysis." *Journal of Political Economy* 78 (March/April): 193–238.

Gurley, John G., and Edward S. Shaw (1960). *Money in a Theory of Finance.* Washington, D.C.: The Brookings Institution.

Harris Memorial Foundation (1931). *Unemployment as a World Problem.* Edited by Quincy Wright. Chicago: University of Chicago Press.

Harrod, R. F. (1951). *The Life of John Maynard Keynes.* London: Macmillan. Reprinted, New York: Augustus M. Kelley, 1969.

* Reprinted or translated works are cited in the text by year of original publication; the page references to such works in the text are, however, to the pages of the reprint or translation in question.

Hegeland, Hugo (1954). *The Multiplier Theory*. Lund: C. W. K. Gleerup.

Hicks, J. R. (1935). "A Suggestion for Simplifying the Theory of Money." *Economica* 2 (Feb.): 1–19. As reprinted in *Readings in Monetary Theory*, selected by a committee of the American Economic Association (Philadelphia: Blakiston, for the American Economic Association, 1951), pp. 13–32.

Hobson, J. A. (1910). *The Industrial System*. New York: Charles Scribner's Sons.

Howson, Susan, and Donald Winch (1977). *The Economic Advisory Council 1930–1939*. Cambridge: Cambridge University Press.

Hutchison, T. W. (1953). *A Review of Economic Doctrines 1870–1929*. Oxford: Clarendon Press.

————— (1968). *Economics and Economic Policy in Britain 1946–1966: Some Aspects of Their Inter-Relations*. London: George Allen and Unwin.

Johannsen, Nicholas A. J. (1908). *A Neglected Point in Connection with Crises*. New York: Bankers Publishing Co. Reprinted, New York: Augustus M. Kelley, 1971.

Johnson, Elizabeth S. (1977). "Keynes as a Literary Craftsman." In Patinkin and Leith (1977), pp. 90–97. As reprinted in Johnson and Johnson (1978), pp. 30–37.

Johnson, Elizabeth S., and Harry G. Johnson (1978). *The Shadow of Keynes: Understanding Keynes, Cambridge and Keynesian Economics*. Chicago: University of Chicago Press.

Johnson, Harry G. (1961). "The *General Theory* after Twenty-Five Years." *American Economic Review* 51 (May): 1–17. As reprinted in H. Johnson, *Money, Trade and Economic Growth* (Cambridge, Mass.: Harvard University Press, 1962), pp. 126–50.

Kahn, R. F. (1931). "The Relation of Home Investment to Unemployment." *Economic Journal* 41 (June): 173–98. As reprinted in Kahn (1972), pp. 1–27.

————— (1932). "The Financing of Public Works: A Note." *Economic Journal* 42 (Sept.): 492–95.

————— (1933). "Public Works and Inflation." *Journal of the American Statistical Association* 28 (March): 168–73. As reprinted in Kahn (1972), pp. 28–34.

————— (1972). *Selected Essays on Employment and Growth*. Cambridge: Cambridge University Press.

Keynes, John Maynard (1911). Review of *The Purchasing Power of Money*, by I. Fisher. *Economic Journal* 21 (Sept.): 393–98.

————— (1913). *Indian Currency and Finance*. As reprinted in Keynes, *Collected Writings*, Vol. I.

————— (1919). *The Economic Consequences of the Peace*. As reprinted in Keynes, *Collected Writings*, Vol. II.

————— (1923). *A Tract on Monetary Reform*. As reprinted in Keynes, *Collected Writings*, Vol. IV.

————— (1924). "Alfred Marshall 1842–1924." *Economic Journal* 34 (Sept.): 311–72. As reprinted in Keynes, *Collected Writings*, Vol. X, pp. 161–231. (See Keynes [1933b]).

————— (1925). *The Economic Consequences of Mr. Churchill*. As reprinted in Keynes, *Collected Writings*, Vol. IX, pp. 207–30.

—— (1929a). "The German Transfer Problem." *Economic Journal* 39 (March): 1–7. As reprinted in *Readings in the Theory of International Trade,* selected by a committee of the American Economic Association (Philadelphia: Blakiston, for the American Economic Association, 1949), pp. 161–69.

—— (1929b). "The Reparation Problem: A Rejoinder." *Economic Journal* 39 (July): 179–82.

—— (1930). *A Treatise on Money, Vol. I: The Pure Theory of Money.* As reprinted in Keynes, *Collected Writings,* Vol. V.

—— (1930). *A Treatise on Money, Vol. II: The Applied Theory of Money.* As reprinted in Keynes, *Collected Writings,* Vol. VI.

—— (1931a). "An Economic Analysis of Unemployment." In Harris Memorial Foundation (1931), pp. 3–42. As reprinted in Keynes, *Collected Writings,* Vol. XIII, pp. 343–67.

—— (1931b). *Essays in Persuasion.* As reprinted with additions in Keynes, *Collected Writings,* Vol. IX.

—— (1932). "The World's Economic Crisis and the Way of Escape." In Arthur Salter *et al., The World's Economic Crisis and the Way of Escape,* pp. 69–88. London: Allen and Unwin. As reprinted in Keynes, *Collected Writings,* Vol. XXI, pp. 50–62. (Halley Stewart Lecture).

—— (1933a). *The Means to Prosperity.* As reprinted in Keynes, *Collected Writings,* Vol. IX, pp. 335–66.

—— (1933b). *Essays in Biography.* As reprinted with additions in Keynes, *Collected Writings,* Vol. X.

—— (1936). *The General Theory of Employment Interest and Money.* As reprinted in Keynes, *Collected Writings,* Vol. VII.

——. *The General Theory and After: Part I, Preparation.* Edited by Donald Moggridge. Vol. XIII of Keynes, *Collected Writings.*

—— *Activities 1929–31: Rethinking Employment and Unemployment Policies.* Edited by Donald Moggridge. Vol. XX of Keynes, *Collected Writings.*

—— *Activities 1931–1939: World Crises and Policies in Britain and America.* Edited by Donald Moggridge. Vol. XXI of Keynes, *Collected Writings.*

—— *Activities 1940–1946: Shaping the Postwar World: Employment and Commodities.* Edited by Donald Moggridge. Vol. XXVII of Keynes, *Collected Writings.*

——. *Collected Writings.* 30 volumes planned. Published to date: Vols. I–VI (1971), Vols. VII–VIII (1973), Vols. IX–X (1972), Vols. XIII–XIV (1973), Vols. XV–XVI (1971), Vols. XVII–XVIII (1978), Vols. XIX–XX (1981), Vol. XXI (1982), Vol. XXII (1978), Vols. XXIII–XXIV (1979), Vols. XXV–XXVII (1980), Vol. XXIX (1979). London: Macmillan, for the Royal Economic Society.

Keynes, John Maynard, and Hubert Henderson (1929). *Can Lloyd George Do It?: An Examination of the Liberal Pledge.* As reprinted in Keynes, *Collected Writings,* Vol. IX, pp. 86–125.

Kuhn, Thomas S. (1970). *The Structure of Scientific Revolutions.* Second enlarged edition, Chicago: University of Chicago Press.

Laidler, David (1982). "Harry Johnson as a Macroeconomist." *Journal of Political Economy,* 90: forthcoming.

Lavington, F. (1921). *The English Capital Market*. London: Methuen. Reprinted, New York: Augustus M. Kelley, 1968.

—— (1922). *The Trade Cycle: An Account of the Causes Producing Changes in the Activity of Business*. London: P. S. King and Staples.

Liberal Industrial Inquiry (1928). *Britain's Industrial Future*. London: Ernest Benn.

[Liberal Party.] (1929). *We Can Conquer Unemployment*. London: Cassell.

Marshall, Alfred (1871). "Money." Manuscript first published in *The Early Economic Writings of Alfred Marshall*, edited by J. K. Whitaker (London: Macmillan, 1975), Vol. 1, pp. 164–75. (For further details see listing under Unpublished Sources.)

—— (1923). *Money, Credit and Commerce*. London: Macmillan.

—— (1926). *Official Papers*. London: Macmillan.

Mitchell, B. R., and P. Deane (1962). *Abstract of British Historical Statistics*. Cambridge: Cambridge University Press, 1962.

Mitchell, Wesley C. (1913). *Business Cycles*. Berkeley: University of California Press.

—— (1927). *Business Cycles: The Problem and Its Setting*. New York: National Bureau of Economic Research.

Moggridge, D. E., and Susan Howson (1974). "Keynes on Monetary Policy, 1910–1946." *Oxford Economic Papers* 26 (July): 226–47.

Myrdal, Gunnar (1939). *Monetary Equilibrium*. London: W. Hodge.

Ohlin, Bertil (1929a). "Transfer Difficulties, Real and Imagined." *Economic Journal* 39 (June): 172–78. As reprinted in *Readings in the Theory of International Trade*, selected by a committee of the American Economic Association (Philadelphia: Blakiston, for the American Economic Association, 1949), pp. 170–78.

—— (1929b). "Mr. Keynes' Views on the Transfer Problem: A Rejoinder." *Economic Journal* 39 (Sept.): 400–04.

Patinkin, Don (1965). *Money, Interest, and Prices*. 2nd edition. New York: Harper and Row.

—— (1969). "The Chicago Tradition, the Quantity Theory, and Friedman." *Journal of Money, Credit and Banking* 1 (Feb.): 46–70. As reprinted in Patinkin (1981), pp. 241–64.

—— (1972a). "On the Short-Run Non-Neutrality of Money in the Quantity Theory." *Banca Nazionale del Lavoro Quarterly Review* 25 (March): 3–22.

—— (1972b). "Friedman on the Quantity Theory and Keynesian Economics." *Journal of Political Economy* 80 (Sept./Oct.): 883–905.

—— (1976). *Keynes' Monetary Thought: A Study of Its Development*. Durham, N.C.: Duke University Press.

—— (1979). "Keynes and Chicago." *Journal of Law and Economics* 22 (Oct.): 213–32. As reprinted in Patinkin (1981), pp. 289–308.

—— (1981). *Essays On and In the Chicago Tradition*. Durham, N.C.: Duke University Press.

Patinkin, Don, and J. Clark Leith, editors (1977). *Keynes, Cambridge and the General Theory : The Process of Criticism and Discussion Connected with the Development of the General Theory*. London: Macmillan.

Pigou, A. C. (1917). "The Value of Money." *Quarterly Journal of Economics* 32 (Nov.): 38-65. As reprinted in *Readings in Monetary Theory,* selected by a committee of the American Economic Association (Philadelphia: Blakiston, for the American Economic Association, 1951), pp. 162–83.

—— (1929). *Industrial Fluctuations,* 2nd edition. London: Macmillan.

—— (1933). *The Theory of Unemployment.* London: Macmillan.

Robertson, D. H. (1922). *Money.* Cambridge: Cambridge University Press.

—— (1928). *Money.* New edition revised, Cambridge: Cambridge University Press.

—— (1933). "A Note on the Theory of Money." *Economica* 12 (Aug.): 243–47. As reprinted in Robertson, *Essays in Monetary Theory* (London: Staples Press, 1940), pp. 92–97.

—— (1948). *Money.* 4th edition. London: Pitman.

Shackle, G. L. S. (1967). *The Years of High Theory: Invention and Tradition in Economic Thought.* Cambridge: Cambridge University Press.

Snyder, Carl (1924). "New Measures in the Equation of Exchange." *American Economic Review* 14 (Dec.): 699–713.

Stigler, George J. (1955). "The Nature and Role of Originality in Scientific Progress." *Economica* 22 (Nov.): 293–302. As reprinted in Stigler, *Essays in the History of Economics* (Chicago: University of Chicago Press, 1965), pp. 1–15.

Tobin, James (1955). "A Dynamic Aggregative Model." *Journal of Political Economy* 63 (April): 103–15.

—— (1963). "An Essay on Principles of Debt Management." In Commission on Money and Credit, *Fiscal and Debt Management Policies.* Englewood Cliffs, N.J.: Prentice-Hall, pp. 143–218.

—— (1969). "A General Equilibrium Approach to Monetary Theory." *Journal of Money, Credit and Banking* 1 (Feb.):15–29.

Warming, Jens (1932). "International Difficulties Arising Out of the Financing of Public Works During Depressions." *Economic Journal* 42 (June): 211–24.

Winch, Donald (1969). *Economics and Policy: A Historical Study.* London: Hodder and Stoughton.

Wright, Harold (1923). *Population.* New York: Harcourt, Brace.

W[right], H[arold] (1927). "[Obituary of] Frederick Lavington." *Economic Journal* 37 (Sept.): 503–4.

Wright, Quincy. See Harris Memorial Foundation.

Government Publications

Great Britain]. (1929). *Memoranda on Certain Proposals Relating to Unemployment.* Parliamentary Papers, Cmd. 3331. London: H.M.S.O.

Serial Publications

Great Britain]. *Ministry of Labour Gazette.*

Unpublished Sources

Clark, Colin. See below, [Great Britain]. Economic Advisory Council.

[Great Britain]. Economic Advisory Council. "Calculations Regarding Possible Expansion in Certain Export Trades." June 16, 1930. Public Record Office Papers. Cab. 58/10, E.A.C.(H)91. (Prepared by Colin Clark.)

Marshall, Alfred. "Money." Unpublished manuscript, dated circa 1871, in the Marshall Library, Cambridge, England. Marshall Red Box 2 (Money and Banking, Exchanges), Item 6 (see above, p. 183, n. 2).

IV Theory and Measurement

9

Keynes and Econometrics: On the Interaction between the Macroeconomic Revolutions of the Interwar Period

1. Introduction

My talk today has a title—and a subtitle. The title is well defined and specific; the subtitle, much less so. The title will lead me to a discussion of the attitudes and practices of John Maynard Keynes with respect to econometrics. And quite apart from the renewed interest of the last few years in the work of Keynes, there is ample justification for discussing this subject on this occasion. First, as we shall see, Keynes was indeed concerned with the econometrics of his time—in the broad sense of empirically oriented economic analysis. Second, and more significant, Keynes' *General Theory of Employment Interest and Money* almost forty years ago defined the framework of research in macroeconomics for many decades which followed; and the relation of this book to

Presidential address delivered before the Econometric Society meetings in San Francisco in December 1974, with subsequent elaborations.

Reprinted by permission from *Econometrica* 44: (November 1976), pp. 1091–1123. Besides the additions which appear in thick square brackets and in the Postscript, some minor changes and corrections have been made.

A preliminary version of this paper was presented in December 1974 before the Economics Department Seminar at the Hebrew University of Jerusalem, and I am grateful to my colleagues for the many helpful and stimulating comments and suggestions which they then provided. In this context I am particularly grateful to Chaim Barkai, Ruth Klinov, and Marshall Sarnat. Similarly, I have benefited from stimulating discussions with Simon Kuznets, to whom I am also indebted for permission to quote from his correspondence with Keynes. I am also grateful to Yoram Ben-Porath, Ephraim Kleiman, Donald McCloskey, Marcus Miller, George Stigler, and Donald Winch for their comments on earlier drafts. Needless to say, however, none of these is to be held responsible for the views presented in this paper.

I am deeply indebted to Lord Kahn, Keynes' literary executor, for his kind permission to make use of unpublished materials in the Keynes Papers, and to Donald Moggridge and Susan Howson for their continuous and gracious help in providing me with requested photocopies from these papers. I am also grateful to many friends abroad to whom I turned at various times to request photocopies of relevant materials.

It is a distinct pleasure to express my appreciation to my successive research assistants, Leonardo Leiderman and Gabriella Brenner, for their invaluable and conscientious help with the large amount of library work, checking of sources, and computations

econometrics is amply attested by the fact that, for example, the most influential interpretation of it—the *IS–LM* interpretation which John Hicks presented in his "Mr. Keynes and the 'Classics' "—appeared as an article in *Econometrica* (1937). Furthermore, and most important in the present context, the desire to quantify the *General Theory* provided the major impetus for the exponentially growing econometric work that began to be carried out in the late 1930s on the consumption, investment, and liquidity-preference functions individually and, even more notably, on econometric models of the Keynesian system as a whole.

But in addition to, and as a reflection of, the impetus that he gave to econometric work, Keynes also had important formal connections with the Econometric Society. Thus he was one of the thirty economists from all over the world selected by the council in 1933 to constitute the first group of Fellows of the Society (*Econometrica* 1 [1933], p. 445). And a year later, at the initiative of Ragnar Frisch, Keynes was elected to the council itself and remained a member of it until his death.

All this might be as expected for one who was a world-outstanding economist of his time. But what was to me less expected was to learn recently that, in 1944, Keynes was elected president of the Econometric Society, though not without first politely protesting[1] that "whilst I am interested in econometric work and have done something at it at different times in my life, I have not recently written anything significant or important along these lines" (from which I infer that Keynes saw himself as one who *had* at one time made contributions to

connected with the preparation of this paper. I must also express my indebtedness to Gwendoline Cohen and to the late Vera Jacobs, who carefully typed the paper through its various drafts.

Might I also take this opportunity to express my appreciation of the excellent facilities of the Jewish National and University Library of the Hebrew University, and for the kind and cooperative spirit with which its staff has always provided its efficient help.

The work on this paper has, in part, been supported by research grants from the Ford Foundation (received through the Israel Foundation Trustees) and the Israel Commission for Basic Research. The paper will be reissued as a research paper of the Maurice Falk Institute for Economic Research in Israel. To all of these institutions, I am greatly indebted.

{With the exception of Keynes, the major protagonists of the story which follows—Colin Clark, Simon Kuznets, Jan Tinbergen, and Richard Stone—are still with us. I have taken advantage of this fact to circulate the final draft of this paper among them and to ask for their comments. Some of these comments are of general interest and—with the kind permission of the aforementioned individuals—have accordingly been reproduced at the appropriate points in this paper in braced footnotes like this one.}

1. In a letter of August 20, 1943, to Alfred Cowles, who was then secretary and treasurer of the Society, and who had written Keynes a month before suggesting that he serve in this position (letter in Keynes Papers). At that time, it was customary to reelect presidents of the Econometric Society for a second year, and, accordingly, Keynes continued in this office in 1945 as well. Afterward, however, this custom was dropped (see list of presidents in *Econometrica* 25: [December 1957], p. 186).

the field!). And so, if we want to, we can regard my address today as a commemorative one, marking the thirtieth anniversary of John Maynard Keynes' having served as president of the Econometric Society.

But my talk also has a subtitle. And the subject described by this subtitle is as broad and complex as it is fundamental, for it deals with the interaction of ideas, and with the subtle and mysterious ways such interactions take place. And it also deals with the equally, if not more, complicated question of the interaction between ideas and institutions.

Let me be more specific: for many years now we have become accustomed to using the term "Keynesian Revolution" to denote the dramatic changes Keynes' *General Theory* effected with respect to macroeconomic theory. I feel, however, that we are much less aware than we should be of the no less significant (though quieter) revolution that began to take place even before the *General Theory* with respect to macroeconomic measurement or, more specifically, with respect to the measurement of national income, which is the general term I shall for simplicity frequently use to denote the measurement of any one or more of the national aggregates (income, product, expenditure), broken down by their respective components. In section 5 below I shall justify the use of the term "revolution" in this context; for the moment let me simply note that it is the one associated primarily with the names of Simon Kuznets in the United States and Colin Clark in England. And it is to the interrelationships between these two revolutions that my subtitle refers. But I have already said that this question is an extremely complex and difficult one; accordingly, I should make it clear at the outset that the present discussion does not even pretend to deal with it in a systematic and comprehensive manner. What I hope to do, however, is to highlight the major aspects of this question, with particular emphasis on the way the aforementioned interrelationships manifest themselves in the work of Keynes.[2]

2. Keynes and Mathematical Economics

Though this is my main concern, I cannot discuss the subject of Keynes and econometrics without first digressing briefly on two other points that always arise in this context: the first is Keynes' attitude toward mathematical economics, and the second is Keynes' famous 1939 debate with Tinbergen.

2. [For the way these interrelationships manifest themselves in the respective works of Lindahl and Kalecki, see above pp. 44, 63.]

On the first point, I can only repeat what I have said elsewhere.[3] We are all familiar with Keynes' oft-cited criticism in the *General Theory* of "symbolic pseudo-mathematical methods of formalizing a system of economic analysis . . . which allow the author to lose sight of the complexities and interdependencies of the real world in a maze of pretentious and unhelpful symbols" (*GT*, pp. 297–98). We should not, however, accept this statement at face value as an absolute and unchanging rejection of mathematical methods. First of all, Keynes' own analysis in his earlier *Treatise on Money* (1930) was in fact largely based on fairly mechanical applications of the so-called fundamental equations. Furthermore, the *Treatise* devoted an entire chapter (20) to "An Exercise in the Pure Theory of the Credit Cycle" in which Keynes explored in a very formalistic manner, and under a variety of alternative assumptions, the mathematical properties of his model of the cycle. Indeed, if ever an author "lost sight of the complexities . . . of the real world in a maze of pretentious and unhelpful symbols," that author was Keynes of the *Treatise* (see *KMT*, chaps. 4–7).

In fact, it may have been Keynes' lack of success with such formal model building in the *Treatise* that led him to the more critical attitude expressed in the passage from the *General Theory* just cited. In any event, it is significant that in the *General Theory,* in contrast with the *Treatise,* Keynes did not present a formal mathematical statement of the theory of employment that constitutes the major theme of the book: such statements were to be provided only by subsequent expositors (e.g., Hicks 1937). Instead, to the extent that Keynes made use of mathematical analysis in the *General Theory,* he did so with respect to such secondary themes as the relationship between the own-rates of interest of different goods (chap. 17, sec. II) and the theory of prices (chap. 21, sec. VI). Even in these instances, the mathematical formulation adds little to Keynes' literary exposition and so could be deleted without much loss of continuity.

Actually, I think it is fair to say that the *General Theory* reveals an ambivalent attitude toward the role of mathematical analysis in economics: for with all his reservations about the usefulness of such analysis, Keynes could not resist the temptation to show that he too could employ it! Thus the famous quotation from the *General Theory* so critical of mathematical analysis with which I began this discussion actually occurs in section III of the same chapter 21 that I have just cited as providing an instance of the use of such analysis; indeed, this quotation appears as part of Keynes' apologia for nevertheless going

---

3. See *KMT*, pp. 21–23, from which this and the following three paragraphs are, with minor changes, reproduced.

ahead and resorting to it in section VI of that chapter. Thus, when all is said and done, I strongly suspect that a comparison of the *General Theory* (and a fortiori the *Treatise*) with the other works on economic theory that were written during that period would actually show Keynes' works to be among the more mathematical of them.

On the other hand, judging from the critical literature which subsequently grew up around chapters 17 and 21 of the *General Theory*, I think it fair to say that the mathematical analysis that appears in these chapters is not only not essential to the argument, but also problematic. And this fact, together with the ineffectualness of the "fundamental equations" of the *Treatise*, makes it clear that whatever may have been Keynes' attitude toward the proper role of mathematical methods in economic analysis, his strength did not lie in the use of such methods (cf. pp. 150–51 above).[4]

3. The Keynes-Tinbergen Debate

Keynes' famous debate with Tinbergen began with Keynes' review in the September 1939 *Economic Journal*[5] of the pioneering statistical study of business cycles which Tinbergen carried out on behalf of the League of Nations in 1939 as a complement to Haberler's earlier study (1937) of business-cycle theory. To place this debate in its proper context, I must first of all emphasize that Keynes' review article was entitled "Professor Tinbergen's Method" and was devoted not to the much better known second volume of this study on *Business Cycles in the United States of America, 1919–1932*, but to the first volume (published a few months earlier), *A Method and Its Application to Investment Activity*, in which Tinbergen set out and exemplified the principles of multiple-correlation analysis. Accordingly, the criticisms Keynes presented in this review were leveled not at Tinbergen's ambitious forty-six–equation model of the United States economy, but at the use of correlation analysis to estimate even a single equation.

Let me also confess that though not all of Keynes' criticisms were well taken (e.g., his "suspicion that the assumption of linearity rules out cyclical factors" [*JMK* XIV, p. 313; see also Tinbergen's reply, 1940, p. 150]), I find it somewhat depressing to see how many of them

4. My colleague Eytan Sheshinski has, however, pointed out to me Keynes' useful economic interpretation of Frank Ramsey's results in the latter's famous "Mathematical Theory of Saving" (1928), as reported on pp. 621–23 of that article.

5. This review, as well as the very interesting correspondence which Keynes carried out with Tinbergen and others in connection with it, is reproduced in *JMK* XIV, pp. 285–320. I am indebted to my colleague Nissan Liviatan for helpful discussions of some of the following points.

are, in practice, still of relevance today. Thus Keynes wrote:

Am I right in thinking that the method of multiple correlation analysis essentially depends on the economist having furnished not merely a list of the significant causes, which is correct as far as it goes, but a *complete* list? For example, suppose three factors are taken into account, it is not enough that these should be in fact *verae causae;* there must be no other significant factor. If there is a further factor, not taken account of, then the method is not able to discover the relative quantitative importance of the first three. If so, this means that the method is only applicable where the economist is able to provide beforehand a correct and indubitably complete analysis of the significant factors. [*JMK* XIV, p. 308, italics in original]

What could be a better description of specification bias? Or, again,

Professor Tinbergen is concerned with "sequence analysis"; he is dealing with non-simultaneous events and time lags. What happens if the phenomenon under investigation itself reacts on the factors by which we are explaining it? For example, when he investigates the fluctuations of investment, Professor Tinbergen makes them depend on the fluctuations of profit. But what happens if the fluctuations of profit partly depend (as, indeed, they clearly do) on the fluctuations of investment? [*JMK* XIV, pp. 309–10]

In brief, what we now call the simultaneous-equation bias.

In his review article, Keynes also referred to the basic difficulty of measuring expectations (*JMK* XIV, p. 309), to the restrictive nature of the assumption of universal linearity (*JMK* XIV, pp. 311–15), as well as to "the frightful inadequacy of most of the statistics employed" (*JMK* XIV, p. 317). And, in what I interpret as an allusion to his *Treatise on Probability*, he stated: "Thirty years ago I used to be occupied in examining the slippery problem of passing from statistical description to inductive generalization in the case of simple correlation; and today in the era of multiple correlation I do not find that in this respect practice is much improved" (*JMK* XIV, p. 315).[6]

Keynes concluded his review of Tinbergen's work with the following comment:

I hope that I have not done injustice to a brave pioneer effort. The labour it involved must have been enormous. The book is full of

6. Though the *Treatise on Probability* had been published eighteen years earlier, in 1921, it was based on the fellowship dissertation for King's College which Keynes had successfully submitted in 1909. Part V of the book is entitled "The Foundations of Statistical Inference." It includes a discussion of the correlation coefficient which begins with an observation by Keynes which is very similar to the one just cited (see *JMK* VIII, p. 461).

intelligence, ingenuity and candour; and I leave it with sentiments of respect for the author. But it has been a nightmare to live with, and I fancy that other readers will find the same. I have a feeling that Professor Tinbergen may agree with much of my comment, but that his reaction will be to engage another ten computers and drown his sorrows in arithmetic. [*JMK* XIV, p. 318]

And if this is what Keynes said at a time when one had to think twice before undertaking the laborious task of estimating a multiple-regression equation on a mechanical desk calculator, what would he say today, in this age of instant estimation?

I would not like to leave this well-known episode in the history of econometrics without first noting that, despite his severe criticisms, Keynes retained the highest regard for Tinbergen. Thus he concluded his Comment (1940) on Tinbergen's reply to his review with the paragraph:

No one could be more frank, more painstaking, more free from subjective bias or *parti pris* than Professor Tinbergen. There is no one, therefore, so far as human qualities go, whom it would be safer to trust with black magic. That there is anyone I would trust with it at the present stage or that this brand of statistical alchemy is ripe to become a branch of science, I am not yet persuaded. But Newton, Boyle and Locke all played with alchemy. So let him continue. [*JMK* XIV, p. 320]

And in a moving letter that he wrote shortly after the end of the war in Europe, Keynes replied in the following words to Alfred Cowles' suggestion that Tinbergen should be elected vice-president of the Econometric Society:

I hope very much indeed that Tinbergen can be elected Vice-President. As it happens, I had the pleasure two days ago to give a luncheon party at Cambridge in honor of Tinbergen and three other Dutch economist statisticians, whom he had brought over with him to this country. I had already heard from him, but his sudden arrival over here took us all by surprise. It was with extreme satisfaction that we renewed contact with him. I felt once again, as I had felt before, that there is no-one more gifted or delightful or for whose work one could be more anxious to give every possible scope and opportunity. He looked no older and was as handsome as ever. Indeed, my experience is that when I meet European friends who have gone through a course of starvation their health has been vastly improved by it. Your troops eat twice as much as you do. You eat twice as much as we do, and we eat twice as much as is either good or necessary for health. However, Tinbergen added that I should not have spoken about him in the same way a month before liberation.

He declared that his life was saved by the packets of food dropped from the air by our airmen.[7]

4. The Use of National Income Estimates in the *General Theory*

Let me now return to my main concern—the interaction between the macroeconomic revolutions of the interwar period. Appropriately enough for this purpose, the impact of the revolution that took place with respect to the availability of national income data can be illustrated most dramatically by contrasting Keynes' two famous works on macroeconomics: the *Treatise on Money* published in October 1930 and the *General Theory* published in February 1936.

The ultimate purpose of the *Treatise* was to explain the fluctuations in output that characterized the business cycle or, as Keynes called it in the *Treatise*, the credit cycle. The vehicles for this explanation were the famous "fundamental equations," in which a crucial role was played by the relation between investment and saving. As is well known, according to Keynes' definitions in the *Treatise*, these two quantities are not generally equal. Indeed, the excess of investment over saving equals the abnormal profits of firms, and the existence of such profits leads firms to expand output. Conversely, when savings exceed investment, there are losses, and output declines. This, in a highly oversimplified form, is the cycle theory of the *Treatise*.[8]

Now the *Treatise* was not only a book on theory; as its title indicates, it was intended to be a comprehensive treatment of monetary economics, dealing with the applied aspects (which is the subject of vol. II of the *Treatise*) as well as the theoretical ones (the subject of vol. I). Correspondingly, in this second volume Keynes attempts to present empirical estimates of the variables that play a key role in the theory presented in the first one.

In this context he presents an index of total output (for the period 1920–29), which, for lack of anything better (and Keynes bemoans "the present deplorable state of our banking and other statistics" [*TM* II, p. 78] that leaves no alternative to such estimates), is simply the average of two existing indices of employment and of industrial use of raw materials, respectively (*TM* II, p. 79, last column of table).

The situation is far worse, and Keynes' complaints are correspondingly greater ("the relevant statistics . . . are few and unsatisfactory. There is no single set of figures which measures accurately what should

---

7. Letter of July 23, 1945 to Alfred Cowles (in Keynes Papers).
8. Cf. pp. 7–8 above. For further details, see *KMT*, chaps. 4–6.

be capable of quite precise measurement" [*TM* II, p. 87]) with respect to estimates of total investment in fixed capital. Keynes rejects the use of data on the volume of new issues for this purpose both because these do not reflect residential construction, a major component of such investment, and because such data do not necessarily reflect the time period when the investment was actually carried out. Accordingly, Keynes suffices with a general reference to Wesley Mitchell's summary (in *Business Cycles* [1927]) of various time series connected with different aspects of investment activity and claims that this summary shows that "the fluctuations [in the rate of investment in fixed capital] are substantial and that they are correlated with the phases of the credit cycle in quite as high a degree as our theory would lead us to expect" (*TM* II, pp. 88–89). Keynes then uses a variety of a priori assumptions to derive an estimate of investment in "working capital" (*TM* II, pp. 92–100). Finally, he combines his estimates of investment in fixed and working capital, as well as of investment abroad, to present a table of total net investment in Britain for the period 1919–24, which he describes in the following words: "The following calculation is not based on statistical data, but is a not unplausible guess as to what may have happened—intended to illustrate my argument rather than to state an historical fact" (*TM* II, p. 101).

In less than six years all this is changed. In particular, when in the *General Theory* Keynes comes to deal with the same basic contention—the crucial role of the fluctuating volume of investment in generating business cycles—he is able to support his views by citing the estimates of total investment that Colin Clark had presented for Britain for the period 1928–31 in his book on *The National Income: 1924–1931* (1932, pp. 117, 138)[9] as well as the preliminary estimates for the United States for the period 1925–33 which Simon Kuznets had presented in his National Bureau of Economic Research Bulletin *Gross Capital Formation, 1919–1933* (NBER Bulletin no. 52, November 15, 1934).[10] Keynes also cites these tables in support of his contention that

9. Actually, Clark had presented such estimates the year before, in his maiden publication in the field (1931, p. 366). Clark's book (1932, pp. 114, 138) also provided the basis for estimates for 1924–27, and it is not clear to me why Keynes omitted these. I might note that Clark's estimate for 1924 was a critical revision of the one that had been presented by Bowley and Stamp in their *National Income, 1924* (1927), and that in a letter which Keynes wrote to Daniel Macmillan in December 1931 recommending the publication of Clark's book, he expressed the opinion that Clark's criticisms were correct. Keynes went on to say: "Indeed, Clark is, I think, a bit of a genius: almost the only economic statistician I have ever met who seems to me quite first-class. He is quite young and this is his first work" (letter in Keynes Papers).

10. As can be inferred from the galley proofs reproduced in *JMK* XIV, Keynes' reference to Kuznets' work appears for the first time in the second proof of the *General Theory*, which dates to the beginning of 1935 at the earliest (*JMK* XIV, p. 351, p. 440, n. 3). The fact that even then national income estimates were not yet a standard tool of

depreciation allowances and the like "normally" bear a high proportion to the value of gross investment; but at the same time he expresses the view that "Mr. Kuznets' method must surely lead to too low an estimate of the annual increase in depreciation" (GT, pp. 102–4).

As a matter of fact, Keynes was not too careful in his use of Kuznets' data, and this led to an intensive correspondence between the two men which culminated in Keynes' publication of a note of correction in the September 1936 Economic Journal.[11] This correspondence was actually sparked by a letter to Keynes from George O. May (a distinguished member of the accounting profession, and one of the major directors of the National Bureau at the time)[12] immediately after the publication of the General Theory, in which May pointed out that Kuznets had explicitly stated that his deductions for depreciation referred only to the business sector, and (for lack of the necessary data) excluded the household and government sectors. Correspondingly, Keynes' justified feeling that the estimates for depreciation were "too low" stemmed not from inadequacies in Kuznets' estimates, but from Keynes' erroneous interpretation of them.[13]

May's letter was followed a month later (March 23, 1936) by one from Kuznets himself, who corroborated May's criticism in detail (JMK XXIX, pp. 188–91). Kuznets also pointed out two minor arithmetical errors—and one major one—in the calculations that Keynes had made from Kuznets' data in order to derive an estimate of

---

economic analysis may be one of the reasons Keynes expressed his theory of effective demand in chapter 3 of the General Theory in terms of N, the level of employment, and not in terms of Y_w, the level of national income measured in wage units. On the other hand, note Keynes' presentation of the consumption function in terms of Y_w in chapter 8 of his book—which is also the chapter in which he presents the respective national income estimates of Clark and Kuznets. Note too that in his restatement of his theory in chapter 18, Keynes specifies his "dependent variables as the volume of employment and the national income (or national dividend) measured in wage units" (GT, p. 245). [On p. 38 of the General Theory, Keynes also claims that there are methodological reasons for not expressing his theory of effective demand in terms of real national income (see also GT, p. 114). These reasons have been cited and rejected on pp. 129–30 above.]

11. This correspondence has, fortunately, been preserved in the Keynes Papers, and I do hope that it will be reproduced in a future volume of Keynes' Collected Writings. [It since has been, in JMK XXIX, to which reference will henceforth be made.] Keynes' September 1936 note is reproduced as appendix 2 to the new edition of the General Theory (JMK VII, pp. 386–93).

12. I am indebted to Simon Kuznets for this information.

13. May's letter (dated February 25, 1936) is not in the Keynes Papers, but it was fortunately located by Solomon Fabricant (to whom I am much indebted) in a volume of May's writings (1936, pp. 408–10) which was published by Price, Waterhouse & Company, the firm with which May was connected. [This letter has since been reprinted in JMK XXIX, pp. 187–88.]

total business depreciation.[14] As a result of these and other considerations, Kuznets firmly disassociated himself from what Keynes had
designated as the estimate of "net capital formation (on Mr. Kuznets'
definition)" (*GT*, p. 103, last line of table), stated that "the use of our
estimates in your book was over hasty," and concluded his letter with
the corollary request that "if you can find any way of amending your
interpretation and correcting the erroneous impression that it is likely
to create, I, and, I am sure, my colleagues at the National Bureau, will
greatly appreciate your doing so" (*JMK* XXIX, pp. 190–91).

In his letter of reply (dated April 6, 1936) Keynes conceded his error
and said that he would publish a note of correction in the *Economic
Journal*. Two months later, he sent Kuznets a first draft of this note for
his comments.[15] By then, Solomon Fabricant's *Measures of Capital
Consumption, 1929–1933* (NBER Bulletin no. 60, June 30, 1936) had
just come from the press. Accordingly, in his reply (dated June 26,
1936), Kuznets made use of it, as well as other of Fabricant's
estimates, to comment on Keynes' draft by means of a detailed nine-
page memorandum which presented numerous tables, including a
summary table with estimates of net capital formation for the economy
as a whole—the desideratum of Keynes' analysis (*JMK* XXIX, pp.
194–201).

One might think that after having erred so grievously in his original
interpretation of Kuznets' estimates, Keynes would have been somewhat hesitant before challenging him again. But such circumspection
was not part of Keynes' character. Instead, in his reply (dated August
3, 1936) to Kuznets' letter, Keynes, of course, thanked him for his
detailed memorandum, but then—with respect to Kuznets' estimates
of inventory accumulation—went on to say, "I have checked the order
of magnitude in your figures by the usual sort of rough tests which I
always apply myself and which are difficult to explain to others, and, as
I say, your figures here make to me no sense" (*JMK* XXIX, p. 202).
And, interestingly enough, this time Keynes was half-right. For, in his
reply (dated August 19, 1936), Kuznets explained that, though the reason for Keynes' reservations was not valid, the estimates in question
were, indeed, incorrect and had been revised in the direction indicated
by him (*JMK* XXIX, p. 205).

From all this—as well as some final revisions which Kuznets, at
Keynes' request, had cabled him—there finally emerged Keynes'
aforementioned note of correction in the September 1936 *Economic*

14. These estimates appear in line 2 of the table on p. 103 of the *General Theory*.
Kuznets pointed out that the last figure in this line should be 6,320, instead of 8,204.
15. This draft has not survived.

Journal. Keynes began this note with a reference to his correspondence with Kuznets and then presented a series of corrected tables which he had more or less transferred bodily from Kuznets' memorandum.[16]

In the *General Theory*, Keynes made use of Kuznets' data on net investment not only to describe the volatility of this variable, but also to derive a "highly approximate estimate" of the marginal propensity to consume. This he did by first using the data to compute an estimate of the multiplier for the United States during the period in question (1925–33), then deducing from it the corresponding estimate of the marginal propensity to consume. Keynes stated that he estimated the multiplier by calculations based on a grouping of the annual data by pairs of years. As he wrote: "If single years are taken in isolation, the results look rather wild. But if they are grouped in pairs, the multiplier seems to have been less than 3 and probably fairly stable in the neighbourhood of 2.5. This suggests a marginal propensity to consume not exceeding 60 to 70 per cent" (*GT*, pp. 127–28).

Let me at this point note that, to the best of my knowledge, this was the first estimate of marginal propensity to consume that was based on an examination of statistical time series.[17] And, in any event, the members of this audience will be particularly interested to note that by virtue of his having derived his estimate of the marginal propensity indirectly from an estimate of the multiplier, Keynes might be said to have been the first person to have made use (even if unintentionally) of a reduced-form equation to derive an unbiased estimate of a structural parameter! And all this several years before Trygve Haavelmo's pathbreaking work (1943, 1944, 1947) on the methodological necessity for such a procedure.

Be that as it may, there are several far more prosaic questions that arise with reference to Keynes' estimate. First, Keynes does not specify what national income data he used in conjunction with Kuznets' investment data to compute the estimate of the multiplier, and it is not at all obvious what they may have been. For Willford King's estimates (1930, p. 77) went only to 1928, whereas Kuznets' pre-

16. Some of the tables in the copy of this memorandum in the Keynes Papers actually show the markings that Keynes made to prepare them for press. One appropriate modification that Keynes did, however, make in these tables was to replace Fabricant's estimates of depreciation on the basis of historical costs (which Kuznets had presented in his memorandum in order to maintain consistency with his estimates in NBER Bulletin no. 52), with Fabricant's newly available estimates of depreciation at current replacement cost (which Kuznets had added in a footnote to each of the tables in his memorandum) (Keynes' letter of August 3, 1936 and Kuznets' reply of August 19, 1936; *JMK* XXIX, pp. 201–2, 204).

17. Unfortunately, the statistical basis of Kahn's original estimate (1931, pp. 13–14) is not specified, except to say that it was supplied by Colin Clark (cf. p. 197 above).

liminary estimates of national income were at that time available for only four of the nine years covered by his investment estimates (*National Income, 1929–1932*, NBER Bulletin no. 49, January 26, 1934; revised June 7, 1934). This mystery has led me to much searching of libraries and questioning of witnesses and to the consequent conclusion that the only relevant national income estimates that could have been available to Keynes at that time (i.e., mid-1935 at the latest) were those published by the National Industrial Conference Board. In particular, the *Conference Board Bulletin* for February 20, 1934 (pp. 15–16) presented estimates of national income for the period 1909–33 prepared by one Edward T. Frankel, described as the statistician of the Board.[18]

But this does not end the mystery. For if I interpret the procedure Keynes describes as one which estimated the United States multiplier for the period 1925–33 on the basis of averages for the pairs of years 1925–26, 1927–28, 1929–30, and 1931–32, then the estimates yielded by net investment as estimated by Kuznets à la Keynes (*GT*, p. 103) and national income as estimated by the Conference Board are, respectively, 25 [*sic*], 1.1, and 1.9. If, instead, we ignore 1925 and take the pairs of years 1926–27, 1928–29, 1930–31, and 1932–33, then the estimates become 2.9, 1.8, and 2.1, respectively. And it is hard to say that these results justify Keynes' conclusion that "the multiplier seems to have been less than 3 and probably fairly stable in the neighbourhood of 2.5" (*GT*, p. 128).[19]

I must also point out that, at the end of his September 1936 note of correction with respect to his use of Kuznets' investment data (see above), Keynes returned to the question of estimating the multiplier by such data and wrote:

> When comparable figures of income are available, we shall be able to make some computations as to the value of the Multiplier in the conditions of the United States, though there are many statistical

18. I am very much indebted to Daniel Creamer of the Conference Board for providing me with a photocopy of this *Bulletin*. In this connection, see also Carol Carson's "History of the United States National Income and Product Accounts" (1975, pp. 63–66, 154–55), which also provides additional information on Frankel.
My statement that Keynes had made this estimate of the multiplier by mid-1935 at the latest is based on the fact that proofs of chapter 10 of the *General Theory* (in which the estimate appears) were circulated for criticism at that time (*JMK* XIII, p. 525; XIV, p. 351), and that these proofs already contained the discussion on pp. 127–28 of this chapter which I have cited in the preceding paragraph (*JMK* XIV, p. 457).

19. If a two-year moving average is used instead, the results become even worse, and range from −1.1 to +11.8. I might note that Keynes' statement about the magnitude and stability of the multiplier was challenged already in 1937 by Lauchlin Currie, who made year-to-year calculations on the basis of a preliminary draft of Kuznets' *National Income and Capital Formation 1919–1935* (1938) and reached estimates of the multiplier which ranged from negative numbers to +21.6 (Currie 1938, p. 21).

difficulties still to overcome. If, however, as a very crude, preliminary test we take the Dept. of Commerce estimates of income (uncorrected for price changes), we find that during the large movements of the years from 1929 to 1932 the changes in money-incomes were from three to five times the changes in net investment shown above. In 1933 incomes and investment both increased slightly, but the movements were too narrow to allow the ratio of the one to the other to be calculated within a reasonable margin of error. [*JMK* VII, p. 392]

But once again, if one carries out the indicated calculations with the national income estimates which Keynes apparently used,[20] the results do not completely accord with his description. In particular, the estimates for the multiplier yielded by the year-to-year changes from 1929–32 are, respectively, 4.4, 5.7, and 3.3.[21] And I also find it characteristic of Keynes that he does not bother to point out that his estimates here, as well as his estimating procedure, differ from those he had presented only half a year before in the *General Theory*.

Another puzzling aspect of Keynes' procedure in the *General Theory* was his failure to take the estimates of British national income that Colin Clark had presented in his 1932 book (pp. 117, 138) together with the estimates of net investment Keynes had cited from his book (*GT*, p. 102), and to derive from them an estimate for the multiplier for Britain corresponding to the one he had derived from Kuznets' data for the United States. It may well be that it was this omission Keynes was trying to justify when he preceded the latter estimate with the comment that "at present . . . our statistics are not accurate enough (or compiled sufficiently with this specific object in view) to allow us to infer more than highly approximate estimates. The best for the purpose, of which I am aware, are Mr. Kuznets' figures for the United States" (*GT*, p. 127). But I suspect that an additional, and not entirely unrelated, reason for this omission was that the application of Keynes' estimating procedure to the data he had cited from Clark's study would have shown that the multiplier implicit in the change from 1928–29 to 1930–31 was slightly less than unity![22]

20. Namely, those presented in Robert Nathan's article "The National Income Produced, 1929–1934" in the November 1935 issue of the United States Department of Commerce, *Survey of Current Business* (p. 17): for the estimates of "national income paid out" (as distinct from "produced") in the *Survey of Current Business* for January 1935 and August 1935 show a decline from 1932 to 1933, and not the slight increase referred to by Keynes. In any event, estimates based on "national income paid out" also depart from Keynes' description.

21. The corresponding estimate for the change from 1932 to 1933 is 15.4.

22. However, the multiplier implicit in the change from 1926–27 (which date Keynes did not cite—see n. 9 above) to 1928–29 is 5.0.

I might note that Keynes' apparent reservations about Clark's estimates, coupled with his general lack of faith in regression analysis that I have already described, had some ironic implications here. For, if only Keynes had been willing to apply such analysis to Clark's estimates of consumption and national income in Britain for the six years 1924 and 1927–31 (Clark 1932, p. 117), he would have obtained just what he wanted: a marginal propensity to consume of approximately 0.7.[23]

The foregoing puzzle is compounded by the fact that in 1933 Colin Clark had apparently made some estimates of the multiplier which Keynes found most satisfactory, but to which he does not refer in the *General Theory*. Thus, in a letter dated January 29, 1933, Keynes wrote to Richard Kahn:

> Colin [Clark] was delighted with the multiplier for secondary employment, but I tell him that all it does is to increase slightly my confidence in the accuracy of his statistics. He has further elaborated . . . [his calculations] but I tell him not to overcook it because, if he succeeds in making the actual and computed curves identical, I shall distrust his statistics again, since I know for certain that the multiplier is not always 2. [*JMK* XIII, p. 413, ellipses and square brackets in source cited]

I have not been able to determine the nature of Clark's calculations,[24] though they may be related to the ones which he later extended and published in his "Determination of the Multiplier from National Income Statistics" (1938)—an article which estimates the multiplier in Britain as equal to 2.07 in the period 1929–33[25] and which contains a diagram that shows a good correspondence between a curve repre-

23. Statistically significant at the 10 percent level. And indeed, Richard Stone and W. M. Stone—with obviously quite a different attitude to regression analysis—made use shortly afterward of the data in Clark's 1937 book to derive an estimate of the marginal propensity to consume of 0.52 for Britain (1938, pp. 15, 19).

24. [They can now be identified with the calculations that Clark made in some correspondence with Keynes in January 1933, which (together with much other material) has recently been discovered. This material has now been reproduced in *JMK* XXIX, with the aforementioned correspondence appearing on pp. 57–61. Together with the diagram of the "actual" and "computed" curves which Clark sent with his letter of January 16, 1933 to Keynes (and to which Keynes referred in his letter of January 29, 1933 to Kahn), he (Clark) also enclosed the data on which the curves were based, saying "I know you fight shy of diagrams" (*JMK* XXIX, p. 61; cf. p. 129 above). I might note that in this correspondence both Keynes and Clark estimate the multiplier not by the method Keynes was to use in the *General Theory*, but in some obscure way by applying Kahn's estimate of a multiplier of 2 to Clark's estimate (1932, pp. 134–36) of the excess of savings over investment as defined in the *Treatise*, and then comparing actual with computed output.]

25. Clark derived this estimate indirectly from the estimates that he made of the marginal propensities to save and import, respectively (Clark 1938, p. 442).

senting "actual gross national income" for the years 1929–37 and one representing this income as "computed from multipliers" (ibid., p. 443).[26]

I hope I will not be considered too cynical if I conclude the discussion of this point by noting that the estimate of the United States multiplier that Keynes made in the *General Theory* on the basis of the national income and investment data which had just become available does not differ too much from those that he had earlier made without the benefit of such data, and solely on the basis of various a priori assumptions. Thus, in his *Means to Prosperity* (1933), Keynes estimated the United States multiplier as "greater than 2, rather than less" (*JMK* IX, p. 345). And in a lecture that he gave in June 1934 he stated that "on a balance of considerations I should be extremely surprised if the multiplier in the United States is less than 3, and it is probably appreciably higher" (*JMK* XIII, p. 461). In all fairness, however, I should add that Keynes of the *General Theory* was sufficiently influenced by the calculations he had made with Kuznets' data as to present an estimate of the multiplier (viz., 2.5–3.0) that was "a lower figure . . . than [he] should have expected" (*GT*, pp. 127–28), which might have been an allusion to the estimate he presented in the June 1934 lecture just cited. On the other hand, the estimate of the multiplier of "three to five" he published at the end of his September 1936 *Economic Journal* does accord with that of this lecture.

I have gone into all this detail about Keynes' use of data in the *General Theory* because I think it reveals certain characteristics of his which are important for an understanding of the story I have yet to tell. Thus it shows, first of all, Keynes' basic concern with integrating his theoretical analysis with the data of the real world. Furthermore, it shows him as a person with strong intuitive feelings for the proper orders of magnitude of the various data—indeed, so strong and so confident that he did not hesitate to pit these feelings against the systematic estimates made by the specialists in the field. Not unrelatedly, it shows him as a person who was not too meticulous in his handling of data, and who sometimes succumbed to the temptation to bend the data to fit his preconceptions.[27]

26. In what was apparently a reference to this article, Keynes wrote to Roy Harrod, in a letter dated July 16, 1938:

> Colin [Clark] . . . has recently persuaded himself that the propensity to consume in terms of money is constant at all phases of the credit cycle. He works out a figure for it and proposes to predict by using the result, regardless of the fact that his own investigations clearly show that it is not constant, in addition to the strong a priori reasons for regarding it as most unlikely that it can be so. [*JMK* XIV, pp. 299–300, square brackets in source cited].

27. Another well-known example that might be mentioned in this context is Keynes' statement in the *General Theory* (p. 10) that "the change in real wages associated with a

I suppose we could say that Keynes was a casual empiricist; but it would then be only fair to ask: how many of the economists of his day were not? And it would also be only fair to add that the bending of economic data to fit preconceptions is not exactly a phenomenon which has since disappeared from the face of the earth.

5. On the Nature of the Statistical Revolution

From the sequence of events I have described above, it is obvious that the statistical revolution as represented by Clark's and Kuznets' national income estimates preceded the "Keynesian Revolution" as represented by the *General Theory*. Let us now look into this story in somewhat greater detail.

Paul Studenski's well-known history of national income estimates (1958) starts with the seventeenth-century estimates of Sir William Petty and Gregory King in England and goes on to describe the construction of such estimates through the eighteenth and nineteenth centuries in France, Russia, Germany, and the United States as well. These long antecedents notwithstanding, there are, I feel, three interrelated characteristics of the interwar national income estimates that justify our use of the term "revolution" with respect to them. First, these estimates were now presented (most notably, in the work of

---

change in money-wages, so far from being usually in the same direction, is almost always in the opposite direction." Keynes may have made this statement under the impact of the immediately preceding period in Britain (where from 1925 to 1933 money wages fell by 7 percent, while real wages rose by 35 percent) and the United States (where from 1929 to 1933 money wages fell by 28 percent [*sic*], while real wages rose by 3 percent). (These calculations are based on the data reproduced in *KMT*, pp. 17, 121.) However, the statement did not stand up under the subsequent systematic examinations of Dunlop (1938), who studied British wages over the period 1860–1937; and Tarshis (1939), who examined United States data for the period 1932–38. See also Keynes' reply (1939), reprinted as appendix 3 to the new edition of the *General Theory*. I might also note Keynes' use of empirical data in his *Tract on Monetary Reform* (1923) in connection with his analysis of inflation (pp. 45–46) and with his presentation of the purchasing-power-parity theory (pp. 81–87). With respect to the latter, note Angell's criticism at the time (in his review of the *Tract*) of Keynes' claim to have verified the theory with the data he presented (Angell 1925, pp. 274–75). On Keynes' concern with data, as well as his intuitive feeling for them, see also Austin Robinson's perceptive memoir (1947, p. 44).

{In a letter to me dated May 25, 1976, Jan Tinbergen has related the following anecdote: "In the Statistical Office of the Netherlands we had attempted to estimate a number of substitution price elasticities for imports. We did find quite a few cases where it was around the famous figure of 2 which Keynes assumed in his study about the transfer capacity of Germany [see Keynes (1929), p. 166]. When I told him about our results I thought he would be glad that his assumption had shown to be true. What he said, however, was: isn't it nice that you found the correct figure?"}

[In this connection I might also mention Keynes' lack of interest in Clark's attempt (1932, chap. XI; see p. 243 below) to test the theory of the *Treatise* empirically, as evidenced by Keynes' failure even to refer to this attempt in the 1933 correspondence with Clark described in n. 24 above.]

Kuznets 1933, and especially 1941) against the background of a systematic clarification of the methodological problems involved in defining such basic concepts as net income, investment, final versus intermediate product, the value of government output, and the like—and this clarification concluded with operational solutions to the problems in question.[28] Second, there took place a rapid development in the detail and variety of these estimates, as well as a vast improvement in their quality. Finally, and most significant of all from our present viewpoint, these estimates no longer resulted from the sporadic research activities of individual scholars using different methods which they respectively applied to different, isolated years, but from the organized activity of official government agencies which systematically produced current annual estimates on as homogeneous a basis as possible. And the facts remain that, with the possible exception of Australia, such estimates did not come into existence until after (and in part, as a result of) World War I, and that only such estimates can provide data helpful for current government policy formulation.[29]

Thus, for example, a major impetus to the establishment in the United States of the National Bureau of Economic Research in 1920—and to the Bureau's initial concentration on the construction of national income estimates—was the experience of several economists in the service of the United States government during the war which led them to feel that their country was lagging behind others in the preparation of such estimates. As was stated in the preface to the two-volume study *Income in the United States: Its Amount and Distribution, 1909–1919* (1921, 1922), the maiden publication of the Bureau: in contrast with the "excellent estimates [that] have been made of the national income of Great Britain and Germany,[30] where well-administered income taxes with low exemption limits provide a solid foundation to build on," United States statisticians before the war (at which time there was no income tax)

> found the American data bulky but miscellaneous and hard to fit together. The war lent the problem pressing importance; and several estimates of the national income, most of them based directly or

28. This is not to deny the importance of Pigou's classic discussion of some of these problems in his *Economics of Welfare* (1924, part 1), though it should be noted that by its very nature this discussion does not contain operational conclusions. Note too Clark's references (1937, chap. 1) to Pigou's discussion.

29. Studenski (1958, vol. 1, p. 151) lists Australia as having started annual estimates in 1886; but in his description of the Australian estimates on pp. 135–37 he refers to what at best seem to be triennial estimates. For other discussions of early national income estimates see Deane (1956, 1957) and Kendrick (1970).

30. In the subsequent pages of the study (1921, pp. 81–88), the authors refer to the work of A. L. Bowley and Josiah Stamp in Britain, and of Karl Helfferich in Germany.

indirectly upon Mr. King's [1915] figures for 1910, were made by men interested in the government's financial policy. These estimates were all rough approximations, hastily constructed. Quite naturally, they differed considerably in their results. [1921, p. viii]

Correspondingly, the first project of the National Bureau was the preparation of better estimates, which led to the publication of the two-volume study just cited, followed several years later by Willford King's *National Income and Its Purchasing Power* (1930), which brought his estimates up to 1928.[31]

Let me now point out that the foregoing estimates—and, as far as I can judge from Studenski's study (1958, vol. 1, especially pp. 141 and 156–57), the pre–World War I estimates of all countries—were of national income by factor shares (wages, profits) or by industrial origin (agriculture, manufacturing). They were not of national income—or, rather, product—by final use (viz., consumption and investment, respectively). In part this was because the first two types of estimates were the easiest to compute from the available data: income tax data (to the extent available) could readily be used for estimates of national income by factor shares; and, similarly, census of manufacturing data for estimates of national income by industrial origin (i.e., net value added of the different industries). In contrast, estimates of national product by final use required that the statistician make additional estimates in order to distinguish between the output of those goods and services destined for final use and those destined for intermediate use, and in order to make allowances for the relevant transportation costs and distributive markups which enter into the price of a good to the final purchaser (Kuznets 1933, pp. 23–24; 1941, pp. 98–99). In brief, such estimates partook of some of the complexities of the later input-output analysis.

But the priority in time of these factor-share and industrial-origin estimates was only in part due to such "technological constraints"; in part it was also due to the "tastes" or "preferences" of the society in which the economists (who reflected these "tastes") prepared their estimates. In particular, these preferences were for learning the answers to questions about the long-term growth of the economy as reflected by the increase in its national income, and/or about the distribution of this income by various categories (e.g., size, labor-capital, farmers–industrial workers). In the words, once again, of the preface to

31. For further details of the beginnings of the National Bureau, see Wesley Mitchell, "The National Bureau's First Quarter-Century" (1945). Because it was the work of the Bureau that ultimately led to the official United States national estimates (see below), I have concentrated in what follows on its contributions. For the contributions of other institutions and individuals during this period, see Carson (1975). See also n. 33 below.

the National Bureau maiden study *Income in the United States* (1921, vol. 1, p. ix), these preferences reflected themselves in "a desire to learn whether the national income is adequate to provide a decent living for all persons, whether this income is increasing as rapidly as the population, and whether its distribution among individuals is growing more or less unequal. . . . ." Similarly, in his preface to his book *The National Income and Its Purchasing Power* (1930, p. 9), Willford King explained his purpose in terms of the fact that "so many questions pertaining to the economic welfare of the citizens and the political policy of the legislators hinge upon a knowledge of the facts concerning the distribution of income among different classes of citizens." And, in the same spirit in England, Bowley had explained in the introduction to his *Division of the Product of Industry: An Analysis of National Income before the War* (1919) that the purpose of his study was "to show the amount and origins of the aggregate incomes of the people of the United Kingdom and the proportions of the aggregate that go to various economic classes" (p. 5). And much the same purpose was designated by Bowley and Stamp in their later study *The National Income, 1924* (1927, p. 95).

Notable by its omission from these declarations of purpose is any reference to the importance of national income data for the study of business cycles.[32] And this omission also manifests itself in the Bowley and Stamp Studies in the fact that they do not provide estimates for a sequence of successive years. But, as evidenced by the publication in 1923 of the National Bureau's volume *Business Cycles and Unemployment*, the study of cycles was rapidly to become a leitmotif of the Bureau's work, as it had been of the pre-1920 discussions which ultimately led to its establishment (N. I. Stone 1945, p. 9). Thus, in Wesley Mitchell's essay "Business Cycles," which opens this volume, there is a description of the volatility of investment, which in part rests on J. M. Clark's classic 1917 article on what was later to be called the "acceleration principle." It is also interesting that Clark's article, in turn, took as its starting point the data Wesley Mitchell had presented in his 1913 volume *Business Cycles*. Again, in what the Bureau published in 1927 as essentially a second edition of his 1913 volume, Mitchell surveyed (inter alia) the theories dating from the turn of the century which assigned a critical role in the business cycle to fluctua-

---

32. Indeed, in their introduction to *National Income, 1924* (1927, p. 93), Bowley and Stamp referred to the "instability of industry" as one of the reasons that had "prevented the construction of any estimate which would have a reasonable degree of permanence," which was, of course, a valid consideration from the viewpoint of their study, whose purpose was to estimate "the change in the national income that resulted from the war."

tions in the volume of investment—namely, the theories of Tugan-Baranowski, Spiethoff, Johannsen, and others (Mitchell 1927, pp. 23–29).

Needless to say, the interest of United States economists in the study of business cycles was sharply increased by the catastrophic events of the Great Depression. So it is not surprising that in the introductory remarks to his preliminary estimates of *Gross Capital Formation, 1919–1933*, in the 1934 NBER Bulletin that has already been referred to, Kuznets explains that estimates of net capital formation are of importance not only as measures of the addition to wealth, but also because "the total flow of commodities which, because of their durable nature represent largely investment, and which account for the bulk of gross capital formation, has been observed to show cyclical fluctuations strikingly different from those in the flow of commodities that are fully consumable within short periods" (Kuznets 1934b, p. 1). And I might also note that at the same time Kuznets was preparing these estimates he was also writing a largely theoretical paper on the acceleration principle (1934c) as his contribution to the Wesley Mitchell *Festschrift*.

Similarly, on the British scene, Colin Clark concluded his 1932 book on national income in an attempt (to the best of my knowledge, unique in the literature) to use his estimates to provide an empirical estimate of the "fundamental equations" of Keynes' *Treatise*, and even to test their validity as against that of the equation Clark attributed to Friedrich Hayek, who was at the time Keynes' chief rival in the field of business cycle theory. (See Clark 1932, chap. 11; 1933a.)

I have elaborated on all this in order to bring out the fundamental point that these national product estimates of the early 1930s were not the outcome of idle curiosity satisfying itself by the mechanical collection of data—not an exercise in measurement for the sake of measurement—but were in varying degrees motivated by the desire to quantify those macroeconomic variables to which the pre–*General Theory* theories of the business cycle had already attached crucial significance.

At the same time, it must be emphasized that the subsequent appearance of the *General Theory*, with its revolutionary analysis of the determination of the equilibrium level of output by means of the aggregate demand for consumption and investment goods, gave a further and decisive impetus to the preparation of national income estimates by these categories. For though Colin Clark had first provided such an estimate in 1932 (p. 117, table 45), it is only after the Keynesian Revolution that we find national income estimates widely presented in the

$C + I + G = Y$ rubric which is the cornerstone of Keynesian economics.[33]

But I have drawn slightly ahead of my story, which, until the outbreak of World War II, proceeds along increasingly divergent lines in the United States as contrasted with England—a divergence I shall later try, in part, to explain. In the United States, the work of the National Bureau was recognized by the political authorities: in particular, in 1932 the Senate requested the preparation of national-income estimates for 1929–31. In response to this request, Simon Kuznets was lent to the United States Department of Commerce to set up a unit whose function it henceforth would be to provide national-income estimates on a current and systematic basis. The first product of this unit was a study carried out under Kuznets' responsibility, with the assistance of Lillian Epstein and Elizabeth Jenks of the National Bureau and Robert F. Martin and Robert R. Nathan of the United States Department of Commerce. This study, *National Income, 1929–32*, was almost simultaneously published in January 1934 as a Senate Document and (in summary form) as Kuznets' National Bureau Bulletin no. 49, to which I have already referred.[34] And a year later the National Incomes Section of the Department of Commerce, under the headship first of Martin and then of Nathan, began to publish annual estimates of national income by factor shares and industrial origin (but not by final use)[35] in the *Survey of Current Business* (see, e.g., Martin 1935 and Nathan 1935a).

In England, however, there was no parallel development during these years. In his 1932 book *National Income, 1924–1931*, Colin Clark complained about "the disgraceful condition of British official statistics" and urged "the centralization and proper co-ordination of the Government's statistical work" (1932, pp. vi–vii). But five years later, in his *National Income and Outlay* (1937), Clark began his introduction by justifying the publication of his new book on the ground that since the appearance of his first book on the subject in 1932, "no other writers have made any contributions to the subject of the determination

---

33. See Studenski (1958, vol. 1, pp. 152–53) and Kuznets (1973, p. 260). For further discussion of Clark's estimates, see below. See also the early use of such a framework by Warburton (1934, 1935), cited by Carson (1975, pp. 161–62). I might, however, note that in neither of these cases was the government component estimated separately.

34. This description is based on the respective prefaces to these two publications. For further details of this development, see Carson (1975, pp. 155–61).

[On the development of official United States national income estimates discussed here and in the following pages, compare also chap. 3, secs. 1–3, of the recent Department of Commerce monograph *Revolution in United States Government Statistics 1926–1976* (1978), prepared by J. W. Duncan and W. C. Shelton. As indicated there (p. 74, n. 1), these sections draw in large part on Carson's work.]

35. I shall return to this point below.

of the national income" (p. v). And he ended the introduction with the following complaint:

Work of the nature involved in the preparation of this book, like experimental work in the natural sciences, cannot properly be done by single individuals, but requires considerable expenditure in the provision of both academic and clerical assistance. Such limited funds as are available for the provision of research assistance in economics are at present fully occupied in other types of work, many of a theoretical nature. As a result I have had to do the entire work of investigation and calculation for this book with the exception of such clerical assistance as I paid for out of my own pocket. The more detailed investigations, which are needed to bring our knowledge of this subject to the extent and precision to which it has been brought in America and Germany, cannot be made by individual investigators. If the saying is true, that economics is eventually capable of benefiting the human race as much as the other sciences put together,[36] it must be equipped not only with the scientific spirit, but also with the financial resources, of the older sciences. [Clark 1937, p. vii]

But this remained a voice crying in the wilderness until the economic pressures of World War II forced the British government to begin to construct current national income estimates. I am, of course, referring to the famous White Paper of April 1941, *Analysis of the Sources of War Finance and an Estimate of the National Income and Expenditure in 1938 and 1940* (Cmd. 6261), for which James Meade and Richard Stone were primarily responsible.[37]

36. Donald Winch has pointed out to me that, in all probability, this was an allusion to the following statement in the Liberal Party's *Britain's Industrial Future* (1928)—the so-called Yellow Book in which the party then set out its political program (cf. p. 192 above):

How can economic science become a true science, capable, perhaps, of benefiting the human lot as much as all the other sciences put together, so long as the economist, unlike other scientists, has to grope for and guess at the relevant data of experience? [P. 123]

This statement appears in a discussion of the inadequacy of official statistics. And for reasons which will become clear in the next section, it may not be entirely a coincidence that Clark chose to allude to a work in whose preparation Keynes, as Harrod (1951, pp. 392–93) tells us, played an active and prominent role.

{In a letter to me dated May 27, 1976, Colin Clark has confirmed that this sentence in his preface "was a reference to the chapter in the Liberal Party's *Britain's Industrial Future* (The Yellow Book, 1928). This chapter was clearly written by Keynes. At that time I expected my readers to recognize the reference." In this letter Clark also explains that "when I complained about lack of help in the preface . . . I had just applied to the British branch of Rockefeller Foundation, and my application had been rejected."}

37. See Harrod (1951, p. 502) and Stone (1951, pp. 83–86). See also Sayers (1956, pp. 67–74) and Winch (1969, pp. 262–63). Unfortunately, no one (to my knowledge) has done for the detailed history of the development of modern British national income estimates what Carol Carson (1975) has recently done for that of the United States. This history is

Thus we can regard the statistical revolution which brought about the introduction of official national income estimates in both the United States and Britain as an example of a technological improvement stimulated by war; except that in the United States it was World War I which (with some lag) fulfilled this function, whereas Britain for some reason had to wait for World War II.

And, as is so frequently the case with technological improvements, on certain fronts the newcomer to the process surged ahead for a time. I say this especially with respect to the development by Meade and Stone (1941) of the broad conceptual framework of social accounting within which the national income estimates were placed. But I also say it with reference to the estimation of national income by the final-product $C + I + G = Y$ rubric Keynes had developed in his *General Theory* (1936) and applied empirically in his *How to Pay for the War* (1940).[38] For, despite the early work on such final-product estimates by Simon Kuznets (1934, 1937, 1938) to which I have already referred, despite the concurrent work of Clark Warburton at the Brookings Institution and of Lauchlin Currie at the Federal Reserve (Carson 1975, pp. 161–71), and despite the pre-*General Theory* emphasis of all these economists on the importance of such estimates as a tool of economic policy, the fact remains that the National Income Unit of the Department of Commerce lagged behind in extending its work to encompass such estimates. Instead, it assigned priority to placing its estimates of national income on a monthly basis (1938) and to preparing them by individual states (1939).[39] Thus it would seem that in the years im-

really outside the terms of reference of—and hence only briefly described in —the Central Statistical Office's *National Accounts Statistics: Sources and Methods* (1968, pp. 32–33). And for the same reason it is even more briefly described in Lewes' *Statistics of the British Economy* (1967, pp. 161–63). Here, then, is a subject worthy of study. [In this connection, see the Postscript below for a discussion of Richard Stone's recent discovery of some official British national-income estimates that were prepared in 1929 and then suppressed.]

38. Which, in turn, drew upon his earlier article in the *Economic Journal* on "The Income and Fiscal Potential of Great Britain" (1939c); see also his supplementary note a year later on "The Concept of National Income" (1940b).

39. On the reasons for this priority, see Carson (1975, pp. 159–60). What increases one's puzzlement about this lag—and, correspondingly, one's impression that the unit during this period was intellectually relatively isolated—is Carson's description (1975, pp. 166–67) of the work on estimates of gross national product and its components which was being carried out elsewhere in the Department of Commerce during 1939 by V Lewis Bassie. Carson notes that Bassie had been one of Currie's assistants at the Federal Reserve in mid-1937.

I might note that once again (see p. 243 above) it is Colin Clark who is to be credited with having been the first one to provide estimates of national income for periods of less than a year. Thus, in his article in the June 1933 issue of the *Economic Journal* (p. 211), Clark provided quarterly estimates of national income from the first quarter of 1927 to the first quarter of 1933 (*sic*). See also his later *National Income and Outlay* (1937, p. 206). Indeed, the presentation of quarterly estimates was a characteristic of Clark's work from its very beginning (1931, p. 366).

mediately following its establishment, the National Income Unit was not sufficiently attuned to the developments in either macroeconomic theory or policy. Indeed, the unit did not develop final-product estimates until 1942 (Gilbert and Bangs 1942a), when the "tastes" for them (to revert to a metaphor I have already used) were heightened by the growing need of the United States, too, to deal with the problems and inflationary pressures of a war economy. I might also note that, in carrying out these final-product estimates, the National Income Unit was to a certain extent apparently also influenced by the example of its British counterpart.[40] On the other hand—and quite unlike its British counterpart, which again lagged seriously behind—within a few months the National Income Unit was (at the request of the War Production Board) already publishing its final-product estimates quarterly (Gilbert and Bangs 1942b).[41]

40. In her unpublished thesis (1971, p. 170), Carol Carson notes that the 1941 White Paper was reprinted in the July 1941 *Federal Reserve Bulletin*. She also reports on an interview in 1969 with Milton Gilbert (who in 1941 succeeded Robert Nathan as head of what was by then the National Income Division), who recalled "lively discussions" with Richard Stone when the latter visited the division's offices during the war. (I am indebted to Dr. Carson for providing me with a copy of her thesis and permitting me to cite from it.)

41. Corresponding quarterly estimates in Britain were first published by the Central Statistical Office in the *Monthly Digest of Statistics* for January 1957 (pp. iv–vi), which provided estimates back to the first quarter of 1954. For additional comments on, and recollections of, the development of national income estimates in the United States Department of Commerce, see the brief articles by George Jaszi, Simon Kuznets, Richard and Nancy Ruggles, and Walter S. Salant in the Fiftieth Anniversary Issue of the *Survey of Current Business* (1971).

{In a letter to me dated May 22, 1976, Simon Kuznets has written: "It may well be that the delay in adoption of the final-products approach by the Department of Commerce is a matter of change in 'tastes.' But it may also be a matter of sheer time needed to shift a new and rather elaborate technique from its pioneering stages within a non-governmental research organization, like the NBER, to the official auspices of a rather large and bureaucratic organization. I do not remember the dates. But the complete manuscript of the capital formation volume, published in 1938, could not have been finished much before that date: and Bill Shaw, who had been my main assistant on it [see Kuznets 1938, p. viii] and also helped with the estimates for earlier decades, shifted to Washington almost immediately thereafter—producing the basic commodity flow tables for the Department of Commerce soon thereafter. The span between completing the work on commodity flow and final product approach and the adopting of it by the Department of Commerce was relatively brief, and was delayed only by the delay in Milton Gilbert's taking over the leadership. . . . In short, I would not ascribe much significance to the time gap involved—considering the speed with which the adoption was, in fact, accomplished. But you might want to check on the dates."

Such a checking has yielded the following results: Shaw continued working at the National Bureau until September 1940, at which time he began to work half-time at the Department of Commerce (NBER Bulletin no. 80, September 9, 1940, pp. 14–15; cited by Carson 1975, p. 1968 n. 51, though with incorrect date). Milton Gilbert was appointed chief of the National Income Division in 1941 (Carson 1975, p. 168). Shaw's article "The Gross Flow of Finished Commodities" appeared in the *Survey of Current Business* for April 1942 and was followed a month later by that of Gilbert and Bangs (1942a) (see the reference inter alia to Shaw and his work in the first two footnotes of the latter article.}

To sum up, this then was the nature of the interaction between the macroeconomic revolutions of the interwar period: the pre-Keynesian theories of the business cycle which assigned a crucial role to fluctuations in investment caused some of the efforts of the statistical revolution to be directed toward measuring this variable; these early-1930 estimates, in turn, provided support for the theoretical revolution then in the making; and the feedback from the theoretical revolution encouraged further elaboration and refinement of the statistical measurements, which, in turn, permitted further theoretical developments. Among such developments in Keynesian economics proper, I include the wartime inflationary-gap literature, of which Keynes himself was again the initiator by means of his already mentioned "Income and Fiscal Potential of Great Britain" (1939) and *How to Pay for the War* (1940). In the postwar period, I include the refinements of the consumption and investment functions, as well as the development of more elaborate Keynesian models. And from a broader perspective I would also include the stimulus to Leontief's work on input-output analysis that was provided by the National Bureau's work on national income (Leontief 1936, pp. 105–6; 1941, p. 10). In brief, we had here the kind of fertile interaction between theory and measurement which had so frequently characterized the progress of science.

6. The Lag in British National Income Statistics

At the end of World War I, as we have seen, the United States looked to Britain as an example to be followed in the field of national income estimation; at the outset of World War II, the opposite was the case. What caused this reversal of roles?

Let me start with personalities. In the usual account of the development of British national income statistics in World War II, and of the 1941 White Paper in particular, Keynes is given major credit. Thus, in his well-known biography, Roy Harrod has provided a vivid description of the crucial role that Keynes played in pushing this "great revolution" (as Harrod denotes it) through the Treasury. "The initiative," Harrod states, "must be attributed to Keynes, but for whose interest the compilation would not have been made and published at that time" (Harrod 1951, p. 502).[42]

42. See also the other references cited in n. 37 above.
[Cf. the interesting correspondence connected with the preparation of this White Paper which has now become available in *JMK* XXII, pp. 325–33. Richard Stone (1978, pp. 67–72) has recently provided some personal reminiscences of this event, including the following edifying description of the way Keynes operated in this context:

[Keynes] did more than anyone else I have known to break down the Cult of the Zeros, by which I mean the practice then common among statisticians of writing

Quite frankly, however, I feel that if we want to praise Keynes for his role in promoting official estimates of national income in 1941, then we should also criticize him for not having used his influence to promote them at a much earlier stage. And he had many opportunities to do so. Thus, Keynes' active role in the establishment of the *Monthly Bulletin* of the London & Cambridge Economic Service in 1923, and his continued connection with it in subsequent years, is frequently, and quite rightly, cited as evidence of his deep concern with economic statistics (cf., e.g., Austin Robinson 1947, p. 44). Yet the basic fact is that, from the statistical viewpoint, this *Bulletin* mainly reported on standard time series such as prices, wages, interest rates, exports, stocks of raw materials, and the like. Furthermore, and in keeping with the fact that it was issued in conjunction with the Harvard Committee on Economic Research, its aggregate time series were of the Harvard A-B-C type at the inception of the *Bulletin*, and remained so throughout the 1930s. It made no attempt to develop new aggregate series and, in particular, made no attempt to develop current national income estimates. This was left for the occasional efforts of the *Economist*.[43]

My criticism of Keynes on this score is even stronger with respect to his activities or, rather, the lack of them, just a decade before the publication of the 1941 White Paper. For in 1931 Keynes was a leading member of the famous Macmillan Committee as well as of the newly established Economic Advisory Council (EAC)[44]—both of which bodies were, in different contexts, charged by the British government with advising it on the causes of and remedies for the deep depression into which the economy had by then fallen. And yet Keynes did not

---

down zero when what they meant was that no reliable information was available. I shall give a typical example. At an early stage in a discussion on estimates of the balance of payments we were presented with a table containing the usual zeros against a number of items. "Look," said Keynes, "you know as well as I do that the change in Commonwealth balances cannot have been zero last year: what do you think it was?" "We really don't know," was the reply, "but probably between three and four hundred million." "Then put it down at £350 million" said Keynes "and try to get some accurate information in the future, for by your own admission it is very important." [ibid., pp. 71–72]]

43. On the nature of the Harvard A-B-C curves, see Mitchell (1927, pp. 200–201, 324–26). See also the expository article by William Beveridge (1923), then chairman of the Executive Committee of the London & Cambridge Economic Service, in the introductory number of its *Bulletin*. On the *Economist*, see the annual estimates for 1920–23 presented in the issue of October 4, 1924 (p. 520), and those for 1920–27 presented in a supplement to the issue of October 6, 1928 by one G. D. Rokeling, with a foreword by Josiah Stamp. Rokeling's work was cited by Keynes in his *Treatise* (II, pp. 76–77).

44. The EAC was established in January 1930 and continued to function until after the outbreak of the war in 1939. Keynes was one of its members throughout its existence. I have made use here of the highly illuminating study of *The Economic Advisory Council 1930–1939* (1977) by Susan Howson and Donald Winch; cf. also pp. 195–96, 204–5, above.

take advantage of his prominent position in both these bodies to further the introduction of official national income estimates on a current basis.

Let me be more specific. The final chapter of the Macmillan Report (1931) was devoted to "Proposals Relating to Information and Statistics"; among them, however, is *not* to be found a proposal for the construction of official national income statistics. Now, Harrod tells us that Keynes "played a big part in the drafting of the Report. His scheme for its general structure was adopted with modifications. He wrote large sections of it, and his style is clearly visible in certain passages" (Harrod 1951, p. 423). And that Keynes bore a good deal of responsibility for the aforementioned chapter in particular can be firmly established from a letter to him in April 1931 from Colin Clark, then a junior staff member of the EAC, fresh out of Oxford (above, pp. 195–96), "returning the draft of the chapter on Statistics in the Macmillan Report together with [his] own additions."[45]

There is also the internal evidence of the chapter itself: for it repeatedly echoes the complaints Keynes had voiced the year before in volume II of the *Treatise* about the inadequacy of the British statistics with reference to money and banking, volume of trade, total volume of investment, and the like. And surely it is the voice of the *Treatise* (see especially vol. II, chap. 37) that we hear in the recommendation to obtain statistics on the value of contracts made in the industries dealing with capital construction (building and contracting, engineering, etc.), which "are of much importance to a Central Bank in determining whether and how far new capital construction needs from time to time to be encouraged or discouraged" (Macmillan Report, p. 183). But there is no explicit reference in this chapter to the integration of such statistics within a framework of national expenditure estimates.[46]

Similarly, despite the active concern of the EAC with economic statistics,[47] and despite its periodical reports on the current economic situation, there is no indication in the study by Howson and Winch (1977) that the EAC attempted to promote the construction of official national income estimates. And this despite the fact that Keynes himself was chairman of the EAC Committee on the Economic Outlook, which issued three reports on the current situation in 1930, and was an active member of the subsequent Committee on Economic Informa-

45. This letter is in the Keynes Papers.
46. This is not to deny that the chapter did strongly recommend the improvement of the census of production and the collection of other data that are necessary for a proper development of national income estimates.
47. Thus it had committees which issued reports on "The Revision of the Cost-of-Living Index Number" (1930–31) and on "Unemployment Statistics" (1930). See Howson and Winch (1977, pp. 33, 36–37).

tion, which over the period 1931–39 issued twenty-seven such reports.[48]

Why did Keynes fail to promote the construction of national income statistics in the early 1930s? My conjecture is that at that time Keynes had little faith in such aggregate estimates and preferred to depend instead on his own sense of proper magnitudes as based on his impressions of individual time series. And I would also suspect that despite Keynes' earlier highly laudatory comments in the letter in which he had recommended the publication of Colin Clark's 1932 book on *National Income*,[49] and despite the latter's acknowledgment to him in his preface to this book, Keynes had even less faith in the aggregate estimates of Colin Clark.

I think there is evidence for both these conjectures in the story that I have already told of the way in which Keynes of the *General Theory* made use of the data of Clark and of Kuznets, respectively, and of the discussions which followed (see section 4 above). And this evidence finds support in a revealing remark that Keynes made in one of his lectures on monetary theory during the fall 1933 term at Cambridge: here, after distinguishing between what we could now designate as ex ante and ex post concepts of income, he went on to say: "Post mortem has no strict meaning & even if it has it doesn't matter—only people interested are the Colin Clarks—to answer inquisitive people who want to know."[50]

Another incident which conforms with my conjectures occurred in 1939 when Keynes persuaded Stamp, then chairman of the EAC Committee on Economic Information, to be very skeptical of some aggregate estimates that had been prepared by one of its staff members, Piers Debenham. In support of his skepticism Keynes wrote Stamp that, as a result of "a quarter of an hour's thought," he had caused Debenham to increase significantly his estimate of investment and that, though he [Keynes] was "not an expert on these matter[s]," he "fancied" that he "could in another quarter of an hour make him [Piers Debenham] make equally large corrections in the figures for savings." And Keynes concluded this letter with the statement that he "used to think that Colin Clark deserved the V.C. for statistical courage, but should now certainly depose him in favor of Piers."[51]

48. See Howson and Winch (1977, appendix 1) for a list of these reports and for the specific pages in their study where they are discussed.
49. See n. 9 above.
50. Cited from Robert Bryce's notes of Keynes' lecture of November 13, 1933 (on the nature of these notes, see *KMT*, p. 73 n. 11; cf. also above, p. 21).
51. This incident is described by Howson and Winch (1977, p. 150). The letter in question is dated July 1, 1939 and is in the Keynes Papers. This incident also serves to point up an aspect of the puzzle of Britain's lag in national income statistics that I have

I must now point out that Keynes was not alone in England at that
time in having reservations about Clark's estimates and that, indeed,
the change which apparently occurred in Keynes' own evaluation of
these estimates may in part have been caused by the critical way they

---

neglected: namely, why neither Arthur Bowley nor Josiah Stamp did more to promote
official national income estimating during the interwar period. Bowley, I suspect, was too
much engrossed for this purpose in the academic world of teaching and research. Thus
R. G. D. Allen writes that though Bowley was "always a severe critic of British official
statistics, and highly respected in official quarters, he was called upon far too seldom to
advise on the development of government statistics" (1968, p. 134a). But that Bowley
was nevertheless concerned with the problem is evidenced by his statement in his 1904
study of *National Progress in Wealth and Trade* that "there is no obvious reason why the
Commissioner of the Internal Revenue should not be requested to prepare an estimate of
the change of national income during recent years" (1904, p. 191). See also Bowley's
concluding recommendations for the collection and publication of additional data (1904,
pp. 84–88). And note too the much later work on the estimation of national income which
Bowley carried out within the framework of the National Institute of Economic and
Social Research (see below). Insofar as Josiah Stamp—that eminent public servant—is
concerned, his work on national income was secondary to his main activities in the field
of public finance, industry, and the like. Thus Jones' full-length biography of Stamp
(1964) barely mentions this work—though I suspect that to a certain extent this reflects
the greater interest of the biographer in Stamp's more public activities. It is also
noteworthy that Stamp's major contribution to the field of national income estimates—
namely, his *British Incomes and Property* (1916)—was essentially a by-product of his
work on taxation, and had its origins as a Ph.D. thesis for Bowley at the London School
of Economics (Jones 1964, pp. 85–89, 273–74). At the same time, I must point out that
Stamp did return on occasion to work on national income, as evidenced by the studies
reprinted in his *National Capital* (1937). So the question of why Stamp did not do more to
promote national income estimates remains.

In this context I should note that in June 1919 Bowley and Stamp were appointed by
the Royal Statistical Society to serve on a five-man "Committee on Official Statistics"
charged with considering "the best method of approaching the Government with a view
to effecting an improvement in the collection and presentation of official statistics."
After deliberation, the committee drew up a "Petition to His Majesty's Government"
(among whose many subsequent signatories was Keynes) which stated that there was
"an urgent need" for such an improvement; supported this statement with several examples of "defects in statistics," including some with respect to wage income and, even
more so, nonwage income, as a consequence of which "the aggregate of national income
can only be roughly estimated"; and requested the appointment of a Royal Commission
or Parliamentary Committee "to enquire into the existing methods of the collection and
presentation of public statistics and to report on the means of improvement" (*Journal of
the Royal Statistical Society* 83 (1920), pp. 131–33, 668). Unfortunately, nothing came of
this petition. For the government instead appointed a Cabinet Committee which prepared
a *Report on the Collection and Presentation of Official Statistics* (1921) that buried the
petition by concluding that "no case exists for an enquiry" and recommending instead
the establishment of "a permanent Consultative Committee of Statistical Officers" for
the purpose of "insuring more effective cooperation and coordination between the different departments in the statistical work" (ibid., p. 13)—a conclusion the Statistical
Society subsequently transmitted to its members with the comment that the *Report* "is
under consideration by the Council" (*Journal of the Royal Statistical Society* 84 [1921],
p. 611). I have not, however, found any indication of further action by the council. For
further discussion of this Cabinet Committee report, see Howson and Winch (1977, p. 8),
to whom I owe this reference.

[See again the Postscript below for a description of some suppressed official national
income estimates from 1929.]

were received by the experts in the field. Thus, one of the editors of the *Journal of the Royal Statistical Society*, E. C. Snow, wrote a devastating review of Clark's *National Income: 1924–1931* (1932) in the pages of the *Journal* (1933). Furthermore, Clark's attempt to reply in a later issue (1933b) succeeded only in provoking Snow to an even sharper attack (1933, pp. 658–59). And though the review by A. W. Flux (whose estimates Clark had in part criticized in his book) in the 1933 *Economic Journal* was moderately favorable, it too indicated certain reservations. Again Bowley (1933) questioned some of the revisions that Clark had made in his book of the Bowley-Stamp estimate for 1924 (see n. 9 above) and, indeed, Clark subsequently (1933a, p. 655n.) accepted the majority of Bowley's criticisms. Similarly, Clark's later *National Income and Outlay* (1937) drew what can at best be described as ambivalent reviews from both Bowley in *Economica* (1937b) and Phelps-Brown in the *Economic Journal* (1937); for, while recognizing the importance and magnitude of the task Clark had undertaken, and admiring the statistical "ingenuity and boldness with which the inquiry had been pursued" (Phelps-Brown 1937, p. 333), they also expressed reservations about some of the methods and assumptions that he had used in deriving certain of his estimates.

Thus, I do not say that Keynes was necessarily wrong in his criticisms of Clark and Debenham; indeed, that is a question worthy of study. Nor do I say that Keynes was wrong in saying in his *How to Pay for the War* (1940), when referring to the estimates of national income with which he had to work, that

> the statistics from which to build up these estimates are very inadequate. Every government since the last war has been unscientific and obscurantist, and has regarded the collection of essential facts as a waste of money. There is no one today, inside or outside government offices, who does not mainly depend on the brilliant private efforts of Mr. Colin Clark (in his *National Income and Outlay*, supplemented by later articles); but, in the absence of statistics which only a government can collect, he could often do no better than make a brave guess. [*JMK* IX, p. 381]

But I do think we have the right to ask whether Keynes himself had done what he could have done to have provided "the Colin Clarks" with the government assistance[52] necessary to develop their work on

---

52. Including, for example, such minor things as the adding machine the Treasury refused to buy for Colin Clark in 1930, when he was on the staff of the EAC! After recounting this anecdote, Howson and Winch (1977, p. 25) add: "Given the tradition of Treasury control, the development of national income estimates in 1940 was no doubt facilitated by the fact that Richard Stone brought his own machine."

firm foundations; whether he had done what he could have done to have implanted Colin Clark's work within an official government framework, just as Simon Kuznets' work in the United States had been so implanted.[53]

But, as important and dominant a role as Keynes played in the British economics profession in the interwar period, and it was dominant, I do not think that we can ascribe Britain's lag behind the United States in national income estimating solely to his personality. Nor do I think we can ascribe it solely to the personality of Colin Clark. For there were also broader forces at work, some of which, however, may also have contributed to the very fact that it was a person of Keynes' characteristics who dominated the scene, and that it was a person of Clark's characteristics (namely, somewhat unconventional) who took on the task of preparing the national income estimates.

The first such force was the greater interest (relative to Britain) in empirical economics, as contrasted with theoretical, that characterized the United States in the first decades of this century. In part, this may have been one of the products of institutional economics, whose counterpart in Britain was much less influential. In any event, it is noteworthy that the first Director of Research of the National Bureau,

---

53. {In a letter to me dated May 27, 1976, Colin Clark has written: "You say that Keynes should have attempted to exert more influence in Whitehall to get national income studies underway. But I do not think that it would have succeeded. Opposition to him was very strong. In the case of the official who would have been principally concerned ([A. W.] Flux, Director of Statistics in the Board of Trade) it was a matter of inertia, and lack of comprehension of any methods other than his own." And in a subsequent letter (dated June 17, 1976) Clark repeated: "I have not expressed and am not expressing any dissatisfaction about Keynes failing to help sufficiently in getting support for work on national income statistics. At that time, I did not think that he could have done much."

In a similar vein, Richard Stone—in a letter to me dated June 21, 1976—has written: ". . . in Britain, non-academic interest in the national income was not aroused before the second world war. The concept of demand management did not exist despite the economic troubles we went through in the 1920's and 30's. Politicians and civil servants simply did not think in these terms and the suggestion that Bowley and Stamp, and above all, Colin Clark were doing work of potential importance for practical policy purposes would have been met with incomprehension and, no doubt, with derision had it been comprehended. Keynes did do a splendid job in 'selling' the national income estimates that James Meade and I made in 1940–41 to the Treasury: by then he had a comprehensible argument for their adoption but you must not suppose that there was no opposition or that anyone would have listened if his arguments had been put forward by us. . . . It must be remembered that Keynes was (a) a very busy man with hundreds of irons in the fire; and (b) in the interwar period, by no means *persona grata* in Treasury Circles. In all the circumstances, therefore, I wonder whether he could be expected to have done much at the time given his attitudes and the objective circumstances I have already described."}

[In his subsequent paper "Keynes, Political Arithmetic and Econometrics" (1978, p. 67), Stone has once again defended Keynes against my criticism by contending (inter alia) that he had "many irons in the fire." To my mind, however, this actually confirms my criticism that Keynes did not attach enough importance to that "iron" known as national income statistics.]

Wesley Mitchell, was one of the "founding fathers" of this movement.[54]

A related fact was the general lag of British economic statistics behind those of the United States. Thus, for example, in the *Treatise*, Keynes compared the abundancy and detail of United States financial statistics with the corresponding inadequacy in Britain, an inadequacy which forced Keynes himself to prepare the estimates he needed of total British demand deposits at the time (*TM* II, p. 9). Indeed, I might point out that, in contrast with national income statistics, even World War II was not enough to bring about the publication of official British statistics of the money supply. This had to await Milton Friedman and (ironically enough) the Radcliffe Committee: for the publication of these statistics was in part a by-product of the improvements in financial statistics that were carried out in the late 1950s and early 1960s as a result of the work and recommendations of this committee, even though the committee itself (in accordance with its well-known view that money does not matter) did not include the money supply in the list of statistics that it recommended publishing (Radcliffe Report, pp. 133–35, 284–302)![55] I might also point out that one of the causes of the aforementioned general lag in British statistics was the reluctance of the British government to compel firms to provide data on confidential

54. See Dorfman (1959, vol. 4, pp. 188–89, 353, 360–77). The reader will also recall Clark's complaint in his preface to *National Income and Outlay* (see n. 36 above) about the priority given in British economics to theoretical work.

55. See, however, p. 170 of this *Report* for a diagram presenting the money supply and its relation to national income for the periods 1930–38 and 1946–58. On the improvement in British financial statistics as a result of the Radcliffe Committee, see Bank of England, *Quarterly Bulletin* 3 (1963), pp. 285–93; Central Statistical Office, *Economic Trends,* February 1964, p. xxviii. The first British estimates of total net deposits were published in the Bank of England's *Quarterly Bulletin* just cited; and the first quarterly estimates of the money supply (currency *plus* net deposits) were published in the Central Statistical Office's *Financial Statistics* for March 1966 (pp. 1, 56), which provided estimates back to the first quarter of 1964. It is noteworthy that both of these journals began their appearance only after the work of the Radcliffe Committee. Estimates of the British money supply for earlier periods have since been made by Sheppard (1971, p. 183).

Another indication of the British disbelief in the importance of money during the early 1960s is the fact that the first British quarterly estimates of national expenditure appeared simultaneously in the *Monthly Digest of Statistics* for 1957 (pp. iv–vi; see n. 41 above) and in the Central Statistical Office's *Economic Trends,* which publication was begun in 1953 for the purpose of conveniently presenting in one place statistical indicators of trends in the economy. In contrast, the quarterly estimates of the money supply appeared in *Economic Trends* only after a five-year delay (ibid., December 1970. pp. viii, 33).

The British history of official monetary statistics should be contrasted with that of the United States, where quarterly estimates of net deposits of all banks (and not just member banks) appeared for the first time in the *Federal Reserve Bulletin* of May 1927 (pp. 314–15, 378; see also p. 546 of the July 1927 issue), and monthly estimates of the total money supply began to appear in the *Federal Reserve Bulletin* of February 1944 (pp. 134, 161). See also Friedman and Schwartz (1963, 1970).

There can be no doubt that this further lagging of British monetary statistics behind those for national income was due to the overwhelming influence of the $C + I + G = Y$ framework of the *General Theory*. I should, however, note that the monetary policy

matters, even when only the respective aggregates of these data were to be published (e.g., profits, certain categories of deposits, etc.; see Macmillan Report, secs. 407, 412–14; Clark 1932, p. vii; Clark 1937, pp. vi–vii).

The lag of British empirical economics behind that of the United States was even more marked with respect to the systematic empirical testing of theoretical hypotheses. Thus, the most influential tests of the specie-flow mechanism of English classical economics were carried out as Ph.D. theses by Frank Taussig's students at Harvard: namely, John H. Williams' study of Argentina (1920), Jacob Viner's of Canada (1924), and Harry White's of France (1933). And a similar statement can be made for the Marshallian demand curve: in the United States, Henry Moore (1914, 1929) and, subsequently, his student Henry Schultz (1938) both made basic contributions to the statistical estimation of this curve;[56] but there were no such contributions emanating from Britain.[57] Or again: in the early 1930s there appeared two classic books under the title *The Theory of Wages;* but whereas Hicks' book (1932) in Britain was almost entirely concerned with an exposition and elaboration of the marginal-productivity theory of wages, Paul Douglas' book (1934) in the United States had as its main objective the empirical verification of this theory.

Even more relevant to my present point was the sharp contrast between the United States and Britain with respect to the empirical testing of the accepted pre-Keynesian[58] macroeconomic theory, read: the

---

which Keynes advocated in the *Treatise* also did not stimulate the preparation of a series on the money supply; for, in contrast with Friedmanian monetary policy of today, that of the *Treatise* took as its critical variable not the quantity of money, but the rate of interest. And in this, Keynes was continuing with a traditional British view, most notably associated at that time with the name of Ralph G. Hawtrey, who had repeatedly expounded it in the Treasury well before the appearance of the *Treatise* (see Guillebaud's [1968] article on Hawtrey). So it is noteworthy that the Macmillan Report's chapter on statistics (see above) also does not specifically recommend the publication of a series on the total money supply; and it is also noteworthy that, in contrast, there is a long British record of good current series on interest rates of various kinds.

[A question which deserves further study is the relation between the changing definition of money over time and the nature of the contemporaneous monetary statistics. Thus in the nineteenth century money was frequently—if not generally—defined to consist only of currency (cf., e.g., the Currency School, Wicksell [above, p. 41]), and this undoubtedly reflected itself in the statistics published. Another—and obvious—example of this relationship is the profusion of M's (M₁, M₂, M₃, . . .) in recent years.]

56. As might be expected, Keynes was almost as critical of Schultz's work as of Tinbergen's. Thus, in a letter to Harrod in July 1938, he wrote: ". . . Schultz's (Tinbergen is a much better example) results, if he ever gets any, are not very interesting (for we know beforehand that they will not be applicable to future cases)" (*JMK* XIV, p. 296).

57. In George Stigler's survey of pre-World War I studies of statistical demand curves, the one closest to being due to a British economist is the study by Lehfeldt in the 1914 *Economic Journal*. Lehfeldt, however, actually signed his article as of Johannesburg.

58. And today some would add "and post-Keynesian"!

quantity of money. Thus, Irving Fisher's classic statement of this theory in his *Purchasing Power of Money* (1911, 1913) devoted the two penultimate chapters to a "statistical verification." And when, a decade later, Warren Persons developed a new and better "Index of Trade for the United States" (1923), Carl Snyder (1924) made immediate use of it to provide a further empirical test of the theory. All this can be instructively contrasted with, say, the casual comparisons Keynes made at the end of his presentation of the quantity theory in his *Tract on Monetary Reform* (1923, pp. 67–68).

There is, however, at least one major exception to the relative neglect of empirical work in Britain, and that is its strong tradition of empirical family-budget studies. But it seems to me that this tradition received its major impetus not from the work of professional economists, but from the desire of such turn-of-the-century social reformers as Charles Booth and B. S. Rowntree to establish the facts about the standard of living of the British working class, with special regard to the degree of poverty which prevailed. And I find it particularly significant that Bowley—that pioneer of modern national income estimates in Britain—came to his work on these estimates from his earlier study of changes in real wages in nineteenth-century Britain, and that he continued to devote a significant part of his scientific efforts over the years to the empirical study of poverty.[59] So I would conjecture that the lead Britain enjoyed in national income estimating in the period immediately preceding World War I may have actually stemmed in part from the statistical budget studies which were the hallmark of its famous turn-of-the-century social reformers.[60]

59. See the respective articles on Booth and Bowley (the latter by Roy Allen) in the *International Encyclopedia of the Social Sciences* (1968). See also Bowley's discussion of "pauperism" in his *National Progress in Wealth and Trade since 1882* (1904, pp. 20–25, 86–87). The reader will also find it instructive to read Bowley's introduction to his *Wages and Income in the United Kingdom since 1860* (1937a). Bowley also continued to be interested in budget studies, as indicated by (e.g.) his later work (together with Allen), *Family Expenditure* (1935).

{In a letter to me dated June 29, 1976, Roy Allen has written: "I knew most of your 'cast' during the 1930's, some of them quite well. . . . I worked very closely with Bowley, almost unique in operating on the border between the economic and the social. But I think he remained what he was originally: a late-Victorian social reformer. His main applied interests throughout were in two fields: prices, wages and earnings; social surveys. (My first work with Bowley—and indeed with Colin Clark too—was on the New London Survey from 1929 onwards.) His specifically economic work was largely derivative from his main interests—or in the form of mathematical exercises—and he was certainly led to work on the national income because of his concern with the distribution between wages and other incomes."}

60. In commenting to me on this conjecture, Peter Mathias has made the criticism that it overlooks the influential work of Robert Giffen, who independently of Booth presented statistical studies both of "The Progress of the Working Classes" (1886, pp. 365–474) and of national income (1880, pp. 161–96; 1889). See the article on Giffen in the *International Encyclopedia of the Social Sciences* (1968); see also Studenski (1958, vol. 1, p. 117).

I have so far discussed the possible influence of general ideas in explaining Britain's lag in national income estimating in the interwar period. Let me now add a few words about the possible corresponding influence of institutions. And if I come to this subject only at the end of this long paper, it is not because of its being less important than others that I have discussed (indeed, the opposite may well be the case), but because of its really lying beyond my field of competence.

It is a well-known fact, which has been further corroborated by the foregoing account, that reliable estimates of national income on a current basis cannot be produced by a single individual working alone; instead, there is a necessity for the kind of organized efforts that only an institutional framework can ensure. But interwar Britain had very little of a tradition of organized institutional research in economics. In the United States, in contrast, the Brookings Institution and the National Industrial Conference Board were founded in 1916 (see Dorfman 1959, vol. 4, pp. 194–200) and (as already indicated) the National Bureau was founded in 1920. But it was only in 1938 that a corresponding institution, in the form of the National Institute of Economic and Social Research, was founded in Britain. And it is significant that one of the first studies undertaken by this Institute was of the national income of the United Kingdom, a study which was, however, delayed by the outbreak of the war (Bowley 1942, p. vii).

A related phenomenon was that in contrast with the situation that already existed in the days of the New Deal in the United States, there were few economists working in a professional capacity within the British government. As Winch has told us: "Economists were drafted into government service during the First World War, but they tended to merge imperceptibly with other temporary civil servants. After the war their services were used mainly on ad hoc committees and Royal Commissions. The chief exception to this, however, was the Economic Advisory Council," and this was not a very effective body. It was only in World War II that this situation changed (Winch 1969, p. 265).

I have come to the end of my fairly long story. But, from a more fundamental viewpoint, it is only the beginning. Thus, we should test my explanation of the interwar lag of British national income estimating behind that of the United States by seeing if it also helps explain why, for example, Britain apparently also lagged behind Sweden and Germany (the influence of the Historical School on the latter?). And we might also try to broaden our perspective and ask whether the differences we have noted between British and United States economics in the interwar period—say, the greater relative emphasis in the latter on empirical work (including the systematic testing of hypotheses) as compared with theoretical, and (even more important) the absence in the former of institutional frameworks within which to organize and carry out research—also characterized other scientific disciplines in these two countries. But this is a task that we must leave for the sociologists of science.[61]

Postscript: Some Suppressed British National Income Estimates from 1929[62]

Richard Stone (1977) has recently made the intriguing discovery that the 1941 White Paper national income estimates were not the first ones to have been officially made in Britain. In particular, in 1929 the Inland Revenue prepared and printed a *Report on National Income* for the fiscal year 1923/24 and for the two subsequent calendar years 1924 and 1925. This *Report,* however, was marked "Confidential," as a result never released, and subsequently sank without trace into the government archives. Thus there is no mention of it in any of the materials I have examined in connection with this study. Similarly, Colin Clark has informed me that though he had in 1931 received a hint of the existence of some suppressed document (on which hint more in a moment), he had no specific information about this *Report* either at the time he was working on his own estimates or subsequently (personal conversation, July 1978).

In his letter of transmission to the Chancellor of the Exchequer which appears at the beginning of the *Report,* Sir Ernest Gowers[63] recommended its suppression in the following words:

As the estimate of National Income presented in the Report is rather less than that obtaining under the authority of Stamp and Bowley, and the lower estimate is partly due to a lower estimate of the National Wages bill, I think it would be desirable to treat the Report as a confidential paper.

It is not clear from this whether the recommendation to suppress was due to the doubts as to the accuracy of the *Report* which were generated by the discrepancy from the Stamp-Bowley estimates (which reason Stone [1978, p. 65], finds "scarcely convincing"), and/or the fear that the publication of a lower estimate for wages could generate labor

61. I can, however, report on illuminating discussions with my sociologist-of-science colleague Joseph Ben-David, who tells me that there were at the time similar differences with respect to some of the disciplines in the physical sciences.

62. Attached to n. 37 above.

63. Who had in 1903 begun his long, varied, and illustrious career in the British civil service with a stint at the Inland Revenue, and who had returned to it in 1927 as chairman of the board (*Who's Who: 1966* [London: Adams and Charles Black, 1966]). Gowers is probably best known today as the reviser of Fowler's *Modern English Usage* (1965).

demands for increasing them. The latter interpretation has been supported by Colin Clark in his aforementioned conversation with me, in
which he explained that, while on the staff of the Economic Advisory
Council (viz., 1930–31), he had received a hint of the existence of
earlier estimates from Cornelius Gregg, then Head of Intelligence and
Statistics in Internal Revenue, who told him that the Federation of
British Industries had objected to the publication of a report which
showed their gross profits as compared with total salaries and wages
(cf. p. 13 of the *Report*) out of fear that this would have weakened their
position in collective bargaining with labor. Stone (1978, p. 65), however, has alluded to such a contention (without reference to Clark) and
has cast doubt on it, saying "how they [i.e., the Federation] could have
known about it [i.e., the *Report*] is a bit of a mystery since it is marked
confidential, I have never seen any reference to it and I have never
known anyone outside the official world who was aware of its existence."

I should note that in the preface to his *National Income: 1924–1931*
(1932, p. vii) Clark himself charged the Federation of British Industries
with having "resisted" the publication of figures for industrial profits
because "they had complained quite candidly that they did not wish
the true figures of industrial profits to be quoted against them in wage
negotiations." This immediately brought forth a letter to him from the
director of the Federation (dated October 22, 1932) hotly denying the
charge. The director admitted that the Federation had, in response to a
query from the Chancellor of the Exchequer in October 1930, objected
to "the continued publication of a table dealing with industrial profits
which had been prepared for the Colwyn Committee," but claimed that
it had done so because the inaccuracies and conceptual problems involved in these estimates made them misleading, and not for the reason
Clark had given. In subsequent letters, the director demanded that
Clark withdraw his charge from the unsold copies of his book—a demand that Clark rejected.[64]

64. I am indebted to Colin Clark for supplying me with copies of these letters from the
Federation; unfortunately, his replies to them have not survived.

Bibliography for Part IV*

Allen, R. G. D. (1968). "Arthur Lyon Bowley." In *International Encyclopedia of the Social Sciences.* Edited by David L. Sills. (New York: Macmillan and Free Press). Vol 2, pp. 134–37.

Allen, R. G. D., and Arthur L. Bowley (1935). *Family Expenditure: A Study of Its Variation.* London: Staples Press.

Angell, James W. (1925). "Monetary Theory and Monetary Policy: Some Recent Discussions." *Quarterly Journal of Economics* 39 (Feb.): 267–99.

Beveridge, William (1923). "Business Cycles and Their Study." *London & Cambridge Economic Service*: (Introductory Number, Jan.): 1–7.

Bowley, Arthur L. (1904). *Statistical Studies Relating to National Progress in Wealth and Trade Since 1882: A Plea for Further Enquiry.* London: P. S. King and Son.

——— (1919). *The Division of the Product of Industry: An Analysis of National Income Before the War.* Oxford: Clarendon Press. As reprinted in Bowley and Stamp (1938), pp. 5–59.

——— (1933). "The National Income of the United Kingdom in 1924." *Economica* 13 (May): 138–42.

——— (1937a). *Wages and Income in the United Kingdom since 1860.* Cambridge: Cambridge University Press.

——— (1937b). Review of *National Income and Outlay,* by Colin Clark. *Economica* 4 (Aug.): 350–53.

——— (1942). *Studies in the National Income 1924–1938.* Cambridge: Cambridge University Press.

Bowley, Arthur L., and Josiah Stamp (1927). *The National Income, 1924.* Oxford: Clarendon Press. As reprinted in Bowley and Stamp (1938), pp. 91–145.

——— (1938). *Three Studies in National Income.* London: London School of Economics.

Carson, Carol (1975). "The History of the United States National Income and

---

* Reprinted or translated works are cited in the text by year of original publication; the page references to such works in the text are, however, to the pages of the reprint or translation in question.

Product Accounts: The Development of an Analytical Tool." *Review of Income and Wealth* 21 (June): 153–81.

Clark, Colin (1931). "Statistical Studies Relating to the Present Economic Position of Great Britain." *Economic Journal* 41 (Sept.): 343–69.

―――― (1932). *The National Income: 1924–1931.* London: Macmillan.

―――― (1933a). "The National Income and the Theory of Production." *Economic Journal* 43 (June): 205–16.

―――― (1933b). "The National Income and the Net Output of Industry." *Journal of the Royal Statistical Society* 96 (pt. 4): 651–59.

―――― (1937). *National Income and Outlay.* London: Macmillan.

―――― (1938). "Determination of the Multiplier from National Income Statistics." *Economic Journal* 48 (Sept.): 435–48.

Clark, J. M. (1917). "Business Acceleration and the Law of Demand: A Technical Factor in Economic Cycles." *Journal of Political Economy* 25 (March): 217–35. As reprinted in *Readings in Business Cycle Theory,* selected by a committee of the American Economic Association (Philadelphia: Blakiston, for the American Economic Association, 1944): pp. 235–60.

Currie, Lauchlin (1938). "Some Theoretical and Practical Implications of J. M. Keynes' General Theory." In the National Industrial Conference Board, *The Economic Doctrines of John Maynard Keynes* (New York: National Industrial Conference Board), pp. 15–27.

Deane, Phyllis (1956). "Contemporary Estimates of National Income in the First Half of the Nineteenth Century." *Economic History Review* 8 (No. 3): 339–54.

―――― (1957). "Contemporary Estimates of National Income in the Second Half of the Nineteenth Century." *Economic History Review* 9 (April): 451–61.

Dorfman, Joseph (1959). *The Economic Mind in American Civilization,* Vol. 4. New York: Viking Press.

Douglas, Paul (1934). *The Theory of Wages.* New York: Macmillan.

Duncan, Joseph W., and William C. Shelton (1978). *Revolution in United States Government Statistics 1926–1976.* Washington, D.C.: U.S. Department of Commerce, Office of Federal Statistical Policy and Standards.

Dunlop, John T. (1938). "The Movement of Real and Money Wage Rates." *Economic Journal* 48 (Sept.): 413–34.

Fabricant, Solomon (1936). *Measures of Capital Consumption, 1929–1933.* New York: National Bureau of Economic Research, Bulletin No. 60.

Fisher, Irving (1911). *The Purchasing Power of Money.* New York: Macmillan.

―――― (1913). *The Purchasing Power of Money.* Revised edition, New York: Macmillan. Reprinted, New York: Augustus M. Kelley, 1963. (Date of edition as given in reprint is incorrect.)

Flux, A. W. (1933). Review of *The National Income: 1924–1931,* by Colin Clark. *Economic Journal* 43 (June): 279–81.

Friedman, Milton, and A. J. Schwartz (1963). *A Monetary History of the United States: 1867–1960.* Princeton: Princeton University Press, for the National Bureau of Economic Research.

―――― (1970). *Monetary Statistics of the United States: Estimates, Sources,*

and Methods. New York: National Bureau of Economic Research.
Giffen, Robert (1880). *Essays in Finance*. First series, second edition. London: Bell and Sons.
—— (1886). *Essays in Finance*. Second series. New York: G. P. Putnam and Sons.
—— (1889). *The Growth of Capital*. London: Bell and Sons.
Gilbert, Milton, and R. B. Bangs (1942a). "Preliminary Estimates of Gross National Product, 1929–1941." *Survey of Current Business* 22 (May): 9–13.
—— (1942b). "National Income and the War Effort—First Half of 1942." *Survey of Current Business* 22 (Aug.): 10–17.
Guillebaud, C. W. (1968). "R. G. Hawtrey." In *International Encyclopedia of Social Science*. Edited by David L. Sills (New York: Macmillan and Free Press). Vol. 6, pp. 328–30.
Haavelmo, Trygve (1943). "The Statistical Implications of a System of Simultaneous Equations." *Econometrica* 11 (Jan.): 1–12.
—— (1944). "The Probability Approach in Econometrics." *Econometrica* 12 (July): 1–115.
—— (1947). "Methods of Measuring the Marginal Propensity to Consume." *Journal of the American Statistical Association* 42 (March): 105–22.
Haberler, Gottfried von (1937). *Prosperity and Depression: A Theoretical Analysis of Cyclical Movements*. Geneva: League of Nations.
Harrod, R. F. (1951). *The Life of John Maynard Keynes*. London: Macmillan. Reprinted, New York: Augustus M. Kelley, 1969.
Hicks, J. R. (1932). *The Theory of Wages*. London: Macmillan.
—— (1937). "Mr. Keynes and the 'Classics'; A Suggested Interpretation." *Econometrica* 5 (April): 147–59. As reprinted in *Readings in the Theory of Income Distribution*, selected by a committee of the American Economic Association (Philadelphia: Blakiston, for the American Economic Association, 1946), pp. 461–76.
Howson, Susan, and Donald Winch (1977). *The Economic Advisory Council 1930–1939*. Cambridge: Cambridge University Press.
Jones, James Harry (1964). *Josiah Stamp, Public Servant: The Life of the First Baron Stamp of Shortlands*. London: Pitman.
Kahn, R. F. (1931). "The Relation of Home Investment to Unemployment." *Economic Journal* 41 (June): 173–98. As reprinted in Kahn (1972), pp. 1–27.
—— (1972). *Selected Essays on Employment and Growth*. Cambridge: Cambridge University Press.
Kendrick, John W. (1970). "The Historical Developments of National-Income Accounts." *History of Political Economy* 2 (Fall): 284–315.
Keynes, John Maynard (1921). *A Treatise on Probability*. As reprinted in Keynes, *Collected Writings*, Vol. VIII.
—— (1923). *A Tract on Monetary Reform*. As reprinted in Keynes, *Collected Writings*, Vol. IV.
—— (1929). "The German Transfer Problem." *Economic Journal* 39 (March): 1–7. As reprinted in *Readings in the Theory of International Trade*, selected by a committee of the American Economic Association (Philadel-

phia: Blakiston, for the American Economic Association, 1949), pp. 161–69.

—— (1930). *A Treatise on Money, Vol. I: The Pure Theory of Money.* As reprinted in Keynes, *Collected Writings,* Vol. V.

—— (1930). *A Treatise on Money, Vol. II: The Applied Theory of Money.* As reprinted in Keynes, *Collected Writings,* Vol. VI.

—— (1931). *Essays in Persuasion.* As reprinted with additions in Keynes, *Collected Writings,* Vol. IX.

—— (1933). *The Means to Prosperity.* As reprinted in Keynes, *Collected Writings,* Vol. IX, pp. 335–66.

—— (1936). *The General Theory of Employment Interest and Money.* As reprinted in Keynes, *Collected Writings,* Vol. VII.

—— (1936). "Fluctuations in Net Investment in the United States." *Economic Journal* 46 (Sept.): 540–47. As reprinted in Keynes, *Collected Writings,* Vol. VII, pp. 386–93.

—— (1939a). "Relative Movements of Real Wages and Output." *Economic Journal* 49 (March): 34–51. As reprinted in Keynes, *Collected Writings,* Vol. VII, pp. 394–412.

—— (1939b). "Professor Tinbergen's Method." *Economic Journal* 49 (Sept.): 558–70. As reprinted in Keynes, *Collected Writings,* Vol. XIV.

—— (1939c). "The Income and Fiscal Potential of Great Britain." *Economic Journal* 49 (Dec.): 626–39.

—— (1940a). *How to Pay for the War.* As reprinted in Keynes, *Collected Writings,* Vol. IX, pp. 367–439.

—— (1940b). "The Concept of National Income: A Supplementary Note." *Economic Journal* 50 (March): 60–65.

—— (1940c). "Comment [on Tinbergen (1940)]." *Economic Journal* 50 (March): 154–56. As reprinted in Keynes, *Collected Writings,* Vol. XIV, pp. 318–20.

——. *The General Theory and After: Part I, Preparation.* Edited by Donald Moggridge. Vol. XIII of Keynes, *Collected Writings.*

——. *The General Theory and After: Part II, Defence and Development.* Edited by Donald Moggridge. Vol. XIV of Keynes, *Collected Writings.*

——. *Activities 1939–1945: Internal War Finance.* Edited by Donald Moggridge. Vol. XXII of Keynes, *Collected Writings.*

——. *The General Theory and After: A Supplement.* Edited by Donald Moggridge. Vol. XXIX of Keynes, *Collected Writings.*

——. *Collected Writings.* 30 volumes planned. Published to date: Vols. I–VI (1971), Vols. VII–VIII (1973), Vols. IX–X (1972), Vols. XIII–XIV (1973), Vols. XV–XVI (1971), Vols. XVII–XVIII (1978), Vols. XIX–XX (1981), Vol. XXI (1982), Vol. XXII (1978), Vols. XXIII–XXIV (1979), Vols. XXV–XXVII (1980), Vol. XXIX (1979). London: Macmillan, for the Royal Economic Society.

King, Willford (1915). *The Wealth and Income of the People of the United States.* New York: Macmillan.

—— (1930). *The National Income and Its Purchasing Power.* New York: National Bureau of Economic Research.

Kuznets, Simon (1933). "National Income." In *Encyclopedia of the Social*

Sciences, Vol. 11. As reprinted in *Readings in the Theory of Income Distribution*, selected by a committee of the American Economic Association (Philadelphia: Blakiston, for the American Economic Association, 1946), pp. 3–43.

—— (1934a). *National Income, 1929–1932*. New York: National Bureau of Economic Research, Bulletin No. 49.

—— (1934b). *Gross Capital Formation 1919–1933*. New York: National Bureau of Economic Research, Bulletin No. 52.

—— (1934c). "Relation Between Capital Goods and Finished Products in the Business Cycle." In *Economic Essays in Honor of Wesley Clair Mitchell*. New York: Columbia University Press. As reprinted in Kuznets, *Economic Change: Selected Essays in Business Cycles, National Income and Economic Growth* (London: William Heinemann, 1954), pp. 47–104.

—— (1937). *National Income and Capital Formation 1919–1935*. New York: National Bureau of Economic Research.

—— (1938). *Commodity Flow and Capital Formation*, Vol. 1. New York: National Bureau of Economic Research.

—— (1941). *National Income and Its Composition, 1919–1938*. New York: National Bureau of Economic Research.

—— (1973). "Data for Quantitative Economic Analysis: Problems of Demand and Supply." In Kuznets, *Population, Capital and Growth: Selected Essays*. New York: W. W. Norton, pp. 243–62.

Lehfeldt, Robert (1914). "The Elasticity of Demand for Wheat." *Economic Journal* 24 (June): 212–17.

Leontief, Wassily (1936). "Quantitative Input and Output Relations in the Economic System of the United States." *Review of Economic Statistics* 18 (Aug.): 105–25.

—— (1941). *The Structure of American Economy, 1919–1939: An Empirical Application of Equilibrium Analysis*. Cambridge, Mass.: Harvard University Press.

Lewes, F. M. M. (1967). *Statistics of the British Economy*. London: George Allen and Unwin.

Liberal Industrial Inquiry (1928). *Britain's Industrial Future*. London: Ernest Benn.

Martin, Robert F. (1935). "The National Income, 1933." *Survey of Current Business* 15 (Jan.): 16–18.

May, George (1936). *Twenty-Five Years of Accounting Responsibility 1911–1936. Essays and Discussions*. Edited by Bishop Carleton Hurst. New York: Price, Waterhouse.

Meade, J. E., and R. Stone (1941). "The Construction of Tables of National Income, Expenditure, Savings and Investment." *Economic Journal* 51 (June–Sept.): 216–33.

Mitchell, Wesley C. (1913). *Business Cycles*. Berkeley: University of California Press.

—— (1923). "Business Cycles." In the National Bureau of Economic Research (1923), pp. 5–18. As reprinted in *Readings in Business Cycle Theory*, selected by a committee of the American Economic Association (Philadelphia: Blakiston, for the American Economic Association, 1944), pp. 43–60.

—— (1927). *Business Cycles: The Problem and Its Setting*. New York: National Bureau of Economic Research.

—— (1945). "The National Bureau's First Quarter-Century." In *The National Bureau of Economic Research Twenty-Fifth Annual Report*. New York: National Bureau of Economic Research, pp. 11–40.

Moore, Henry Ludwell (1914). *Economic Cycles: Their Law and Causes*. New York: Macmillan. Reprinted, New York: Augustus M. Kelley, 1967.

—— (1929). *Synthetic Economics*. New York: Macmillan.

Nathan, Robert R. (1935a). "National Income Increased Five Billion Dollars in 1934." *Survey of Current Business* 15 (Aug.): 16–18.

—— (1935b). "The National Income Produced, 1929–1934" *Survey of Current Business* 15 (Nov.): 16–18.

National Bureau of Economic Research (1921). *Income in the United States: Its Amount and Distribution, 1909–1919, Vol. 1: Summary*. New York: National Bureau of Economic Research.

—— (1922). *Income in the United States: Its Amount and Distribution, 1909–1919, Vol. II: Detailed Report*, edited by W. C. Mitchell. New York: National Bureau of Economic Research.

—— (1923). *Business Cycles and Unemployment: An Investigation under the Auspices of the National Bureau of Economic Research Made for a Committee of the President's Conference on Unemployment*. New York: McGraw-Hill, for the National Bureau of Economic Research.

Patinkin, Don (1976). *Keynes' Monetary Thought: A Study of Its Development*. Durham, N.C.: Duke University Press.

Persons, Warren (1923). "An Index of Trade for the United States." *Review of Economic Statistics* 5 (April): 71–78.

Phelps-Brown, E. H. (1937). Review of *National Income and Outlay*, by Colin Clark. *Economic Journal* 47 (June): 333–34.

Pigou, A. C. (1924). *The Economics of Welfare*, 2nd edition. London: Macmillan.

Ramsey, Frank P. (1928). "A Mathematical Theory of Saving." *Economic Journal* 38 (Dec.): 543–59. As reprinted in *Readings in Welfare Economics*, selected by a committee of the American Economic Association (Homewood, Ill.: Richard D. Irwin, for the American Economic Association, 1969), pp. 619–33.

Robinson, E. A. G. (1947). "John Maynard Keynes, 1883–1946." *Economic Journal* 57 (March): 1–68. As reprinted in *Keynes' General Theory: Reports of Three Decades*, edited by Robert Lekachman. (New York: St. Martin's Press), pp. 13–86.

Sayers, R. S. (1956). *Financial Policy 1939–1945*. London: H.M.S.O. and Longmans, Green.

Schultz, Henry (1938). *The Theory and Measurement of Demand*. Chicago: University of Chicago Press.

Shaw, William H. (1942). "The Gross Flow of Finished Commodities and New Construction, 1929–41." *Survey of Current Business* 22 (April): 13–20.

Sheppard, David K. (1971). *The Growth and Role of UK Financial Institutions 1880–1962*. London: Methuen and Co.

S[now], E. C. (1933). Review of *The National Income: 1924–1931*, by Colin Clark. *Journal of the Royal Statistical Society* 96 (pt. 1): 110–15, 658–59.

Snyder, Carl (1924). "New Measures in the Equation of Exchange." *American Economic Review* 14 (Dec.): 699–713.

Stamp, Josiah (1916). *British Incomes and Property*. London: London School of Economics.

—— (1937). *The National Capital and Other Statistical Studies*. London: P. S. King and Son.

Stigler, George J. (1954). "The Early History of Empirical Studies of Consumer Behavior." *Journal of Political Economy* 62 (April): 95–113. As reprinted in Stigler, *Essays in the History of Economics* (Chicago: University of Chicago Press, 1965), pp. 198–233.

Stone, N. I. (1945). "The Beginnings of the National Bureau of Economic Research." In *The National Bureau of Economic Research Twenty-Fifth Annual Report*. New York: National Bureau of Economic Research, pp. 5–10.

Stone, Richard (1951). "The Use and Development of National Income and Expenditure Estimates." In *Lessons of the British War Economy*, edited by D. N. Chester (Cambridge: Cambridge University Press).

—— (1977). *Inland Revenue Report on National Income 1929*. Cambridge: University of Cambridge, Department of Applied Economics.

—— (1978). "Keynes, Political Arithmetic and Econometrics." *Proceedings of the British Academy* 64: 55–92 (published 1980).

Stone, Richard, and W. M. Stone (1938). "The Marginal Propensity to Consume and the Multiplier: A Statistical Investigation." *Review of Economic Studies* 6 (Oct.): 1–23.

Studenski, Paul (1958). *The Income of Nations*. New York: New York University Press.

Tarshis, Lorie (1939). "Changes in Real and Money Wages." *Economic Journal* 49 (March): 150–54.

Tinbergen, Jan (1939a). *A Method and Its Application to Investment Activity*. Vol. I of *Statistical Testing of Business Cycle Theories*. Geneva: League of Nations, Economic Intelligence Service.

—— (1939b). *Business Cycles in the United States of America 1919–1932*. Vol. II of *Statistical Testing of Business Cycle Theories*. Geneva: League of Nations, Economic Intelligence Service.

—— (1940). "On a Method of Statistical Business-Cycle Research: A Reply." *Economic Journal* 50 (March): 141–54.

Viner, Jacob (1924). *Canada's Balance of International Indebtedness*. Cambridge, Mass.: Harvard University Press.

Warburton, Clark (1934). "Value of the Gross National Product and Its Components, 1919–1929." *Journal of the American Statistical Association* 29 (Dec.): 383–88.

—— (1935). "How the National Income Was Spent 1919–1929." *Journal of the American Statistical Association* 30 (March): 175–82.

White, Harry D. (1933). *The French International Accounts 1880–1913*. Cambridge, Mass.: Harvard University Press.

Williams, John H. (1920). *Argentine International Trade under Inconvertible*

Paper Money 1880–1900. Cambridge, Mass.: Harvard University Press.

Winch, Donald (1969). *Economics and Policy: A Historical Study.* London: Hodder and Stoughton.

Government Publications

[Great Britain]. (1941). *An Analysis of the Sources of War Finance and an Estimate of the National Income and Expenditure in 1938 and 1940.* Parliamentary Papers, Cmd. 6261. London: H.M.S.O.

[Great Britain]. Cabinet Committee (1921). *Report on the Collection and Presentation of Official Statistics.* London: H.M.S.O.

[Great Britain]. Central Statistical Office (1968). *National Accounts Statistics: Sources and Methods.* Edited by Rita Maurice. London: H.M.S.O.

[Great Britain]. Committee on Finance and Industry (Macmillan Committee) (1931). *Report.* London: H.M.S.O.

[Great Britain]. Committee on the Working of the Monetary System (Radcliffe Committee) (1959). *Report.* London: H.M.S.O.

[Great Britain]. Inland Revenue (1929). *Report on National Income 1929.* (Printed in 1929, but not published until 1977; see Stone 1977 above.)

Macmillan Committee. See [Great Britain]. Committee on Finance and Industry (1931).

Radcliffe Committee. See [Great Britain]. Committee on the Working of the Monetary System (1959).

U.S. Congress, Senate (1934). *National Income, 1929–32.* S. Doc. 124, 73rd Congress, 2nd session.

U.S. Department of Commerce, Office of Federal Statistical Policy and Standards (1978). *Revolution in United States Government Statistics 1926–1976.* By Joseph W. Duncan and William C. Shelton. Washington, D.C.: U.S Government Printing Office.

Serial Publications

Bank of England. *Quarterly Bulletin.*

The Economist.

[Great Britain] Central Statistical Office. *Economic Trends.*

[Great Britain] Central Statistical Office. *Financial Statistics.*

[Great Britain] Central Statistical Office. *Monthly Digest of Statistics.*

London & Cambridge Economic Service. *Monthly Bulletin, Special Memoranda.*

National Bureau of Economic Research. *Bulletin.*

National Industrial Conference Board. *The Conference Board Bulletin.*

U.S. Department of Commerce. *Survey of Current Business.*

U.S. Federal Reserve Board. *Bulletin.*

Unpublished Sources

Bryce, Robert B. Notes on Keynes' lectures at Cambridge, Autumn term 1932, 1933, and 1934. Handwritten notes deposited at Carleton University, Ottawa. Typewritten version (with some inaccuracies) filed in the Keynes Papers (see below).

Carson, Carol (1971). "The History of the United States Income and Product Accounts: The Development of an Analytical Tool." Unpublished Ph.D. thesis, George Washington University.

J. M. Keynes Papers. Deposited in the Marshall Library, Cambridge, England.

Appendix

Page References to Other Editions of the *Tract* and *Treatise*

Pages Cited in This Book	Corresponding Pages in Other Editions	

	Tract on Monetary Reform	
Collected Writings Edition (1971)	Original Edition (1923)	United States Edition (1924)
4–6	5–8	7–10
12	13	16
40ff.	45ff.	50ff.
45–46	51–53	57–59
62	75–76	83
63	77	84–85
64	78–79	85–86
64, n. 1	79, n. 1	86–87, n. 1
67–68	83–84	91–92
68	85	93
81–87	99–106	108–16

	Treatise on Money, Volume I	
Collected Writings Edition (1971)	Original Edition (1930)	
xvii	v	
31–32	36	
113–14	126	
121	134	
124	138	
127	141	
127–29	140–43	
127–31	140–46	
132	146–47	
139	154–55	

Treatise on Money, Volume 1 (cont.)

Collected Writings Edition (1971)	Original Edition (1930)
159–60	177–78
167	186
171	190–91
175–78	196–99
177, n. 3	198, n. 3
178, n. 2	199, n. 2
184	206
186	208
189	211
207–8	231–32
209, n. 1	233, n. 1
222–30	248–57
264	294–95
271–75	302–7

Treatise on Money, Volume II

Collected Writings Edition (1971)	Original Edition (1930)
9	10
76–77	86–87
78	88
79	89
87	97
88–89	99
89–90	100
90	100
92–100	103–12
101	113–14
162–65	181–89
334	372–73
336, n. 1	375, n. 1
337–38	376–77

General Theory

The pagination of the *Collected Writings* edition and the original editions is practically the same, except for the preface.

Index of Names

Index of Subjects

Acceleration principle, 242, 243

Balanced budget, 167
Banana plantation parable, 15, 49
Bank rate, 41
Business cycles, 6, 24; in *Treatise*, 7; theory of (Kalecki), 78; theory of (Ohlin), 53; Tinbergen's study of, 227; statistics for, 242; Hayek's theory, 243; pre–*General Theory* theories, 243, 248; in *General Theory*, 231

Cambridge economists, 90, 176–78; view of *General Theory*, 37; quantity theory, 165–68, 170, 171–74; cash-balance theory, 165; optimum portfolio approach, 174–75; differences from Keynesian theory, 175, 176, 179–80; Cambridge equation, 174, 184, 187–88
Capitalists: consumption of, in Kalecki's analysis, 63–64, 67–68, 72–73, 97, 98; as savers and investors, 69, 75
Cash-balance approach, 4, 91, 165
Central banks, 203, 205, 250
"Central message," 17–18, 82–86, 92, 153. *See also individual writers*
Chicago, University of, 57 n, 79, 91, 180; monetarism, 190; Harris Foundation lectures at, 23–24, 205
Circulation of money, 171
Cobb-Douglas function, 134
Confidence, 178, 186
Consumption: and income, 8, 20, 22, 35; in Ohlin, 55; in Kalecki's Marxian analysis, 63–64, 67–68, 72–73
Consumption function, xxi, 22, 32, 190, 199, 248; in Lindahl, 44; in terms of na-

tional income, 130, 232 n; quantification of, 224
Cycles: Kalecki's concentration on, 83, 85; in *Treatise*, 7, 226, 230–31. *See also* Business cycles

Definitions, 95; in *Treatise*, xx, 7, 28, 230
Demand, aggregate, xxi, 5, 9, 14–15; and aggregate supply, 9, 11, 43, 80, 81, 128, 134, 142–43, 154; equilibrated by changes in output, 70, 88; theory of aggregate demand in *General Theory*, 156, 243
Demand for money, 11, 74, 170–74; Marshall's statement on, 173, 181–83; Pigou on, 184; Lavington on, 185–86; in quantity theory, 186; Robertson on, 187
Demand function: and supply function, 124–29, 139; Marshallian demand curve, 143, 256
Demand price, aggregate, and aggregate supply price, 124–27
Deposits, 187–88
Depreciation, 232–33
Depressions, 167; of twenties and thirties, 88; ended by wars, 211–12; in United States, 138, 200, 243. *See also* Public works; Unemployment
Diagrammatic analysis, Keynes' objection to, 129
Dynamic market mechanism, 142, 143, 152

Econometrics, 223–25, 229
Economic theory: and economic policy, 213–14; mathematical economics, 225–27; empirical economics, 256–57; institutional research, 258–59